The news interview has become a major vehicle for presenting broadcast news and political commentary, and a primary interface between the institutions of journalism and government. This much needed text examines the place of the news interview in Anglo-American society, and considers its historical development in the United States and Britain. The main body of the book discusses the fundamental norms and conventions that shape conduct in the modern interview; it explores the particular recurrent practices through which journalists balance competing professional norms that encourage both objective and adversarial treatment of public figures. It also explores how, in the face of aggressive questioning, politicians and other public figures struggle to stay "on message" and pursue their own agendas. Through analyses of well-known interviews, the book illuminates the simultaneously symbiotic and conflictual nature of the relationship between journalists and public figures, and reveals the tensions lying beneath the surface of the nightly news. This comprehensive and wide-ranging book will be essential reading for students and researchers in sociolinguistics, media, and communication studies.

STEVEN CLAYMAN is Associate Professor of Sociology and is affiliated with the Communication Studies Program at the University of California, Los Angeles. His research lies at the intersection of talk, interaction, and mass communication. Much of his work concerns various forms of broadcast journalism, with an emphasis on news interviews and presidential press conferences. His articles have appeared in *American Sociological Review; American Journal of Sociology; Journal of Communication; Media, Culture, and Society;* and *Research on Language and Social Interaction.*

JOHN HERITAGE is Professor of Sociology at the University of California, Los Angeles. He works in the field of communication and interaction with particular reference to health care and political communication. In the latter field, he has researched extensively on news interviews, political rhetoric, and its relationship to audience reactions and presidential press conferences. His publications include *Garfinkel and Ethnomethodology* (1984); *Structures of Social Action*, co-edited with Max Atkinson (Cambridge, 1984); and *Talk at Work*, co-edited with Paul Drew (Cambridge, 1992).

Studies in Interactional Sociolinguistics

EDITORS
Paul Drew, Marjorie Harness Goodwin, John J. Gumperz,
Deborah Schiffrin

The News Interview
Journalists and Public Figures on the Air

STEVEN CLAYMAN
and
JOHN HERITAGE
University of California, Los Angeles

CAMBRIDGE
UNIVERSITY PRESS

PUBLISHED BY THE PRESS SYNDICATE OF THE UNIVERSITY OF CAMBRIDGE
The Pitt Building, Trumpington Street, Cambridge, United Kingdom

CAMBRIDGE UNIVERSITY PRESS
The Edinburgh Building, Cambridge CB2 2RU, UK
40 West 20th Street, New York, NY 10011-4211, USA
477 Williamstown Road, Port Melbourne, VIC 3207, Australia
Ruiz de Alarcón 13, 28014 Madrid, Spain
Dock House, The Waterfront, Cape Town 8001, South Africa

http://www.cambridge.org

First published 2002

Printed in the United Kingdom at the University Press, Cambridge

Typeface Sabon 10/13 pt.   *System* LʌTEX 2$_\varepsilon$ [TB]

A catalogue record for this book is available from the British Library

ISBN 0 521 81259 3 hardback
ISBN 0 521 01191 4 paperback

Contents

Acknowledgments

This project turned out to be a more ambitious and time-consuming undertaking than we anticipated when we began. Many colleagues and associates provided crucial advice and inspiration along the way.

First and foremost out thanks go to David Greatbatch, whose own pioneering research helped open up the news interview to systematic study and set an agenda for the work that would follow. We had hoped that he would be able to work on this book with us, but unfortunately his busy schedule did not permit this. His work has nourished our own in innumerable ways, and his many contributions to this book are beyond straightforward inventory or acknowledgment either here or in the notes to the text. We are most indebted to him for his support over very many years. Without him, this book would not have been written.

David Olsher and Andy Roth both did important work on news interview materials while this book was in progress. Their research enlightened our own and their insights have substantially enriched the book.

Emanuel Schegloff and Michael Schudson read parts of the manuscript and contributed both constructive feedback and moral support. Paul Drew generously read the entire manuscript at a critical juncture in its development. His comments helped give final shape to this book and made it a much better one.

Lisa McConnell edited the manuscript, formatted and streamlined the transcript excerpts, and constructed the index. These were daunting tasks, and we are deeply indebted to her meticulous work. We are also grateful to Andrew Winnard, Jacqueline French, and everyone at Cambridge University Press whose professionalism made the production of this book such a pleasant experience.

At various stages in their academic careers, Elizabeth Boyd, Liana Manukyan, Olga Solomon, Tanya Stivers, and Jennifer Strand provided us with the kind of research assistance that every researcher dreams of.

Finally, we are grateful to Nancy and Margaret for their steadfast support and encouragement. Their presence in our lives helped make the project that much more meaningful.

1

Introduction

If you sit down in front of your television to catch up on the news, or if you turn on the radio for the same purpose, you will very likely be treated to a series of stories narrated by an anchorperson or correspondent. However, at least some of what you hear is apt to appear in a different form altogether – not a narrated story, but an interactional encounter between a journalist and one or more newsworthy public figures.

The news interview has come to occupy a prominent place in the landscape of broadcast journalism and political communication. Interviewing has long been a basic journalistic tool – perhaps the most important tool[1] – for gathering information, the raw material that will later be worked up into finished news stories. What is new is its increasing use as a finished news product in its own right. Whether live or taped, in studio or via remote satellite links, as one segment of a news program or the overarching format for the program as a whole – the interview is now a common form in which broadcast news is packaged for public consumption, and hence an alternative to the traditional narrative or story form of news presentation. Although the news story remains important, a significant proportion of news content now consists of a journalist asking questions of politicians, experts, or others who are "in the news."

Numerous factors have contributed to the growth of the news interview. Technological innovation is part of the mix. The advent of cable has greatly increased the number of channels and news outlets,

---

[1] Both Gans (1979: 138) and Hess (1981: 18, 52) find that reporters get most of their information, not by witnessing events directly or by consulting documents, but by interviewing sources.

while satellite feeds and electronic newsgathering equipment now permit live interactions with newsmakers from virtually anywhere in the world. These changes have expanded opportunities for the development of new forms of news and public affairs programming.

At the same time, increasing competitive pressures have encouraged broadcasters to exploit these opportunities. The older commercial television networks are now competing with a growing array of cable channels, as well as VCRs and the Internet, with predictable consequences for each content provider's market share and profitability. Meanwhile the US networks have each been taken over by conglomerates that have assumed substantial debt and have been much less willing to allow their news divisions to remain insulated from the pressures of the bottom line (Auletta 1991; Hallin 1997). All of this has had a substantial impact on the ethos of broadcasting, with producers much more concerned about production costs and audience ratings, and hence willing to experiment with new formats for news and public affairs programming. Against this backdrop, formats based on spoken interaction – panel discussions, informal debates, various forms of audience participation, and of course news interviews – are particularly attractive. Such formats are inexpensive to produce, and they embody qualities of "spontaneity" and "liveliness" that audience members are believed to like.

The rise of the news interview has made it a significant component of the contemporary public sphere, and hence worthy of social scientific attention. It is a locus of direct and essentially unscripted encounters between journalists and a wide range of public figures, including government officials at the highest levels. It is an arena in which journalists perform certain core democratic functions: soliciting statements of official policy, holding officials accountable for their actions, and managing the parameters of public debate, all of this under the immediate scrutiny of the citizenry. If journalists have traditionally discharged these tasks through practices of storytelling and narration, now they also do so through practices of questioning and interrogation. Correspondingly, public figures' ability to deal adeptly with journalists' questions has become an essential prerequisite for successful political communication. Just as speechmaking skills were crucial in the days of the public square, the capacity to field questions has become a core skill for public figures in the television age.

To underline these points, consider that both journalistic and political careers are now contingent on performance in news interviews and their close cousins, press conferences. If journalists previously gained professional status and popular renown mainly by virtue of their investigative and literary abilities, their ranks have been joined by journalists known mainly for their skills at questioning and interrogation: Sam Donaldson and Ted Koppel in the USA, Robin Day and Jeremy Paxman in the UK. Correspondingly, politicians who can "think on their feet" and deal effectively with unexpected and difficult questions (John Kennedy and Margaret Thatcher) receive praise and admiration, while those who have difficulty in this forum (Ronald Reagan and John Major) are criticized for their interactional failings.

It is not difficult to find cases where career prospects have been substantially boosted – or hindered – on the basis of performance in a single news interview. When revelations about Gennifer Flowers threatened to undo Bill Clinton's first run for the presidency in 1992, a joint appearance by the Arkansas governor and his wife on *60 Minutes* did much to resurrect his campaign. Conversely, Bob Dole's 1996 campaign suffered an important setback when, in an interview on *The Today Show*, he expressed a seemingly cavalier attitude about the addictiveness of tobacco.

One remarkable illustration of the power of the contemporary news interview is Jeremy Paxman's 1997 encounter with Michael Howard on the BBC's *Newsnight* program. Howard was formerly Home Secretary under Prime Minister John Major, and at the time of the interview he was a principal challenger for the leadership of the Conservative Party. As Home Secretary, his responsibility for the British prison system had previously become a contentious political issue. Two years earlier, following a well-publicized prison escape, Howard appeared before the House of Commons, and while he admitted setting policy for the prison service, he denied any involvement in operational matters. His denial was subsequently contradicted by numerous authoritative sources, raising the specter of having willfully misled the House.

In the 1997 interview, Paxman zeroed in on an event that had a direct bearing on the veracity of Howard's claim to having had no operational role in the prison service – namely the firing of a prison official. Paxman asked whether Howard had overruled the Director

General of Prisons (Derek Lewis) by instructing him to fire the official. If Howard had actually given such instructions, it would directly contradict his prior claim to having been operationally un-involved. When Howard refused to give a straightforward answer, Paxman pursued the matter with extraordinary tenacity, asking essentially the same question another thirteen times! Perhaps never has a single act of evasiveness under questioning been so massively pursued and placed on display before the viewing public.

The Howard–Paxman interview has been described as "a watershed in political interviews and a new low in relations between the Tory government and the BBC" (Gibson 1999), and the ramifications were indeed substantial. The interview received much subsequent news coverage, it was seized upon and exploited to good effect by Howard's challengers for the Conservative Party leadership (Cordon 1997), and it marked a turning point in his political fortunes. Howard would eventually lose his bid for the leadership, and his party would lose the election, ushering in the ascendancy of the Labour Party under Tony Blair.

Howard's waning political standing was matched by Paxman's veneration as a broadcast journalist. Paxman was subsequently named Interviewer of the Year by the Royal Television Society (Summerskill 1998). The following year, the interview was featured and commemorated on *Newsnight's* twentieth anniversary program.

The Howard–Paxman interview rebounded to the benefit of the journalist and the detriment of the public figure, but news interviews can also have just the reverse effect. Consider Dan Rather's encounter with George Bush during the 1988 presidential campaign.[2] The political stakes could not have been higher: Bush was a front-runner for the Republican presidential nomination, the race was just getting underway, and he was about to be interviewed on the CBS *Evening News* – then the most highly rated television news program in the USA. The interview started out routinely enough, but it soon developed into a sharply acrimonious confrontation over Bush's involvement in what came to be known as the Iran-Contra

---

[2] This interview was the focus of a series of articles in a special section of the journal *Research on Language and Social Interaction* (1988/89) edited by Anita Pomerantz. See especially the contributions by Clayman and Whalen (1988/89) and Schegloff (1988/89).

scandal. That nine-minute interview had substantial repercussions for both parties.

Bush's campaign got a substantial boost. He was widely perceived to have dispelled his unflattering image as an obedient and "wimpy" second fiddle to President Reagan. Thus, *Time* magazine – which featured the encounter as its cover story – characterized it as "video High Noon" and described Bush as follows: "Bush had shot down the legendary media gunslinger from black rock. It was the new George Bush. Not Bush the perpetual stand-in, but Bush the stand-up guy. Bush unbound. Bush unwimped" (Stengel 1988: 17). More-over, a *Time* magazine poll indicated that a majority felt that Bush had indeed strengthened his public image, and that he had "won" the battle with Rather (Stengel 1988: 17–19). It was by no means a total victory – he failed to fully dispel doubts about his knowledge of the arms-for-hostages deal (Toner 1988), and he was questioned further about the scandal on Ted Koppel's *Nightline*. That later interview prompted an eerie sense of déjà vu when Bush adopted the same defensive stance and mistakenly referred to Ted Koppel as "Dan"! These were minor setbacks, however, as Bush went on to win the Republican nomination and later the presidency by a landslide.

The interview had quite the opposite effect on Dan Rather's career. CBS received 6,000 telephone calls that evening, most of them expressing disapproval of Rather, and poll results suggested that a majority of viewers thought Rather had been "rude" (Stengel 1988: 19). The CBS affiliates also expressed dissatisfaction with Rather at the annual affiliate convention (Auletta 1991: 500–1). Later in the campaign when the presidential debates were held, Rather was the only network news anchor who was not on any panel of questioners – it was feared that Bush might use the incident to beat back Rather's aggressive questions, or that Rather might be inhibited from raising such questions (Weintraub 1988). At about the same time, Rather began to lose influence at CBS when a CBS News president took charge who was determined to impose greater discipline and to ensure that the news division focus on covering the news rather than making it (Auletta 1991: 536–8). Finally, while the CBS *Evening News* would remain the leading network news pro-gram through most of 1988, it began to lose viewers and slipped into third place the following year (Goldberg and Goldberg 1990).

The causes of this steady decline are undoubtedly complex, but it is significant that some commentators (e.g., Du Brow 1990) have attributed the problem, at least in part, to lingering memories of that unseemly but ultimately fateful interview.

These cases demonstrate one final point regarding the distinctiveness and import of the news interview. Unlike the traditional news story, the news interview is essentially unscripted and unpredictable. Of course, interviewers and interviewees may each have a preconceived agenda in mind at the outset, a more or less developed idea of what they would like to say and do. However, each party's capacity to realize his or her agenda is thoroughly contingent on the conduct of the other party. The actual course of an interview is thus by no means predetermined; it is an emergent product of how the participants choose to deal with each other then and there, move by move, moment by moment. Part of the appeal of the news interview is precisely this spontaneous quality, the sense of liveliness and even danger arising from the spectacle of a powerful public figure matching wits with a seasoned journalist. This is why some interviews – like the Bush–Rather and Howard–Paxman encounters – become news events in their own right, the focus of subsequent news coverage that further enhances their impact.

If the news interview is not scripted in any strong sense of the word, neither is it a disorganized free-for-all in which "anything goes." Indeed, as we will be arguing throughout the book, the parties to a news interview observe an elaborate set of social conventions associated with the roles of interviewer and interviewee. These conventions are largely tacit and taken for granted – they are rarely commented upon within interviews themselves, and they receive only cursory and superficial attention in journalism textbooks and manuals of interviewing technique. And yet, these conventions of interaction are very real and very powerful. Adherance to the conventions is what distinguishes the news interview from other genres of broadcast talk and other forms of interaction more generally. These conventions are robust and remarkably similar in both Britain and the United States, although they are subject to cross-cultural variation and historical change. In all of these ways, the news interview can be understood as an organized social institution in its own right.

At the same time, the news interview is deeply intertwined with other societal institutions, most notably journalism and politics. It is a public arena in which representatives of these institutions encounter one another and strive to pursue their respective goals and agendas. Accordingly, what transpires within a news interview both reflects and contributes to the current state of journalism, politics, and their co-evolution over time.

Our primary objective in this book is to examine the inner workings of the news interview in Anglo-American society – the roles, norms, and elementary practices that sustain it. We will also explore aspects of its relationship to the larger social world – the forces within journalism and politics that first gave rise to the news interview and continue to shape its development in both Britain and the United States, as well as its consequences for news, political communication, and the public sphere.

The news interview as a genre

The news interview is a familiar and readily recognizable genre of broadcast talk. But what makes it so? What sets news interviews apart from talk shows, panel discussions, debates, audience participation programs, and other interaction-based genres of broadcast programming? Like most ordinary language categories, the "news interview" has fuzzy bounderies – its members share a loose family resemblance rather than a rigid set of defining attributes. Nevertheless, certain attributes do tend to characterize instances of this programming genre.

The prototypical news interview involves a distinctive constellation of participants, subject matter, and interactional form. The interviewer is known as a professional journalist rather than a partisan advocate or celebrity entertainer. Interviewees have some connection to recent news events, either as primary actors (e.g., government officials) or as informed commentators (e.g., certified experts). The audience plays no active role in the interaction. The discussion normally focuses on matters related to recent news events, is highly formal in character, and is managed primarily through questions and answers. In the USA, prototypical news interviews are featured on nightly programs such as *Nightline* (ABC) and *The NewsHour* (PBS), and weekly programs such as *Meet the Press*

(NBC), *Face the Nation* (CBS), and *This Week* (ABC). In the UK, prototypical news interview-based programs include *Newsnight* (BBC2), the Sunday *Breakfast With Frost* (ITN), and various radio programs produced by BBC Radio 4: *The Today Programme*, *The World at One*, and *PM*.

The boundaries of the news interview genre can be clarified by considering some marginal cases. Consider CNN's *The Larry King Show*. It is news-oriented, features politicians and other newsworthy guests, and largely maintains the question–answer format. On the other hand, Larry King's background is in talk radio rather than traditional journalism, and he takes telephone calls from viewers during the show. The resulting program is thus a hybrid of the news interview and radio call-in genres.

A closer relative of the news interview is the press conference, which shares most of the news-interview attributes outlined above, but with a few important differences. Press conferences are held at the behest of the public figure rather than the news media, and involve large numbers of participating journalists instead of just one or two. The latter difference may not seem particularly significant, but the participation of numerous journalists fundamentally alters the conditions of interaction, reducing the opportunity of each journalist to ask follow-up questions, and thus making it easier for public figures to be less than fully responsive and to pursue their own agendas. Thus, while news interview questioning is often under the control of a single journalist who can counter self-serving or evasive responses, in press conferences the journalistic role is fragmented, making it somewhat less effective as an instrument of public accountability.

The news interview in disciplinary context

The research reported in this book falls within an interdisciplinary field of study concerning the news media in contemporary society. More specifically, it builds upon a long line of research dealing with Anglo-American newsmaking institutions and the social processes through which news is produced.[3]

---

[3] For more comprehensive reviews of this extensive literature, see Schudson (1996), Shoemaker and Reese (1996), and Tuchman (1988).

Although research of this sort now crosses disciplinary boundaries and includes important work in communication studies and political science, its deepest roots are within sociology. Max Weber ([1910] 1976), in a speech delivered at the first Congress of Sociologists meeting in Frankfurt, advanced what is perhaps the first fully developed proposal for research into the social organization of the press. Many of the questions Weber raised concerned the significance of the commercial basis of news organizations – the need for newspapers to serve both consumers and advertisers, the rise of newspaper trusts and monopolies, and the impact of all of this on news output. However, Weber also called attention to reporters' routine everyday practices – including, most notably, where and how they obtain the information that is subsequently relayed to the public as news.

This research agenda problematizes the social process by which news is constructed. In so doing, it runs contrary to the view of news offered by journalists themselves and perhaps assumed by many news consumers in their unreflective moments: that news is best explained as a more or less straightforward representation of "reality." Journalists occasionally assert that news reflects reality pure and simple, but most offer the more sophisticated view that news is a judicious selection of the most newsworthy events of the day (Epstein 1973: 13–37; Gans 1979: 79–80). This view is founded on the assumption that journalists are autonomous professionals who are insulated from extraneous pressures and are trained to report news objectively in accordance with established standards of newsworthiness. This viewpoint has not held up well against research into the various practical constraints and institutional circumstances under which journalists actually operate.

Such research would take considerable time to develop. Although important work followed Weber's proposal, studies of newsmaking institutions and production processes remained few and far between from World War I through the 1950s. Work in this area all but died out altogether by the early 1960s, prompting Herbert Gans (1972) to comment on "the famine" in institutional media research. This state of affairs was due in part to the early dominance of the Columbia school of media studies associated with Paul Lazarsfeld and his colleagues. Their work was concerned mainly with the "effects" side of the media equation, conceived in social psychological terms as the impact of news on individuals' attitudes and behaviors. Moreover, because that work revealed media effects to be more modest and limited than had previously been assumed, it probably contributed to a general waning of academic interest in the news media. Interest would re-emerge with a vengeance in the early 1970s. On both sides of the Atlantic, a plethora of monographs, edited collections, and articles in leading academic journals appeared within the span of a few years. This burst of attention was due, at least in part, to a growing suspicion that the theory of minimal media effects was premature and probably overstated. That theory appeared increasingly implausible in the face of the dramatic expansion of television as the dominant source of information and entertainment. The rise of television seemed, to many, to fill a void created by the declining influence of political parties in election campaigns and as mediators of political meaning, and it happened to coincide with an equally dramatic increase in social turbulence in the late 1960s and early 70s. In addition, the popular writings of Marshall McLuhan had a less direct but nonetheless tangible influence on the intellectual ferment of the time. Accordingly, researchers began to develop new ways of conceptualizing media effects,[4] thus resurrecting – albeit cautiously and not without controversy – notions of media power.

Another reason for renewed interest in the news media was particular to the US context. Journalists came under sustained attack during the first Nixon administration when both President Nixon and Vice President Agnew, with the aid of a young speechwriter named Patrick Buchanan, accused them of widespread "liberal bias." These well-publicized attacks appeared to gain support from an ostensibly systematic study of the 1968 presidential election (Efron 1971) which argued that network news broadcasts strongly favored liberal Democrat Hubert Humphrey over conservative Republican Richard Nixon.

The liberal bias thesis set an agenda for subsequent research in the USA, much of which refuted that thesis by directing attention to constraints on newsgathering that transcend the partisanship of individual reporters, constraints inherent in the bureaucratic, professional,

---

[4] See, for example, discussions of agenda setting (McCombs and Shaw 1972), the spiral of silence (Noelle-Neumann 1974), and cultivation theory (Gerbner and Gross 1976).

and cultural environments in which reporters operate. Most of the British studies during this period tended to be theoretically oriented and emphasized the broader political–economic framework in which news organizations are embedded.[5] However, important empirical work was produced on both sides of the Atlantic, offering insight into the culture of the journalistic profession, the bureaucratic structure of news organizations, and the day-to-day practices of working journalists.[6] Notwithstanding each author's unique background and interests, the findings were remarkably convergent: that journalists, being limited in time and space, must somehow routinize the newsgathering process, that they do so in part by relying on certain bureaucratic locales where news is predictably available, that their decisions are also shaped by entrenched professional values, as well as external pressures from interested parties in the wider society.

A central contingency shaping the production of news is the relationship between reporters and their sources. It was repeatedly shown that reporters restrict their attention to a relatively narrow range of government officials and certified experts, whose actions and accounts form the basis for most news stories.[7] Similar observations have been made about the range of sources that appear on programs devoted to live interviews (Croteau and Hoynes 1994). The social relationship between reporters and sources has also been the subject of sophisticated theoretical analysis (Blumler and Gurevitch 1981).

Notwithstanding this attention to source recruitment patterns and reporter–source relationships, comparatively little is known about how reporters and sources actually deal with one another on a day-to-day basis. And yet, it is through such routine dealings that the raw material of what will become "news" is generated. For the case of the broadcast interview, such dealings are themselves news – the "news" in a news interview consists entirely of mundane interactional transactions between journalists and their sources.

---

[5] See, for instance, the papers collected in Curran, Gurevitch, and Woolacott (1977) and Gurevitch, et al. (1982).

[6] Important British studies include Halloran, Elliott and Murdock (1969), Elliott (1972), Hall, et al. (1978), Schlesinger (1978), and Tunstall (1971). American studies during this same period include Altheide (1974), Epstein (1973), Fishman (1980), Gans (1979), Gitlin (1980), Molotch and Lester (1974; 1975), Sigal (1973), Tuchman (1978).

[7] Almost all of the studies cited in note 6 make this point.

Recently, however, these transactions have begun to be explored by scholars committed to examining the inner workings of the news interview as a journalistic form. Some researchers have focused their attention on journalists and the arts of questioning and interrogation.[8] Others have examined public figures and their techniques for dealing with journalists' questions and with one another.[9] Still others have examined the overarching system of interaction that constitutes the news interview and distinguishes it from ordinary conversation.[10] Finally, interviewing practices have been examined for the manner in which they are distributed across individual participants and sociohistorical contexts.[11]

This line of research has provocative implications, calling into question many cherished dichotomies in social science and media studies: the split between interpersonal and mass communication, between news content and production processes, and between public and private spheres of social life. The news interview is plainly a vehicle for communicating to a mass audience, but it is, at the same time, a form of interpersonal communication between interviewer and interviewee. It is both a consumable news product, and an emergent process of news production. It is an important platform within the public sphere, but it is constituted through mundane practices of talk and interaction that have been adapted from those of ordinary conversation. These attributes make the news interview a fascinating and theoretically fruitful object of study, but they also pose special challenges for the analyst of news interview discourse.

Analyzing the news interview

Studying the news interview requires a distinctive mode of analysis appropriate to its distinctive character. To clarify this point, it is useful to begin by considering, by way of contrast, how news

---

[8] Adkins 1992; Bull, et al. 1996; Clayman 1988, 1991, 1992, 2002, Forthcoming; Greatbatch 1986b; Harris 1986; Heritage Forthcoming a, Forthcoming b; Heritage and Roth 1995; Jucker 1986; Macaulay 1996; Olsher Forthcoming; Roth 1998a; Roth and Olsher 1997.

[9] Bavelas, et al. 1988; Clayman 1993, 2001; Greatbatch 1986a, 1992; Harris 1991.

[10] Clayman 1989, 1991; Greatbatch 1988; Heritage 1985; Heritage and Greatbatch 1991. See also Bull 1994.

[11] Bull and Elliott 1998; Bull and Mayer 1988, 1993; Clayman and Heritage 2002; Elliott and Bull 1996; Harris 1991.

is typically analyzed when it appears in story form. Traditional content analyses tend to focus on matters such as the themes that predominate within a given range of stories, and the balance and diversity of viewpoints represented therein. For example, studies of election news are concerned with the proportion of coverage devoted to each candidate, and the tendency for stories to concentrate on the theme of the horse race (e.g., who's ahead, campaign strategy, publicity efforts, etc.) to the exclusion of more substantive matters (e.g., the candidates' qualifications, issue positions, policy proposals, etc.). Studies of political news beyond the confines of the campaign have revealed a similar emphasis on political strategy over policy substance.

When we turn from the story form of news to consider the news interview, a different mode of analysis is in order. While overarching themes – such as political strategy – are highly significant to the organization of news narratives, they are rather less central within a mode of discourse that is organized interactionally rather than thematically. The news interview is, first and foremost, a *course of interaction* to which the participants contribute on a turn-by-turn basis, for the most part by asking and answering questions. Of course, particular themes are expressed within each successive contribution, but these contributions are not merely understood in terms of their thematic content. They are also understood in terms of how they bear on the unfolding interactional "game" being played by interviewer and interviewee.

To illustrate this point, consider the questions that interviewers ask. The sense and import of any given question depends in part on how it functions as a "move" within the interview game at a particular point in its state of play. Each question has a retrospective import – some questions accept and build upon the interviewee's previous remarks in a way that moves the discussion along, while other questions subject prior remarks to challenge. Each question also has a prospective import – some questions are relatively open-ended and allow the interviewee maximum leeway to respond, whereas others narrow the parameters of an acceptable response and exert pressure on the interviewee to answer in a particular way. Correspondingly, the sense and import of an interviewee's response depends in part on how it deals with the agenda established by the question – whether it is dutifully answering, or resistant in some way, or downright

evasive. Clearly, how these questioning and answering activities get
realized represents a significant level of meaning in news interview
discourse, one that is available both to interview participants and
to the media audience. Indeed, the ability to track the interactional
game as it unfolds is one of the pleasures of interview spectatorship
and in part accounts for the distinctive appeal of the news interview
as a genre.

The significance of the interactional dimension rests in part on
the fact that while it is analytically independent of a news interview's
content, it is necessarily consequential for the latter. Interaction between interviewers and interviewees is the generative process by
which news interview content, whatever its character, gets created.
No topic, theme, or perspective can find its way into a news interview except through the vehicle of an interactional move by one of
the participants – and each such move is shaped and constrained by
the moves that preceded it, just as it in turn affects what gets said
and done in subsequent moves. Thus the *content* of a news interview is thoroughly contingent on the generative *process* of interview
interaction.

Furthermore, the interactional dimension is responsive to, and
consequential for, various aspects of the social context in which interviewing takes place. Varying styles of play tend to be characteristic of particular journalists and public figures, who become known
for their manner of questioning and answering respectively, and
who thereby acquire a distinctive public persona. For journalists,
this is a major source of professional reputations – the cautious restraint of Jim Lehrer and Brian Walden, the challenging aggressive-
ness of Sam Donaldson and Jeremy Paxman, the probing intimacy
of Barbara Walters, and the imperious dominance of Robin Day and
Ted Koppel. Correspondingly, although public figures are seen in a
much wider range of social contexts, their personae are also inflected
by interview conduct. While in office, President Bill Clinton's way of
handling questions was at least one ingredient in his janus-faced image as both sincerely empathetic and shrewdly calculating. In short,
the public images of both interviewers and interviewees derive in
part from the distinctive ways they play the interview game.

Varying styles of play also distinguish the institution of journalism as it is constituted in different historical and national contexts.
To take one noteworthy example that will be explored further in

the next chapter, comparatively deferential styles of questioning in the 1950s have given way to much more adversarial encounters in recent years, especially in British news interviews and in American presidential press conferences. This shift resulted from a host of changes in the political, economic, and institutional environment of broadcast journalism. Thus, just as the underlying form of the news narrative can reflect the larger sociohistorical context (Schudson 1982; Hallin and Mancini 1984),[12] the whole manner in which the broadcast interview is conducted can be an index of much broader developments in journalism and national politics.

Finally, systematic variations in the way interviewers treat particular interviewees and categories of interviewees can be a means by which ideological bias enters into the interviewing process. Indeed, disproportionately hostile treatment can constitute some interviewees as "beyond the pale" and can function to dramatize and reinforce the boundaries of legitimate opinion in public discourse.

Given its manifold significance, how does one go about analyzing the interactional game of the news interview? In light of the preceding, it may be tempting to begin by examining how the game is played differently by different participants and in different social environments. For instance, focusing on the interviewer's role in the game, one could chart the relative prevalence of polite or deferential styles of questioning versus more aggressive or adversarial styles of questioning across particular interviewers, interviewees, news programs, broadcasting media, national boundaries, or historical eras.

However, a comparative analysis of this sort cannot proceed without a thorough understanding of the various practices that constitute deference or adversarialness in this context. Such practices are numerous, complex, and by no means transparent. To take just one example (explored further in chapter 6), one way of expressing adversarialness is via questions that are opinionated or assertive – such questions display an expectation about the type of answer that would be correct or preferable, and thus exert pressure on the interviewee to answer in a particular way. Pressure of this sort can be

---

[12] The formal properties of the news narrative have been explored by discourse analytic approaches to the news. For a sampling of work in this area, see Bell (1991), Fairclough (1995), Fowler (1991), van Dijk (1988), and Weaver (1975). For an overview of discourse analytic approaches to the news, see Bell and Garrett (1998).

encoded in a variety of ways, some of which may be available to a priori intuition while others most certainly are not. For example, it turns out that when yes/no questions are negatively formulated (e.g., "Didn't you," "Aren't you," "Isn't it true that") they embody so strong a preference for an affirmative answer that they are often treated by interviewees as if they were expressing an opinion rather than merely asking a question. To the extent that the analyst's a priori understanding of such basic practices is incomplete or misguided, the comparative results will be suspect.

More generally, any attempt to document systematic variations in interview conduct presupposes that one already has a grasp of the broad array of practices that comprise such conduct, and the sense and import that such practices have for the participants themselves (Schegloff 1993). These elementary practices are the axes along which variation of whatever sort will occur, so they must be thoroughly understood before variations can be described and their significance fully appreciated. Just as advances in chemistry and physics were contingent on the development of the periodic table of elements, and current advances in biology are contingent on cracking the genetic code, progress in analyzing the news interview requires similar attention to fundamentals. Priority must be given to isolating and describing the elementary practices that constitute the basic building blocks of news interview interaction.

What are these practices? How do they affect the conduct of interviewers and interviewees? What are the institutional norms to which they are responsive, and what happens when these norms are transgressed? Once these practices have been described, what can they tell us about how the news relates to its social context and how it has evolved over time? Clearly no analysis of the news interview can come to terms with its journalistic, political, and cultural power without attending seriously to such questions. Accordingly, these questions will be our principal preoccupation throughout this book.

Methodology: conversation analysis

Anyone seeking to understand how the interactional game of the news interview works must confront data like the following. This is a detailed transcript of the first few exchanges in an interview with

Bob Dole during his 1996 campaign for the Republican presidential nomination. The transcript captures not only the words themselves but also how they were articulated, including silences (denoted by numbers in parentheses), overlapping speech (denoted by square brackets), points of emphasis or stress (denoted by underlining), and so on (see Appendix).

(1)   US ABC *This Week*: 18 Feb 1996: New Hampshire Primary
      IR: John Cochran   IE: Bob Dole

```
 1  IR:   Are you: hh running scared,
 2  IE:   .hh Not really. I've- uh- I'm- my I think my
 3        attitude's better too: in- in 1996. uh: .hh I'm
 4        not as tense, I'm not as tight, I'm not- I'm
 5        relaxed, .hh What will happen will happen,
 6  IR:   You said earlier this week tha:t (0.2) whoever
 7        wins New Hampshire_ (0.5) in all likelihood: is
 8        going to be the nominee:. (.) Di- Do you wish
 9        you hadn't said that,
10  IE:   Y=I prob'ly shoulda said if Bob Dole: wins the
11        New Hampshire Bob Do(h)le'll be the nominee but
12        that's alright you gotta be confident.
13        (.)
14  IR:   Mm hm,
15  IE:   If we d- If we don't win New Hampshire, (0.7) uh
16        we'll win North and South Dakota.
17        (.)
18  IR:   Is it getting personal between you and Buchanan?
19  IE:   I don't think so:.=uh Pat 'n I have been
20        friends=I just don't agree with him. .hh I don't
21        agree with his view of women. I don't agree that
22        we oughta give .hh as he said years ago, his
23        writings (tuh) the nuclear weapons maybe to (.)
24        Japan: 'n th- South Korea .. hh Uh: [:-
25  IR:                                        [Do you think
26        he's a racist? or anti Semitic,
27  IE:   Oh I don't know. I don't th- I don't believe so:
28        but:=uh: (0.5) .hh uh:: I do believe that:=uh:
29        (0.5) some of his views are not in=h not in
30        accord with th- where th' mainstream Americans
31        are.
```

At the level of topical content, this interview is straightforward and not particularly complicated. It is about the current state of

Dole's candidacy, and in particular his level of confidence and his relationship with his principal Republican adversary Pat Buchanan. However, if we consider the underlying interaction through which this topic is addressed – the particular practices that the interviewer is using to raise various issues, the practices that Dole is using to deal with them, how each set of practices relates to and manifests the speaker's strategic considerations, and the basic ground rules that both participants are mindful of over the course of the exchange – the picture becomes much more complex and by no means straightforward.

To explore these issues, we employ the methodology of conversation analysis. Although conversation analysis originated within sociology in the United States, it is now practiced across a wide range of academic disciplines and national contexts. Conversation analysis (henceforth CA) is an approach to the study of human interaction that involves, at its core, the direct observation of naturally occurring interaction as captured on audio and videorecordings.[13]

The value of recorded data cannot be overstated. Once recorded, a segment of interaction can be examined repeatedly, and re-examined as new information becomes available, and even slowed down for frame-by-frame scrutiny. It can thus be analyzed with much greater detail and precision than would otherwise be possible if it were observed only once in real time. The import of recorded data in CA is rather like that of slow motion "instant replay" in televised sporting events.[14] While spectators in the stands may have only a vague grasp of the fleeting events in a particular play, television viewers can, by virtue of the instant replay, achieve a much deeper and more precise understanding of the specific sequence of behaviors that combined to produce the play's outcome. This applies as well to the academic study of human interaction when it has been preserved on audio or videotape.

---

[13] More thorough introductions to conversation analytic methodology may be found in Clayman and Gill (Forthcoming), Heritage (1995; 1997), ten Have (1999), and Zimmerman (1988). For a broader overview that touches on both methodology and empirical findings, see Heritage (1984a: chapter 8). For introductions that deal specifically with the study of talk in institutional settings, see Zimmerman and Boden (1991) and Drew and Heritage (1992). Those interested in the intellectual origins of the field and its relationship to allied fields should consult Schegloff (1992a) and Clayman and Maynard (1995).

[14] For this analogy we are indebted to Max Atkinson (1984: 7–9).

Recordings have an additional advantage in that they can be transcribed in detail, shared with other researchers, and even reproduced in the final research report. Printed transcript excerpts serve as concrete illustrations of points that the author would otherwise have to make abstractly. In this way, transcripts also provide readers with independent access to the events in question, so that they can check what the author is claiming against an actual record of what transpired. Thus, to return to the sports analogy, just as television viewers can use the instant replay to assess the accuracy of the referee's call and the broadcast commentary, CA readers can consult the transcript excerpts to evaluate the author's analysis. This serves as a powerful constraint on what a researcher can plausibly and justifiably assert in print.

Transcript excerpts are used throughout this book. They are intended to be accessible to a general audience, but they do contain a few specialized symbols to capture important interactional details like silences, overlapping speech, and so on. A key to the transcription symbols can be found in the Appendix.

Although CA is often characterized as a qualitative method, this is somewhat misleading. Conversation analysts typically deal with numerous examples of a given interactional phenomenon, and these are examined systematically to arrive at a general understanding of the phenomenon in question. However, unlike formally quantitative approaches, CA does place much greater emphasis on the close analysis of individual cases, and it is this case-by-case method which forms the backbone of the CA approach.

Analyzing single episodes of interaction is more difficult than it may appear at first glance. One may have a lively intuitive sense of the meaning and import of a particular utterance, but intuition is not always a reliable guide to interaction and at times it can be downright misleading. Thus, within CA every effort is made to ground any analysis in the understandings and orientations of the participants themselves. To this end, a crucial analytic resource is the response that a given utterance receives subsequently. Because interaction unfolds sequentially, turn by turn, each successive utterance ordinarily responds to and hence deals in some way with the one that came just before it. Correspondingly, each utterance displays that speaker's analysis and understanding of what preceded it. The sequential organization of interaction thus provides a kind of "running index"

(Heritage 1988) of the interactants' own understandings of one another's conduct, and this can in turn serve as an important resource for the professional analyst.

Generalizations are arrived at by working case by case in this manner through all candidate instances of a given phenomenon that are available. As the analyst begins to develop an initial sense of a pattern or organizational principle that cuts across the collection, close attention is paid to seemingly "deviant" or anomalous cases that appear to depart from the pattern. An anomalous case may turn out, upon closer inspection, to be beyond the scope of the core phenomenon under investigation. Alternatively, it may lead the investigator to revise his or her initial analysis in a way that encompasses both the anomalous case and the regular cases. Finally, the anomalous case may turn out to be entirely consistent with the original analysis if, for example, it is negatively sanctioned or is otherwise treated by the participants as a departure from normality. Anomalous cases can thus turn out to provide the strongest evidence in support of a given generalization. In any event, by progressively examining both regular and anomalous cases, the analyst is driven to specify more clearly the scope, character, and normativity of the conventions that govern interaction (Clayman and Gill Forthcoming; Heritage 1984: chapter 8; Schegloff 1968; ten Have 1999).

Finally, when CA methods are used to analyze talk in institutional environments – such as law courts, hospitals, classrooms, and of course broadcasting studios – the analysis must take an additional step: to link documented interactional conventions to the institutional context at hand and the specialized tasks, roles, and relevancies that comprise it (Drew and Heritage 1992).

Establishing the relationship between talk and its institutional environment is by no means straightforward.[15] For example, what might seem at first glance to be a convention specific to the news interview may in fact be a highly general feature of interaction whenever and wherever it occurs, so that the institutional environment is neither relevant nor consequential for its production. For this reason, research on institutional forms of talk often proceeds by

---

[15] Useful discussions of the relationship between talk, social institutions, and other aspects of social structure may be found in Schegloff (1987; 1991; 1992b), Wilson (1991), Zimmerman and Boden (1991), and Drew and Heritage (1992).

comparative reference to ordinary or "casual" conversation, which appears to be the predominant and fundamental form of interaction in the social world. Notwithstanding the many varieties of conversation (e.g., talk at family dinners, poker parties, telephone chat, etc.), these varieties do share a common core of organizational features (Schegloff 1999). If practices of institutional talk can be shown to depart systematically from parallel practices in ordinary conversation, then there are grounds for concluding that those practices are indeed adaptations to the local institutional environment, and that they result from the participants' orientation to specialized aspects of that environment. Indeed, it is through the specialized adaptation of conversational practices that a course of interaction betrays its "institutional" character, and that social institutions are ultimately talked into being.

Levels of analysis

Although the study of interaction may be regarded as a form of "micro-analysis," this domain can in fact be examined at varying levels of scale. Our approach to the news interview is multidimensional in this respect, ranging from relatively "micro" levels involving the design of individual turns and actions, to more "macro" levels involving the encompassing system of speech exchange and its relationship to the broader institutional and sociopolitical environment. In the following we provide a preview of the main levels of analysis employed in this book.

Speech exchange system

The news interview can be understood in its entirety as a system of speech exchange that differs from other systems such as debates, lectures, and ceremonies, as well as from the basic system of ordinary conversation. The distinctiveness of each speech exchange system rests upon the underlying method by which the participants take turns at talk. In ordinary conversation, turn-taking is a thoroughly unscripted affair – how long any given speaker will retain the floor, and who will speak next, remains to be worked out by the participants themselves on a turn by turn, moment by moment basis. In contrast, other speech exchange systems are more "formal" in character, with the construction of turns and the order of speakership proceeding in accordance with a more or less predetermined format (Sacks, Schegloff, and Jefferson 1974). To take one familiar example, formal debates are organized as a series of position statements and rebuttals, with the maximum length of each turn and the order of speakership fully known in advance. Much less familiar are various ceremonial occasions such as those of Burundi society, in which participants take the floor in order of descending social status (Albert 1972). Then there are routine business meetings, in which turns at talk are allocated by, and addressed to, the chair. Whatever its specific character, a system of turn-taking defines the basic ground rules for interacting in any social setting.

We explore the news interview as a speech exchange system in chapter 4. This system seems at first to be exceedingly straightforward – turn-taking is organized in terms of the simple rule that interviewers should ask questions while interviewees should answer them. However, when one considers what the participants must actually do to follow this rule, it becomes apparent that the processes involved are really quite complicated and by no means obvious. They include both interactional practices that are particular to the news interview, as well as the systematic avoidance of practices that would be normal and natural in ordinary conversation. In chapter 4 we analyze the systematic matrix of practices underlying this speech exchange system, the way in which the system defines the boundaries of permissible conduct, and the institutional functions that it serves.

Action sequences

The news interview can also be examined at the level of the sequences of action that comprise it. Some action sequences are very tightly organized, so that the initial action is routinely followed by a very particular response with little room for variation under normal circumstances. Greetings are organized in this way – an initial greeting ordinarily receives a return greeting, and any departure from this pattern is likely to generate special inferences about the motives or intentions of the recipient (e.g., "he's angry at me"). Other action sequences are more loosely organized. News announcements, for example, may be followed by a range of responses – expressions of surprise ("oh really"), evaluative assessments ("that's great"), questions that probe for further information, and so on. At the level of sequences, analysis focuses on the various environments in which some focal action-type gets introduced, and how that action is consequential for the range of actions that may follow.

The analysis of sequences and their organization is not confined to any particular chapter, but is a running theme throughout most of the book. It arises most prominently in chapter 3, which deals with the sequences through which interviews are opened and closed, and in chapter 8, which deals with how disagreements between interviewees are elicited and expressed. In both cases, focal sequences are organized in ways that are strikingly different from parallel sequences in ordinary conversation – some are more compact, others more elaborated – and these differences are indicative of the highly distinctive orientations that guide participation in a news interview.

Actions and their accomplishment

One step below the level of action sequences is the analysis of individual actions and the various practices through which they are accomplished. These practices include characteristic lexical choices, phrasings, interactional behaviors involving both speaker and recipient, and indeed any practices relevant to the recognizable accomplishment of some focal action.

This level of analysis is most prominent in chapters 5 and 6, which deal with the design of interviewers' questions, and chapter 7 which deals with interviewees' answers. Question design concerns matters such as the maintenance of interviewer neutralism, and various techniques used to exert pressure on recalcitrant interviewees. Answer design focuses on how interviewees indicate that they are indeed being responsive to a given question, as well as various evasive maneuvers deployed to resist the question.

The news interview and society

The news interview does not exist in a vacuum; it is embedded within institutional, cultural, and sociohistorical environments that give shape to it and are in turn shaped by it. As a primary locus for direct and public confrontations between journalists and officials at the highest levels, the news interview is an important aspect of the contemporary public sphere, as well as a bellwether of the state of broadcast journalism and national politics.

We explore the relationship between the news interview and society at various points throughout this book. In chapter 2 we chart the historical evolution of the broadcast news interview in the postwar era, with an emphasis on the distinctive developmental trajectories the interview has taken in Britain and the United States. In chapters 4 and 5 we consider how the conventions of the news interview turn-taking system and allied practices reflect certain institutional features of broadcast journalism, including the norm of formal neutrality that interviewers are obliged to uphold. Finally, in chapter 9 we consider the current state and future prospects of the news interview as an instrument of journalism, a medium of political communication, and an aspect of the public sphere.

The database

This study is based primarily on an analysis of approximately 250 news interviews broadcast over the past twenty years. The analysis focuses exclusively on prototypical news interviews broadcast on national news programs involving professional journalists and newsworthy public figures engaged in discussion of recent news events. Roughly equal proportions of the data were drawn from American and British national contexts. The American interviews are slightly fewer in number, but they tend to be longer than their British counterparts. The American data were drawn mainly from programs that feature live interviews – in particular, the nightly news programs *The NewsHour* (PBS) and *Nightline* (ABC), and the Sunday news programs *Meet the Press* (NBC), *Face the Nation* (CBS), and *This Week* (ABC). A smaller number of interviews and interview segments were taken from the news magazine program *60 Minutes* (CBS), the radio show *All Things Considered* (NPR), and various other sources. The British data were drawn primarily from *Newsnight* (BBC2), *The Today Programme* (BBC Radio 4), and *The World at One* (BBC Radio 4).

Although the database is spread across a twenty-year period, this represents a relatively stable era in the history of the broadcast news interview. As we will see in the next chapter, the most dramatic changes in interview conduct took place in earlier decades. Correspondingly, while the data were drawn from both American and British programs, there is a striking level of similarity across these national contexts (Heritage and Roth 1995). There are thus grounds for treating the primary database as an essentially cohesive subject for study.

The game in action

The metaphor of the news interview as a game has been explicit in this introduction. In some ways, this metaphor may seem inappropriate; while most games are insignificant diversions from the serious business of life, the news interview is both serious and deeply consequential. But in other ways the metaphor is quite apt. Like true games, the news interview is a distinct form of activity that is bounded off from the ordinary run of social life. It is organized by well-established rules, although the rules here are much more complex and more deeply taken-for-granted than in most games. It is played through a series of moves and counter-moves. Its participants are locked in competition, and with varying levels of skill they deploy their moves strategically in pursuit of divergent goals and objectives. At the end of the game – and this sets the news interview apart – there may be ramifications for personal careers, for public affairs, and sometimes for the march of history.

To understand how the news interview game works, we will examine it in action, as it is played by prominent and skillful journalists and public figures. This will involve both a telescopic look at interviewing practices as they vary across institutional, cultural, and historical contexts, as well as a microscopic look at particular practices in considerable detail. Since the microscopic level of analysis is (as we argued earlier) fundamental, and since there is much more continuity than variation across the data set, more space is devoted to this mode of analysis. We will endeavor to show that singular practices of interviewing do indeed matter – for the course of the interview itself, and for the social world that it reflects and embodies.

2

The news interview in context: institutional background and historical development

According to the Oxford English Dictionary, the term "interview" entered the language in 1514, from the French *entre voir* (meaning "to be in sight of"), hence referring to a "meeting of persons face-to-face, especially one sought or arranged for the purpose of formal conference at some point" (p. 1740). These first interviews were normally between high ranking individuals and, in a world where travel was difficult and most diplomatic communication was conducted by letter, they were rare events accompanied by high ceremony. The extraordinary 1520 extravaganza, when Henry VIII of England entertained Francis I of France so lavishly that the event (and its location) came to be known as the Field of the Cloth of Gold, may have been one of the first "interviews" ever to be so named.

By the end of the nineteenth century and the rise of modern journalism, the term interview came to have a different and more current meaning. Webster's dictionary of 1913 defined an interview as "a conversation, or questioning, for the purpose of eliciting information for publication," noting that this is a "recent use, originating in American newspapers, but apparently becoming general" (Webster 1913: 781). A more recent Webster notes that the term "interviewee" emerged in 1884. By this point, the term had lost its older ceremonial associations, and acquired its primary modern meaning as a journalistic practice.

The news interview is the invention of American print journalists, and grew to prominence in the last quarter of the nineteenth century. By the early twentieth century, English and other European journalists began to accept it, often under American instruction (Schudson 1994). Early interviews were usually done without notes, and their results were paraphrased and summarized in newspaper articles.

As the interview became institutionalized, however, direct quotation became more common and the interview increasingly became an "on the record" affair. In a parallel but delayed fashion, US presidential press conferences also evolved from off-record background conversations with journalists, to the full-scale on-record sessions we know today.

The emergence of the news interview was a product of changes in newspapers in the middle of the nineteenth century when factual reporting became a more important feature of newspaper content than partisan commentary, and was associated with the professionalization of journalists that accompanied this development. News interviews were disliked by proprietors who preferred their newspapers to be organs of opinion, and by editors who disapproved of the reporter's increasing independence from editorial control (ibid.). Interviews were also disliked by their subjects. In addition to their understandable resentment of journalistic ambushes on their own doorsteps, public figures found they had to accommodate to a new and more uncertain method of communicating with the public. The direct expression of their views in speeches or in writing that was typical before 1850, was supplanted by journalistic mediation concocted out of quotation and paraphrase. Because the result is a product of the questions the journalist chooses to put, the source's responses, and the reporter's selective representation of them, public figures found the expression of their opinions entangled in an uneasy process of collaboration. New dependencies emerged – on the wit and motivation of the reporter to ask the right questions, and to understand and represent the import of the answers. And collaboration brought with it a taint of manufacture and artifice – the "joint construction of . . . a hack politician and . . . a journalist," as one nineteenth-century critic described it.[1]

What began in the newspaper business spread to broadcasting shortly after the development of radio. Once radio producers discovered that broadcasting the spoken word was more than a matter of simply reading the printed word aloud, they used mediating interviewers to help public figures and others "in the news" to get their message across. The use of interviewers solved the problem of "address." As early as 1928, experiments conducted at the BBC led

---

[1] Schudson (1994: 76).

to the conclusion that it was "useless to address the microphone as if it were a public meeting, or even to read it essays or leading articles."[2] Interviews solved this problem of address: the public figure simply responded to the interviewer's questions. In this way, an element of conversational informality and spontaneity was injected into broadcasting, while the rigors of directly addressing the broadcast audience were reserved for newscasters, advertisers, and electioneering politicians.

The same techniques were later imported directly from radio to television, and with even more urgency. As President Franklin Roosevelt's "fireside chats" demonstrated, it is certainly possible to create an "informal" script and read it so as to simulate spontaneous talk. However, while this practice is workable on radio, it is impossible on television. Here, before the development of the teleprompter, "the speaker, being seen, was seen to be reading" (Wyndham Goldie 1977: 198). Moreover, it would be many years before public figures developed any real competence in using the teleprompter in a natural way (Cockerell 1988). Thus, almost from the beginning, interview techniques were a significant feature of television current affairs shows. In America, *Hear it Now*, Edward R. Murrow's interview-based magazine show for CBS radio, became *See it Now* on CBS television in 1951. NBC's *Meet the Press* started as a radio show in 1945 and moved to television in 1947. The program endured many changes of slot, but it has deviated little from its original interview format. It has now become the longest running show on American television. In Britain, news interview techniques pioneered by Robin Day and others from 1958 onwards have since become a staple feature of television news and current affairs.

In this chapter, we review the normative context of the broadcast news interview, the regulatory constraints that shape its production, and trace the evolution of the news interview in Britain and America.

The "interview contract"

The growth and institutionalization of interviewing, for both newspapers and broadcast media, is built on a coincidence of interest between public figures and journalists. Journalists need access to

---

[2] Matheson 1933 (75–6), quoted in Scannell (1991: 3).

public figures for their livelihood, while public figures need journalists to gain access to what Margaret Thatcher once called "the
oxygen of publicity." Thus an informal and unspoken contract exists between the two parties in which journalists exchange access to
publicity for the kind of news content that will keep readers reading
and viewers watching. These incentives also imply the sanctions that
underlie the bargain: boring or uncooperative interviewees do not
get a second invitation, and aggressive journalists can be boycotted.[3]
These sanctions are a valuable reminder of the tensions just below
the surface of the "joint construction" of news.

Underlying these tensions are specific journalistic values and interests which are quite frequently at odds with the objectives of
politicians. According to veteran British interviewer Robin Day,
writing in 1961, the interviewer

is there to elicit opinions, regardless of his own. He is giving the person
interviewed an opportunity to deal with attacks or misconceptions. The
interviewer has a duty to see that a person with controversial views has
the other side of the problem put to him. An interview must not degenerate
into a platform for a man's unchallenged opinions...A TV interview does
not exist to glorify the person interviewed. Nor does it exist to glorify
the interviewer. It is for the information of the public. The interviewer
should stick to this principle undeterred by charges of bias or self-assertion.
(Day 1961: 105)

As this statement suggests, broadcast journalists ordinarily attempt to strike a balance between two competing conceptions of
"objectivity." On the one hand, there is objectivity as impartiality:
journalists are expected to be disinterested and neutral in their questioning of public figures. They are expected to have respect for the
facts and the perspectives that their sources communicate, and to
work to bring these into the public domain. On the other hand, there
is objectivity as adversarialness. To achieve factual accuracy and a
balance of perspectives, journalists should actively challenge their
sources, rather than being simply mouthpieces or ciphers for them
(Weaver and Wilhoit 1991; Tunstall 1971). In the news interview
context, this second norm is one that pushes interviewers not to let
the interview become a kind of platform or soapbox from which

---

[3] Politicians on both sides of the Atlantic have recurrently drawn up "friends and
enemies lists" of interviewers and producers (Cockerell 1988; Friendly 1967;
Fallows 1997).

public figures can get away with their own preferred, possibly misleading, and often self-serving spin on events. These two ideals are
of course just that, and there are no absolute standards for the evaluation of either. Because questions inevitably encode points of view
and decisions about relevance, they can never be strictly neutral.
Nor is there adversarialness that does not involve judgments about
what is, and what is not appropriate.

The two ideals, moreover, are not always equally balanced, especially among the elite journalists with whom we are primarily concerned. Successful journalists tend to be those who impart their own
"take" on events, and whose interpretations of the background and
motivations of political actors are conveyed to the viewing public.
As Zaller (Forthcoming) argues, this drives journalists to take a more
adversarial stance towards politicians in both print and television.[4]
In the broadcast interview context, this means asking public figures
questions they would rather not answer, and using questions to
imply versions of events that are unflattering to politicians. It is no
accident that many of the most celebrated television and radio interviewers of the last thirty years – for example, Mike Wallace, Dan
Rather, and Sam Donaldson in the USA and Robin Day, David Frost,
and Jeremy Paxman in the UK – made their reputations through
highly aggressive styles of questioning. Aggressive questioning led
to "heavyweight" celebrity status, counter-balancing and sometimes
exceeding the status of their interviewees. There are thus real career
incentives for journalists who wish to achieve or maintain elite status to engage in the kind of questioning that public figures are most
inclined to dislike and resist.

Setting aside career incentives, journalists tend to hold politicians
in low esteem. According to Epstein:

> The working hypothesis almost universally shared among correspondents is
> that politicians are suspect; their public images probably false, their public
> statements disingenuous, their moral pronouncements hypocritical, their
> motives self-serving, and their promises ephemeral.   (Epstein 1973: 215)

In terms of news interviewing, this can translate into a distinctly
adversarial frame of mind. Sam Donaldson put it this way:

---

[4] This trend towards adversarial reporting is documented in Patterson (1993) and
Zaller (Forthcoming).

As to what questions are appropriate and how they should be asked, well, let's put it this way: If you send me to cover a pie-baking contest on Mother's Day, I'm going to ask dear old Mom whether she used artificial sweetener in violation of the rules, and while she's at it, could I see the receipt for the apples to prove she didn't steal them. I maintain that if Mom has nothing to hide, no harm will have been done. But the questions should be asked. Too often, Mom, and presidents – behind those sweet faces – turn out to have stuffed a few rotten apples into the public barrel.   (Donaldson 1987: 20)

Jeremy Paxman of BBC Television's *Newsnight* was characteristically more succinct:

When he started as a young man on *The Times* Louis Heren was given a piece of advice by an old hack. He was told you should always ask yourself when talking to a politician: "Why is this lying bastard lying to me?" I think that is quite a sound principle from which to operate.[5]

Thus, in addition to the career attractions of taking up an adversarial stance towards politicians, journalists entertain quite deep-seated sub-cultural beliefs which can license such a stance.

There is, in sum, a conflict of interest that underlies the "interview contract." Most public figures would prefer the kind of straightforward dispassionate questioning that is typical of the PBS *Newshour* "newsmaker" interviews, even though they may recognize that such interviews do not make for exciting television. Elite news interviewers, often under pressure from ratings, are impelled to take a more lively and contentious stance. The last thirty years in particular have witnessed a shift from "lapdog" journalism (Sabato 1991) to "attack dog" journalism. As one component of this, the drive towards more adversarial interviewing both reflects and embodies an unavoidable conflict of interest between broadcasters and their subjects, one that injects friction into an otherwise symbiotic relationship.

Controlling the playing field: regulatory constraints on news

The conflicts of interest between journalists and sources do not exist in an institutional vacuum. Broadcasting in both the USA and the UK is subject to a complex regulatory environment which, before the advent of cable and the Internet, arose from a fundamental

---

[5] Jones (1992: 53).

shortage of broadcasting frequencies. From the 1920s, both countries addressed this problem by licensing and regulating access to bandwidth, though they did so within different philosophies of broadcasting. The regulation of broadcasting in the United States emerged within a strongly market-oriented framework in which it was believed that, subject to safeguards against monopoly, consumer choice should largely determine the content of radio and television programming. Accordingly, regulation by the Federal Communications Commission (FCC) has been relatively light and unobtrusive. Since the late 1970s, FCC constraints – on ownership, access to bandwidth, and program content – have been progressively relaxed as cable, satellite and the Internet have increased bandwidth and weakened the basic rationale for regulation in media markets. In Britain, by contrast, the bandwidth problem was addressed by establishing a broadcasting monopoly – the British Broadcasting Corporation – whose potential power was limited by statute, formal powers of appointment to the governing boards of the BBC, and other, more informal, means of control. For these reasons, the history of broadcasting in Britain is one in which relations between governments and broadcasters assume a much greater significance than in the USA.

United States

In the United States, the Federal Communications Commission was established by Congress in 1934 to license broadcasting stations, and thereby to control access to the airwaves. The FCC's policies were historically centered on the development of an informed public opinion, and "on the right of the public to be informed, rather than any right on the part of the government, any broadcast licencees or any individual members of the public to broadcast his own particular views on any matter" (Franklin 1981: 587). FCC policy focused on maintaining a diverse range of broadcast news sources by limiting the total ownership of radio and television stations, and by preventing overlapping ownership or control in the same market. From the emergence of television until the mid-1970s, the FCC strongly favored news programming – a generally less profitable, if not actually unprofitable, component of television broadcasting. Indeed, it was FCC pressure at various points in the 1960s that led to the expansion of news and current affairs programming on American television (Epstein 1973: 53–9).

Although the FCC has the power to revoke licenses, it has historically exerted pressure on stations more indirectly. Until the later 1970s, license renewals involved an audit of news programming, and stations which fell below a certain minimum were required to justify their programming decisions. Negotiations often followed in which renewal was made contingent on an increase in news programming. Similarly, in competitive hearings, the FCC clearly favored news programming in allocating licenses (Epstein 1973: 61). This more interventionist stance by the FCC gradually eroded during the 1970s, and was essentially abandoned in the anti-regulatory atmosphere of the 1980s.

Between 1949 and 1986, the FCC also exerted some influence on various aspects of news content. Most importantly, it enforced standards of balance and fairness in news programming under the "Fairness Doctrine." This required broadcasters to present contrasting points of view on controversial public issues. Also enforced indirectly – the FCC did not actively monitor news programming and mainly responded to complaints – the "Fairness Doctrine" nonetheless induced the networks to take steps toward achieving a measure of balance in their news and documentary programming. It did so by obligating affiliates to balance one-sided programs with later, additional programming (Epstein 1973: 65). Consumed with the necessity of avoiding this kind of costly and unprofitable programming, affiliates insisted that contrasting viewpoints be included in network news. This significantly impacted news interview content. Epstein notes, for example, that in the coverage of a 1968 New York City teachers' strike,

> executives at NBC ordered a number of stories prepared for the Evening News to be reshot or canceled because the views of black community leaders were not adequately "balanced" by filmed interviews with teachers and union officials. And it is quite common for producers to order correspondents to insert "pro" or "con" material in their voice-over narration. (Epstein 1973: 67)

And the "balance" provision of the Fairness Doctrine was supplemented by the "attack rule" which provided that public figures whose honesty, character, or integrity was impugned had the right to be notified of the program, to a script or tape of its content, and access to the broadcaster's facilities to reply. Taken together, these two provisions had a significant, and dampening, impact on the use of controversial interview material on network news.

The membership of the FCC is by presidential appointment and in 1986 – six years into the strongly deregulatory Reagan presidency – the FCC systematically dismantled many of the content regulations which had been enforced during the preceding thirty years including the "Fairness Doctrine." Underlying these changes was the fundamental fact that, with the emergence of cable and satellite transmissions, bandwidth was no longer a scarce resource. In this new context, the argument that bandwidth was a resource of which the broadcasters were temporary stewards lost its force. In place of the older paternalistic conception of broadcasters as community trustees, the Reaganite conception stressed the role of market forces in bringing the public the programming it chooses (Aufderheide 1999). As FCC head Fowler put it, "the public's interest... defines the public interest" (Fowler and Brenner 1982). One result has been an increasing tendency for more politically slanted news and public affairs coverage, especially on cable and in the recently emergent Fox News owned by Rupert Murdoch. While traditional journalistic values continue to stress balance and fairness, new cable news channels, such as MSNBC, strongly promote aggressive "attack dog" interview shows. The result has been an exacerbation of the "argument culture" (Tannen 1998) of journalism, and a general expansion of adversarial interviewing styles. The newly deregulated environment of journalism provided a context for Dan Rather's highly aggressive prime-time interview of George Bush on the CBS *Evening News* and may have contributed to its tenor.

In 1967, a new kind of television network – the Public Broadcasting Service (PBS) – took its place alongside the existing commercial stations. Created by the Public Broadcasting Act signed into law by President Lyndon Johnson, public television was pieced together from over a hundred local educational stations mainly financed by state and local government (Hoynes 1994). Its formation was a response to the sense that the commercial pressures on existing radio and television companies created real obstacles to their ability to serve cultural, informational, and educational functions – in a word, the public service function of the broadcast media. Public television was financed by congressional allocations, determined every three years, by membership of local stations and increasingly by commercial sponsorship and advertising. From the start, government funding was a source of conflict with the Nixon administration which replaced Johnson in 1968. Since the 1980s, the financing for public broadcasting has been heavily contested and uncertain during a period in which free market conservatism and the deregulation of broadcasting have been increasingly in the ascendancy in Washington. Persistent difficulties over the congressional allocation of funds, which can be vetoed by the President, have increased the sensitivity of PBS to the political and moral preferences of the Congress, which today constitute a pressure favoring self-censorship by the broadcasters that in some ways parallels the pressures experienced by broadcasters in Britain.

Britain

From the outset, the British Government handled the bandwidth problem within a quite different philosophical framework from the USA. In contrast to the competition of voices encouraged by US policymakers, British legislators concluded that "the broadcasting service should be conducted by a public corporation acting as a trustee for the national interest and that its status and duties should correspond with those of a public service."[6] This stance favored a single broadcaster – the British Broadcasting Corporation (BBC) – which, from its founding in 1922 until 1955, enjoyed a monopoly of the airwaves. The BBC is funded through an annual license fee, at first paid by owners of radios and, subsequently, television sets. The BBC's remit was summarized by its first Director General Lord Reith as "to inform, educate, and entertain." Similar principles informed the national broadcasting systems developed in Canada, Australia, and a number of European countries.

In 1954, in a major shift in policy, the Broadcasting Act was passed by Parliament permitting commercial television broadcasts. The Act established the Independent Television Authority[7] to

[6] Crawford Committee 1926.
[7] Later termed the Independent Broadcasting Authority with the advent of commercial radio in 1972, and was further restructured in 1990 to become the Independent Television Commission.

ensure that the commercial companies maintained a broad public service broadcasting policy and that they provided fair, objective, and balanced reporting in news, current affairs, and documentary programs. Since this committee, like the FCC in the USA, can change the allocation of television franchises, it can exert similar indirect pressures on news producers to be careful in matters of balance and objectivity. Unlike the BBC, commercial television is primarily funded through advertising revenue and sales of programs.

The British broadcasting system is one in which government plays a key role, and one which is in many ways more overt than in the USA (Cockerell 1988). All the main structural changes in broadcasting – the advent of television, the introduction of commercial television, and subsequent expansions in the number of channels – have followed reports of government committees which resulted in legislation to implement the changes. In addition to legislation, the government of the day has other resources with which to exert influence on the broadcasters.

First, there is the power to appoint. In the case of the BBC, the government appoints the chair and the twelve governing board members of the BBC. This power is one which permits politicians to exert both direct and indirect influence on the policies of the BBC. On two occasions prime ministers have sanctioned the BBC by removing its chairman although, as in the case of some US Supreme Court appointments, they have not always found the direction set by the new chair as palatable as they had hoped. The government has identical powers of appointment of the committee overseeing commercial television, including the important matter of the allocation of broadcasting licenses.[8]

Moreover governments set the BBC's license fee. Decisions to raise this fee are never popular with the British public and legislators are understandably reluctant to raise them any more than necessary. The license fee is thus an inbuilt source of friction between government and the BBC which is continually in search of programming resources. Although withholding increases in the license fee has sometimes been overtly used as a sanction (Cockerell 1988: 133–4), it is also an area where it can be difficult to discern the dividing line

[8] Franchise reallocations took place in 1968, 1982, and 1990. While most of the commercial companies retained their franchises, significant reallocations occurred at each of these points.

between understandable reluctance to court electoral unpopularity, and tacit pressure on the BBC to engage in programming that is more favorable to government interests.

Finally, governments of both political parties have objected directly to particular news and current affairs programs. The most infamous reaction was to a 1971 BBC program titled *Yesterday's Men* about the Labour opposition leadership, which led to a long-term deterioration in the relationship between broadcasters and politicians and an intensification of the hostile relationship between the BBC and the Labour administration that took power in 1974. During the 1980s, government anger at a string of programs dealing with the IRA and other Irish terrorist organizations issued in various forms of pressure: explicit attacks on program makers, monitoring broadcasts for political bias, and informal – but overt – threats to limit revenue from license fees. More generalized attacks on "media bias" – particularly in the six-month run-up to general elections – have also been a recurrent means through which both major British political parties have attempted to restrict the autonomy of broadcasters, often with some success.

Participation

Although balance, impartiality, and objectivity are commonly enjoined on US and UK news and current affairs broadcasts, both by journalistic norms and legal frameworks of broadcasting, this does not mean that all potential participants have equal and unfettered access to news programming. The ideal of "balance," whether required by the US Federal Communications Commission's "Fairness Doctrine" or by British norms of "public service" broadcasting, has never embraced "equal time" or "equal treatment" for communists (Epstein 1973), or terrorist organizations such as the IRA (Schlesinger, Murdoch, and Elliott 1983). Indeed for a six-year period ending in 1994 the British media were not permitted to broadcast the voices of IRA spokespersons – an injunction which they circumvented by having the relevant statements read by "voice doubles" so similar to the main protagonists that the prohibition was rendered vacuous.

Leaving aside these explicit restrictions on participation, it is clear that the major news shows favor "establishment" guests. Research by Croteau and Hoynes (1994) on participation in ABC's *Nightline* and PBS's *Newshour* – both major US news shows that rely heavily on interviews – documents the unmistakable dominance of their guest lists by Washington and establishment "insiders." Both shows predominantly feature members of elites, less than 10 percent were labor, public interest, or racial/ethnic leaders, less than 20 percent were female, and the vast majority were white. These guest lists did not "look like America." Similar British findings were reported a decade earlier by the Glasgow Media Group (1976). This preference for "insider" political actors and experts has its defenders. As Robert McNeil put it: "We are a news program. When we are mounting a debate, it is at the point of action in the debate. We don't take into consideration on the air, as represented by the guests, all the various points of view that have fed the people who are going to make the decision."[9] Other considerations also shape participation. Interviewees should preferably be intelligent and articulate, criteria that many potential interviewees do not meet. As one British media insider observes, broadcasters need:

> people who can make the language get up and walk from the first sentence. Content has to be fairly good but above all it's the way it's said rather than what is said which is important. Those who are sufficiently plausible and voluble, who know how to fashion little bullets of the right length and content and deliver them "live" will be invited time and time again. That's why you see the same people on *Newsnight* night after night. Remember that out of 650 MPs a fair number will be ruled out on grounds of age, dreariness, alcoholism and so forth, so it's quite a small pool of those who can perform, who can shine.[10]

Similar sentiments have been repeatedly voiced in relation to American news interview participants. More recently this concentration of participation has been exacerbated by the increasing interchangeability of the roles of political "insiders," experts, and broadcasters, which may also have contributed to the erosion in public confidence in the objectivity of broadcasters (Fallows 1996).

Even when they gain access to the media, not all political actors are given equal treatment. Even distinguished public figures can be

---

[9] Croteau and Hoynes (1994: 53).
[10] Peter Hennessey, quoted in Jones (1992: 57–8). Similar views were expressed by Reuven Frank when he was head of NBC News: "Most people are dull. That is, they communicate ineptly. If they are dull, their description of interesting events will be dull" (Epstein 1973: 157–8).

treated harshly, as the biochemist and Nobel Prize winner Linus Pauling found when he was interviewed on NBC's *Meet the Press*. Pauling, who had organized a scientific petition against the testing of nuclear weapons, received the kind of hostile grilling that is rarely meted out to distinguished guests. Still harsher treatment can lie in store for more marginal figures such as Nazi sympathizers, representatives of militia or survivalist groups, strike leaders and others.

Daniel Hallin (1994) has observed that the domain of journalism can be divided into three regions, each of which involves the application of different journalistic standards:

The first can be called the sphere of consensus. This is the region of motherhood and apple pie; in its bounds lie those social objects not regarded by journalists and most of society as controversial. Within this region journalists do not feel compelled to present opposing views, and indeed often feel it their responsibility to act as advocates or ceremonial protectors of consensus values. The discussion of patriotism that marked coverage of the homecoming of the hostages after the Iranian crisis is a good example...

Beyond the sphere of consensus lies what can be called the sphere of legitimate controversy. This is the region where objective journalism reigns supreme: here neutrality and balance are the prime journalistic virtues. Election coverage best exemplifies the journalistic standards of this region.

Beyond the sphere of legitimate controversy lie those political actors and views which journalists and the political mainstream of society reject as unworthy of being heard... Here neutrality falls away again and the media become, to borrow a phrase from Parsons, a "boundary maintaining mechanism": They play the role of exposing, condemning, or excluding from the public agenda those who violate or challenge consensus values, and uphold the consensus distinction between legitimate and illegitimate political activity. The anti-war movement was treated in this way during the early years of the Vietnam period.   (Hallin 1994: 53–4)

In a parallel discussion, Stuart Hall (1971) divided news interviews and features into areas of consensus, toleration, and conflict. While consensus interviewees, he observes, are the "accredited witnesses," areas of toleration involve "more maverick witnesses" who are treated with an "off-beat sympathetic human interest" approach. Finally, "areas of conflict have their unaccredited cast of witnesses too: protesters of all varieties; shop stewards, especially if militant, more especially if on unofficial strike; squatters; civil rights activists; hippies; students; hijackers... In dealing with these issues and actors, interviewers are noticeably touchier, defending their flanks against any predisposition to softness" (Hall 1973: 88). These observations speak to the fact that news and news interview questioning are characteristically produced from a broadly "centrist" or "majority" political and social stance. The effect of this is to marginalize those whose perspectives are perceived to be significantly distanced from the center. This process of marginalization was dramatically highlighted in the media treatment of British Labour politician Tony Benn during the 1980s. Benn, who had been a successful and effective cabinet minister in previous Labour administrations, had subsequently radicalized his political stance and his policy positions were treated in a progressively more skeptical way during this period. Benn eventually became so distrustful of media questioning and editing that he personally tape-recorded every interview that he gave. In the USA, Patrick Buchanan, who served in the Reagan White House and in recent years has taken increasingly populist right-wing positions culminating in his departure from the Republican Party, has undergone a similar process of marginalization.

The evolution of the broadcast interview

Despite the rather similar normative and, as we shall see, interactional frameworks that shape news interviews in the USA and Britain, news and current affairs production has been impacted differently by the distinctive regulatory and competitive environments in the two countries. This distinctiveness is particularly marked when we consider historical aspects of news interviews. There is no history of "the news interview" that is clearly common to these two national contexts. Instead, the development and use of news interviews have emerged and been given shape by quite different legislative, economic, and social pressures.

The United States: development by fits and starts

Network news in the USA has rarely carried a significant amount of news interview content. From the late 1940s until the early 1960s network news occupied a fifteen-minute slot and, deducting time for advertising breaks, the nightly news ran for just twelve minutes of airtime. There was no opportunity, within this short compass, to include the kind of time-consuming multiple question-and-answer sequence that makes up a real "interview." Matters were little better when, in 1963, CBS and NBC expanded the news slot to thirty minutes (expanding advertising time to eight of them).[11] Network news carries around twenty items per broadcast, and these items must be squeezed into a twenty-two-minute time frame. Thus, with the exception of special events such as Dan Rather's interview with George Bush on CBS prime-time news in 1988, interview content has remained sparse.

Behind these facts lies a basic conflict of interest between the networks and their affiliates. FCC rules make the networks dependent on their independent affiliates for the "clearance" of their news and current affairs programming.[12] While the affiliates must share the advertising revenue arising from national news with the networks, they have no such obligation in connection with their own more popular, and more profitable, local news broadcasts (Epstein 1973). Understandably, affiliate stations resisted the expansion of network news for as long as possible. Indeed the expansion of network news in the early 1960s was as much a product of fear of reprisals from the FCC, as of any other factor. In 1961, then FCC Chairman Newton Minow commented that: "Unfortunately too many television stations reject the public affairs programs offered by the networks because they can make more money rerunning old movies. This kind of broadcasting raises serious questions about responsibility and the public interest." The implication was clear: refusal to accept national network news and current affairs programming could lead to reprisals for the affiliates when their licenses came up for renewal. The expansion of network news in 1963 was a consequence of this stance. As one NBC executive commented: "Without the FCC we couldn't line up enough affiliates to make a news program or documentary worthwhile,"[13] and it seems clear that, as Epstein concluded, any alteration in FCC support for network news product would undermine the prospects for its "clearance" and its ultimate viability.

---

[11] ABC, the weakest of the three networks in terms of resources, did not expand its network news to thirty minutes until 1967.

[12] For this reason the "clearance" of particular network current affairs and news documentary programs can vary quite widely, according to the topic and the outlook of the affiliates involved – impacting their profitability to the networks and the preparedness of networks to address particular topics.

[13] Epstein (1973: 54).

Moving away from news broadcasting into current affairs, matters are somewhat different for the main network interview shows – NBC's *Meet the Press*, CBS's *Face the Nation*, and ABC's *This Week*. These three shows are broadcast weekly on Sunday mornings, and attract a roster of highly placed politicians and administration officials. *Meet the Press* started as a radio show in 1945, and had its television premiere in 1947. It is America's longest running television show. Originally thirty minutes long, *Meet the Press* was given a press conference format in which a political newsmaker was interviewed by a panel of journalists. Subsequently, it evolved into a news interview program with three interview segments, followed by a roundtable discussion. The host, currently Tim Russert, is joined by two other journalists during the interview segments, and three others during the roundtable discussion. *Face the Nation*, CBS's rival show first aired in 1954, was discontinued between 1961 and 1963, and has since continued to the present day. Its format has undergone a similar evolution to that of *Meet the Press*. Somewhat later, ABC countered with *Issues and Answers* which ran between 1960 and 1981, when it was replaced with the successful *This Week with David Brinkley* which drew on Brinkley's prestige as a reporter and news anchor. Guests were interviewed by Brinkley, conservative columnist George Will, and Sam Donaldson, the liberal "balance" to Will. It is currently co-hosted by Sam Donaldson and Cokie Roberts.

These interview shows had a difficult time establishing their current positions. Initially they aired at times when ratings were low, and their time slots were quite frequently shifted. Indeed there were periods when their survival owed something to the networks' and affiliates' need to accommodate the public affairs programming preferences of the FCC. Latterly, they have established a clear niche in Sunday morning programming. Their audience, though far from large, includes a concentration of "insiders" to politics (including print journalists), national and local opinion leaders, and persons who are likely to vote. Thus their influence may be more substantial than their audience share suggests. Additionally, statements made in the course of these interviews often appear in Monday morning newspapers (and occasionally in network news), widening their impact and relevance.

Perhaps because they were initially modeled on the press conference format, and employed distinguished print journalists including White House correspondents seasoned in questioning presidents, the style of questioning in these "Sunday morning" shows from the outset was robust and at times combative. Here, for example, is an excerpt from an interview with the Secretary of Agriculture in January 1960:

(1) US NBC *Meet the Press*: 17 Jan 1960: Egg Farmers
     IR: Lawrence Spivak   IE: Sec. of Agriculture, Ezra Benson

1	IR:	An important sentence of the 1952 Republican
2		platform said this: "The Republican Party will
3		create conditions providing for farm prosperity
4		and stability." Do you think the Republican
5		administration has made good on that promise?
6	IE:	Yes, I do, to a very large extent, as far as we
7		can within the limitations...
8	IR:	Your critics insist that the seven years of your
9		administration of the Agriculture Department
10		have resulted in failure, since the farmers'
11		income has reached a 19-year low, and our
12		surpluses are at an all time high. How do you
13		answer that, Sir?
14	IE:	In the first place, four fifths of our
15		agriculture today is free of controls, and is
16		in fairly good balance and doing fairly well...
17	IR:	You say you are in difficulty in the one fifth,
18		but isn't it true that there are no price
19		supports for eggs and the egg farmers are in
20		serious difficulty.
21	IE:	We produce 250 commodities commercially in this
22		country. There are only 21 of those
23		supported... but generally speaking over the
24		years the poultry industry has made good
25		progress and has made a reasonable profit.
26	IR:	Mr. Secretary, I had a telegram from a group of
27		egg farmers in New Jersey who say they are going
28		into bankruptcy at a rapid rate... Would you
29		say that they are in good shape?
30	IE:	No I would not...
31	IR:	These egg farmers are operating in a free
32		market, which is what you would like to see for
33		most farmers. How are they going to solve their
34		problem?

This is a substantially hostile style of questioning, considering the date and the fact that the interviewee is a senior Cabinet member. The interviewer comes close to contradicting the Secretary, and manages to imply that his tenure at Agriculture has been a failure. Both the individual questions and their accumulation are substantially more hostile than presidential press conferences of the same period, and also more aggressive and "forensic" than comparable British interview content during the 1950s. Other, equally robust styles of questioning emerge in different contexts. For example, Mrs. Eleanor Roosevelt, questioned on *Meet the Press* on a conversation which she had had with the Soviet leader Nikita Khrushchev, was asked the following:

(2)   US NBC *Meet the Press*: 20 Oct 1957: Khrushchev
       IR: May Craig   IE: former First Lady Eleanor Roosevelt

  1   IR: You have been quoted as describing Khrushchev as
  2   being cordial, simple, outspoken. How can you
  3   think that any Communist, particularly a top
  4   official, can be simple?
  5   IE: I meant when I said that of course, that in his
  6   manner and in the way of receiving you he was
  7   simple...
  8   IR: You also are quoted as saying you found him very
  9   likeable though you disagreed with his views.
 10   How could you like anybody who has done what he
 11   did in supporting murder?

Here, in a context where a British interviewee of comparable stature would undoubtedly have been addressed in a more bland and deferential way, the former First Lady's judgment is questioned in terms that verge on moral outrage. Questioning on *Meet the Press* is scarcely more adversarial than that today.

The 1970s witnessed the emergence of two major news programs that made maximum use of the news interview format. The first of these was PBS's *MacNeil-Lehrer Report* (now the *Newshour*) which began as a thirty-minute news show in 1975, and expanded in 1983 to an hour-long program – the only nightly one-hour news show on American television. The *MacNeil-Lehrer Report* was the first major essay in news production by PBS. It emerged from PBS's coverage of a major American crisis – the Watergate Affair. PBS's Robert MacNeil, then on leave from the BBC, and Jim Lehrer covered the

Senate Watergate hearings gavel to gavel, and supplemented this coverage with extensive commentary and interview segments. The coverage had a wide impact – effectively putting public television on the map (MacNeil 1982). MacNeil and Lehrer exploited the break by arguing for, and getting, a news show that was quite different from network news. The original conception was that the show would be a supplement to commercial television news, and it was scheduled accordingly – at 7.30 PM – after the network news had aired (MacNeil 1982: 309). In place of the network's twenty topics in twenty-two minutes, the *MacNeil-Lehrer Report* offered one major news topic in a thirty-minute show. The result was an unhurried and in-depth treatment which relied extensively on interviews with a series of guests conducted, in an echo of NBC's *Huntley-Brinkley Report*, by MacNeil in New York and Lehrer in Washington. After its expansion to a one-hour slot, the renamed *MacNeil-Lehrer Newshour* covered more stories. It includes a brief news summary, with foreign news taken from Britain's Independent Television News, and is now formatted to include four items, three of which are substantial news stories. Interviews on the *Newshour* are divided between "newsmaker" interviews with single highly placed government and foreign officials, and discussion and debate interviews involving a mix of experts in a particular field. The interviewers themselves are rarely adversarial, and the conflicts that emerge on the program are normally originated by the guests themselves.

The second news interview show to emerge during the 1970s – ABC's *Nightline* – also arose from extensive coverage of a political crisis. In November 1979, after Iranian militants invaded the American Embassy in Tehran, ABC reacted with a series of late-night shows called *America Held Hostage*. The show was part of a long-running campaign by ABC's head of news, Roone Arledge, to increase its news coverage. Having lost the battle for a one-hour prime-time news show (once again vetoed by ABC's affiliate stations), Arledge believed that the 11.30 PM time slot, immediately after the affiliates' local news shows, could be a place at which more in-depth news coverage could be aired. The problem was that: "Arledge knew he needed a real crisis – one with 'legs' to it – a story so compelling, so potentially profitable, and just long enough, that watching late-night news would become an American habit" (Koppel and Gibson 1996: 7). The Iranian hostage crisis was the "hook" that brought the initial audience to ABC, and its frontman, Ted Koppel, would become the anchor for the new show – *Nightline* – that grew directly from it 142 days after the start of the crisis.

ABC promoted *Nightline* with the slogan "Bringing people together who are worlds apart." As Koppel himself notes (Koppel and Gibson 1996) this was true both literally and figuratively. It was true literally because *Nightline* made extensive use of newly operational satellite links to create debate interviews with participants from around the world. It was true figuratively because the accent of the *Nightline* interviews, in contrast to those on the *Newshour*, was debate and controversy. The first *Nightline* featured a discussion between the Iranian chargé d'affaires in Washington and the wife of the imprisoned American ambassador to Iran, and many highly charged interviews were to follow. In significant contrast to the more urbane *Newshour*, Koppel himself does much more to probe and to elicit the points of friction between interviewees than the *Newshour* interviewers, and he is certainly more prepared both to ask the truly difficult adversarial questions of interviewees, and to sanction them when their responses are unsatisfactory. At the present time, despite some blunting of the original cutting edge of Koppel's interviewing style, he and his show remain a formidable instrument of journalistic inquiry.

Reviewing the American experience as a whole, it is striking that the news interview has struggled to find a niche in news and current affairs programming. This is particularly so for the "live" interview. Outside of talk shows and "human interest" interviews of the type epitomized by Barbara Walters' show *One on One*, which have consistently attracted larger audiences and advertising profits, interview shows have tended to air considerably outside "prime-time" slots and have generally had to be insulated from profit considerations. The longest running "Sunday" interview shows owe their existence in part to the networks' desire to address FCC policy preferences, while the later arrivals have achieved their successes by building audiences from major crises that occupied the headlines over many weeks and months. Moreover, news interview shows do not attract the same level of public interest and specialist commentary in the USA that they have in Britain. One factor in this divergence may derive from a competitor institution in the USA – the presidential press conference – which is absent in Britain. While American presidents since John Kennedy's day have ordinarily used the tele-vised press conference as a primary channel of communication with the American public, British prime ministers have done so through parliamentary questions and the one-on-one news interview. In the American context, the significance of the news interview is some-what attenuated by the general absence of the chief executive from the roster of potential participants, and by the existence of an insti-tutionalized and prestigious alternative channel of communication. In the British context, the significance of news interviews and news interviewers is enhanced by the fact that prime ministers have no effective alternatives to this medium of communication.

Britain: the growth of adversarial interviewing

British broadcasting has always been more centralized than the US, and broadcast news production has always involved a more direct interface between broadcasters and politicians than its American counterpart. Perhaps for these reasons, the history of the news in-terview in Britain has a less diffuse developmental trajectory, and one which is shaped both by the changing institutional context of British broadcasting and relations between broadcast journalists and British political elites.

The news interview is a much more prominent feature of daily British broadcasting than it is in America. Its very real significance as a means by which British people come to know their political leaders is in part explicable by the absence of other channels of communi-cation. British parliamentary proceedings were not broadcast until 1989, and the equivalent of the presidential press conference has never been a feature of British political life. Moreover, in a political system characterized by three-week election campaigns and an ab-sence of paid political advertising, news interviews (and particularly the big "set piece" television interview pioneered by Robin Day) are a primary means for political leaders to connect to the electorate.

The role of the television interview is further and powerfully sup-plemented by radio. The BBC's radio network is a major force in news programming, presenting one- and two-hour news shows dur-ing news radio's prime time – the morning and evening drive-time commutes. BBC radio coverage offers a large national audience to politicians and other public figures. In particular, BBC Radio 4 runs

three major news shows every day – *Today*, *The World at One* and
PM – which are largely composed of interview content, frequently
with cabinet ministers, major government officials, and commentators. Its presenter/interviewers, which have included Robin Day,
Brian Redhead and John Humphrys, are major public figures in their
own right, and have moved freely between television and radio. The
relative weighting of the more workaday radio interviews and their
television counterparts is quite well caught by the Conservative former Finance Minister, Kenneth Clark. Referring to *Newsnight* –
BBC Television's flagship nightly current affairs program – Clark
observed that appearing on *Newsnight* is "a big risk – bigger than
the *Today* programme...I'd only go on the programme if I thought
I'd made a pig's ear (of other interviews) during the day."[14]

But if major "set piece" television interviews are the equivalent
of the American press conference, they carry the potential to be
significantly more attention-grabbing, dramatic, and risky. Whereas
the press conference involves a large number of questioners often
pursuing quite different news agendas, the one-on-one news interview permits more sustained and pointed lines of questioning than
are normally possible in the press conference. The emergence of the
news interview progressively introduced a dimension of justification
and political accountability that could be dramatic and confrontational. For the politician, the risks of failure in this context were
balanced by the very substantial benefits of doing well.

The starting point in the British story, as in America, is the early
1950s. At this point the BBC was the monopoly broadcaster and
took an intensely conservative view of its role in news production. This conservatism had its origins in its statutory obligation
to maintain balance and impartiality in the presentation of news
and current affairs. This was interpreted by the BBC's first and
most influential Director-General, Lord Reith, to mean that the
BBC should avoid all forms of political controversy. The result was
"impartiality on the side of the government." Reithian attitudes per-
sisted after his retirement in 1938 well into the post-World War II
period. The then Director-General, Sir William Haley, believed that
television was inappropriate as a medium for political discussion,
debate, or news presentation, and he forbade the use of pictures in

---

[14] Reported in the *Independent* newspaper (London) 22 January 2000, p. 7.

television news. The BBC's first postwar news division head, Tahu Hole, equally insisted on an essentially passive approach to news gathering. Jonathan Dimbleby describes his regime in the following terms:

> he imposed rules and restraints on the staff of the News Room which sti-
> fled talent and strangled enthusiasm. Under him the search for truth was
> destroyed by the demand for accuracy; the slogan "if in doubt, leave out"
> was elevated to the status of a divine commandment. An obsession for po-
> litical "balance" made a mockery of proper journalism; investigation was
> impossible; "scoops" were forbidden; the authority of the News Agencies
> was absolute; and no report by a BBC foreign correspondent could appear
> in a bulletin unless it had been first confirmed by at least two Agencies.
> (Dimbleby, 1975: 270).

The net result was a news program "so bland and timeless that a recording of Monday's newsreel would be repeated verbatim the following Wednesday" (Cockerell 1988: xiii). A second restriction during this period was the Fourteen-Day Rule. Initiated during World War II, this mandated that topics that would be discussed in Parliament during the next fourteen days, or which were in any bill currently before either House, could not be discussed on the airwaves. Hundreds of potential topics of immediate topical relevance were thus embargoed and, since parliamentary business was ordinarily published only a week in advance, the list of excluded topics was potentially infinite. This was not a context favoring investigative, adversarial, or even meaningful current affairs interviewing. In his memoirs, Robin Day (1989: 104) reprints a parody of "the deferential pat-ball interview of the pre-ITN days":

```
 1  IR:   Sir, would you say that your visit to Timbuktu
 2        had been worthwhile?
 3  IE:   Oh yes, I would definitely say my visit had been
 4        worthwhile. Yes, certainly.
 5  IR:   Ah, good, well, could you say what topics you
 6        discussed, sir?
 7  IE:   No, I'm afraid I couldn't do that. These talks
 8        were of a highly confidential nature, you
 9        understand, and you wouldn't expect me to
10        reveal anything that might prejudice our future
11        relations.
```

12   IR: No, of course not, sir. Well, sir, you must be
13   very tired after your talks and your journey –
14   may I ask, sir, are you going to take it easy
15   for a while now – a holiday, perhaps?
16   IE: Ah, if only one could. But you know a minister
17   in Her Majesty's Government can never take it
18   easy, never rest, not really, you know. They're
19   waiting for me now.
20   IR: Well, thank you very much, sir.

Although this is parody, it is based on the real journalistic practices of
the period. Chapter 6 (example 1) shows an interview with Labour
Prime Minister Clement Attlee in 1951 that certainly converges in
spirit with it. This, then, was a period in which the news interview
languished, and commentators are united in their characterization of
the few interviews that did take place as benign and deferential, with
interviewers functioning as "respectful prompters" (Wedell 1968)
who asked public figures "soft soap" questions (Day 1961).

   This state of affairs was ended, not by an autonomous evolution of the BBC's stance and policies, but rather as a direct result
of the end of the BBC's television monopoly in 1955. The independent television companies that emerged began with an approach
to news and current affairs broadcasting that aimed to be lively,
investigative, and entertaining, and they hired a new breed of interviewers to do it – including most notably the young Robin Day
who, with his "forbidding appearance and fierce approach" (Day
1989: 80), rapidly became the dominant news interviewer of his
time. Amid a rapidly growing television market (ownership of television sets multiplied sevenfold during the 1950s to 70 percent of
British households), new battle lines were drawn in British news
and public affairs programming. An early casualty of the new competitive atmosphere in news broadcasting was the Fourteen-Day
Rule, which was simply ignored without repercussion, and subsequently quietly abandoned by Parliament. More significantly, news
interviews became more adversarial, and the independent companies abandoned the BBC practice of submitting lists of questions in
advance to ministers, who would then give rehearsed answers. "Unscripted" interviews became the order of the day. In this context,
the obligation of impartiality became interpreted more actively as

enhancing, rather than restricting, the right to cross-question. As Day put it, "having been a shackle, impartiality became a sword" (Day 1989: 181).

Perhaps the key interview during this period was Day's interview with then-Prime Minister Harold Macmillan which flatly departed from the previous deferential style with which senior politicians had been treated. One newspaper described it as "the most vigorous cross-examination a Prime Minister has been subjected to in public." While the interview got mixed reviews in the press, it struck a chord with the viewing public and Macmillan himself found that surviving Day's more aggressive cross-questioning gave him enhanced credibility with the electorate. He was not the only Prime Minister to embrace the new style of news interview for these reasons. Former British Labour Prime Minister James Callaghan recalls that

I often used to say to the BBC when they wanted me to have an interview, "could it be Robin Day?" He was my favourite interviewer. I liked his tough manner of questioning and although he could be a bit of a bully if his victim seemed to flinch, I hardly ever found he took unfair advantage. I rather like a rude TV interviewer – I am not saying that is why I asked for Robin – because the public sympathy would be on the side of the man being heckled rather than the man doing the heckling.   (Cockerell 1988: 232)

The truth of Callaghan's last remark was later demonstrated in the United States, with devastating consequences for Dan Rather, after Rather's famously aggressive interview with then-Vice President George Bush.

The changes initiated by the independent television companies were soon taken up by the BBC, which had lost audience share to its new rival. The motivation for these changes was simple for, as John Whale notes, "a news organization working on its own can swallow uninformative explanations of official or commercial blunders, and even the refusal to explain them at all, without any great discomfort...the moment there are rivals in the field it is afraid of appearing more gullible, less enterprising than them, lest its audience diminish" (Whale 1977: 29).

During the early 1960s, under the visionary leadership of a new Director General Hugh Greene, the BBC took the lead in further dismantling the climate of deference in news and current affairs. And, by 1963, BBC interviewers were every bit as acerbic as their

independent television rivals.[15] A significant contribution to this
process was made by the satirical news show *That Was The Week
That Was* (TW3). Part of a wave of satire that swept Britain in the
last days of a long-running, but politically exhausted, Conservative
administration, the show was developed by a team that had previously worked on the BBC's early evening news magazine show
Tonight, and was fronted by David Frost among others. It discussed
and analyzed the week's news and newsmakers in highly irrever-
ent terms and pushed back the barriers of acceptable comment on
television. Sketches listed MPs who had not spoken in the House of
Commons for ten or fifteen years, and exposures of incompetent and
hypocritical government decisions. Although it only ran between
1962 and 1963, the show further raised the stakes for more conventional news shows including, increasingly, BBC Radio news shows
such as *The World at One* (a forty-minute show airing at 1.00 PM).
As Ian Trethowan, later a Director General of the BBC, commented:
"Although at times anarchic, and on occasion contemptibly unfair,
TW3 swept through British broadcasting as a cleansing agent, scour-
ing away the last of the bland and banal."[16] Among politicians, it
had a mixed reaction. Robin Day, in a striking anecdote, recalls
sitting with major Labour Party officials at the party's annual conference watching TW3:

They revelled in the pillorying and abuse of the Tory government. This
produced shrieks of delighted laughter... Those Labour politicians knew
perfectly well that much of what they had applauded was a gross breach
of the BBC's obligation to be impartial. Some of them could see the dangers for a Labour government... Dick Crossman MP, in one of his en-
joyable moments of appalling frankness, said to me about *That Was The
Week That Was*: "Marvellous stuff! Marvellous! But of course the BBC
won't be allowed to get away with it when Labour are in power." (Day
1989: 224–5)

---

[15] Grace Wyndham Goldie (1977: 256–7) quotes the following from a 1963 interview with the new Conservative premier, Sir Alec Douglas-Home. The interviewers
were Robert McKenzie and Robin Day. The first question deals with the unaccountable process by which he was elevated to the leadership: "Could I bring you
to the question of how you got your job, which has been really controversial? *The
Times* said today 'Many Conservatives in high places are extremely angry and
resentful at the way Lord Home got the leadership.' Now do you yourself think it
was a democratic process?" This was a question every bit as challenging as those
of "Meet the Press" quoted earlier.
[16] Cockerell 1988: 86.

While initially liberating, TW3 also contributed to a distrust of broadcasters that increasingly focused on the BBC during the subsequent Labour administration (1964–70), headed by Harold Wilson. Wilson distinguished between ITV, which he saw as playing by the rules, and an arrogant and unaccountable BBC. In 1967, he imported Lord Hill, the Chairman of the Independent Television Authority, to chair the BBC's Board of Governors. His aim was to bring the BBC into line, and to force its Director General, Hugh Greene, to resign (Cockerell 1988). He was only partially successful. The Director General served out his term until 1969, and in 1971 the BBC under Hill went on to broadcast a documentary – *Yesterday's Men* (1971)[17] – that dealt mercilessly with ex-Labour Cabinet ministers and outraged Wilson, who was later re-elected as Prime Minister in 1974. The program had long-term consequences for the BBC. Broadcaster David Dimbleby detected "a rather hideous softening" in television's approach to politicians after this broadcast,[18] and the Annan Commission on Broadcasting supported this general verdict. Angela Pope, the program's producer, observed that "I have had my fingers burnt. I wouldn't try it and no one else should try it for a very long time. Nobody must do *Yesterday's Men* again. You mustn't. Better be safe than imaginative."[19]

The BBC responded to the political pressure which built up after *Yesterday's Men* by setting up a complaints commission. Far from stemming the tide of criticism, however, this move, which was subsequently emulated by the ITA, only served to reinforce the belief that the broadcasting authorities were no longer capable of safeguarding the public interest. And, as a result, with a significant number of politicians calling for overt Parliamentary control of broadcasting in order to rectify this situation, both the BBC and ITV reacted by assuming a more cautious role. Writing of the BBC in 1975, Kumar noted how: "Current BBC metaphors show a dramatic shift from those involving leading and directing, to those involving far more neutral concepts: essentially, the BBC is seen as the 'register' of the many different 'voices' in society, as the 'great stage' on which all the actors, great and small, parade and say their piece" (Kumar 1975: 246). As the broadcasting organizations moved to pursue a

---

[17] The title echoed an election slogan that Labour had used to describe the Conservatives in the 1970 election campaign which Labour lost.
[18] Cockerell 1988: 180.   [19] Ibid.

policy of holding "the middle ground" (ibid. 248), the parameters
of the permissible in British television and radio interviewing dis-
cernably narrowed.

Moreover, by the 1980s, British politicians had learned how to
deal with news interviewers. Prime Minister Margaret Thatcher employed American-style media advisors, who negotiated the format
of programs. She and her ministers avoided specific interviewers,
and they and other politicians have learned to influence the terms of
interviews. As Jeremy Paxman, currently Britain's best-known interviewer, observed: "There are politicians who say 'If you ask me that
question you will regret it. If you ask me that question I will take it
up with the DG (Director General). If you ask me that question I will
walk out.' Now clearly it does concentrate the mind when you are
on the air in twenty seconds and a politician is saying that to you."[20]
Prior to the 1987 general election campaign, Conservative politician
Norman Tebbit set up a well-publicized "bias-monitoring" unit at
Conservative Party headquarters. While the extent of BBC anxiety
about this unit and other more covert forms of political pressure
is unknown, the BBC did hold back a major error committed by
the Prime Minister in a live interview with David Dimbleby on the
day before the general election. Thatcher criticized her opponents
as people who "just drivel and drool that they care," a phrase that
was picked up by Dimbleby and for which she apologized on air. As
Cockerell (1988: 331) relates, videotape of this revealing interview
segment was held back until it was too late for opposition comment:

Mrs. Thatcher, who had expected the BBC to make much more of the
exchange, was delighted. It seemed that the browbeating of the past year
had worked. The Prime Minister rewarded BBC News with the first long
interview after the campaign: in previous elections this had been given to
ITV. She came to the studios, ended the interview with "my pleasure" and
stayed for lunch.   (Cockerell 1988: 331)

Her opponent, Neil Kinnock, the Labour leader, was not so fortu-
nate. Kinnock had responded to a question by David Frost on a
Sunday morning interview in a way that acknowledged that a non-
nuclear Britain could be invaded by the Soviet Union. His remarks
were extensively recycled through the airwaves and became a major
object of Conservative campaigning.

[20] Jones 1992: 62.

During the 1990s, friction between government and the broadcasters mainly centered on the financing of broadcasting, which the Conservative administration under John Major sought to reform. Interviewers have remained highly robust in their approach to politicians, particularly during the waning years of the Conservative administration when they were able to exploit deepseated differences among Conservative politicians over Europe. On BBC Television's *Newsnight*, Jeremy Paxman remains an absolutely formidable interrogator, and his aggression is matched on BBC Radio by John Humphrys and others. Survey research commissioned by the BBC shows that the British public actively approves of aggressive interviewing.[21] Certainly British interviewing remains consistently more adversarial than its American counterpart.

At the present time, British television is undergoing a process of marketization in which the old certainties of the BBC/ITV duopoly are eroding. Satellite and cable, especially Rupert Murdoch's BSkyB, are beginning to cut into ratings and have intensified the competition between the older adversaries. News and current affairs have, as in the USA, been victims of this ratings war, and have increasingly been shortened and shifted out of prime time. The longer Sunday shows remain sites of interviews that can be probing and intelligent but, as in the USA, ratings tend to be low. Nonetheless the overall tone of British news interview seems to have been decisively set by Robin Day's pioneering work, and British political life is undoubtedly the better for it.

Conclusion

In this chapter, we have aimed to sketch the different institutional contexts that have shaped the broadcast news interview in America and Britain, and to sketch the general development of news interview programs in the two countries. Taken as a whole, the development of the news interview appears quite different in the two countries. In contrast to the presidential press conference which, during the 1960s and 1970s, moved away from an older deferential style to become increasingly adversarial (Clayman and Heritage 2002), the American adversarial television news interview

---

[21] *Daily Telegraph*, 17 September 1998, p. 5.

seems to have emerged more or less fully armed in *Meet the Press* and *Face the Nation* – programs which CBS's Fred Friendly once described as verbal fencing bouts "in which a wary but nimble politician spends the half hour trying to prevent his interrogators from getting him to put his foot in his mouth" (Friendly 1967: 147). Indeed, it was not until the *MacNeil-Lehrer Report* that American viewers could tune into nonadversarial news interviews on a regular basis. Quite the reverse has been true in Britain, where the evolution has been closer to developments in the presidential press conference – from deference to adversarialness, albeit with periods of retrenchment.

Notwithstanding these different trajectories of development, and continuing regulatory and cultural differences between interviews in the two countries, there are also remarkable similarities in the underlying structures and functions which give the modern interview the shape it has. In part, this is because all news interviews have to address fundamentally common tasks. Every news interview has to be opened and closed; there must be means for managing when, and for how long, the participants speak; at least in democratic countries interviewers must have means with which to show the simultaneous independence and nonpartisanship of their questions; there must be means of highlighting and dealing with evasive answers and so on. These tasks, we argue, are handled through sets of systematic interactional practices that give common shape to the contemporary news interview in both Britain and America. These practices, as we will show, are overwhelmingly similar, though their distributions and configurations vary from program to program and from context to context. In the following chapters, we aim to describe this underlying structure of the news interview – the fundamental and very general resources, practices, and actions through which specific interviews and programs are assembled in all their particularity.

3

Openings and closings

In 1982, John Nott, then the British Minister of Defense, was interviewed live on television after it was announced that he would retire from politics. When the interviewer began to question Nott's credibility and technical expertise, the Minister angrily announced that he was "fed up with this interview." He then rose from his chair and removed his microphone, thus bringing the interview to an abrupt and unceremonious close. The interviewer, in an effort to normalize what was ostensibly a major breach of interview etiquette, responded with a brisk "thank you Mister Nott." This incident was regarded as highly newsworthy and received substantial coverage by both broadcast and print journalists. It also stimulated much commentary and analysis in op-ed pieces and letters to the major British newspapers and periodicals. At year's end, the incident was included in BBC Television's review of its news and current affairs coverage.

Similar incidents have made headlines in the United States. During the 1992 presidential campaign, Ross Perot momentarily stormed out of an interview on the CBS program *60 Minutes*. Although that particular segment of the interview was not aired initially, it was included in a special program commemorating the 25th anniversary of *60 Minutes*.

These brief interactional episodes became newsworthy events because each was widely perceived as extraordinary, a massive departure from normal interview conduct. But what is "normal" in this context? More specifically, how do journalists and public figures normally enter into, and exit from, a news interview?

At first glance, it might seem that nothing very interesting or significant takes place within the opening and closing phases of the news interview. These moments might be regarded as peripheral to the "main event," the substance of the interview itself. Moreover, what happens within them appears to be utterly routine and rather obvious: the topic of discussion is announced, the guests are introduced, and at the conclusion of the interview they are thanked for taking part.

However, when news interview openings and closings are contrasted with their counterparts in ordinary conversation, it becomes apparent that the former are governed by a robust and highly distinctive set of social conventions. Why this distinctive arrangement? The conventions for opening and closing a news interview are best understood as adaptations to the specialized task of interviewing and to various contingencies posed by the complex institutional environment in which interviewing takes place. News interviews are of course unlike ordinary conversations in many ways – interviews are prearranged for the benefit of an overhearing audience, interaction within them is comparatively formal and impersonal, and should be completed within a fixed time limit. Given these special and in some respects peculiar circumstances, special work is required to launch a news interview and to bring it to a close. At the same time, because opening and closing practices here are so very distinctive, they combine to mark the interaction at its boundaries as something other than a casual conversation, as in essence a distinctive genre of media discourse.

In many ways, the analysis of openings and closings in this chapter exemplifies the approach taken throughout this book. Using ordinary conversation as a comparative reference point, we examine the conventions that govern a particular aspect of news interview conduct, and pay close attention to the actual practices that sustain and, at times, breach those conventions. We also draw linkages between interviewing conventions and the broader environment – in this case the institutional environment of broadcasting – in which interviewing is embedded. Because openings and closings are often edited out of prerecorded interviews, our observations in this chapter are based primarily on interviews conducted "live" for unedited broadcast.

News interview openings

Let us begin at the beginning, with the opening phase and its overall structure. The following is a straightforward example of the way in

which news interviews typically get off the ground. Notice that the
first question, which does not appear until lines 23–5, is preceded
by an extended spate of preliminary talk.

(1) UK BBCTV *Newsnight*: June 1989: Soviet Nuclear Weapons
     IR: Peter Snow   IE: David Howell

1	IR:	Well President Gorbachev has done it again.
2		(0.2) He's announced yet another unilateral
3		cutback in Soviet forces in Europe. (0.2) Once
4		again this is 'n area in which the Soviets <u>have</u>
5		an admitted super<u>ior</u>ity over the West, .hhh
6		the Soviet leader says he'll withdraw f<u>i</u>ve
7		h<u>u</u>ndred nuclear warheads from Eastern Europe
8		this year. .hhh The unil<u>a</u>teral reduction, (.)
9		coming on top of <u>o</u>ther planned cuts in Soviet
10		forces, .hhh was announced in Moscow tonight.
11		.hh at the <u>e</u>nd of a <u>two</u> day visit by the
12		American Secretary of State James Baker. .hhh
13		But on arr<u>i</u>ving in Brussels this evening Mister
14		Baker t<u>o</u>ld reporters the S<u>o</u>viet proposal was
15		<u>not</u> enough. .h to dr<u>a</u>w the U<u>ni</u>ted States into
16		neg<u>o</u>tiations <u>on</u> these weapons.
17		((Taped background segment))
18	IR:	.hhh Margaret Gilmore: Margaret Gilmore
19		reporting.=
20		=Well um .hh I'm joined now uh by David H<u>o</u>well,
21		from the Commons, who is the chairman of the:
22		Commons Select Committee on Foreign Affairs.=
23		=Mister Howell. .hh eh=What d'<u>you</u> think about
24		this.=D'you think it's uhs- just a sm<u>a</u>ll st<u>e</u>p as
25		Mister Baker was saying?
26		(0.8)
27	IE:	Well it's uh- it's a bit hard to tell until we
28		have the: (0.2) clearer figures in the
29		morning...

Openings stand apart from the main body of the interview in some
rather fundamental ways. Rather than *interactional* exchanges between interviewers (or IRs for short) and interviewees (or IEs), openings normally consist of an extended *monologue* produced by the IR
alone (at times supplemented by a taped background segment prepared in advance – see line 17 above). In addition to its distinctively
monologic character, the opening spate of talk is *addressed explicitly to the audience* rather than to the IE. Thus, even when guests are

actually present in the television studio (as in the preceding example), IRs usually face the camera as they deliver their initial remarks. They also refer to their guests in the third person while introducing them to the audience (e.g., "I'm joined now by David Howell . . ." in lines 20–22). This will change once the questioning begins, at which point the parties become engaged interactionally and address one another directly from that point on (lines 23–29). However, everything that precedes the first question remains monologic and overtly audience-directed.

Three basic tasks are accomplished through this pre-questioning spate of talk, each within a separate segment of the opening. These tasks may be seen in the preceding example, which begins with (1) a news announcement or statement of topic, which will be termed the *headline* (lines 1–3), after which (2) *background* information is detailed (lines 3–17), and then (3) the IR *leads in* to the interview proper, often by formally introducing the IEs (lines 20–22). Only upon completion of these tasks does the IR issue the first question (lines 23–25). We shall briefly examine each of these components in turn.

Headline

Journalists generally begin by offering a global characterization of the topic to be discussed. In its simplest form, this initial headline may consist of a single sentence that encapsulates the topical news item, as in the following two excerpts.

(2)   UK BBCTV *Newsnight*: May 1989: China Unrest
      IR: Peter Snow

1   IR: We beg<u>in</u>: with the conti- kint- continuation of
2   mo<u>men</u>tous ev<u>en</u>ts in Ch<u>in</u>a:_ where there's now
3   increasing evidence of a s<u>er</u>ious power struggle
4   .hh in the Chinese leadership . . .

(3)   UK BBCTV *Newsnight*: June 1989: Labour Party Policy
      IR: Donald MacCormick

1   IR: Tod<u>ay</u>: Labour began an internal debate that will
2   have a critical <u>bear</u>ing on the party's ch<u>an</u>ces
3   of winning the next election . . .

Headlines are designed in such a way as to capture the audience's attention and draw them into the unfolding discussion. Consider the terms used to formulate the topic – such terms tend to be selected so as to highlight the dramatic or newsworthy character of the subject matter. Thus, in (2) above, the subject of unrest in China is characterized as "momentous," while in (3) a debate within the Labour Party is characterized as having a "critical bearing" on the party's election prospects.

Beyond word selection, there are other methods of capturing the audience's attention. One such method is to pose a puzzle of some kind, one that projects a resolution – or at least something bearing on a resolution – in subsequent talk. For instance, in the next example a puzzle is posed by raising an initial question (lines 1–2) about how to catch perpetrators of housing discrimination.

(4) US PBS *NewsHour*: 13 June 1985: Housing Discrimination
     IR: Robert MacNeil

1 IR: How do authorities catch landlords or realtors
2   who discriminate against minorities? There's an
3   interesting proposal before Congress and it's
4   what we look at first tonight.

An initial puzzle may also be posed by the use of a referentially ambiguous statement. In (1) above, the IR starts off by observing (line 1) that "President Gorbachev has done it again," thereby posing a puzzle as to the specific nature of Gorbachev's action ("it").[1] Whether the puzzle is established via a question or a referentially ambiguous statement, the effect is much the same – it focuses the audience's attention on what gets said next, which must be monitored in order to resolve the puzzle (Heritage and Greatbatch 1986; Goodwin 1996). Puzzles are thus inherently engaging, with attention-getting properties that journalists exploit to draw audience members into the ensuing discussion.

Beyond characterizing the topic of discussion, some headlines also indicate who the participating interviewees will be. In the following example, after an initial puzzle is established (lines 1–4), the subsequent talk both projects an agenda for the interview and identifies the IEs (lines 6–13).

---

[1] Goodwin (1996) refers to such utterances as "prospective indexicals" because their sense is not initially available to recipients. Recipients must then monitor subsequent events in order to clarify and elaborate upon the meaning of the antecedent indexical.

(5)   US ABC *Nightline*: 4 June 1985: Espionage
      IR: Ted Koppel   IE1: Bobby Inman   IE2: Christopher Boyce
1   IR: From the A-bomb of forty years ago to the most
2   sophisticated undersea weaponry of today, what
3   has motivated Americans to steal US military
4   secrets for the Soviet Union? Good evening. I'm
5   Ted Koppel in Washington and this is Nightline.
6   Our topic, the Walker family spy case and its
7   role in the continuing cloak and dagger war
8   between the CIA and the KGB. Our guests include
9   a former deputy director of the CIA, and from
10   the federal penitentiary at Marion, Illinois,
11   Christopher Boyce, the so-called Falcon of
12   "Falcon and the Snowman" fame, now serving forty
13   years for spying for the Soviets.

This information may also be deferred until just before the first
question, but senior-level officials and other prominent individuals
are often identified at the outset. This pattern may reflect an assumption on the part of news producers that "big name" public
figures will keep audience members tuned in and should be mentioned at the earliest opportunity. The headline segment is thus expanded accordingly.

Background

Following the headline is a segment that details relevant background
information. These segments vary greatly in length and organization, and they will not be examined in detail here.[2] It will suffice
to observe that the transition from headline to background may be
marked in a variety of ways. The transition can entail a shift to another journalist or to a taped segment, in which case the boundary
may be quite obvious. In the following, it is explicitly announced
(arrowed).

(6)   US PBS *NewsHour*: 11 June 85: Southern Baptists
      IR1: Robert MacNeil   IR2: Charlayne Hunter-Gault
1   IR1:   As we reported earlier, the Reverend Charles
2   Stanley was re-elected president of the
3   Southern Baptist Convention today in a

---

[2] See Pomerantz (1988/89) for an analysis of the background segment which preceded the infamous Bush–Rather interview.

4	political struggle that happened not in the
5	world of politicians but in the ranks of the
6	nation's largest Protestant denomination.
7	→ Charlayne Hunter-Gault has our story.
8	Charlayne?
9 IR2:	Robin, it's been described as a holy war, but
10	what it really is is a fight between different
11	factions of Southern Baptists ...

More often, the transition from headline to background is evident in more subtle ways – generally by a shift in the description's level of detail or "granularity" (Schegloff 2000), and sometimes also by shifts in verbal tense or temporal reference. For example:

(7)   US PBS *NewsHour*: 15 Oct 1992: Currency Crisis
        IR: Unknown

1 IR:	1→	Now the currency crisis in Europe.
2	2→	It started last month when Great Britain pulled
3		its pound sterling from the system that links
4		the European currencies ...

Here the move from an extremely general and tenseless summary statement (arrow 1) to a detailed chronological narrative (arrow 2) clearly marks the transition from headline to background.

Lead-in

The final segment of the opening prepares for entry into the questioning proper. It is at this point that the interviewees are formally introduced to the audience, although as we have seen, information about their identities may also be conveyed earlier within the opening. If that information has already been provided (as in the following example at arrow 1), then the lead-in to the interview may be managed simply by noting that the interviewee is present and ready to talk (arrow 2).

(8)   UK ATV *Today*: 11 May 1979: Tony Stocks Released
        Anchor: Unknown   IR: Richard Hudson Evans   IE: Tony Stocks

1 Anc:	The case of a Shropshire man who was given a ten
2	year jail sentence for armed robbery is to be
3	reopened by the police.
4	1→ The man, forty year old Tony Stocks, served six

5   years of the sentence. He now runs a carpet
6   business. Mister Stocks was...
7   ((12 lines omitted))
8   2→   ...Mister Stocks is now in the studio with
9   Richard Hudson Evans, talking about what
10   happened way back in 1970.

Alternatively, the lead-in may include a more elaborate introduction in which the interviewee's identity and credentials are formally presented. When multiple interviewees are present, all may be introduced at this point, or they may be introduced one at a time as each is brought into the discussion. In either case, introductions resemble the following (see lines 6–14)

(9) US PBS *NewsHour*: 22 July 1985: South Africa
     IR1: Robert MacNeil   IR2: Jim Lehrer
     IE1: Herbert Beukes   IE2: Nthato Motlona

1   IR1:   Our major focus section tonight is South Africa
2   and the declaration of a state of emergency over
3   the weekend. We look first at recent events
4   that have led to the declaration.
5   ((Taped report; 24 lines))
6   IR2:   We hear first from the top South African
7   official in the United States, the Ambassador
8   designate, Herman Beukes.
9   ((Interview with HB; 70 lines))
10   IR1:   A different view on events in South Africa now
11   from Doctor Nthato Motlona, chairman and founder
12   of the Committee of Ten, an activist civic
13   association in Soweto, the black township near
14   Johannesburg.

Once again it is noted that the IEs are present and ready to go (lines 6, 10), but in this case each is explicitly introduced by name and title along with other descriptive items (lines 7–9, 11–14).

Plainly such introductions are designed to indicate how the interviewee is qualified to comment on the present topic, and in what capacity he or she will be speaking. Thus, while there is an infinite number of correct characterizations which could in principle be applied to any interviewee (e.g., "Jones is male, Caucasian, left-handed, vegetarian, etc."), journalists tend to select only those which are germane to the present topic of discussion (Roth 1998a). In the preceding example, the topic is the South African Government's declaration of a state of emergency (lines 1–2), and the first IE is linked to South African affairs as that government's official spokesperson (lines 6–7), while the second IE is linked as a representative of blacks in that country (lines 11–14). Introductory descriptions are thus chosen with an eye toward their relevance to the present agenda.

Moreover, these introductory descriptions are geared specifically for the viewing audience. This audience-directedness is apparent in the fact that descriptive items are selectively elaborated in a way that enables audience members to grasp their topical relevance (cf., Sacks and Schegloff 1979). For example, when the second IE is initially described as "chairman and founder of the Committee of Ten" (lines 11–12), this rather obscure affiliation (at least, obscure to American viewers) is subsequently elaborated in stages to clarify its relevance to South African racial affairs. First the Committee is elaborated by characterizing it as "an activist civic organization in Soweto" (lines 12–13). Then an item within that elaboration ("Soweto") is, in turn, further elaborated (lines 13–14) in a way that identifies its racial composition ("a black township") and locates it in relation to a larger and presumably more familiar South African city ("near Johannesburg"). By way of contrast, commonly known descriptive items are not so elaborated (cf., lines 6–8). Introductions are thus designed to establish each interviewee's relevant credentials in terms that the audience might be expected to recognize.

Interviewees normally remain silent during the introductions, and indeed throughout the entire opening discourse. This enables the journalist to proceed unilaterally through the various components of the opening segment and on to the first question.

Comparisons and institutional circumstances

If news interview openings are contrasted with parallel processes in ordinary conversation (cf., Schegloff 1986), a number of important differences may be discerned. In addition to gross differences in overall form discussed above – interview openings are monologic rather than interactional, and are addressed outward toward the audience – there are further differences in the *specific actions* which comprise the opening. Many of the most routine and familiar conversational practices simply do not appear in the news interview context. For instance, only rarely do the parties to an interview exchange greetings – *hellos* and *good evenings* are almost entirely absent. Also absent are personal inquiries such as *how are you?* Finally, the very first step in any conversational encounter is that preliminary process through which the parties first indicate that they are available and ready to interact – e.g., by issuing and responding to a summons (e.g., "Hey Jim!" "Yeah?"), or engaging in a parallel nonvocal process (e.g., a wave and a move toward proximity and mutual gaze) (Schegloff 1968). This preliminary process of coordinating entry into a state of talk is also absent from news interviews, in which participants appear onscreen poised and ready to interact.

The only conversational practice that *does* regularly appear in news interviews is the practice of identifying or recognizing the interactional participants. However, that process unfolds very differently here. While conversationalists take steps to identify/recognize one another, interview participants do not. Introductions are addressed to a nonparticipating third party, the media audience.

These systematic differences are adaptations to the institutional circumstances at hand – to the specialized task of interviewing and contingencies posed by the environing context of broadcast journalism. Consider first the fact that *news interview talk is normally restricted to questions and answers.* We will explore this pattern at length in the next chapter, but we mention it now as a factor that goes some way toward explaining the absence of various action sequences common in conversation. Greetings, for example, plainly do not fit within a question–answer framework. By declining to exchange such items, the parties adhere systematically to the requirement that they restrict their talk to questions and answers only. Correspondingly, much of the opening talk that *is* produced can be understood as necessary background for subsequent questioning, and forms the immediate context in which the first question is launched.

Secondly, *interview participants act under the auspices of impersonal institutional roles.* An orientation to impersonal role-based identities – namely interviewer and interviewee – is quite unlike much casual conversation, where the participants often know each other as "whole persons" and interact under the auspices of an ongoing personal relationship. This circumstance in part accounts for the absence of both greetings and *how are you*s. These "access rituals" (Goffman 1971: 79–94) acknowledge and honor the participants' shared biography and relational ties, so they are mainly relevant in interactions between acquaintances – although telephone salespersons often knowingly exploit the personalizing import of such practices! In a news interview, while the parties may have a personal acquaintanceship that transcends their professional personae, this is generally disattended, and the rituals which might otherwise be evoked by that relationship become inappropriate and are omitted. There are occasional exceptions to this rule – some morning news interview programs include a brief greeting sequence (arrowed below), which imparts a slightly more "personal" tone to the encounter.[3]

(10) US NBC *Today Show*: 27 Jan 1998: Lewinsky Scandal
       IR: Matt Lauer   IE: Hillary Clinton

1 IR: On close up this morning the First Lady of the
2   United States, Hillary Rodham Clinton.
3   (.)
4 IR: → Mrs. Clinton, good morning.
5 IE: → Good morning Matt.

By declining to engage in such rituals in the vast majority of interviews, the participants constitute the occasion as an impersonal encounter between occupants of the institutional roles of interviewer and interviewee.[4]

The third and perhaps most distinctive institutional factor has to do with the way in which *news interview encounters have been prearranged for the benefit of the media audience*. Interviewees are invited to participate far in advance, and they arrive at the studio or are placed before remote cameras or microphones before the broadcast begins. In some instances the participants may talk briefly prior to airtime. The opening that the audience witnesses is thus in many respects a "false" beginning. This has consequences for virtually every aspect of the opening. It makes a mutual identification process, greetings, and *how are you*s potentially redundant, for these activities may have been performed prior to airtime. Also redundant is the preliminary process of coordinating entry into a state of talk. Since

---

[3] Greetings also appear to be more common on radio interviews, perhaps because IEs are linked to the studio by telephone only, and the greeting fulfills the latent function of establishing that the IE is indeed on the line and ready to talk.

[4] Greetings and "how-are-yous" are also absent in other institutional settings, such as citizen calls for emergency service, except in rare cases when the caller and call-taker happen to be acquainted (Whalen and Zimmerman 1987). In this respect, doctor–patient interactions represent an interesting borderline case (Robinson Forthcoming).

interview participants are placed before microphones and cameras prior to airtime, they have already been primed to interact, so any further work of this sort becomes superfluous and is omitted on the air.

The distinctive features of news interview openings are thus not mere happenstance; they reflect the special circumstances under which interviews are conducted. Correspondingly, these features are rich in implications for the interaction to follow. The shape of the opening segment provides in part for the qualities of formality, impersonality, and theatricality that are such familiar attributes of the broadcast news interview. From the very outset it comes across to the audience as something other than a private conversation among friends – it appears as a "strictly business" encounter that has been planned in advance and is now being orchestrated on behalf of the media audience.

Interviewee identities and interview genres

Thus far we have focused on what elements of ordinary conversation get left out of news interview openings. What remains, however, is equally significant, for it conveys information about the substance of the interview to follow. In some respects this is obvious – openings announce the upcoming topic of discussion and who will be taking part. But what is less obvious is that openings also foreshadow the *form* that discussion will take. There are various genres of interview discourse, and audience members can anticipate the type of interview to follow mainly by observing how the interviewees are introduced. While interviewees generally are presented as having authority to comment on the subject at hand, authority is not a binary, all-or-nothing characteristic. There are different forms of authoritativeness, and openings vary in terms of the epistemological status they bestow upon interviewees. As a consequence different openings project different perspectival treatments of the topic and hence different genres of interview discourse.

The interviewee as participant and the "newsmaker interview"

Some interviewees are identified as central participants in the events under discussion. Leading government officials and political candidates are perhaps the prime examples of "newsmakers" who are intimately involved in shaping news events. This status is reflected in the manner in which newsmaker interviewees are identified within the opening. Rather than identificatory information being withheld until the lead-in component of the opening, newsmakers are typically identified at the outset, within the initial headline component. For example, an interview with Pat Buchanan is opened with a headline/news announcement of his appointment as President Reagan's White House Communications Director (lines 5–9). Buchanan is further characterized by an elaborate puzzle-type headline (lines 1–5) which casts him as highly controversial.

(11)   US ABC *Nightline*: 3 June 1985: Pat Buchanan
          IR: Ted Koppel   IE: Pat Buchanan
1   IR: His comment on feminists: "Send those chicks
2   back to the kitchen where they belong." On
3   Walter Mondale: "A jar of jelly." And on the
4   press: "It's ridiculous for them to say they
5   speak for the American People." Throughout the
6   years Patrick Buchanan has always been
7   controversial, but now he holds one of the most
8   sensitive posts on the Reagan White House
9   staff...
10   ((Background segment omitted))
11 IR: Joining us now live in our Washington bureau,
12   White House Communications Director, Pat
13   Buchanan...

And in an interview conducted at the height of the 1992 presidential campaign, maverick candidate Ross Perot is identified straightaway as a featured guest.

(12)   US PBS *NewsHour*: 18 Sep 1992: Ross Perot
          IR: Judy Woodruff   IE: Ross Perot
1   IR: First up tonight i:s a newsmaker interview with
2   Ross Perot...
3   ((Background segment omitted))
4   .hhh Mister Perot joins us now:...

This type of opening projects a "newsmaker interview" in which a prominent person in the news will be featured.

The interviewee as expert and the "background interview"

Interviewees may also be characterized as having specialized knowledge of the subject. They are thus certified to comment on the events in question even though they are not involved in shaping them first hand. Typically, knowledgeable experts are not identified until the lead-in segment of the opening, when they are formally introduced. At that juncture, the interviewee's expertise may be asserted straightforwardly (see lines 5–6 below), but it is more commonly demonstrated by enumerating organizational affiliations (lines 6–8), publishing activities (lines 8–10), and other relevant credentials.

(13)   US PBS *NewsHour*: 14 June 1985: Hijacking
         IR: Judy Woodruff   IE: Neil Livingston

```
 1  IR:    Our first focus section is on the major news
 2         story of the day, the hijacking of a TWA plane
 3         in the Middle East. Joining us to try to shed
 4         some light on how this happened and to piece
 5         together events there is an expert on terrorism,
 6         Neil Livingston. He is president of the
 7         Washington based Institute on Terrorism and
 8         Subnational Conflict. Mr. Livingston has
 9         written two books on terrorism and America's
10         ability to combat it.
```

The interviewee's knowledge may also derive from being an eyewitness to the events at hand. In the following, while the IE's expertise is also noted, her status as a direct witness is emphasized (arrowed).

(14)   US ABC *Nightline*: 26 July 1985: Argentina
         IR: Charles Gibson   IE: Lynda Schuster

```
 1  IR:    Twenty-five thousand people disappeared. Men,
 2         women, and innocent children, assumed murdered
 3         in a reign of terror in Argentina ... Tonight,
 4         a unique inside look at an old ally but a new
 5         democracy, Argentina.
 6         ((Background segment – 150 lines))
 7         ((Commercial break))
 8         With us now live in our Miami bureau, Wall
 9         Street Journal correspondent Lynda Schuster,
10         whose area of expertise is Latin America and
11         the economy of Argentina.
12    →    Ms. Schuster has recently returned from
```

13	Argentina, where she witnessed the climate of
14	the ongoing trial and Argentina's economic
15	situation.

Whether identified as a certified expert or eyewitness, the interviewee is aligned to offer comments as one with specialized knowledge of the subject under examination. This form of authority projects what is sometimes referred to as a "background interview" or "backgrounder," in which knowledgeable sources offer informed commentary on events of the day.

The interviewee as advocate and the "debate interview"

Some openings convey more than just the interviewee's relevant credentials. When the topic is treated as a matter of controversy, the opening may also include some mention of where the interviewee stands on the issue. For example, in a discussion of newly proposed legislation for detecting discriminatory housing practices, one IE is identified as a supporter of the legislation (arrow 1) and the other as an opponent (arrow 2).

(15) US PBS *NewsHour*: 13 June 1985: Housing Discrimination
        IR: Robert MacNeil   IE1: Phyllis Spiro
        IE2: William North

1	IR:	How do authorities catch landlords or realtors
2		who discriminate against minorities? There's an
3		interesting proposal before congress and it's
4		what we look at first tonight. The idea is to
5		stage tests by sending people with similar
6		incomes but different racial or ethnic
7		backgrounds to buy or rent housing...
8		The Reagan administration is pushing a new fund
9		of some four million dollars to help community
10		groups set up such tests. But the move is being
11		fought by the National Association of
12		Realtors...
13		We have both sides of the argument now. Phyllis
14		Spiro of the Open Housing Council here in New
15	1→	York City supports federally funded testing.
16		William North, general counsel of the National
17	2→	Association of Realtors, opposes it.

When political positions are noted (and they may be suggested in far more subtle ways than in this example), the interviewees are aligned as *advocates* prepared to defend a particular point of view. Advocates are commonly introduced in pairs representing opposing sides of an issue, thereby projecting a "debate interview" in which divergent points of view will be exhibited and made to clash.[5]

A debate interview may also be foreshadowed still earlier within the opening, in the headline and background components, insofar as the subject is initially cast as a controversial and hence debatable "issue." In the previous example, the background segment depicts recent events as a clash between the Reagan administration's efforts to implement the new legislation (lines 8–10), and opposition by the National Association of Realtors (lines 10–12). Correspondingly, the lead-in to the introductions – "We have both sides of the argument now" (line 13) – portrays the interview to follow as a continuation of this ongoing controversy.

The three basic interview genres outlined above have become institutionalized among news producers. On *The NewsHour*, interview segments are explicitly identified and categorized in these ways; similar genres can be discerned on news interview programs generally. It bears emphasis that the identity categories (participant, expert, advocate) do not simply reflect the "objective" character of any given interviewee. "Experts" can also be treated as "advocates" and vice versa, and "participants" can be consulted for their expertise and not just their first-hand knowledge. Accordingly, rather than *reflecting* the interviewee's identity, interviewee introductions should be understood as *constituting* that identity in a particular way for the occasion of the interview. Such identities may then subsequently shift and evolve as the interview progresses (Roth 1998a, 1998b).

News interview closings

This chapter began with a discussion of two interviews – involving John Nott and Ross Perot, respectively – whose endings were extraordinary, so much so that the ending itself became a noteworthy incident and the focus of subsequent media attention. What was so unusual? In both cases they were brought to a close prematurely and at the initiative of the interviewee rather than the interviewer. Such occurrences would be unremarkable in the context of an ordinary

---

[5] This type of interview will be explored in chapter 8.

conversation, where time constraints are less rigid and where any conversationalist can launch the closing process. However, in the news interview context, this involved a major breach of etiquette.

News interview closings, like openings, adhere to conventions which are strikingly different from their counterparts in ordinary conversation (cf., Schegloff and Sacks 1973), and these differences are bound up with various institutional circumstances and contingencies. One such contingency is paramount: namely, the need to end the encounter at or near a prespecified point in time. The overall length of an ordinary conversation is not normally determined in advance, and conversations as a group do not have a standardized length. Most interviews, in contrast, are constrained by the scheduling requirements of broadcasting, which allot a specific length of time for each program. This constraint is not absolutely rigid – some leeway for additional time can be gained by, for example, shortening postinterview program segments and announcements, increasing the "scrolling speed" of the closing credits, and so on. In some circumstances, a program may be permitted to run overtime, although such incidents are rare and are treated as exceptional. Granting these avenues for flexibility, regularly scheduled interviews are conducted within an essentially predetermined and fixed time frame.[6]

This time frame must somehow be realized in practice, and the interviewer is uniquely positioned to manage this complex task. As the official agent of the broadcast organization, interviewers are responsible for keeping the discussion moving forward, and for ensuring that it ends on time. To facilitate this process, most interviewers have earphones through which production personnel can keep them apprised of the temporal situation and can let them know when time is running out. Interviewers are also interactionally positioned to manage the closing process – as the one who asks the questions, the interviewer is in the interactional driver's seat, launching all sequences of action including those that bring about closing.

As we shall see, a great deal of the closing process can be understood as a solution to the problem of how to bring an unscripted

---

[6] For the special case of nonscheduled on-the-spot interviews in the midst of live media events such as political conventions, termination may be driven by emergent external events, so that the timing of termination is less predictable but still relatively inflexible.

interaction to a close in accordance with a prearranged schedule. This process will be examined in reverse order, beginning with the task of actually terminating the interview, and then proceeding to the advance work of preparing for termination.

Terminating

No interaction is over until the participants recognize it as such, and display that recognition to one another (Schegloff and Sacks 1973). Of course, in ordinary conversation this is accomplished by exchanging ritualized farewells such as "goodbye" or its equivalent. News interview closings, in contrast, are distinguished by the wholesale absence of ritualized farewells – interviewers and interviewees simply do not say "good bye" to one another! Closings are instead launched by interviewers and usually involve thanking the interviewees for their participation.

(16)   US PBS *NewsHour*: 13 June 1985: Artificial Heart
          IR: Judy Woodruff   IE: Allen Lansing
1   IR: → Doctor <u>A</u>llen Lansing, we tha̲nk you for being
2   with us.
3   IE: Thank you. It was my pleasure.

This form of closing can be understood in terms of the impersonal, task-oriented character of the encounter. Just as greetings and *how are you*s are stripped out of the opening phase, ritualized farewells are omitted from news interview closings. In their place is an action – an expression of gratitude – that is responsive to and evokes, not the participants' personal relationship, but rather their role-based identities and the task in which they have been engaged.[7]

It is also common for the interviewer to state the interviewee's name, and sometimes his or her full name and title, in the course of expressing thanks. This is presumably done with an eye toward the media audience, some of whom may have tuned in late or forgotton who has been speaking, and hence would benefit from reiterated identificatory information.

Not only is the use of *thank you* as a means of termination distinctive, but so is the manner in which it is responded to. Although

---

[7] Also relevant is the fact that what is being closed is the on-air interaction only. IRs and IEs may be able to talk again once the broadcast ends.

thankings are normally acknowledged in ordinary conversation, in the news interview context a response appears to be more or less optional. IEs sometimes reciprocate or otherwise acknowledge the *thank you* as in the preceding example; in other cases, however, the IR's terminal *thanks* receives no response. For example:

(17)   UK BBCTV Special: 27 Sep 1981: Labour Party Election
       IR: Robin Day   IE: John Silkin

1   IR: <u>N</u>ow I must <u>thank</u> you Mister Silkin,=
2   =and <u>n</u>ow to <u>D</u>avid <u>D</u>imbleby in the <u>ha</u>:11.

(18)   US ABC *Nightline*: 7 June 1985: Josef Mengele
       IR: Charles Gibson

1   IR: I th<u>ank</u> all three of you and .h Doctor Snow for
2   joining us,='n I'll be back in a moment.

Looking more closely at these examples, it is apparent that the IR's *thank you* is not designed to allow for a response. Rather than wait for a response, the IR proceeds straightaway to other noninterview business. In (17) above, after thanking his guest (line 1), the IR immediately proceeds to relinquish the floor to another journalist (line 2). And in (18), the IR moves immediately from his terminal *thanks* (line 1) to a commercial break (line 2). In this latter example the IR actually "rushes" to the next item without pausing to take an inbreath, and the pivotal word ("and") is contracted to facilitate this rapid move to other business. Plainly no response from the IEs is expected or required here.

   Interviewees, for their part, sometimes remain unresponsive even when there is a bit of time to do so. For example:

(19)   US PBS *NewsHour*: 22 July 1985: South Africa
       IR1: Robert MacNeil   IR2: Jim Lehrer
       IE: Nthato Motlona

1   IR1:   Doctor Motlana, thank you for j<u>oi</u>ning us.
2   →   (2.2)
3   IR2:   Still to c<u>ome</u> on the NewsHour tonight . . .

Although there is a gap (arrowed) after the "thank you" during which the camera remains focused on the IE, he declines any vocal response. He does produce a very tiny head movement, perhaps the ghost of a nod, but refrains from offering anything more substantial than that.

Finally, news producers, camera operators, and other production personnel also seem to treat the interviewee's response as unnecessary. It is not uncommon for the camera to remain focused on the interviewer throughout the closing process, rather than switching to the interviewee as would be appropriate if a response were expected. Moreover, when the interview has been taped for later inclusion in a news program, the tape is often cut immediately following the interviewer's *thanks*.

(20)   UK BBC Radio *World at One*: 15 Feb 1979: UK Economy
         IR: Brian Widlake   IE1: Sam Brittan   IE2: Peter Jenkins
1   IE2:   . . . which is which- which party can best deal
2   with the: trade unions,=and which party can best
3   manage the economy.=
4   IR: =Gentlemen,=thank you very much.=
5   =((Tape cut))

Clearly, a response to the IR's terminal "thanks" is treated, both by the immediate participants and by backstage production personnel, as optional rather than obligatory. Why would this be? A plausible explanation is that the participants are mindful of the pressing temporal constraint under which they are operating. An orientation to this constraint is even more transparent in the earlier process by which the participants prepare for termination.

Winding down

Closing an interview generally involves more than just issuing a final *thanks*; there are also efforts to "wind down" the discussion before proceeding with its termination. A similar process occurs in ordinary conversation, consisting at minimum of an exchange of short tokens such as *okay* or *all right* before saying *goodbye*. These have been termed "passing turns" (Schegloff and Sacks 1973) because in producing them a speaker declines to continue the preceding topic of discussion, or to begin some new topic, in effect "passing" the opportunity to add anything of substance to the conversation. When all parties pass a turn in succession, they display a mutual readiness to close and thus provide for the appropriateness of the exchange of farewells.

News interview closings also involve a preliminary process of winding down, although it is organized very differently. As (20) above illustrates (see also excerpts [21]–[22] below), passing turns are completely absent from the closing phase of the news interview. It is not difficult to explain this systematic absence – passing turns would be doubly inappropriate in this context. First, because such turns are neither questions nor answers, they are incompatible with the most basic principle of interview talk, which specifies that the participants should restrict themselves to the activities of questioning and answering (see chapter 4). Second, passing turns are also incompatible with the inflexible time frame in which interviews are conducted. If a pre-closing sequence of passing turns provides each party with an opportunity to say more and extend the interaction, or to "pass" and make way for termination, such a sequence becomes irrelevant in a context where time constraints do not permit the encounter to be extended.

How, then, do news interviews wind down? Not through a separate pre-closing sequence devoted exclusively to that task; here the practices that prepare for termination are not distinct from the course of the interview itself. The relevance of termination is established through practices that occur as components of, or are embedded within, turns devoted to some other business – either within the interviewer's final *thanks*, or within earlier questioning turns.

Prefaces to the final thanks
Interviewers may prepare for termination just before launching into the final *thanks*. One way of doing this is to *announce that termination is necessary* (arrowed) prior to thanking the IE.

(21)   US PBS *NewsHour*: 22 July 1985: South Africa
           IR: Robert MacNeil   IE: Nthato Motlona

1   IR: → We have to end it there Doctor Motlana, thank
2   you for joining us.

(22)   US ABC *Nightline*: 22 July 1985: South Africa
           IR: Charles Gibson   IE1: Rev. Allan Boesak
           IE2: Ambassador Herbert Beukes

1   IR: → I am afraid we could go on forever. I am afraid
2   → that we have to stop at some point, and it's
3   → gonna have to be this point. Reverend Boesak and
4   Ambassador Beukes, thank you both ever so much
5   for joining us.

Such announcements generally have an imperative character, and at least imply that time has run out. This procedure clearly establishes the relevance of termination, but it does little to wind down the discussion in progress.

An alternative prefatory procedure is for the interviewer to briefly *comment on what has been said in the course of the interview*. In the following example the IR builds on the IE's final assertion in order to briefly summarize (line 5) and evaluate (line 6) his overall remarks. By referring to what the IE has said "tonight" (line 6), the IR is clearly targeting the IE's cumulative remarks over the course of the interview.

(23)   US ABC *Nightline*: 4 June 1985: Espionage
       IR: Ted Koppel   IE: Christopher Boyce

1 IE: . . . and the G<u>o</u>vernment is <u>d</u>erelict in its <u>d</u>uty if
2   it does <u>not</u> comm<u>uni</u>cate to the four million with
3   security clearances <u>that</u> <u>fact</u>. That sh<u>ou</u>ld be
4   d<u>one</u>.
5 IR: →   Christopher Boyce, I think you've d<u>one</u> it.
6   →   And done it very <u>e</u>loquently tonight. Thank you
7   very much for talking with me.
8 IE: Very good. Good night.

In a similar vein, another IR briefly comments on the "upshot" or significance of the discussion (lines 1–3).

(24)   UK BBC Radio *Today*: May 1993: Social Security Reform
       IR: John Humphrys   IE: David Howell

1 IR: →   Well I think Mister Howell the Chancellor
2   →   obviously has a great deal to occup<u>y</u> him when he
3   →   does come back from his holidays.
4   [Thank] you very much for coming into=
5 IE: [Yes]
6 IR: =the studio to discuss it with us and thank you
7   too to Paul Combree. Thank you both. .hhh

One hallmark of these comments is that they deal with the *cumulative* sense or import of what has been said over the course of the discussion, rather than merely responding to the IE's most recent statement. In effect, the IR withdraws from a turn-by-turn engagement with the IE to comment on the interview in its entirety. The significance of this move is that it effectively caps off the discussion and provides for the relevance of closing (Heritage and Watson 1980).

A less elaborate type of preface involves a single word such as "well" or "all right" (arrowed).

(25)   US ABC *Nightline*: 23 July 1985: South Africa
       IR: Charles Gibson
1   IR: → All right, thank all thr<u>ee</u> of you for joining us,
2   I appreciate it very much.

(26)   US PBS *NewsHour*: 10 June 1985: Arms Control
       IR: Robert MacNeil   IE: Kenneth Adelman
1   IR: → Well Mister Adelman, thank you for j<u>oi</u>ning us.
2   IE: You're welcome.

It may not be obvious at first glance, but these brief items also prepare for closing, albeit in an exceedingly subtle way. In other contexts, "well" often precedes talk that diverges from the topical or perspectival orientation of the previous turn (Pomerantz 1984; Schiffrin 1987). "All right" is used in a similar manner in both ordinary conversation (Beach 1993) and in news interviews – interviewers often say "all right" just before asking a question that begins a new topic.[8] These items are thus specialized for use at disjunctive points in the development of interaction, where they serve in effect as boundary markers. Hence, while they do not specifically project termination as the next action to be pursued, these items lay the groundwork for it nonetheless by closing down the prior line of talk and marking what is to follow as a new departure.

Perhaps the most minimal type of closing preface involves the production of only the IE's name before the final *thanks*.

(27)   UK BBC Radio *Today*: June 1993: Bosnia Camps
       IR: John Humphrys   IE: Ian Smedley
1   IR: → Ian Smedley thank you very much.

(28)   US PBS *Newshour*: 25 July 1985: South Africa
       IR: Jim Lehrer   IE1: Sheena Duncan   IE2: John Chettle
1   IR: → .hhhhh Miz Duncan Mister Chettle thank you both.

Notice that these proper names are displaced from what might be regarded as the syntactically "normal" position within the sentence. They are objects of the IR's expression of gratitude, referenced by

---

[8] It is notable that similar items also occur in conversational pre-closings, although in conversation they are free-standing and "pass" a turn at talk, while here they are prefatory items.

the "you" in "thank you," and yet they appear in sentence-initial
position. This rather unusual syntactic construction serves specific
interactional functions (Duranti and Ochs 1979). One such function, in the present context, is to provide some advance warning
that closing is imminent. Interviewers may of course address interviewees by name at any point in the course of an interview; but to
use the IE's full proper name (as in [27] above), or to address all the
participating IEs in turn (as in [28]) is specialized for the environment of closing. When the interviewer launches into such a mode of
address, it tacitly projects that closing is in the works.

One final point concerns the manner in which the more elaborate
closing prefaces (announcements and summaries) are implemented.
In some cases the interviewer constructs the prefatory remark out
of material supplied by the interviewee's preceding talk. Thus, when
one IE ended his turn by noting that President Reagan had described
the Strategic Defense Initiative as "my baby" (line 2), the IR borrows
this phrase and modifies it for use in his own closing announcement
(line 4).

(29) US ABC *Nightline*: 13 Oct 1986: Summit
         IR: Sam Donaldson   IE: George Will

1   IE: ... program that the president has described over
2   →   'n over as <u>my</u> baby.
3   IR: Okay. (.) and on <u>that</u> note, (.) we're gonna
4   →   hafta leave <u>our</u> baby. .hhh That's our report
5   for tonight ...

Another example of this practice occurred in (23), which was examined earlier for its summarizing preface. Notice how this summary
("I think you've done it") incorporates material supplied by the IE's
final remark ("That should be done").

(23) US ABC *Nightline*: 4 June 1985: Espionage
         IR: Ted Koppel   IE: Christopher Boyce

1   IE: ... and the G<u>o</u>vernment is <u>derel</u>ict in its <u>duty</u>
2   if it does <u>not</u> com<u>mun</u>icate to the four million
3   with security clearances <u>that</u> <u>fact</u>.
4   →   That sh<u>ould</u> be d<u>one</u>.
5   IR: →   Christopher Boyce, I think you've d<u>one</u> it. And
6   →   done it very <u>el</u>oquently tonight. Thank you very
7   much for talking with me.
8   IE: Very good. Good night.

Such borrowings are not merely clever or witty. They impart a sense of coherence to the closing process, enabling the IR to segue smoothly from the IE's previous remarks, whatever they might be, and on to termination.

In summary, these prefatory practices, each in their own way, prepare the way for closing. Moreover, in whatever form they may appear, closing prefaces neither project nor receive any response from the interviewees. Interviewers simply produce the closing preface and then launch immediately into the final *thanks*.

Earlier efforts at winding down

The interviewer may also indicate that closing is imminent in advance of his or her final closing turn, in an antecedent question. For instance, the IR may characterize a given question as the "last" or "final" question of the interview (arrowed).

(30)   US PBS *NewsHour*: 12 June 1985: Credit Card Fraud
          IR: Judy Woodruff   IE: Rudolph Giuliani

```
 1  IR:  →  Just one last thing. Is there any word of
 2           advice you would give to the consumer on how to
 3           protect himself or herself from this sort of
 4           thing? Or is it the credit card companies that
 5           are really having to .hhhhh
 6  IE:     It's- it's both. Uh from the point of view of . . .
 7           ((8 lines omitted))
 8           because the costs are largely passed along.
 9  IR:     Rudolph Giuliani, thank you for being with us.
10  IE:     Thank you very much.
```

(31)   UK BBCTV *Newsnight*: June 1989: Labour Party Policy
          IR: Donald MacCormick   IE: David Blunkett

```
 1  IR:  →  Just a just a last very quick question if I may.
 2           Are you saying that . . . ((question continues))
 3  IE:     .hhh (1.0) The balance of votes is very
 4           difficult . . . ((answer continues))
 5  IR:     David Blunkett thank you very much indeed for
 6           joining us tonight.
```

Even without an explicit characterization, certain questions come across as "last questions" by virtue of their content. For instance, questions about future plans or prospects have an air of finality about them.

(32) US PBS *NewsHour*: 13 June 1985: Artificial Heart
       IR: Judy Woodruff   IE: Dr. Allen Lansing
1   IR: → Can you give us any idea ah when your next
2   implant may- may be?
3   IE: No, we have not set a date, we have not picked a
4   candidate. Uh we have several possibilities...
5   ((3 lines omitted))
6   over to the uh apartment for convalescents.
7   IR: Doctor Allen Lansing, we thank you for being
8   with us.
9   IE: Thank you. It was my pleasure.

Here, after discussing the present state of the artificial heart program
with a noted physician, a question about plans for the next implant
nicely caps off the discussion and thus prepares for closing.

Interviewers may of course begin to turn the discussion
"downhill" even earlier in the course of the interview, before the last
question–answer exchange. But the general point is that they normally make some effort to wind down the discussion before launching into the closing itself. Unlike ordinary conversation, where the
process minimally involves each interactant declining an opportunity to say more, in the time-limited context of the news interview
it primarily involves one party – the interviewer – taking steps to
forecast that closing is imminent, and when possible to minimize its
abruptness by constructing it as following "naturally" from whatever the interviewee has just said.

Micro-managing the final answer's length

The process examined thus far is not always sufficient to achieve a
punctual closing. Consider that the parties to an interview are not
equally knowledgeable about the temporal situation under which
they are operating. As noted above, only the interviewer is aware
of specifically when the time limit is being approached due to an
audio link to the control room; interviewees lack this knowledge,
and their answers are generally quite lengthy.[9] These circumstances
raise the possibility that time will run out while the interviewee is
talking. How do interviewers deal with this potentially problematic
situation? As it turns out, there are a variety of methods whereby

---

[9] For a discussion which bears on the length of IE's answers, see chapter 4.

interviewers can attempt to exert some control over the length of the interviewee's final remarks.

Cutting the IE off

Perhaps the most straightforward practice is to initiate the closing turn interruptively, thereby truncating the interviewee's developing response to make way for termination. For example (arrowed):

(33)   UK BBCTV *Newsnight*: June 1989: Defense
         IR: Peter Snow   IE: David Howell

```
 1  IE:      ...Uh we can offer to the Russians if they come
 2            down to (.) the same level as the western allies
 3            that's fine (.) Of course: (.) this latest move
 4            by Gorbachev doesn't .h begin to move that far:
 5  IR:       m
 6  IE:       He'd have to offer a .hh a reduction of twelve
 7            hundred short range missi:les as well as the
 8            nuclear artillery (.) to come down to our level,
 9            but=
10  IR:  →   =Listen Mister Howell thank you very much I'm
11            afraid we must end there thank you very much for
12            joining us.=
13  IE:      =O:kay.
14  IR:      Thank you so much.
15  IE:      Yum
```

Here the IR initiates a closing turn (arrowed) at a point where the IE was clearly not yet finished, having just produced a conjunction ("but") projecting further talk that would elaborate upon and contrast with what he has said thus far.

From a purely instrumental standpoint, interrupting may be an effective means of micro-managing the length of the final answering turn. This practice creates other difficulties, however. It is aesthetically jarring and disrupts the orderly "winding down" of the interview that interviewers otherwise strive to achieve. Perhaps more importantly, interviewers are in danger of being seen as "brusque" or "rude" if they interrupt their prominent guests.

A powerful illustration of these difficulties occurred when CBS News anchor Dan Rather interviewed Vice President George Bush about his involvement in the Iran-Contra affair during the 1988 US presidential campaign. Both parties were contentious and

argumentative throughout the interview, but Rather's abruptness
in closing was singled out for criticism in subsequent commentaries.
It is not difficult to see why. Rather initially projects that closing
is imminent (lines 1–4), but he then goes on to ask a final question about whether Bush would be willing to hold a news conference to explain his role in Iran-Contra (4–11). As Bush starts to
respond (10–13), Rather cuts him off (line 14) to initiate the closing
turn. In Rather's own account of the incident (Rather 1994: chapter
4), he was compelled to close at this juncture – the interview had
already run substantially overtime, and the producer was urging
Rather (via earphone) to close then and there.

(34)   US CBS *Evening News*: 25 Jan 1988: Iran-Contra
        IR: Dan Rather   IE: George Bush

```
 1   IR:     Mister Vice President, (.) I appreciate you
 2           joining us tonight, I appreciate the
 3           straightforward way: in:: uh (0.2) which you've-
 4           (.) engaged in this exchange.   eh- clearly some
 5           unanswered questions [remain. ARE YOU willing,]=
 6   IE:                          [(                        )]
 7   IR:     =.hh are you willing (0.2) to go to a news
 8           conference.=before the Iowa caucuses, .hhh
 9           [answer ques]tions   [from a: ll comeh- all]=
10   IE:     [I've been to]       [eight (six) news     ]=
11   IR:     =[comers ]
12   IE:     =[confere]nces since March:  uh-
13           [.hh eighty (six- seven)  since   March   ]
14   IR:     [I gather that the answer is no:. .hh Thank] you
15           very much f'being with us Mister Vice President.
```

Whatever considerations may have motivated Rather to interject,
he did not handle it adeptly. In addition to truncating the answer,
Rather also provides a markedly unsympathetic characterization of
it. Bush was apparently moving to reject Rather's call for a special
press conference, citing the large number of press conferences he
had already held (lines 10–13). Although this comment implicates
rejection, it also exhibits a general attitude of openness to the news
media. Rather, however, translates this nuanced answer into a flat
"no." This interruptive and ungenerous closing was the last image
viewers were left with, and it may partially explain the widespread

criticism that Rather received. In subsequent reflections even Rather himself, though inclined to defend his overall conduct that evening, has been self-critical of his handling of the closing (Rather 1994: chapter 4).

When interviewers find themselves having to interrupt their guests, they usually work to minimize or compensate for the abruptness of such a move. The following example contains a variety of such mitigating practices. The IE begins his response (line 3) with a statement projecting a two-part answer – "maybe yes, and maybe no" – but he has produced only the "no" component of the answer when the IR begins to close (line 8).

(35) US ABC *Nightline*: 7 June 1985: Josef Mengele
      IR: Charles Gibson   IE: Simon Wiesenthal

```
 1   IR:       You've watched them so closely. Do you think
 2             the family will step forward
 3   IE:       Uhm maybe yes, and maybe no. Because the family
 4             is following the directions of the lawyer, of
 5             Rolf Mengele. And Rolf Mengele says to the
 6             prosecuter yesterday or two days ago, no comment
 7             today, and no comment later
 8   IR:  →    All right. I have to interrupt 'cuz we've run
 9             outta time, but you leave us with a key phrase,
10             maybe yes and maybe no, and maybe that does stay
11             uncertain for a long time. I thank all three of
12             you and Doctor Snow for joining us, and I'll be
13             back in a moment.
```

The IR here takes various steps to soften the abruptness of his closing move. First, he begins to speak only after the IE has completed a recognizable unit of talk – both a complete sentence, and a possibly complete "no" component of the answer. Thus, although the IR has interrupted and truncated the IE's projected answer, he continues to honor the integrity of the syntactic and pragmatic components which comprise it. He also invokes the time constraint to account for having interrupted (lines 8–9), portraying himself as compelled by circumstances over which he has no control, and thus countering the appearance of motivated rudeness (see also except [33] above). Finally, he builds his closing preface (lines 9–11) out of the IE's prior remarks, borrowing a particular phrase ("maybe yes

and maybe no") and pronouncing it a "key phrase" that encapsulates the current state of knowledge. In so doing, he casts the IE's
truncated remark as a "natural" and "appropriate" place at which
to end.

Warning in advance

Interviewers can avoid the potentially disruptive practice of cutting
interviewees off, and yet still exercise some control over the final
answering turn, by indicating in advance that time is short. Advance
time warnings of this sort may be introduced in the midst of the final
answer-in-progress, as in the following (arrowed).

(36)   US ABC *Nightline*: 5 June 1985: Corporate Mergers
       IR: Ted Koppel   IE: Walter Adams

```
 1  IR:      . . . w:ith whom is: competition these days.
 2            Aren't we talking about competition within the
 3            United States any more or is it only .hh
 4            competition with these (0.2) other multinational
 5            corpor[ations. ]
 6  IE:             [Well it-] uh- uh- obviously competition
 7            is both domestic (.) and international. But
 8            look at the record of General Motors to come
 9            back to the GM uh- eh- Hugh:es uh-
10            [MER:ger   .hh       ]
11  IR:  →   [Lemme ca- lemme cau]tion you we're down to our
12            last minute so [give it quickly please.]
13  IE:                      [O k a y  wha-  what] 'as
14            General Moters done. .hh It'as abandoned the-
15            the small car field . . .
```

Here the IR interjects to indicate that closing is imminent, and then
withdraws, permitting the IE to continue. Notice that this warning
is not initiated haphazardly, for it occurs just after the IE projects
that a lengthy answer may be forthcoming. His call to "look at the
record of General Motors" (line 8) implies that an extended corporate history is about to be elaborated, and this is what prompts the
IR's warning. A similar sequence of events occurs in the following,
when the IE's comment that he will be elaborating on a list of two
items (lines 3–4) immediately prompts the IR to interject with a time
warning (line 5).

(37)   UK BBCTV *Newsnight*: May 1989: China Unrest
     IR: Peter Snow   IE: Denis Healey

```
1  IE:     ... I'll go out on a limb and say: I think it's
2          likely to be increased further .hh by future
3          events but I would like to make two very quick
4          points.=
5  IR:  →  =Very quickly if you would.
6  IE:     There's a genera:tional thing here ...
```

In both of these examples, the IR warns that closing is imminent, interjects that warning while the IE's turn is unfolding, and does so just after the IE projects substantial talk to come.

Although the IEs are permitted to continue speaking in the preceding examples, each is still subjected to an interruption of sorts. To avoid interruptions altogether, IRs may issue a time warning still earlier, in conjunction with the last question. This enables the IEs to design their responses from the outset with the temporal situation in mind. The warning may include an actual report of the time remaining (arrowed).

(38)   US ABC *Nightline*: 23 July 1985: South Africa
     IR: Charles Gibson   IE: Frank Wisner

```
1   IR:  →  All right Mister Wisner, final twenty seconds.
2          How does America look in all this?
3   IE:    Well, I think America is looking good. The
4          problem in South Africa is apartheid. The
5          problem ...
6          ((4 lines omitted))
7          ... that's the best way to go, not by punitive
8          actions.
9   IR:    All right, thank all three of you for joining
10         us, I appreciate it very much.
```

Alternatively, the warning may contain a more general injunction to keep the response brief (arrowed).

(39)   US PBS *NewsHour*: 11 June 1985: Southern Baptists
     IR: Charlayne Hunter-Gault   IE1: Russell Dilday
     IE2: Paul Pressler

```
1   IR:    Specifically this fight, Mister Dilday, how
2          badly do you think this hurts the denomination
3          in the eyes of the convention as well as the
```

```
4        →  world? Very briefly.
5   IE1:    A tragic disruption of what our main purpose is
6           in reaching our world for Christ and
7           accomplishing bold mission thrust goals, this
8           kind of interjection came at the insistence of a
9           political organization >six years ago. =right at
10          the time whem we were on the verge of moving
11          forward as a denomination to accomplish these
12          goals=of the Bible. [.hh] an' we been=
13  IR:                       [Ar-]
14  IE1:    =sidetracked ever since then.=an' it's tragic
15          indeed.
16  IR:     Well Mister Pressler and Mister Dilday,=I thank
17          you very much- ah both for being with us.
```

Such warnings are clearly issued to encourage the interviewees to limit their responses, but how effective are they? This is difficult to determine, since there is no actual record of what would have been said in the absence of a warning. However, in some instances interviewees do indicate that they are at least trying to "hurry up." Looking more closely at the previous excerpt, notice that in the context of the prior question, the first part of the answer ("A tragic disruption..." at line 5) lacks an initial subject and verb (e.g., "*It is* a tragic disruption..."), departing from what might seem to be the "normal" way of answering, and thus displaying an effort to abbreviate the response. Later on (line 9) the IE increases the pacing of his speech beginning at the point marked ">," and he rushes from the downwardly intoned "ago." (a possible utterance completion point) and into the next unit of talk without an intervening silence. This acceleration occurs just as the IE projects that he may be launching into a lengthy historical digression ("six years ago..."). Finally, after the IR begins and then quickly aborts a closing move (line 13), the IE continues (lines 14–15) with an item that is specifically *not* a blow-by-blow recounting of the "history" begun at line 9, but is a quick completion of it: "an' we been sidetracked ever since then.=an' it's tragic indeed." In sum, by eliding utterance components, quickening the pace at specific points, and so on, interviewees can present themselves as "hurrying" and thus dutifully responsive to the interviewer's warning.

Interspersed response tokens

Perhaps the most subtle means of micro-managing the interviewee's final turn involves the production of brief acknowledgments (e.g., *hm, uh huh, yes*) and aborted turn initiations. It is not uncommon for interviewers to sprinkle such tokens of response over the course of an interviewee's turn when closing is imminent. In the next example, the IR first produces an acknowledgment (arrow 1) and then two aborted turn initiations (arrows 2 and 3) before actually closing the interview. The response at arrow 2 ("We") begins just after the IE has projected two items of further talk ("The two basic difficulties are...").

```
(40)   US PBS NewsHour: 13 Oct 1986: US/USSR Summit
       IR: Jim Lehrer   IE: McGeorge Bundy
 1  IE:        ...It's a ver:y har:d business. .hh to [get .h=
 2  IR:  1→                                          [Hm
 3  IE:        =agreements that are (0.4) reliable: (.) in
 4             the terms 'n conditions that both sides see:.
 5             The two basic difficulties are .hhh a
 6             [Soviet fear: of American high technology, and=
 7  IR:  2→    [We
 8  IE:        =an American fear::, .hh [of what the Soviets=
 9  IR:  3→                             [We have
10  IR:        =Jeh- Mister Bundy, we hafta leave it there.
11             Gentlemen, thanks- thanks to all of you.
```

As a general rule, interviewers refrain from producing all acknowledgment tokens and other receipt items while an interviewee is speaking. The significance of this pattern of withholding will be explored in the next chapter, but for now it may be observed that it is extremely common throughout news interviews in both Britain and the United States. However, one of the very few environments in which interviewers can be found departing from this pattern is just prior to closing. These acknowledgment tokens show interviewers to be monitoring the unfolding talk and treating particular junctures within it as places where they could in principle assume the floor. When the interviewer begins and then aborts a more substantial turn at talk, this displays an even more active interactional stance. And when these aborted responses begin with "We" or "We have," as in the preceding extract, they strongly suggest that the interviewer intends to bring about closure.

Taken together, these various bits of interjective talk indicate that, at the very least, the interviewer is preparing to take the floor, and at most that the interviewer is poised to close the interview entirely. This can in turn serve as a subtle hint to interviewees to wind down their remarks.

Contested closings

As we have seen, the primary initiative for closing the interview rests with interviewers, and interviewees generally collaborate in this process. However, interviewees are not always so cooperative – they may resist the interviewer's closing efforts, sometimes quite strenuously. Such resistance is particularly common in debate interviews involving advocates for opposing sides of a political issue (see chapter 8). Debates often become highly charged, and in the heat of battle each interviewee may strive to have the last word and, correspondingly, to deny that opportunity to the opposing interviewee.

This occurs in the following excerpt, where the IR makes three attempts to close (arrowed), but the first two are overridden by IEs locked in conflict with one another. The issue is corporate mergers – the critic is economist Walter Adams, and the defender is financier Malcolm Forbes.

```
(41)  US ABC Nightline: 5 June 1985: Corporate Mergers
      IR: Ted Koppel   IE1: Walter Adams   IE2: Malcolm Forbes
 1  IE1:      ....h These multina:tional corporations are
 2             not aMER:ican corporations .hh they're not
 3             serving the public interest in the United
 4             States .hh they're loyal to only ONe flag .h
 5             that's their own flag. .h General Moters
 6             salutes its own flag it does NOT respect the
 7             stars 'n stripes
 8  IR:   1→  All [right Mister-]
 9  IE1:         [a n d  i t ] [does   not   serve   the]=
10  IE2:                       [Ya know ya don't-  .hh]=
11  IE1:      =[stars n  stripes.]
12  IE2:      =[ ya don't meet ] many red necked economists
13             yer duh: quite'n exception Professor hhh
```

```
14              [heh-heh-heh-heh-heh   .hh-hhh-.hhh ]=
15   IE1:       [Well (.) I'm a PAtriot Mistuh- Forbes]
16   IE2:       =.h hh .h uh .hh This country's stronger then
17              it's ever been an more prosperous then it's
18              ever been it's pulling the rest o' the world
19              .hh back up into an economic health.   .hh And I
20              th- I would say .hh when companies .h by their
21              growth en their multiplicity .hh (.) m-multiply
22              jo:bs en more people er workin=then=ever=before
23              (.) that's patri[o t i s m.]
24   IR:    2→              [All [right] Mister Forbes]
25   IE1:                   [Yes but the JOBS]=
26   IR:    2→  =[Professor Adams and gentlemen I'm-]
27   IE1:       =[ARE BEING CREATED BY THE] SMALL
28              companies and not by the giants. The giants
29              er merging an the sma:ll companies are:
30              creating the jobs.
31   IR:    3→ I'm afraid we're out of time. I thank you all
32              gentlemen very much, Mister Forbes, Professor
33              Adams, Senator Metzenbaum, (.) appreciate you
34              coming in. (.) I'll be back in a moment.
```

The first closing attempt (arrow 1) begins just as Adams appears to be winding down a very strong criticism of multinational corporations (lines 1–7), which he attacks as unpatriotic and un-American. This closing move (line 8) is overridden by Adams (line 9) who adds an increment to his previous criticism. This criticism prompts Forbes to attack Adams personally (lines 10, 12–13), and then to praise multinationals (lines 16–23). The IR's second closing move (at arrow 2) is also interrupted by Adams, this time in an effort to refute Forbes' previous point. Here the IR grows more aggressive in striving for closure – he begins a bit before Forbes has finished speaking, and when he is subsequently interrupted he actively competes for the floor by pressing on with his closing turn (lines 24, 26). However, he eventually aborts his turn and relinquishes the floor to Adams. Only the third attempt (arrow 3) is finally successful.

A similar struggle for the last word took place at the conclusion of a heated debate over an Oregon religious "cult." A critic of the cult (IE1) is attacking the credibility of cult members (lines 1–3) when an outspoken member (IE2) interjects to assert that the critic is "full of shit" (lines 4–5 and 7). At this point the IR attempts to close (lines 10–11, 13), noting that he had earlier promised the last word to the critic "Mister Fawbush." However, the cult member resists this closing move, interjecting with an appeal to have the last word for herself (lines 12, 14–15).

(42)   US ABC *Nightline*: 15th Anniversary Program: Oregon Guru
       IR: Ted Koppel   IE1: Wayne Fawbush   IE2: Ma Anand Sheela
1   IE1:   I̲f we had a̲ny reliability that what these folks
2   are sayin .hh we could beli̲e:ve, (0.3)
3   th[at would be one thing. (.) Bu̲:t I- let me-]
4   IE2:   [O̲h: (0.2) yo̲u: are fu̲ll of shit.]
5   You don't know a̲nything a[bout what reah-]=
6   IE1:   [Let me just (0.3)]=
7   IE2:   =[(0.2) reliability is.]=
8   IE1:   =[let me just point out Ted]
9   IE2:   =[You want him
10 IR: [I said that Mister Fawbush would have the
11   final word, (0.3) and he wi̲ll [:, and if]=
12 IE2:   [Uh (.) But]=
13 IR: =[you're not quiet we'll just cut the mike off.
14 IE2:   =[I would like to tell you what Mister
15   Fawbu[sh (say:) the first (year he went to the)
16 IR: [In that case we'll cut the microphone off
17   right now, Thank you very much all of you for
18   jo̲ining us.

In the battle to achieve closure, some IRs have a decisive technological advantage over their guests: control over the microphones. When this guest stubbornly continues to talk, the IR first threatens to turn off her microphone (line 13), and then does just that (line 16), thus effectively if unceremoniously bringing the interview to an end.

Battles for the last word involve efforts to extend an interview *beyond* the length desired by the interviewer. However, interviewees may also be uncooperative by walking out of an interview *prematurely*, before the interviewer has moved to close. We began this chapter by recounting two dramatic walkouts – one involving John Nott, the former British Minister of Defense, and the other involving US presidential candidate Ross Perot. Walkouts tend to occur under rather different circumstances. While efforts to continue typically occur in debate interviews involving opposing interviewees struggling for the last word, walkouts typically occur in newsmaker interviews involving a single interviewee. This pattern is not coincidental.

In the latter type of interview, interviewers have sole responsibility for subjecting the interviewee's views to challenge, and this often results in an adversarial stance which the interviewee may find objectionable. One way for an interviewee to register dissatisfaction is to end the interview prematurely.

Both walkouts and battles for the last word are exceptions to the rule that usually governs interview closings. What makes them exceptional is that they involve interviewees intervening in a process that is usually managed primarily by the interviewer. In short, contested closings of both kinds involve deviations from normality, and this is why they receive so much attention. Contested closings are often included in special anniversary programs commemorating noteworthy interview moments from that program's past – the Nott and Perot walkouts, and the closing battle over the Oregon cult, were both immortalized in this way. Furthermore, when high-ranking officials or celebrities are involved, contested closings can become news events in their own right, the subject of journalistic commentary and analysis which greatly overshadows the substance of the interviews in which they occurred.

Conclusion

It should be clear by now that the processes of entering into and exiting from a news interview, however brief and perfunctory such processes might seem, actually fulfill a variety of important journalistic functions. Openings set an agenda for the interview and project the form that discussion will take. They also regulate interviewees' access to the interaction and establish the identities that will inform their participation. Closings are structured in such a way as to allow for the imposition of an inflexible time limit with a minimum of abruptness and without trampling unnecessarily on the participants' talk. Moreover, the practices necessary to accomplish these various tasks are complex and subtle, and mastery of them is an important craft skill that broadcast interviewers must possess to be effective.

Furthermore, when contrasted with parallel processes in ordinary conversation, it becomes apparent that there is nothing "natural" or inevitable about how these processes work within the news interview. They represent one particular and distinctive way of managing the task of opening and closing an occasion of interaction. The conventions that organize openings and closings are sensitive to the unusual circumstances under which broadcast news interviewing takes place. Adherence to these conventions is in part what marks the interaction at its boundaries as a prescheduled, impersonal, and highly formal encounter that is geared toward the media audience. As a consequence, audience members who happen to stumble upon the program as it begins can presumably tell, just from the initial spate of talk, and just from the form of that talk, that they are witnessing neither a purely private conversation nor a celebrity chatfest, but a mode of journalism being orchestrated on their own behalf.

4

Basic ground rules: taking turns and "doing" news interview talk

In June 1973, John Ehrlichman, recently fired from President Richard Nixon's White House staff, was interviewed by Mike Wallace on CBS's *60 Minutes*. The drumbeat of criticism of White House crimes and misdemeanors that would eventually topple the President was then intensifying and Ehrlichman's firing was only one of the most recent, and desperate, of Nixon's responses. As the camera moved into a tight close-up of Ehrlichman's face, Wallace intoned the litany of White House wrong-doing: "Plans to audit tax returns for political retaliation. Theft of psychiatric records. Spying by undercover agents. Bogus opinion polls. Plans to fire bomb a building. Conspiracy to obstruct justice. All of this by the law and order administration of Richard Nixon." Eight long seconds passed as the camera focused on a stony-faced Ehrlichman. Then, with a slight smirk, he responded: "Is there a question in there somewhere?" Here, in the midst of the most serious crisis for the White House this century, Ehrlichman focused not on the substantive issues raised by Wallace, but on whether they had been appropriately expressed – in the form of a question.

Nothing could be more obvious than the fact that news interviews are made up of questions and answers. Yet it is this unremarkable fact that is central to the way that interview talk is organized. The question–answer format of news interviews is central to their structure and crucial to analyzing their dynamics in at least three ways.

First, the particular, and in many ways peculiar, manner in which the question–answer format of the news interview is constructed and used is *constitutive* of the news interview as a form of interaction. By maintaining this format, the participants construct their interaction – turn by turn – as something that is recognizably a news interview. They "do news interview talk." The question–answer format is a relatively simple and incontestable set of interactional rules which provide that interviewers properly ask questions and interviewees properly answer them. But these simple rules are only the tip of the iceberg. For underlying them is a much more complex and contestable substrate of conventions and practices through which the appropriateness of a question and the necessity of answering it are negotiated by the participants. Both the rules and the practices that underlie them are largely tacit and out of conscious awareness, but they are central both to the participants' production of "news interview talk" and also to their recognition of appropriate conduct in the interview context. Moreover, at times the participants may become more actively conscious of the rules and, like Ehrlichman, they may appeal to them at key moments as a means of complaint or prevarication about what is happening.

The rules and practices of news interview conduct are not simply resources for the participants. They are also resources with which audience members discriminate between a "news interview" and its more conversational "chat show" cousin or again, as in the infamous Bush–Rather encounter, tell when a news interview is degenerating into something else. Adhering to them creates a highly recognizable interactional format. Even in the case of radio shows, which lack visual or other contextual information, most listeners can recognize that a "news interview" is in progress within seconds of switching on (Atkinson 1982).

Second, the question–answer (Q–A) structure of news interviews distinctively shapes the opportunities the participants have to achieve their ends. It does so asymmetrically. The rules and practices that structure questioning and answering in the news interview provide the main protagonists – interviewer and interviewee – with different resources for dealing with one another. In the Roman arena, gladiators fought with trident and net against shield and short sword. In the modern news interview, the ground rules equip the protagonists with similarly asymmetric resources for attack and defense: the interviewer's resources for capturing and pinning down the interviewee may be matched by the latter's capacity for deflection and pointed riposte.

Finally, the rules and practices of news interview interaction shape the conduct of the participants in ways which meet basic institutional demands that are made of broadcasters and their organizations. Two of these are particularly important: (i) the talk should be managed as "talk for overhearers" so that audience members do not feel that they are hearing an essentially private conversation, but can feel instead that interviews are being conducted for their benefit; and (ii) interviews should not be occasions in which interviewers (and, by extension, the broadcasting organizations which employ them) editorialize about public issues. As we will see, the rules of the news interview game are an institutionalized means of meeting these very basic constraints that are faced by news producers and broadcasting organizations.

In this chapter, we describe the rules and practices that shape the production of questions and answers in news interviews as a *turn-taking system*. We want to demonstrate the very distinctive nature of social interaction when it is shaped by the tasks of asking and answering questions in the news interview context. We investigate the sort of practical work the participants do to stay within the bounds of the system. This chapter will focus on the ways in which news interview turn-taking procedures function as a means for the participants to deal with some of the basic tasks, and also the legal and moral constraints that shape this form of talk. It will also show the ways in which these rules shape the "boundaries of the permissible" for both interviewers and interviewees and some of the ways in which the participants encroach on these boundaries in the heat of conflict.

News interview turn-taking: basic preliminaries

Although the famous British interviewer Sir Robin Day claimed that his task was to engage public figures "in conversation," even the most cursory look at the news interview reveals dramatic differences from a conversational framework. In conversation, topics can emerge freely, the participants are free to make diverse contributions to the subject at hand, and anyone can initiate a new line of departure. In the news interview, by contrast, the participants are fundamentally constrained. Interviewers restrict themselves to questioning, and interviewees restrict themselves to answering interviewer questions, or at least responding to them.[1]

---

[1] IEs can, of course, be evasive in their responses to questions and, in this sense, fail to "answer" them appropriately. A careful formulation of the Q–A structure

This constraint shapes the form taken by the participants' talk and the order in which they talk to the following pattern:

IR: Question
IE: Answer
IR: Question
IE: Answer

This form of turn-taking involves what Atkinson and Drew (1979) have called "turn-type preallocation" in which the activities of asking and answering (or responding to) questions are pre-allocated to the roles of interviewer and interviewee. With minor exceptions, this preallocated pattern holds regardless of the number of interviewers or interviewees involved in the encounter (see chapter 8).

Although this pattern is familiar enough, it is worth pausing for a moment to consider what basic kinds of conduct are excluded by it. The short answer is that the participants – interviewers and interviewees – refrain from a wide variety of actions that they are free to do in the give and take of ordinary conversation. If interviewers restrict themselves to asking questions, then they cannot – at least overtly – express opinions, or argue with, debate, or criticize the interviewees' positions nor, conversely, agree with, support, or defend them. Correspondingly, if interviewees restrict themselves to answers (or responses) to questions, then they cannot ask questions (of interviewers or other interviewees), nor make unsolicited comments on previous remarks, initiate changes of topic, or divert the discussion into criticisms of the interviewer or the broadcasting organization. As we shall see, the strict Q–A format of the news interview rules out even small responsive acts, such as "mm hm," "yes," "oh," "really," and so on, that are normally used to show attentiveness to what is being said, or surprise at it, or agreement with it. In practice, of course, some of these actions occasionally turn up in news interviews but, as we shall see, only as departures from the rules of news interview turn-taking and therefore only as noticeable, problematic and possibly sanctionable courses of action.

One major consequence of these restrictions is, in principle at least, to place interviewers firmly in control of the interactional

of news interviews might suggest that IEs "answer, or otherwise respond to, IRs' questions." The use of the term "answer" in this book should be taken as inclusive of this wider and more careful formulation. See chapter 7 for an elaboration of these issues.

management of the interview. It is the interviewers' questions that
set the agenda for interviewees' responses, and provide a context
in which they will be evaluated as honest, truthful, appropriate, or
dishonest, evasive or combative. Further, where there are two or
more interviewees, interviewers' questions will generally determine
which interviewee is selected to speak next and whether, and when,
other interviewees will be permitted to address the topic under discussion. Moreover, interviewers can take the lead in moving to new
topics and in deciding when, finally, the interview will be closed.
All this is, to repeat, a normal product of adherence to the turn-
taking rules and conventions of the news interview and it represents
a significant potential for interactional power and control.

The value of this control is obvious when we consider that an interview is not designed to be simply a platform for interviewees' preferred spin on events, but rather a context in which their judgments,
opinions, and actions are tested in a process of interrogation. The
interviewer's control of the topical agenda, though far from complete, is a means of restraining politicians and other experienced
interviewees who would otherwise treat the interview situation as
a kind of soapbox from which to deliver a pre-packaged message.
At the other end of the scale, broadcasting organizations must deal
with many interviewees who may never have been interviewed before and may never be interviewed again. These interviewees may
need a strong interactional framework to get through the interview
without mishap. These benefits also have certain costs. The inex-
perienced or unassertive interviewee can be restricted to an agenda
that is limited by the imagination and ability of the interviewer. And
the control exerted through interviewer questioning is, of course, a
major point of friction with interviewees who object to the agenda
that an interviewer is pursuing, or who wish to impose their own
agenda on the encounter.

Interviewer questions

When we look at interviewer questions, it is useful to follow linguists in making a distinction between the grammatical form of
spoken utterances, and the meaning of those utterances when spoken in a particular context (Levinson 1983). Linguists use the terms
"declarative" and "interrogative" to describe the grammatical form

of utterances, and they use the terms "statement" and "question" to name the actions which these utterance types normally accomplish in context. This distinction is important because there is not an absolute one-to-one correspondence between the grammatical form of an utterance, and the action it performs. As we shall see, declaratively formatted utterances can function as questions, and interrogatively formatted utterances can accomplish many non-questioning actions – including assertions, agreements, and accusations. This discrepancy between form and function is often a product of context (Schegloff, 1984), but there are also interrogative formats which normally perform actions other than "questioning." Consider these two grammatical interrogatives:

> – "Where did you lose your computer?"
> – "How could you lose your computer?"

It is evident that while the first seeks information and is designed to "question," the second is designed to "criticize" or "accuse." These distinctions are significant because, though interviewers and interviewees are not linguists, they must look at the grammatical form, the content and the context of an utterance to decide whether it is a "legitimate" bona fide "question" that should properly be "answered" within the news interview framework, or whether, alternatively, it is an assertion or accusation which can be addressed and/or resisted in some other way.

With this said, the vast majority of interviewers' turns at talk in our database involve some kind of question. Analysis of a sample of over 600 interviewer utterances shows that over 85 percent of them end in a question of some kind. The figures are remarkably uniform for British and American news interviews.

These questions take a variety of forms. They include, firstly, all the main types of interrogatively formed questions:

(a) "Wh" questions

(1)   US PBS *Newshour*: 4 Dec 1989: US–Soviet Summit
      IR: Jim Lehrer   IE: Senator George Mitchell
1 IR: → .hhhh Senator Mitchell, what's your overview
2   → of the summit from President Bush's point of
3   view.
4   (.)
5 IE: It was positive . . .

(b) "Yes/No" questions

(2) UK ATV *Nationwide*: 30 Sep 1981: Labour Defense Policy
    IR: David Dimbleby   IE: Brynmor John
1 IR: → Was it intentional not to call you?
2 IE: Well I- (.) I don't think it was mali: :gn,=but
3   it was intentional in the sense that he- he
4   referred at the e:nd to the fact that I had put
5   in a note asking to be calle:d, .hh and couldn't
6   be called.=So it obviously was intentional.=It
7   wasn't .hh an o:versight on his part.

(c) Polar alternatives

(3) UK BBC Radio *World at One*: 14 Feb 1979: Tony Benn
    IR: Brian Widlake   IE: Peter Jenkins
1 IR: If the Prime Minister were to drop Mister Benn
2   → would this be a political plus or a political
3   minus in terms of the coming election and votes
4   (hhh) er generally.
5 IE: .hhhh (.) I think it would be: a political minus
6   in Labour Party ter:m:s.

News interview questions are also sometimes produced in a
"declarative + tag" question format, as in (4), where the tag "has
she" qualifies the declarative "She's been no pushover."

(4) UK BBCTV *Newsnight*: June 1989: European Elections
    IR: Peter Snow   IE: Bryan Gould
1 IE: .hhh Because although Missus Thatcher constantly
2   says how tough she's going to be: (.) .h and indeed
3   she does: us:e the language which an:tagonizes
4   everybody in Europe.=
5 IR: → =She's been no pushover has she.

And in (5) the tag question is simply the question-intoned "Fair?"

(5) US ABC *Nightline*: 22 July 1985: South Africa
    IR: Ted Koppel   IE: Reverend Boesak
1 IR: Reverend Boesak (.) Ambassador Beukes makes the
2   point (.) that you can't have any discussions
3   you can't have any progress in South Africa
4   until the violence stops. .hhh An therefore
5   → the state of emergency is necessary. Fair?
6   (0.4)

```
7  IE:    tch .hhh Well: I would agree with the Ambassador
8         in the sense that you cannot h.hhh have
9         discussions or negotiation 'til the violence stops.
```

In addition to interrogative syntax, interviewers draw on other resources to build their turns as questions. Prominent among these are declaratives that refer to what Labov and Fanshel (1977:100) term "B-events," events about which the recipient of the statement has unique or privileged knowledge (see also Pomerantz 1980). In news interviews, common "B-events" that interviewers refer to, include interviewees' subjective states, such as their feelings, attitudes or intentions, and areas in which the interviewee has particular knowledge, expertise or authority. Declaratives about such matters function as questions seeking confirmation, as in (6), which concerns whether British politician David Owen has any regrets about forming a new political party (the now defunct SDP), breaking away from the Labour Party:

```
(6)  UK BBCTV Newsnight: 29 Sep 1981: Labour Party Split
     IR: John Tusa   IE: David Owen
1  IR: → So in a very brief word David Owen,=you in no
2      → way regret what you did er despite what has
3         (happened) in Brighton this week in the Labour Party.
4  IE:    n- In no way do I regret it.=
```

"B-event" questions also include hypothetical or future-oriented statements about the interviewee's likely actions or policies, as in the following example where a Labour politician is questioned about the party's plans for a settlement of problems in Northern Ireland:

```
(7)  UK BBCTV Newsnight: 29 Sep 1981: Northern Ireland
     IR: John Tusa   IE: Don Concannon
1  IE:    All we've said is that it is our view that a
2         lasting (settlement) in Northern Ireland will
3         come about by reunification. .hh We know we've
4         got a hard task. (.) We know we've er a long
5         plough to furrow er er on this. .h We know we've
6         got to win a lot of hearts and minds. .h I'm not
7         saying it's impossible.=A lot of people tell me
8         it's impossible. I don't think it's impossible
```

9   or else I wouldn't be (a party) to it.
10   (.)
11   IR: → It's not something you're going to force on the
12   Northern Ireland people.
13   IE: er You can't force ((continues))

They can also include formulations that summarize the gist or
upshot of earlier interviewee statements (Heritage 1985):

(8) UK BBC Radio *World at One*: Feb 1979: Agricultural Policy
     IR: Brian Widlake   IE: Christopher Tugendhat
1   IE: I'm all for having a common agricultural policy,
2   (0.6) but I think it's ab<u>surd</u> to suggest that
3   decisions of (.) im<u>mm</u>ense economic magnitude
4   .hhh should be taken en<u>ti : re</u>ly by .hh (.)
5   the ministers who are (.) most int'rested in one
6   particular segment of the community,=I wouldn't
7   want ministers d-defence to take all the
8   decisions on de<u>fe</u>nce and I wouldn't want
9   ministers of .hhhh educ<u>a</u>tion to take all the
10   decisions on education,=
11   IR: → =.hhh So you're suggesting there that the f<u>a</u>rm
12   → ministers shouldn't decide this all entirely
13   → amongst thems<u>e</u>lves, that it should be .hhh
14   → <u>spr</u>ead across the board amongst all ministers.
15   IE: Exactly.=I'm saying that one m<u>u</u>st find some way
16   . . .

Finally, though relatively infrequently, interviewer questions may
be managed through rising intonation, as in the following inter-
jected phrasal question that seeks to clarify a point the interviewee
is making about political reforms in China:

(9) UK BBCTV *Newsnight*: May 1989: China Reforms
     IR: Peter Snow   IE: David Shambaugh
1   IE: So f- I: (.) I see him as: uh f- (.) doing
2   several things first of all (.) briefly .hh um:
3   instituting a system where the national <u>people</u>'s
4   congress becomes a mor : e real<u>i</u>stic parliament
5   perhaps with multiple slate elections to it
6   .hhhh the rule of law: .hh u[h:.
7   IR: →   [Multiple slate
8   → multiparty?
9   IE: ih- No: multiple multiple <u>can</u>didates.

Table 1: *Distribution of main types of interviewer turns*[2]

Interrogative questions (%)	Tag questions (%)	Declarative B-events (%)	Rising intonation (%)	3rd-party statements (%)	1st-party statements (%)	
UK: 67.4	3.9	12.4	3.9	3.6	8.8	N = 304
US: 68.8	4.3	10.5	1.6	7.0	7.8	N = 256

Here the questioning intonation imparted to a declarative utterance gives it the import of what linguists term 'declarative questions' (Quirk *et al* 1972).

Table 1 shows the distribution of these types of questions in a representative subset of our British and American news interview data. It shows that 70 percent of news interview questions are formed using interrogative syntax, and a further 12–16 percent of them use the related forms that are illustrated above.

In addition to the various question types we have described, a substantial minority of interviewer turns consist of first-party and third-party attributed statements. We will discuss the nature of these statements and how they come to be produced later in this chapter and in chapter 5.

Prefaced questions and their interactional construction

So far, the examples of interviewer questions we have shown are relatively simple. In most of them, a single question makes up the entire interviewer turn with no other turn components of any kind. Some interviewer turns, however, are not of this simple type. Just under half of them embody a more complex design that involves more than a single questioning unit.[3] These more complex questions normally take a *prefaced* form which involves additional statements that lead up to the question itself. Examining these prefaced questions gives a

---

[2] The figures making up this table exclude cases in which the IR engages in speaker selection and other interview management activities without asking a question or making a statement. Percentages are subject to rounding effects. For a discussion of some of the coding decisions involved in creating this table, see Heritage and Roth (1995).

[3] More technically, these are turn constructional units, the main types of which are described in Sacks, Schegloff, and Jefferson 1974.

better sense of the special nature of the turn-taking rules for news interviews. It will also begin to show the ways in which the turn-taking rules give news interview interaction its distinctive shape.

A straightforward example of this more complex, prefaced form of interviewer question is (10) below which concerns a museum's efforts to buy the letters of a British explorer. Here the initial "prefatory" sentence (arrow 1) supplies background information for the news audience, presenting it as a simple fact known to the parties, and establishes a context for the subsequent question (arrow 2).

(10)   UK BBC Radio *World at One*: 25 Jan 1979: Letters
       IR: Anna Sebastian   IE: Harry King, Librarian
1 IR: 1→ .hhh <u>The</u> (.) <u>p</u>rice being asked for these letters
2   is (.) three thousand <u>pou</u>: :nds.
3 IR: 2→ Are you going to be able to <u>r</u>aise it,
4   (0.5)
5 IE: At the moment it ... (continues)

In a conversational context, the interviewer's initial statement could readily be treated as a completed turn in its own right and responded to as such. In the news interview, by contrast, where the expectation is that whatever the interviewee does will be produced as a response to a question, interviewees very rarely respond to these kinds of statements.

The delivery of this prefaced question, then, involves a subtle form of collaboration between interviewers and interviewees. By withholding any response until a recognizable question has been produced, interviewees display their understanding that the initial statement is intended to be "prefatory" to a question, and is not to be responded to in its own right. Moreover, by not responding or intervening in the interviewer's turn, they also collaborate with the interviewer's effort to arrive at a question. In turn, interviewers can rely on that collaboration so as to produce "long" multi-unit questions free of "early" or "interjective" interviewee responses.

More generally, by withholding responses to prefatory statements, interviewees embody the expectation that the interviewer's turn should properly consist of a question (Clayman 1988; Greatbatch 1988; Schegloff 1988/9). They thus orient to, and collaborate in producing, the "interview" character of the interactions in which they are engaged. They do "interview talk." Further, these withholdings embody the interviewees' acknowledgment that, in the context of an interview, they do not have rights to a turn until the interviewer has come to a question, and correspondingly that their own talk should properly emerge as an "answer" to a question.

The extent of this interviewee collaboration in the production of interviewer questions and the maintenance of the interview framework can be seen in examples like (11) below in which no response is made to a transparently hostile question preface. Here the IR is Robin Day and the IE is British trade union leader, Arthur Scargill. The election referred to at line 10 was for the leadership of the then powerful National Union of Mineworkers:

(11)   UK BBC Radio *World at One*: 13 Mar 1979: NUM Election
        IR: Robin Day   IE: Arthur Scargill

```
 1  IR:      .hhh er What's the difference between your
 2           Marxism and Mister McGahey's communism.
 3  IE:      er The difference is that it's the press that
 4           constantly call me a Ma:rxist when I do not, (.)
 5           and never have (.) er er given that description
 6           of myself.[.hh I-
 7  IR: 1→            [But I've heard you-
 8      1→   I've heard you'd be very happy to: to: er .hhhh
 9      1→   er describe yourself as a Marxist.
10      2→   Could it be that with an election in the offing
11      2→   you're anxious to play down that you're a
12      2→   Marx[ist.]
13  IE: 3→       [er ] Not at all Mister Da : y.=And I:'m (.)
14           sorry to say I must disagree with you,=you have
15           never heard me describe myself .hhh er as a
16           Ma:rxist.=I have o:nly ((continues))
```

Here, Day's prefatory statement (arrow 1) directly counters Scargill's previous denial that he is a Marxist. The end of this statement is a place where, in conversation, Scargill would likely initiate a disagreement. Yet rather than moving immediately to reject Day's initial statement as an object in its own right, Scargill instead waits for him to come to a question (arrow 2) before initiating a response (arrow 3). Moreover the initial part of his response deals with the question as put, and only after this does he turn to reject the IR's initial assertion.[4] Here, as in other less problematic multi-unit IR

---

[4] Scargill's conduct here illustrates a much more general orientation in conversation (Sacks 1987) and in news interviews (Heritage and Roth 1995) to produce initial

questions, the IE waits in anticipation of a question over the course of the IR's turn and withholds any response until a recognizable question has been produced. In all such cases, interviewees collaborate (and interviewers rely on their collaboration) in the production of multi-unit questioning turns. That collaboration is, of course, consistent with, and conducted within, the basic constraints of the turn-taking system for news interviews.

Interviewee forbearance and self-control in the face of hostile question prefaces is strong evidence for the significance of the turn-taking constraints that we have outlined. Sometimes the effort at self-control is fleetingly visible in the fine-grained detail of interviewee behavior. In (12), the South African Ambassador to the USA, Herbert Beukes, is on the receiving end of a question preface that is sharply critical of the apartheid regime of his government:

(12) US ABC *Nightline*: 22 July 1985: State of Emergency
       IR: Ted Koppel   IE: Herbert Beukes

```
 1  IR:      As Peter Sharp said in that piece it is a lot
 2            easier to impose a state of emergency than it is
 3            to lift it . . hhh You still have the root cause
 4            when you lift it. And black leaders in that
 5            country have made it very clear .hhhh that this
 6            kind of situation there's no way of stopping
 7            this kind of situation unless there is an end to
 8            apartheid. It seems to me .hh that by doing
 9            this by eh imposing I guess this kind of
10            repression you- .hh you really set up uh system
11            where you can do nothing it seems to me
12   1→       #.hh when you lift it# except to change the
13            system that exists there (.) the basic system.
14   2→       #.hhh# Is that unfair? er
15  IE:       Uh I- I would think it's unfair what is being
16            said . . .
```

At each of the arrowed moments, the IR has come to what, in a conversational context, could be a possible turn transition point (Sacks, Schegloff, and Jefferson 1974) – a point at which a sentential or other kind of turn constructional unit in progress is complete. At each of these points, the IE visibly gets geared up and ready to speak. Within the '#' marks at arrow 1, the IE licks his lip, opens his mouth

responses directed to the most recent turn constructional unit (TCU) in another's turn and only subsequently to respond to earlier TCUs in that turn.

(with a possible inbreath) and then closes his mouth again. Within the '#' marks at arrow 2, he opens his mouth (again, with a possible inbreath) but withholds speech until the IR produces the subsequent question. In each case, the IE's action in taking a breath and getting geared up to speak is a *conversationally organized* action. His subsequent suppression of this action is organized by a timely recovery of his orientation to the more restricted turn-taking system for *news interviews*. Here, then, the IE visibly inhibits a "conversational" response so as to act appropriately in the news interview context. Cases like this show that although conversational turn-taking procedures are fundamental in organizing interaction, interviewees make extensive and finely detailed efforts to inhibit their "conversational" responses so as to comply with the special rules of turn-taking in the news interview.

The constraint that interviewees should wait for the interviewer to come to a question before initiating a response operates in other subtle, but important, ways. For example, interviewees systematically avoid many of the kinds of actions performed by recipients of talk in conversation. These actions include acknowledgments of what is being said (such as "mm hm," "uh huh," or "yes") which are "continuative" in that they also indicate an understanding that the informant has more to say (Schegloff 1982). They also include other kinds of acknowledgment tokens (such as "oh," "really," and partial repeats such as "did you") that address the content of what has been said as informative, newsworthy, or interesting (Heritage 1984b; 1985). These kinds of acknowledgments are densely present in ordinary conversation. In the following case, for example, the recipient (S) of a narrative acknowledges each new chunk of information – producing an acknowledgment token at the boundary of nearly every unit produced by her informant:

(13)   Ordinary Conversation: Frankel: TC:I:1:2–3

```
1   S:      =.hhh Uh:m: :, .tch.hhhh Who w'you ta:lking to.
2           . . .
3           . . .
4   G:      I: wasn't talking to a:nybody. Bo-oth Martin'n
5           I slept until about noo:n,=
6   S: 1→   =O[h.
7   G:        [.hhhh An' when I woke up, I wanted to call
```

```
 8          my mother.
 9   S: 2→  Mm[hm
10   G:        [.hhhh An' I picked up the pho:ne, a:n' I
11             couldn't dial out.'n [I thought our phone was
12   S: 3→                         [Oh: ( ),
13   G:     out'v order. ['n I-
14   S: 4→                [Yeh,
```

A similar pattern emerges in the modern talk show, which is designed to simulate a more conversational style of interaction. In the following sequence from the *Oprah Winfrey Show*, the guest describes how a colleague simulated illness as part of a campaign against the smokers in her office building:

(14)   US ABC *Oprah Winfrey Show*: Apr 1991: Passive Smoking
       IR: Oprah Winfrey   IE: Lenora

```
 1   IR:   =Uh you: uh::: (.) say she fakes it?
 2         (.)
 3   IR:   Lenora she fakes it, she faked a heart attack.
 4   IE:   Yeah she faked a heart attack.
 5   IR:   Uh huh. Faked it.
 6         (0.2)
 7   IE:   Faked it.
 8   IR:   How. Fell out on the floor: the whole d- deal?
 9         (.)
10   IR:   Fa[ked it.
11   IE:     [No she: (0.4) said she was havin' uh:: (.)
12         hard time abreathin'.=She was uh: havin'
13         palpitation of the heart,
14   IR:   Mmhm?=
15   IE:   =Called paramedic, they came down. .hhh They
16         examine her but she refused to go to
17         th'hospital.
18   IR:   Mmhm.
19         (0.5)
20   IE:   So: then: (0.2) next week she did the same
21         thing.
22   IR:   Mmhm.
23         (0.5)
24   IE:   Then: (.) she didn't go to th'hospital.
25   IR:   Mmhm.
26   IE:   Then she went to: .hh the fire department, and
27         had them atake her a (.) bou- (0.2) mm (.) three
```

28   weeks later.
29   (1.0)
30   IR: [To:
31   IE: [But they didn't f- (.) to the hospital. [.hhhh
32   IR: [For
33   the heart attack?
34   (0.2)
35   IE: Yes::.
36   IR: Mmhm.

Here, as in (13), Oprah Winfrey acknowledges the overwhelming majority of the statements that this guest makes.

In the news interview, by contrast, interviewees rarely produce these acknowledgments. If we return to (10) for a moment, it is striking that the IR's statement of a fact, which the IE seems to have every right to confirm before the IR moves to her question, is not acknowledged in any way.[5]

(10)   UK BBC Radio *World at One*: 25 Jan 1979: Letters
        IR: Anna Sebastian   IE: Harry King, Librarian

1   IR: .hhh The (.) price being asked for these letters
2   →   is (.) three thousand pou::nds.
3   IR: Are you going to be able to raise it,
4   (0.5)
5   IE: At the moment it... (continues)

A more substantial illustration of the same phenomenon comes from an interview in which a British Conservative Cabinet minister responds to a question about whether government controls will weaken the autonomy of Conservative-held local government agencies. Here the IR begins by referring to the likely truth of the "preamble to his question" (lines 2–3), thereby clearly projecting a substantial block of talk prior to the "question" which he projects as upcoming.[6] At each of the arrowed points (a–e) in the prefacing segment of the IR's turn, the IE passes on an opportunity to respond

---

[5] Note in particular that, by this withholding, the IE does not orient to the IR's statement as a "B-event question" that would require confirmation. This is despite the fact that, in principle, the IE might have stronger rights to know this information than the IR. Statements which IRs aim to have responded to as "B-event questions" are overwhelmingly constructed in a specific format that includes "you + progressive/imperfective verb." Declaratives that do not have these constructional features are generally not responded to as "B-event" questions by IEs.

[6] The projection of an action (such as a question) that the speaker aims to perform after an intervening spate of talk is discussed in Schegloff (1980).

to the IR's turn-so-far. Five of these points are passed and it is only at the sixth point (f), when the IR comes to the completion of a recognizable question, that the IE begins a response (line 24).

(15) UK LWT *Weekend World*: 1984: Controls
     IR: Brian Walden   IE: Unknown

```
 1  IR:       I tell you what I would like to press you
 2             o:n,=and it's this,=and I think you know that at
 3             least the preamble to this question is tru:e.
 4             .hh We'll see what you think of the question in
 5             general. .hhh Your admission you see (0.8) that
 6             there is a trade off here between the nee:d to
 7             reduce this expenditure (0.2) and formally use
 8             democratic rights .hh will upset some Tories.
 9  a→        .hhh Not all Tories agree: with the Government's
10             policy in trying to reduce expenditure like
11  b→        that. .hh There might even be some Torie:s .hh
12             who unlike even me: don't think that public
13             expenditure is an important issue anyway.
14  c→        .hh But what they do think is hellish important
15             (0.2) is local democracy
16  d→        (0.2)
17             and running their own shi : re : s in their own way.
18  e→        .hh Aren't you afra:id that by what you have
19             said to me: .h you may have made a rod for your
20             own back and simply strengthened the arguments
21             of those people .h especially in the Lo : rds .hh
22             who think that local democracy is much more
23             important than cutting expenditure.=
24  IE:  f→   =tch Well .hhh e:r anybody who … (continues)
```

At each of the arrowed points, the IE could reasonably produce a continuative acknowledgment (or "continuer" [Schegloff 1982]) such as "mm hm" that overtly passes on an opportunity to talk, or in fact initiate a fully-fledged turn of his own. In reality, he does none of these things. The IE's withholding of any response across these opportunities constitutes his contribution to the final outcome which is a turn transfer at a question. Thus, what is ordinarily thought of as an action under the direction of a single agent (in this case, the IR), is in fact the joint construction of *both* participants.

Why is it that interviewees inhibit even continuers that would not prevent the interviewer from getting to a question, and indeed might even seem to facilitate it? Acknowledgments, as we have noted, are very common in ordinary conversation and their presence there is closely related to the way conversational turn-taking is managed. In brief, speakers taking a turn in ordinary conversation are treated as having initial rights to only a single unit of talk before another speaker may take a turn (Sacks, Schegloff, and Jefferson 1974). Other participants, however, may cede their opportunity to speak so as to permit the current speaker to continue. The production of acknowledgment tokens (such as "yeh" or "mm hm") is an explicit and very frequent way for a speaker to pass on their turn at talk in favor of the current speaker and, hence, to show a commitment to hearing what the other has to say. This conversational role for "continuers" is predicated on the fact that each speaker in ordinary conversation is initially rationed to one unit of talk.

Given this, we can see that the absence of interviewee acknowledgments in the news interview is also closely related to the news interview turn-taking system. Recall that interviewers are required to engage in questioning, and that interviewees generally, and properly, withhold their responses to interviewer talk until a recognizable question is produced. Because interviewees do not have the right to respond to prefatory statements, acknowledgments which overtly "withhold" such responses have no role. Indeed, the reverse is true, their production tends to be "aggressive" in that, if they are used, they assert an implied claim to the right to intervene at any point in the interviewer's utterance – a right which specifically departs from the news interview Q–A turn-taking framework. It is no surprise then to find that interviewees' use of acknowledgments in the news interview is very commonly a hostile act that foreshadows subsequent aggressive or argumentative interventions. This is well illustrated in the following example in which then Vice-President George Bush crosses swords with CBS anchor Dan Rather:

(16)   US CBS *Evening News*: 25 Jan 1988: Iran-Contra
         IR: Dan Rather   IE: George Bush

```
1  IR:      You said tha' if you had known this was an arms
2           for hostag[es  sw]ap, .hh that you would've=
3  IE: →              [ Yes ]
4  IR:      =opposed it. .hhhh You also [said thet-]=
5  IE: →                                [E x a c t ]ly
6  IR:      =[that you did NOT KNOW thet y-]
```

```
 7  IE:    [(m-   may-   may   I-)   may I   ] answer that.
 8         (0.4)
 9  IE:    (Th[uh) right  ( )-]
10  IR:        [That wasn't a ] question.=it w[as a]=
11  IE:                                      [Yes ]=
12  IR:    =[statement eh-]
13  IE:    =[it   was   a ] statement [and   I'll   ]=
14  IR:                                [Let me ask]=
15  IE:    =[answer it. The President ] created this=
16  IR:    =[the question if I may first]
17  IE:    =program, .h has testified er s:tated publicly,
18         (.) he did not think it was arms fer hostages.
```

Here Bush twice intervenes with acknowledgments (lines 3 and 5) in the very first prefatory sentence of Dan Rather's question. He then follows these with a highly aggressive intervention long before Rather arrives at his question. The example illustrates that interviewees' use of continuers in news interviews is associated with (i) the abandonment of news interview turn-taking procedures, and (ii) an incipient escalation into either disagreement with the interviewer and/or attempted interdiction of the interviewer's turn at talk.

Answers as a joint construction

We have seen that interviewers' questions are often the product of an intimate collaboration between interviewer and interviewee. The same holds true of interviewees' answers. Consider, to begin with, that news interview answers are expected to be lengthy. Interviewees rarely offer brief responses and tend to do so only in retaliation to questioning that they object to. Thus in the following case, US Attorney General Janet Reno is asked, in effect, whether she plans to engage in television censorship. Her response to this hostile question is brief, and is evidently disconcerting to her interviewer:

```
(17)  US NBC Meet the Press: Oct 1993: Television Violence
      IR: Tim Russert   IE: Janet Reno
  1  IR:    .hh Madam Attorney General you've testified
  2         this week- u- in front of Congress abou:t .h
  3         violence and television. .hhh And said that if
  4         the TV industry didn't in effect clean itself
  5         up, clean its act up, .hhh there may be
  6         government intervention. Government regulation.
```

7   (0.4) The New York Ti:mes in an editorial said
8   that (.) you embarked ona quote <dangerous
9   embrace of censorship.>   (0.3) Did you?
10 IE: → No.
11   (0.2)
12 IR: .hhhh Wha:t kind of government intervention are
13   you thinking about? Would you <u>b</u>an: programs
14   like NYPD: Law and Order, would you [uh:
15 IE: →   [No.
16   (.)
17 IR: W- Wh:at are we talking about.
18 IE: We're talking about (.) <u>a</u>sking the media to
19   <u>st</u>op talking (.) about what it promises to do,
20   and do it . . .

The fact that news interview answers are extended poses a puzzle that interviewers recurrently have to resolve: how to determine when an answer is complete and another question is due? In effect, the interviewer must parse the unfolding answer, unit by unit, to determine where and when a new question can be appropriately asked. While prefaced questions, even those with several prefatory sentences (e.g. [15] above) normally end unambiguously with a grammatical question, the conclusions of answers are significantly more difficult to determine. Thus as an answer emerges, it is essentially a joint construction between the interviewee, who chooses to continue with another unit, and the interviewer who, by withholding questions, permits this to happen. While there are a variety of resources by which answerers can indicate a conclusion, ranging from facial and bodily comportment through to quite specific language practices, the joint construction of "complete answers" is a distinctly inexact science. It is made more so in the context of meandering or vacillating answers. And when interviewees like Margaret Thatcher determinedly take breaths in the middle of sentences in order subsequently to rush from one sentence to the next (Bull and Mayer 1988), the interviewer is virtually condemned to "interruption" as a condition of asking questions at all!

One practice that is used to indicate the completion of an answer is a return to the terms of the question. This can involve verbatim repetition of the words in a question (Roth 1996; Schegloff 1998), as in the following:

(18)   UK BBC *Newsnight*: 21 Oct 1993: Arming the Police
         IR: Jeremy Paxman   IE: David Brady

```
 1   IR:  →  ...Is: it your: view that the police should now
 2             be armed?
 3   IE:  →  .hhh But definitely. .hhh Ahm we: wuh- (.) we
 4             have no rights as a society .hh to expect young
 5             men (.) .hh to enter situations wh:ere (.) the
 6             there is a fair: percentage, (.) of: arm:ed (.)
 7             people against them. It's- it's wrong: that they
 8             should- we should ask them .hhh to risk their
 9             lives, and to risk being shot, .hhh and the
10             chances of th- of them meeting an armed: uh:m
11             assailant is so much in- increase: .hh (.) that
12        →  police should definitely be ar[med.
13   IR:                                     [And you don't
14             worry that arming the police might actually...
```

Here the IE responds immediately and affirmatively to the question
put to him about the arming of British police. He then proceeds
to justify this response, returning in the final clause to the words
"police should .. be armed" that concluded the IR's question. The
IR is thus enabled to begin very promptly, in fact in slight overlap,
with a new question (line 13).

Sometimes it is clear that an answer is complete without a return
to the exact language of the question. In the following case, a representative of a human rights organization is asked how his organization knows about the circumstances inside the internment camps in
Bosnia. The IR's question makes reference (with "you don't have a
very large presence there") to the number of people his organization
has in place to monitor the situation:

(19)   UK BBC Radio *Today*: June 1993: Bosnia Camps
         IR: John Humphrys   IE: Ian Smedley

```
 1   IR:  →  How do you know what is going on.=Because you
 2        →  don't have a very large presence there do you.=
 3   IE:     =.hhh Well it's very difficult to authenticate
 4             any reports. .hh ah in the former Yugoslavian
 5             states at the moment obviously it's a very
 6             difficult situation .hhhh But we have wherever
 7             possible tried to .hhh cross check and double
 8             check (.) our reports .hhh Ah we do have a
 9             number of u- affiliated groups and other people
10             with whom we're in regular contact .hhh ah in
```

11   Sarejevo and also other parts of former
12   Yugoslavia .hhh including (Kosovo) .hhh Ah
13   → so we do have quite good contacts on the ground.
14   IR: Do you <u>wo</u>rk like Amnesty International wo: :rks?

In his response, the IE acknowledges the difficulties of authenticating information, but then moves to describe a range of observers and groups his organization can draw on. His turn culminates in a "So" prefaced sentence which presents the upshot of his reply ("we do have quite good contacts on the ground") which effectively addresses both matters – numbers and quality of information – that the IR raised. At this point, when the IE has clearly completed his response, the IR shifts topic somewhat.

In the absence of the kinds of practices shown in (18) and (19), it is not always easy to determine when an interviewee's answer is complete. In the following case, Ross Perot gives an almost over-compact answer to the IR's question.

(20)   US PBS *Newshour*: 18 Sep 1992: Candidacy
       IR: Judy Woodruff   IE: Ross Perot

1   IR: So <u>why</u> don't you go ahead and (.) say: I'm (.) a
2   candidate for pr[esident?
3   IE: →   [Because that's not (.) where
4   → the organi<u>za</u>tion is now. Our organization (.)
5   is <u>to</u>:tally focused on try:ing to get both
6   parties to do the job.
7   (0.7)
8   IE: → That's why.

Seeing from the pause at line 7 that the IR has not recognized that his answer was complete, Perot recompletes his answer, which responded to a "why" question, with a repeat of the word "why" ("That's why.") and thus unambiguously signals that his answer is complete.

At the opposite end of the scale are lengthy answers. In (21), the IE is an opponent of President Reagan's proposal to introduce the "line item veto" as a means of curbing the then-ballooning budget deficit. The line item veto, which would have required a consitutional amendment, was touted as a method of countering profligate "pork barrel" spending in which members of Congress funnel federal funds to their districts. The co-IE, Mack Mattingly, is a supporter of the proposal:

(21) US PBS *Newshour*: July 1985: Line Item Veto
     IR: Jim Lehrer   IE: Senator Weicker

```
 1  IR:   Now Senator Weicker what would be the harm in
 2         tha:t?
 3         (0.5)
 4  IE:   tch .hh Well (.) first of all lemme say that
 5         you've got a very delicate balance between the
 6         three branches of government. .hh °uh° between
 7         the judicial bra:nch an' the executive branch
 8         an the legislative branch...
 9         ...(12 sentences)...
10  IE:   .h So I- the President doesn't need any more
11         power than he presently has. <Believe me he just
12         doesn't come in at the last act. .hh He is uh
13         part of this budget process. .hh What the
14         President's confronted with is tryin' to shift
15         (.) the ga:ze of the American people from these
16         deficits. .hh Which are mainly [due to large=
17  IR:                                   [We-
18  IE:   =tax cuts an big defense spending, .hh shift
19         the ga:ze .h to what would be a panacea_ an
20         easy way out_ (0.2) without in any way causing
21         any discomfort to the American people=an'
22         that's not possible. .hh [An' Mack Mattingly=
23  IR:                             [How will-
24  IE:   =is- ya know .h he's an ho:nest politician.=This
25         guy does (I-)/(li-) he sits on the
26         appropriations committee with me. .hh This guy
27         balances his budgets. .hhh So I'm not referring
28         to Mack but I'm saying as far as the President
29         is concerned this really .hh is abou:t the
30         ultimate (this an' th-) balance the- (.) budget
31         constitutional amendment .h is the ultimate in
32         hypocrisy when compared to the Reagan re(p)-
33         record on spending.
34         (.)
35  IR:   How would he: ...
```

After an extended turn at talk, the IE comes, at lines 13–16, to
what is the apparent core of his response: Reagan's proposal is an
attempt to divert Americans from his own budgetary indiscipline.
At line 16 he comes to a completion of this point with full terminal
intonation (indicated by the period). The IR starts up, only to find
that the IE is adding a further clause to the previous, apparently

complete, sentence. At line 22, the IE again comes to a clear possible completion of his turn, and again the IR begins a question. Again the IE continues with a conjoined sentence, apparently motivated by a desire to exempt his co-IE (a Senate colleague) from the criticism, before finally coming to an upshot with the claim that the proposal is "the ultimate in hypocrisy when compared to the Reagan re(p)-record on spending." At this point, the IR is finally able to initiate a question.

If some turn-taking problems arise from the sheer difficulty of jointly constructing a conclusion to the interviewee's turn, other turn-taking glitches are more transparently motivated by the interviewer's objectives. In the following case (from chapter 3) the IR, under time pressure, repeatedly attempts to close the interview:

(22)   US PBS *NewsHour*: 13 Oct 1986: US–Soviet Agreement
        IR: Jim Lehrer   IE: McGeorge Bundy
1   IE: . . . It's a ver:y har:d business. .hh to [get .h=
2   IR: 1→   [Hm
3   IE: =agreements that are (0.4) reliable: (.) in the
4   terms 'n conditions that both sides see:. The
5   two basic difficulties are .hhh a [Soviet fear:=
6   IR: 2→   [We
7   IE: =of American high technology, and an American
8   fear: :, .hh [of what the Soviets will=
9   IR: 3→   [We have
10 IE: =do in secret.
11 IR: 4→ Jeh- Mister Bundy, we hafta leave it there.
12   Gentlemen, thanks- thanks to all of you.

And a return to (11) also illustrates a rapid intervention:

(11)   UK BBC Radio *World at One*: 13 Mar 1979: NUM Election
        IR: Robin Day   IE: Arthur Scargill
1   IR: .hhh er What's the difference between your
2   Marxism and Mister McGahey's communism.
3   IE: er The difference is that it's the press that
4   constantly call me a Ma:rxist when I do not, (.)
5   and never have (.) er er given that description
6   of myself. [.hh I-
7   IR: [But I've heard you- I've heard you'd
8   be very happy to: to: er .hhhh er describe . . .

Here Scargill would have expanded his answer but Day, eager to contradict him, intersects his continuation with a new question.

In sum, interviewee answers are clearly a joint construction, unit by unit, composed of a determination to continue and a preparedness to permit continuation. However, unlike questions, which generally have a determinate grammatical structure that clearly indexes completion, answers often have built-in indeterminacies that recurrently make for difficulties in establishing when they are complete. The result is that turn transition from interviewees' answers to interviewer questions is often messy and conflictual.

So far, we have been concerned to sketch an outline of the turn-taking system for news interviews. We stress that the overwhelming mass of news interview conduct is compatible – and compatible in fine detail – with this turn-taking system. This system is, both distinctive and restrictive. By respecting the provisions of this system, the parties collaborate in building their talk as "interview talk" and also their roles within it as interviewer and interviewee. And they do this pervasively and collaboratively, turn-by-turn, over the course of the interaction. We now turn to the journalistic tasks and constraints that this turn-taking system helps to manage.

News interview turn-taking in context

It is no accident that news interview conduct is organized by a distinctive turn-taking system. In fact, it is clear that this system is a product both of the general tasks of broadcast journalism and of the place of broadcasting within the political and economic systems of the Western democracies. In the next two sections, we will look at news interview turn-taking in relation to two major professional tasks of broadcast journalists. The first of these derives from the fact that the primary recipients of news interview talk are the members of the news audience for whose benefit the talk is ultimately produced and involves *the production of talk that is targeted for an overhearing audience*. Second, interviewers must manage this task while meeting the constraint that they retain a broadly balanced, impartial, or neutral stance towards the statements and opinions presented by the interviewee. However, interviewers' questions often – and unavoidably – embody assumptions that accept or resist interviewees' stated positions (see chapter 6) and cannot, strictly speaking, be regarded as neutral. Accordingly, we will speak of this stance as embodying a position of "formal neutrality" or, more simply, as a "neutralistic" stance.[7] So the second feature of the news interview we will be concerned with is *the interviewer's management of a "neutralistic" stance towards the interviewee's statements, positions, and opinions.*

Producing talk for an overhearing audience

Adherence to news interview turn-taking procedures embodies a special "footing" (Goffman 1981; Levinson 1988) in which the parties treat their talk as geared to the "overhearing" news audience. This is a generic product of the news interview turn-taking system. The audience is, however, only an *indirect* target of news interview talk. Both interviewer and interviewee address their remarks to one another, and avoid looking into the camera and addressing the audience in a direct way by gaze. And yet the participants do orient to the presence of the audience in more subtle ways which cast the audience as the intended target of the talk. To see how this is done, we begin by looking at how interviewers treat the talk of interviewees.

Talk for overhearers: interviewer conduct

The news interview turn-taking system ensures that, because interviewee talk is produced in response to interviewer questions, interviewers are overwhelmingly the direct addressees of interviewee talk. It is significant, however, that interviewers, like interviewees, systematically avoid the kinds of vocal acknowledging actions (such as "mm hm," "uh huh," "yes," "oh," "really," and partial repeats such as "did you") that are very common and densely present in ordinary conversation. The following case is prototypical: it contains three clear points (arrowed) that represent moments at which some kind of acknowledgment could easily be due in ordinary conversation. In this news interview context, however, no acknowledgments are produced at all.

---

[7] This term parallels Robinson and Sheehan's (1983) distinction between objective and objectivistic news reporting.

(23)   US ABC *This Week*: May 1996: Gasoline Prices
       IR: David Brinkley   IE: Robert Rubin
```
 1  IR:    =Well tell me where you would like (for) it to
 2         go.
 3         (.)
 4  IE:    We:ll David let me take it- a s:lightly
 5         different approach if I ma:y,=And that is tha:t
 6         (.) the President took sensible action this
 7         past week, and I think action that was very
 8         sensitive, (.) to the concer:ns of very large
 9         numbers of Americans with respect to gas prices,
10   →     (0.3)
11         He ordered an accelerated sale of: twelve
12         million barrels of oil that C:ongress had
13         mandated that we sell.=As part of the budget,
14   →     (0.3)
15         As a consequence I think we'll get good prices
16         for the ta:xpayers,
17   →     (.)
18         He asked the secr'tary of energy to take a look
19         at the whole situation, report back in forty
20         five days, .hh and independently (0.2) I
21         (re)stress: independently, (.) the Justice
22         Department to try to take a look at
23         the situation: and (0.2) draw their own
24         conclu:sions.
```

Here then is a very considerable departure from conversational conduct: of the many vocal acknowledgment opportunities that emerge and are taken up in ordinary conversation, probably less than one in a thousand is taken up by interviewers in news interviews.[8]

The interactional import of these withholdings is quite straightforward. The interviewers' questions elicit responses which are addressed to the interviewer. However, by withholding vocal acknowledgments, interviewers decline to act as the primary recipients of interviewee responses and thereby "deflect" them towards

---

[8] As usual, some exceptions to this observation can be noted. "Big name" IRs, such as Dan Rather or Sir Robin Day, may have more latitude to do continuers and indeed other kinds of marginal actions. It is this which, in part, distinguishes them from their more restricted junior colleagues. Moreover a higher incidence of continuers and related actions may be found in more "relaxed" interview settings such as the Sunday interview shows (on both sides of the Atlantic) and on breakfast television interviews. The deployment of these marginal actions may also be used to constitute the IR–IE relationship as itself more relaxed or "personal" rather than formal or professional.

the news audience. This permits the news audience to treat itself as the intended, albeit unaddressed, target of interviewee talk (Heritage 1985).[9]

The effectiveness of this "deflecting" procedure plainly depends on two contingencies: (i) that interviewees' talk responds to interviewers' questions and is therefore addressed to interviewers, and (ii) that although interviewers are thus the addressees of interviewees' remarks they do not act as addressed recipients. This process of deflection is threatened when interviewees talk "out of turn" by responding directly to one another's remarks rather than waiting to be asked a question. In this context, they are normally careful to use various secondary procedures to maintain the interviewer as the addressee of their remarks and, by extension, the news audience as their target. Most commonly, they do this by continuing to direct their gaze at the interviewer and by referring to co-interviewees in the third person as in (24) below:

(24)   UK BBC Radio *World at One*: 15 Feb 1979: UK Economy
       IR: Brian Widlake   IE1: Sam Brittan   IE2: Peter Jenkins

```
 1  IE1:    The most important thing .hhh is that Mister
 2           Healey .h should stick to his gu:ns.=
 3  IE2:    =[You s ] ee
 4  IR:      [Well I-]
 5           (.)
 6  IE2: →  I disagree with- with Sam Brittan on a- in a
 7           most (.) fundamental way about this, (.) because
 8           (0.2) it may well be so.=I mean he would arg-
 9        →  Sam Brittan would argue from a monetarist point
10           of vie:w.=But what Mister Healey does about the
11           money supply . . . (continues)
```

By referring to his co-IE as "Sam Brittan" (lines 6 and 9) and subsequently as "he," rather than "you" (line 8), IE2 sustains his footing as an IE who is addressing his remarks to the IR and, through the

---

[9] This management of the news audience as the primary addressee of news interview talk is significant. The following item from the *Los Angeles Times* (15 October 1988, V/2) complains of "on air" conduct among members of the broadcasting community that is conspicuously absent from the news interview form:

"Why do TV reporters in the field talk directly to the anchor people when they give their reports? And why do sports announcers talk only to each other, as if they're alone at a game? And why are reports of "news only" radio stations directed at one of the staff members? The airwaves are supposed to be public. We, the audience, have been reduced to eavesdroppers and voyeurs."

IR, to the overhearing audience. This secondary procedure (Heritage and Greatbatch 1991) of third-person reference to a co-present interviewee is a central means by which an interviewee can depart from ordinary interview turn-taking procedures while sustaining the footing, and the mode of address, of an interviewee.

In some interviews, normally involving escalating disagreement between interviewees, the participants come to abandon both the Q–A format and this secondary procedure of addressing the interviewer. At this point, where the interviewees are essentially arguing with one another rather than addressing the interviewer and are not hearably producing their talk for the overhearing audience, the interview framework has essentially been abandoned. Excerpt (25) below, which is part of a debate interview between Jill Knight and Oonagh MacDonald concerning changes to the abortion legislation in Britain, is a case in point. Here Knight's initial "out of turn" disagreement (arrow 1) with her co-IE (MacDonald) is countered at line 5 by MacDonald with an incremental continuation of her earlier remarks (arrow 2). This continuation is then heckled with a series of interjective disagreements by Knight (arrows 3, 4, and 5). It can be seen that, with her remark "unless they come under pressure from the kind of counselling organization that you have in mind such as Life" (lines 5, 7, and 9–10) MacDonald abandons the IR as the addressee and directly addresses her co-IE. Thereafter both IEs address one another, rather than the IR, in overlap and in sustained disagreement.

(25)   UK ATV *Afternoon Plus*: 22 Jan 1980: Abortion Limits
        IR: Unknown   IE1: Oonagh MacDonald   IE2: Jill Knight

```
 1  IE1:      The point i:s .hhh that by and la:rge when
 2             people seek out an agency like that they have
 3             made up their mi:nds.=
 4  IE2: 1→  =Not necessarily because .hhh [certainly the=
 5  IE1: 2→                                [Unless they=
 6  IE2:      =ones ]
 7  IE1:      =come] under pressure from [the kin]d of=
 8  IE2: 3→                              [ N o ]
 9  IE1:      =counselling organisation that you
10             ha[ve in mind, such as Life,] [ which ]=
11  IE2: 4→   [No I- I- I've u- this  is no- [there's ]=
12  IE1:      =[tries to make a woman feel guilty and] takes=
13  IE2: 4→  =[no pressure at all,=no.  e:r  (    )  ]
```

```
14  IE1:      =no respons[ibility ] for the [consequences]=
15  IE2: 5→              [N o : ]      [          ]=
16  IR:                               [Now can I put=
17  IE1:      =[ (           ) ]
18  IE2:      =[            ]
19  IR:       =[one point to you,] that I- I- I- as I hear
20            you arguing yet again,=
```

In this case, where both IEs have abandoned news interview turn-taking procedures, and abandoned the footing which is associated with these procedures, it is the IR who terminates the sequence (at lines 16 and 19–20) with a question whose preface sanctions the parties as "arguing yet again" (see chapter 8 for more discussion of these kinds of arguments).

As we have seen, interviewers' withholdings of acknowledgments establish the news audience as an intended recipient of interviewee talk. However, these withholdings are important in an additional and significant way. Plainly, some acknowledgments verge on agreement with the interviewee's position or imply acceptance of its truth. Even the more bland acknowledgments (such as "mm hm") could, by their placement, imply support for the interviewee's point of view. Thus the interviewer's neutralistic stance, which is sustained by doing questioning and nothing else, can be compromised by seemingly minor acknowledgments of interviewee talk. The interviewer's avoidance of acknowledgments thus has a double motivation. It avoids an interactional alignment as the primary recipient of the interviewee's talk, and it avoids subtle impairments to the interviewer's neutralistic position. We develop this last point on interviewer neutralism in more detail below.

Talking for overhearers: interviewee conduct

Just as interviewers withhold acknowledgments during interviewee answers, so – as we have seen – interviewees for their part withhold acknowledgments during interviewer turns at talk. In (10) and (15) that we discussed earlier it was clear that this withholding is systematic. Excerpt (26) further illustrates this phenomenon. Here the interviewer paraphrases two recent public pronouncements by the interviewee (Democratic Senator George Mitchell). Paraphrasing another speaker's public statements – especially when the individual in question is a US senator or some other public figure – is an activity that normally strongly invites confirmation. Yet in this case, completions of the talk attributed to Mitchell (lines 5 and 7) are allowed to pass without comment from Senator Mitchell himself:

(26)   US PBS *Newshour*: 4 Dec 1989: US–Soviet Summit
        IR: Jim Lehrer   IE: Senator George Mitchell

```
 1   IR:       .hh Senator Mitchell (.) you said u::h some
 2              weeks ago: some time ago you criticized
 3              President Bush and his administration for being
 4              .hh possibly d- u::h nostal- almost nostalgic
 5       →      about the cold war .hh you uh used the word
 6              timidity in moving u:h to- on i:n u:h in this
 7       →      whole area .hhh Uh picking up on this the
 8              exa:mple that Secretary Kissinger just outli:ned
 9              that if in the next few days or weeks suddenly
10              there's no government in East Germany .hh should
11              the United States be prepared to move in take
12              steps and uh .hh and uh use some leadership even
13              if it means u:h a reunification of Germany wa:y
14              ahead of (.) everybody else's timetables?
15   IE:       .hhh Well I don't think it's up to the United
16              States to: hh dictate the (.) timing or terms of
17              the eventual reunification.
```

Interviewees overwhelmingly withhold from acknowledging interviewer prefaces, and this withholding has a similar function to the interviewer withholdings we described earlier. The interviewee is the direct addressee of statements describing background information that is known in common by interviewer and interviewee. By withholding acknowledgment of these statements, interviewees contribute to the management of those statements as in reality targeted at the members of the news audience.

In sum, because the Q–A framework for news interviews mandates *only* the production of questions and answers, interviewers and interviewees produce relatively large blocks of talk without any form of acknowledgment from the other. By this means, the news interview talk that results is understood as targeted at an overhearing audience. While departures from this turn-taking system certainly occur, they are commonly associated with the use of secondary procedures for the maintenance of this stance. When the parties depart from this framework in a sustained way, the interaction begins to lose its audience-directed character as an interview, and starts to resemble a form of conversation that is most often conflictual. Correspondingly, the participants become less recognizable as interviewer and interviewee and become increasingly visible as simply "arguing among themselves."

Maintaining neutralism

We now turn to look at the Q–A format of the news interview in relation to the second dimension of the interviewer's task which was mentioned earlier: the maintenance of a "neutralistic" stance. As noted in chapter 2, legal pressures and professional norms constrain broadcast journalism in both Britain and the United States to maintain impartiality and balance in their coverage of news and current affairs. In the news interview, where professional journalists are treated as representatives of their employing news organizations, these pressures effectively translate into the primary requirement, noted above, that interviewers should (i) avoid the assertion of opinions on their own behalf and (ii) refrain from direct or overt affiliation with (or disaffiliation from) the expressed statements of interviewees.

There are a number of ways in which news interview turn-taking contributes to this neutralistic stance. First, as noted earlier, the constraint that interviewers restrict themselves to asking questions is one which limits their ability to express opinions, and agree or disagree with interviewees. As we have seen, while interviewers do produce assertions, these are generally restricted to a single "legitimate" environment: prior to, and in conjunction with, a subsequent question.

This restriction on the conduct of interviewers is matched by a related restriction on the interpretation of interviewer conduct by interviewees. In our news interview data, even quite combative questions are not treated as asserting the interviewer's point of view and are not treated, therefore, as compromising interviewer neutralism. Instead, they are generally treated as designed to solicit the interviewee's viewpoint on the issue which the question addresses. This stance is massively preserved regardless of the extent to which the questions may be understood as "hostile" or as presuppositionally loaded against the position of the interviewee. This is clear, for example, in the following exchange which we briefly examined earlier between Sir Robin Day and Arthur Scargill who was, at the time of the interview, a rival with the Scottish mineworkers' leader Michael McGahey for the presidency of the National Union of Mineworkers:

(11)   UK BBC Radio *World at One*: 13 Mar 1979: NUM Election
       IR: Robin Day   IE: Arthur Scargill

```
1  IR:   .hhh er What's the difference between your
2        Marxism and Mister McGahey's communism.
3  IE:   er The difference is that it's the press that
4        constantly call me a Ma:rxist when I do not, (.)
5        and never have (.) er er given that description
6        of myself.[.hh I-]
7  IR:             [But I]'ve heard you- I've heard...
```

In his response to the question, the IE (Scargill) rejects its – hostile and damaging – presupposition that he is a Marxist. But it is noticeable that he manages this response without challenging the IR's neutralistic position. First, he explicitly frames his response as an answer to the IR's question by repeating its frame ("the difference is"). He thus plays "the interview game." Second, his response deals with the presupposition of the IR's question by treating it as an error of fact (which he ascribes to "the press"), and not by treating it as the expression of the IR's opinion. As this example illustrates, by responding in these ways to interviewer questions, interviewees – regardless of their private opinions about the questions or their motivations – legitimate them as part of the ordinary give and take of the news interview. In particular, they generally treat interviewer questions – no matter how hostile or in other ways prejudicial to their positions – as activities which do not involve the expression of opinions.

   The constraint that interviewers restrict themselves to questioning, involves more than just the avoidance of assertions. It also excludes various kinds of responsive conduct which are commonplace in ordinary conversation from the news interview context. As noted earlier, such actions as news receipts and newsmarks (such as "oh" or "really") which accept, or project acceptance, of the factual status of the statements to which they respond (Heritage 1984b, 1985) and assessments which overtly affiliate or disaffiliate with stated positions (Pomerantz 1984) also have no place within news interview conduct in Britain or the USA and are almost completely absent from the data corpus we have worked with.[10] Moreover, as we have seen, turn-taking in news interviews does not provide even for the production of acknowledgments such as "mm hm" which, if they were produced, would not only undermine the footing of the interview (as discussed above) but could in addition be treated as offering support for an interviewee, or as exerting an inappropriate influence on the shape and trajectory of interviewee responses.

In general, if interviewers stick to questioning, their conduct will be treated as appropriate at least within the "on air" confines of the interview.[11] Only rarely do interviewees publicly protest that a line of questioning is slanted or biased. For example, in the following case, from a 1996 interview in which Patrick Buchanan, then competing with Bob Dole for the Republican presidential nomination, is questioned by the conservative columnist George Will on ABC's *This Week*:

(27) US ABC *This Week*: 2 Feb 1996: Bob Dole
      IR: George Will   IE: Patrick Buchanan

1 IR: .tlkhh One of your- One of your criticisms of
2   Bob Dole is his participation in the: (.)
3   commission th't- in eighty two̲ 'n eighty three̲

---

[10] In some extreme instances, IRs may affiliate briefly with IEs but normally only on highly consensual topics that very often involve international issues. For example, in the following case, a US Army General is describing the difficulties of determining the status of MIAs (servicemen missing in action) from antiquated Vietnamese records:

[MacNeil – Lehrer: 10-23-92]
IE: Ah:: How̲ l:ong will it take? (0.6) It's
         hard to say. I(h): I h: :ad a look̲ at the:
         cataloguing system in the:: central̲ (0.3)
         ah:: military museum in Hano̲i:. .hhh
         Ah: and it's (.) not̲ on a computer, there's
         no: punching in:: ah:: [heh h a h a h h=
IR: →   [somebody's na: :me and=
IE   =[a n a::m e and ha   ] ving [somethi]ng pop up.
IR: →   =[somethin' comin' up]   [Oh boy.]
IE: [.hhh A]nd- and it is not̲ catalogue:d
IR: →   [W o w.]

We note the way in which the IR here provides a completion for the IE's first turn at talk and subsequently offers a brief assessing response to the information he has received. Here the IR assumes a more affiliative posture towards the IE on a tender topic that is a matter of consensual national concern.

[11] As we saw in chapter 2, however, IEs often vigorously protest lines of questioning after the end of a broadcast.

```
4              resulted in accelerating [the already=
5  IE:                             [°Mm hm,°
6  IR:         =legislated (.) tax increases for social
7              security.
8  IE:         M[m hm,
9  IR:          [.hh The commission was appointed by Ronald
10             Reagan, it [was chaired by Alan Greenspan:=
11 IE:                    [Right,
12 IR:         = not- hn- uh: real [ly uh
13 IE:                            [(#Right, #)
14 IR:         leader of the liberal establishment,
15 IE:         [Mm hm,
16 IR:         [.hh Uhm_ (1.0) How can you fault=h the: the
17             conclusions they came to.
18 IE:    →    tlk -hh George stop (holdin' water) for Bob
19             Dole. Lemme tell ya. .hh Back in nineteen eighty
20             two an' eighty three I oppo:sed Ronal' Re↑ agan's
21             tax increase . . .
```

Stung by Will's attempt to present his criticism of Dole as also a criticism of Reagan, Buchanan criticizes the political motivation of the question as "holding water for Bob Dole." Even in highly adversarial exchanges, however, such responses are extremely rare.

Finally, if questioning itself provides a first order of defense against the charge that interviewers have overstepped the limits of neutralism, it also provides the basis for a second order of defense in which challenges can be rebutted by the interviewer's claim to be just "asking questions." In the following case, the topic is the handling of the US Savings and Loan financial rescue by President Bush's Office of Management and Budget (OMB) whose head, Richard Darman, is the interviewee. Just before this sequence, veteran television journalist Sam Donaldson has implied that the OMB was misleading the public about the rescue by setting up a corporation to take the funds involved out of the federal budget. At the beginning of this sequence, Donaldson quite forcibly raises the question of whether, as a result of this maneuver, interest payments will cost taxpayers more. Darman's response is to reject this as a "technical argument" (line 4).

(28)   US ABC *This Week*: Oct 1989: Savings & Loan Rescue
        IR: San Donaldson   IE: Richard Darman

```
1  IR:    Isn't it a fact, Mister Darman, that the taxpayers
2          will pay more in interest than if they just paid
3          it out of general revenues?
```

```
 4  IE:     No, not necessarily. That's a technical
 5          argument –
 6  IR:  →  It's not a – may I, sir? It's not a technical
 7       →  argument. Isn't it a fact?
 8  IE:     No, it's definitely not a fact. Because first
 9          of all, twenty billion of the fifty billion is
10          being handled in just the way you want –
11          through treasury financing. The remaining –
12  IR:  →  I'm just asking you a question. I'm not
13       →  expressing my personal views.
14  IE:     I understand.
```

At line 6, Donaldson directly counters Darman's dismissive response
to his previous question: in response to Darman's claim that the
problem of increased costs to the taxpayers is just "a technical argument," Donaldson interjects and flatly contradicts Darman – though
he goes on to soften the contradiction by adding the question: "Isn't
it a fact?" (line 7). Darman then reasserts his viewpoint and sup-
ports it by reference to the amount of money that is being handled
in "just the way you want" (line 10). By this phrase, Darman of
course means that some of the money is being paid out of "general
revenues." But he also, and simultaneously, challenges Donaldson's
neutralistic stance by insinuating that the previous question was
"loaded" in favor of Donaldson's own personal biases. It is at this
point that Donaldson intervenes to defend his journalistic neutrality
(lines 12–13) on the basis that he had *asked a question* rather than
expressed a personal opinion. This defense is accepted (line 14).
Here, in a generally argumentative Sunday morning news show, we
begin to encounter the limits of questioning as a neutralistic practice
but, even here, Donaldson's claim that a question, rather than an
opinion, was being aired remains an acceptable line of journalistic
defense.

In general then, maintaining the Q–A format of the news interview in itself sustains the interviewer's neutralistic stance. As long as
interviewers engage in "questioning," then, within certain limits at
least (see below), they will be treated as appropriately neutralistic.
Although some questions are a source of friction between interviewers and interviewees and are not permitted to pass unproblemati-
cally, challenges to completed questions are normally managed, as
in the Darman interview above, within the framework of answering. Interviewees thus respect the normative obligations imposed

on them by their questioners and do not subvert the fundamental format of the interview. And, when challenged, interviewers have the ready-made line of defense that their role is to "ask questions." Given this connection between questioning and neutralism, it is not surprising that most major departures from interviewer neutralism, therefore, also involve a departure from questioning. In what follows, we will look at how these more major and problematic challenges are engineered and handled. They can be initiated by the interviewer, or contrived by the interviewee. We begin with those initiated by the interviewer.

Turn-taking norms: departures and their management

The frequency distribution of interviewer questions in Table 1, taken together with the detailed features of turn management described above, is powerful evidence for the fact that interviewers and interviewees generally restrict themselves to questioning and answering, and that interviewees often collaborate in the interactional production of interviewers' questions by restricting their own behavior. The result is a turn-taking system that is very different from conversation.

This turn-taking system, of course, is not a law of nature and it can be departed from and returned to. However, the departures provide strong evidence that the parties regard the Q–A turn-taking system as normative. As we shall see, the persons who launch the departures often treat them as sensitive and problematic, while their recipients commonly treat departures as sanctionable.[12] To return to (15), for example, the rules of news interview turn-taking are invoked as part of a dispute between then Vice-President George Bush and CBS anchor Dan Rather:

(15)   US CBS *Evening News*: 25 Jan 1988: Iran-Contra
         IR: Dan Rather   IE: George Bush

```
1  IR:     You said tha' if you had known this was an arms
2          for hostag[es swap, .hh that you would've=
3  IE:               [ Yes ]
4  IR:     =opposed it. .hhhh You also [said thet-]=
5  IE: 1→                              [E x a c t ]ly
6  IR:     =[that you did NOT KNOW thet y-]
```

---

[12] For discussion of the role of "deviant case" analysis in conversation analysis, see Heritage (1984a; 1988) and Clayman and Maynard (1995).

```
 7  IE:  1→  [( m-  may-  may  I-)  may  I  ] answer that.
 8           (0.4)
 9  IE:      (Th[uh) right (   )-]
10  IR:  2→      [That wasn't a ] question.=it w[as a]=
11  IE:  3→                                    [Yes ]=
12  IR:  2→  =[statement eh-]
13  IE:  3→  =[it was    a   ] statement [and   I'll  ]=
14  IR:  4→                              [Let me ask]=
15  IE:  3→  =[answer it. The President] created this=
16  IR:  4→  =[the question if I may first]
17  IE:      =program, .h has testified er s:tated publicly,
18           (.) he did not think it was arms fer hostages.
```

Here, at each of the arrowed points, both the IR and the IE assert
their respective rights to speak by explicitly invoking the relevance
and normativity of news interview questioning and answering. Bush
begins (arrow 1) with a request to "answer" Rather's initial statement. In this turn Bush orients to the institutional roles of IR and
IE by requesting permission to "answer" the IR at a point where an
IE would normally withhold talk but a conversational participant
would simply proceed to talk without requesting to do so. Moreover, in framing his intervention as a request to "answer" Rather,
he casts his prospective action as in at least formal compliance with
the conventions of news interview talk. Rather's response – a defense
of his right to continue (arrow 2) – rests on the implied claim that
his turn at lines 1–2, 4, and 6 has not yet reached a question and
suggests that it is therefore not complete. While Rather in effect resists interruption, he does so specifically by invoking his institutional
right as IR to ask a question and not the ordinary interactional right
to complete an utterance in progress. Moreover, finally, when Bush
insists on "answering" the statement (arrow 3), Rather continues
to resist (arrow 4) with an explicit appeal to be allowed to "ask the
question . . . first."

In the next sections, we first examine the relatively infrequent departures from questioning that interviewers initiate, and then turn to
a wider range of interviewee-engineered departures from answering.

Interviewer initiated departures from questioning

As Table 1 shows, professional interviewers do not often depart
from their questioning stance to produce turns that simply make

assertions about interviewee positions or arguments.[13] Moreover, the overwhelming majority of news interview turns that are shaped as questions are treated as interactionally neutralistic. Interviewer statements, by contrast, can be much more problematic. While some departures from questioning involve assertions that are ignored or are treated as innocuous, others involve the interviewers in taking a position on their own behalf. Such actions can be both challenging to interviewees and risky for interviewers who may be drawn into overt conflicts and disagreements with interviewees, further compromising their professionally neutralistic stance. In what follows, we identify a number of ways in which interviewers come to address interviewees with statements, the challenges and risks associated with these activities, and the ways in which both challenge and risk can be mitigated.

---

[13] Departures from a questioning stance can be found in non-professional interviews. The following example derives from a series of interviews in which British (Labour) ex-Cabinet minister, Shirley Williams, interviewed a number of prominent politicians for a BBC series that, significantly, was broadcast under the general title "Shirley Williams in Conversation." By this title, the BBC indicated, not only a departure from the normal procedures adopted by professional IRs, but also that – because Williams was not a professional IR employed by the BBC – it was not to be treated as accountable for her expressed opinions. At the time of these interviews (1980), Williams had recently lost her parliamentary seat in the 1979 general election, but had not yet left the Labour Party (in 1981) to join the SDP. In this interview, she is interviewing ex-Labour Prime Minister James Callaghan who had been a Cabinet colleague six months previously. Here she briefly affiliates with an assertion from Callaghan about another ex-Cabinet colleague, Tony Benn:

(*Williams in Conversation* 1980: 240)

Callaghan:	There is at the moment a gap (0.2) in our
	thinking. I think that's got to be filled.
	.hh er- Because a number of the things for
	example that uhm .h Tony Benn says have got
	a lot to be be- er- er- er- have got a lot
	in them.=I mean some of his analysis has
	got a .hh great de[al in it.
Williams: →	[Oh yes.=He- he's got
→	a great deal of er of ( )
	think[ing. There's] no=
Callaghan:	[O h y e s]
Williams: →	=doubt about [it his are new ideas.]
Callaghan:	[he's a- he's-] he's
	a very fertile- well uh he- he- he expounds
	these new and fertile i- ideas. .hh uhm And
	I think that we shouldn't neglect them wherever
	they come from.

Here Williams departs briefly from the standard neutralistic stance of an IR with a turn that overtly agrees with Callaghan's assessment.

Interviewer assertions that buttress a question
Sometimes interviewers conclude questioning turns with assertions
designed to buttress the questions they ask. In each of the cases below
the interviewer comes to a question but then goes on to supplement
it with a more general factual or "quasi-factual" assertion that supplies further relevance and weight to the question that precedes it.
A straightforward instance is from the following interview with an
IRA fundraiser, Martin Galvin, who is interviewed in Dublin after
a trip to Northern Ireland which the British authorities have tried
to stop with an "exclusion order":

(29)   UK BBC Radio *World at One*: 21 Aug 1984: Exclusion Order
       IR: Ann Cadwallader   IE: Martin Galvin

```
 1  IE:     I went to the nor:th I went through whatever it
 2           was I went through (0.2) precisely because: I
 3           want to see peace in Ireland.=And I recognise
 4           that the only way that can come about .h is for
 5           the British to withdraw:, to leave Ireland .hh
 6           in peace and freedom,=for the terrorist to get
 7           out of Ireland.
 8  IR:  →  .hh Will you be coming back next year.=The
 9       →  exclusion order still stands against yo[u.
10  IE:                                            [.hhh
11  IE:     Well it is up to the British, . . .
```

Here the IR finds herself having produced an apparently bland
question whose relevance may be unclear to the radio audience.
To convey the significance of the question, she adds the contextual
information that conveys that the IE could be arrested, and thus
gives her question its point.

   A somewhat more interpretive, or "quasi-factual" background
point is made by the IR in the following interview with Sir Ian
Gilmour, a Conservative critic of then British Prime Minister
Thatcher's Conservative administration. Here a question about
whether the IE will have to break ranks and threaten to vote against
his own party (arrow 1) is followed by the generalizing assertion
that all of the Conservative critics will have to consider the same
(arrow 2).

(30)   UK BBCTV *Newsnight*: 14 Oct 1981: Conservative Splits
       IR: John Tusa   IE: Sir Ian Gilmour

```
 1  IE:     . . . my own belief is that there- that there will
 2           be changes because I regard the present policies
```

```
3              as quite unsustainable.
4   IR:  1→   But won't you have to consider threatening to
5              vote against the government,=
6        2→   That's surely what (.) what all the critics now
7              have to face.
8   IE:       We: :ll I don't know, no I- I think the: the
9              we're still at the (.) stage of the intellectual
10             argument which I think .hh we're winning, . . .
```

Although the generalization concludes the IR's turn, it evidently states a premise that, among other things, provides for the relevance of the question: Conservative critics of the Government have reached the point where they have lost the argument inside the party and may simply have to threaten to vote against the policies they disagree with. What is the stance of this particular critic? The post-positioned statement might just as easily have done its work before the question as after it but, occurring as it does after the question, it can be heard not to replace the preceding question but rather to upgrade the pointedness of the question and to enhance its significance.

Sometimes however, post-positioned statements of this type can be deployed more aggressively. In the following interview, a British Labour politician is questioned on how the Labour Party will present its policy on the controversial issue of nuclear weapons. In a context in which previous Labour Party defense policy (favoring nuclear disarmament) proved electorally unpopular, the IR raises the issue of whether most Labour Party members believe in their party's new election platform on defense (keeping nuclear weapons, pending negotiations with the then Soviet Union). He uses a question design which strongly favors a response that would agree that "most people" do not believe in the policy. He then pursues this question with a second-party referred "B-event" statement that focuses on the IE's personal beliefs, and comes close to asserting flatly that the IE does not believe in his own party's policy:

(31)   UK BBCTV *Newsnight*: Sep 1990: Nuclear Weapons Policy
       IR: Donald MacCormick   IE: David Blunkett

```
1   IR:   But . . . isn't the party in the position, either
2         way, that you're going to the electorate with a
3         policy on this (0.2) crucial issue, in which
4         most people, including you, don't really
5   →     believe. You don't believe in keeping them at
```

6   → <u>all</u>, really.
7 IE: Well, whhh, we're faced with uh an interesting
8   position, . . .

Here the assertion gives added weight to a skeptical stance that
the IR's questioning maintains both before and after this sequence.
Nonetheless in this case, as in all the others, the IE does not contest
the legitimacy or appropriateness of the IR's overall turn.

Playing devil's advocate
Interviewers may also use assertions, rather than questions, to play
"devil's advocate" in relation to the interviewee's position. In these
contexts, interviewers characteristically find ways to mitigate these
assertions. For example, in the following case, the IR temporarily
abandons questioning to make statements of this kind. This case,
from a very long interview about the perils of nuclear waste, involves
Ted Koppel in this technique:

(32)   US ABC *Nightline*: 6 June 1985: Nuclear Waste
       IR: Ted Koppel   IE: Dr. Rosalyn Yalow

 1 IE: .hh Okay now let's get back to this: uh w-what
 2   I think is an exagge<u>ra</u>tion .hh as 'uh the
 3   problem of radioactive waste disposal. .hh
 4   <u>Ce</u>rtainly the scientific comm<u>u</u>nity (.) be<u>lieves</u>
 5   thet it can be dealt with (0.2) rather <u>r</u>eadily.
 6   .hh The: (.) r:<u>ea</u>son (.) why: (0.3) re<u>a</u>ctor fuel
 7   is staying at the site o' the re<u>a</u>ctor .hh is
 8   not thet they don't know <u>what</u> to do with it.
 9   (0.4) They <u>do</u> know what to do with it but et
10   the <u>mo</u>ment .hh our country is not (.) d-doing
11   rep<u>ro</u>cessing. .hh An be<u>fo</u>re one would want tuh
12   (.) <u>per</u>manently- uh dis<u>po</u>se of these materials
13   .hh one want to- re<u>mo:</u>ve the <u>va</u>luable plutonium
14   en uranium .h <u>from</u> them.=
15 IR: =Lemme stop you right <u>the</u>re: and uh:: we're
16   doing <u>un</u>equal combat here, but that's fine
17   → because I- I <u>wan</u>ta hear what <u>you</u> have to say,
18   → <u>my</u> understanding is thet the re<u>pro</u>cessing (0.2)
19   → <u>pro</u>cess .hh is so expensive thet et least from
20   → an eco<u>nom</u>ic point of view (.) it's not viable.
21   (0.8)
22 IE: At the present time because uranium is cheap,
23   (.) it is not worthwhile repro<u>ce</u>ssing. On the
24   other hand . . .

Here, where the IE has asserted that the nuclear waste problem is
exaggerated and that the scientific community knows how to deal
with it (lines 1–5), Koppel counters with a claim that the process
is not economically viable. It is notable here that Koppel's assertion is elaborately framed to highlight his relative lack of expertise
on the complex topic of nuclear waste. Having won a space from
the IE with "=Lemme stop you right there:," Koppel asserts "we're
doing unequal combat here, but that's fine because I- I wanta hear
what you have to say,". While this remark frames his exchanges
with his expert in a combative metaphor, Koppel clearly asserts
his lack of competence in the field and asserts his commitment to
hearing the IE's point of view. His subsequent assertion about the
viability of uranium reprocessing is directly framed by the words
"my understanding is..." Koppel thus avoids asserting this position as a flat factual rebuttal of the IE's position, but rather offers it as a further issue to be considered. In this way, he mitigates
the challenge to the IE's position that his remarks could otherwise
convey.

A systematic form of mitigation in this context involves a shift
of footing in which interviewers provide that the interviewer's claim
is presented on behalf of others, thus preserving the interviewer's
neutralistic stance. The following illustrates this procedure:

(33)   UK BBC Radio *World at One*: 27 Sep 1981: Labour Policy
        IR: Robin Day   IE: Neil Kinnock

```
 1  IE:     Because of the seriousness of the position.  .hh
 2            the fate of the people of this country,=and the
 3            fact that we're the only alternative
 4            government.=And they've gotta let that transcend
 5            .hh any contest that they have among
 6            themselves.=
 7  IR:  →  =There will be quite a lot of Social Democrats
 8       →  watching who will say that the: .hh you are not
 9       →  the only alternative government.
10  IE:     Well I heh huh you don't expect me to say
11            anything good about the Social
12            Democrats.=There's nothing good to say about
13            them. (.) I mean they're not an alternative
14            government...
```

Here, while challenging government policy in response to an earlier question, the IE makes an impassioned statement that his party

(the Labour Party) is the only alternative to the governing Conservatives. Although the IR produces an assertion which directly counters
this, he specifically avoids asserting it on his own behalf. Rather he
offers it as the standpoint of a segment of the news audience – specifically, those who support a third party, the Social Democrats. In this
way, the IR avoids making factual claims on his own behalf about
the counter-assertion and hence avoids direct disagreement with the
IE (see chapter 5).

In general, interviewer-initiated departures tend to be brief, transparently motivated by the immediate exigencies of the interview, and
mitigated in various ways. As a result they often pass without comment from the interviewee. The same cannot be said for interviewee
departures, to which we now turn.

Interviewee departures from answering

Intervening in ongoing talk

Interviewee departures, by definition, involve initiating some action
before a new question has emerged on to the interactional "floor." A
common, and relatively benign form of departure, emerges in multi-
interviewee interviews where a currently unaddressed interviewee
seeks to comment on some aspect of the talk in progress – in breach
of the turn-taking provision that interviewee turns should properly be produced as responses to interviewer questions. In (34), IE2
(Henry Kissinger) requests permission for such a comment (line 4)
and only proceeds (line 8) after permission has been granted by the
IR (line 7).

(34)   US PBS *Newshour*: 4 Dec 1989: US–Soviet Summit
         IR: Jim Lehrer   IE1: Egon Barr   IE2: Henry Kissinger

```
 1  IE1:     ...as long as the two systems exist and we need
 2            them for stability .h we will have no:: .h uh
 3            unification. This is absolutely clear.
 4  IE2: →   May I say something,
 5  IR:      Yes sir.=
 6  IE2: →   =on the subject?
 7  IR:      Yes sir.
 8  IE2:     Uh (.) ahem I think it is a big mistake. to
 9            equate the NATO alliance and the Warsaw
10            Pact...
```

Here the IE, notwithstanding his status and expertise, clearly orients
to his restricted rights to volunteer a contribution to the topic on the
floor of the interview and, even after his request is granted (line 5),
bolsters his request with the claim (line 6) that he wants to say something "on the subject" of the prior IE's turn. A similar orientation is
also visible in "token" requests for permission to speak, as in (35).
Here, immediately after a turn component that requests permission
to speak, the IE proceeds to make his contribution without waiting
for the IR to respond to his request.

(35)   UK ATV *Afternoon Plus*: 7 Mar 1979: Crime Penalties
         IR: Unknown   IE1: Lord Longford   IE2: Michael Williams
1   IE1:   . . . there was no evidence whatever that stiffer
2   penalties di- diminish crime.=
3   IE2:   → =Can I make a point about that.=.hhh which is
4   that (.) if only this country . . . (continues)

By proceeding to make his contribution before the IR responds to
his request, IE2's request effectively has only a pro forma status.
Here the grammatical continuation of his utterance that is engineered with "which," means that his initial remark also functions as
a prefatory statement, drawing attention to the remarks he is about
to make. In this case, although the IE issues only a "token" request,
he nonetheless acknowledges that his action represents a departure
from the turn-taking provisions of the news interview which, by this
acknowledgment, he treats as normative.

   A similar orientation is manifested in the following case where,
rather than merely seeking to make a comment, IE2 initiates a Q–A
sequence addressed to a co-IE.

(36)   UK BBCTV *Panorama*: 28 Sep 1981: Socialist Credentials
         IR: David Dimbleby   IE1: Arthur Scargill   IE2: Roy
         Hattersley
1   IE1:   . . . the sooner they join the Social Democrats the
2   <u>bet</u>ter f[o r   u s] and better for them?=
3   IE2:   [Well let me a-]
4   IE2:   → =David may I ask Mister Scargill a question you
5   asked him and he didn't answer a moment ago.
6   I've been in the Labour Party for thirty two
7   yea:rs.=I was cam<u>paigni</u>ng for it in South
8   <u>York</u>shire when you were campaigning for a

```
9        different pa:rty. .hhhh I think my socialist
10       credentials stand up against yours in any an-
11       analysis. .hh Do you think people like me ought
12       to leave the Labour Party. (.) Do you want us
13       in.=
14  IE1:  =That's a decision that you have to make...
15       (continues)
```

Here IE2's request both seeks permission from the IR to ask his question and partially offsets its impropriety by describing it as a renewal of the IR's previous question. The request also serves to project his upcoming question to IE1, and provides for the relevance of his intervening statements about his "socialist credentials" (lines 6–11) as accomplice to his question.

Attacks on interviewers

Much more serious are interviewee interventions that are directed at the interviewer, and which can maneuver interviewers away from the safety of a questioning stance. These fall into two main types. First, interviewees can disagree with or deny the statements that interviewers regularly preface their turns with, thus drawing interviewers into a situation of disagreement. Second, and comparatively rarely, interviewees may simply attack interviewers' actions, their questions, television programs or broadcasting organizations either by direct assertion or by pointed questioning. These actions threaten interviewers by requiring them to abandon questioning in order to defend themselves. We will deal with each of these in turn.

Attacks on question prefaces

We have already seen that interviewees usually collaborate in the interviewer's production of a question by withholding response to the prefatory components of interviewer questions. This collaboration is not inevitable, however. Interviewees can initiate disagreements on question prefaces with significant consequences for the interview's trajectory. First, they forestall the production of the question the interviewer was aiming at and which would validate the deployment of the prefatory statements. Second, the disagreement formulates the interviewer's prefatory remarks as assertions in their own right rather than as part of a questioning turn. Hence, third, they treat the interviewer as offering contentious statements of opinion rather than merely relevant "background information."

For example, in (37) below, the IR's question is abandoned in the face of a determined attack on the question preface. Here it can be noticed that the IR attempts to proceed with the question preface (lines 6 and 8) across the IE's first two "interjective" disagreements (lines 4–5 and 7), only subsequently acknowledging them at the end of line 9. In this interview, the IE, British peer Lord Longford, is a noted advocate of prisoners' rights.

(37) UK ATV *Afternoon Plus*: Mar 1979: Victims' Rights
      IR: Unknown   IE: Lord Longford

```
 1  IR:      .hhhh Lord Longford erm (0.5) we- we- we do take
 2            a lot of trouble (0.8) rehabilitating (0.5)
 3            criminals. .hhh er: [and long]
 4  IE:  →                       [Well I d]on't- I
 5            [don't ( )-]
 6  IR:      [long term ] scheme for the criminals.
 7  IE:  →   No I don't agree wi[th that at all (sir).]=
 8  IR:                         [But we don't seem] to
 9            [Sorry.]
10  IE:      =[(    )-] er [Sorry (  ) I] don't agree with=
11  IR:                   [I-I see. Well-]
12  IE:      =that statement not a-no way. [We d]o very=
13  IR:                                    [ Well-]
14  IE:      =little to rehabilitate criminal[ s ]
15  IR:                                      [W]ell we seem
16            to spend a lot of money on it even if we do
17            little.=
18  IE:      =Very little.=
19  IR:      =erm ((coughs)) What are your recommendations to
20            giving the victim a better deal.
```

Here the IR's preface (lines 1–3, 6 and 8) is moving towards a contrast between the (allegedly substantial) efforts that are made to rehabilitate criminals and an assertion (initiated at line 8 but not completed) about the relatively little effort made to help crime victims. This turn-in-progress is attacked by the IE at lines 4 and 7. This kind of early disagreement is highly dispreferred (Pomerantz 1984) and its placement definitely contributes to the force of the IE's stated disagreement (see chapter 8). Notably here, the IR attempts to complete his question (lines 6 and 8) competing in overlap with the IE. Following the IR's abandonment of this tack (line 9), the IE emphatically reasserts his disagreement (lines 10, 12, and 14). In his revised question preface (lines 15–17), the IR abandons the projected contrast. His new contrast (between the resources devoted to the rehabilitation of criminals and the actual achievements of the program) backs down from his earlier assertion by accommodating the IE's position. It also supplies information which can be heard to warrant the earlier, disagreed-with assertion from which he has retreated. It is only after this revised question preface, and after the IE has upgraded the IR's backdown by his intensification of the IR's new position (line 18), that the IR is able to proceed to his question without further contest (lines 19–20).

From an interviewer's point of view, the dangers of this kind of attack are clear. They risk drawing the interviewer into direct disagreement with the interviewee and a wholesale abandonment of a professional, neutralistic stance. In this case, the interviewer competes in overlap with the interviewee's early response with the objective of getting to the question. Though he is unsuccessful, the interviewer's efforts are geared to avoid being drawn into a direct response to the interviewee, while simultaneously establishing – by the production of a question – a neutralistic object to which the interviewee should properly respond.

It is notable that prefatory statements that relay third-party positions are very rarely attacked in this way and, as chapter 5 shows, they are a solid means of defending the integrity of interviewer questions. Prefaces which are not guarded in this way are, by contrast, at systematic risk of interviewee interdiction.

In the ideal case, interviewers will respond to attacks on question prefaces by a rapid resort to a question. Though this is not always possible when a full preface is required to set up a question, this tactic is effectively deployed in the following case. Here the IE interjectively challenges (arrow 2) a lengthy question preface in overlap with the initiation of the questioning component of the IR's turn (arrow 1). The IE's challenge is expressed in an idiom that treats the IR's reported "noticing" as small-minded, even mildly malicious. In this case, the IR responds by abandoning the projected question in favor of one that counter-challenges the IE (arrow 3).

(38)   UK BBCTV *Newsnight*: 16 Oct 1981: Geoffrey Howe Speech
        IR: Peter Snow   IE: Francis Pym

```
1  IR:    . . . I couldn't help notici:ng when uh .hhh Sir
2          Geoffrey Howe was speaking this afternoon how
3          while all your other ministerial colleagues were
```

```
4              clapping uh .hh during his speech in between
5              many of the things he was saying .hh you hardly
6              clapped at all.=You hardly applauded at all.
7              =Sitting as you were beside Mister Heath.
8        1→ .hhh [Do you:]
9   IE:  2→      [Come o]ff it.
10  IR:  3→ d- (.) Well is it not true.=
11  IE:       =cu- Come off it.=(   ) I clapped... ((continues))
```

Thus the IR maintains a neutralistic stance by a "retreat" to a revised question that addresses the contested facts. He thus overtly offers the IE a chance to rebut an assertion which he had presented as "background information" in his previous turn but, in the process, he also restores the Q–A format of the interview.

General attacks on interviewer conduct

Direct attacks on the interviewer's conduct in an interview or on interviewer questions create a difficult dilemma for interviewers. The attacks compromise interviewer conduct and professionalism by representing them as deficient. While a defense of their conduct and integrity may appear the interviewer's most desirable and natural response, such a defense involves an abandonment of the neutralistic stance which is the hallmark of the professional interviewer. On the other hand, by ignoring the accusation, the interviewer may seem to have no response and may thus appear to the news audience to be "guilty as charged." A systematic solution to this dilemma involves interviewers in justifying their conduct by reference to their central professional task: questioning. For example, in the following case, a scientist accuses ABC's Ted Koppel of falsely raising viewers' anxieties about increased cancer rates after the Three Mile Island nuclear accident:

```
(39)   US ABC Nightline: 6 June 1985: Nuclear Waste
       IR: Ted Koppel   IE: Dr. Rosalyn Yalow

1  IE:    ...On the other hand there was one horrible
2          thing that happened tonight that you have- .h in
3          addition extended. .hh And that is the notion
4          that there is an increased incidence of cancer
5          associated with th' Three Mile Island accide[nt.
6  IR:  →                                              [No=
7      →  no=no I rai[sed the- I raised the QUEStion]=
```

```
 8   IE:                 [And it is A B s o l u t e l y]=
 9                    =[not ] so.
10   IR:              =[and-]
11   IR:        → Well fine. Then- then tell us how you know it is
12                    not so.=
13   IE:              =The reason why I can tell you it's not so is
14                    we have considerable: experience .hh with uh
15                    survivors of three m- of the Hiroshima Nagasaki
16                    eh bombing...
```

Koppel's escape from this criticism involves two steps. The first (lines 6 and 7) is to deny that he "extended" the idea that the Three Mile Island accident has resulted in an increased incidence of cancer, and to assert instead that he merely "raised the question" (see [28] above). He then retrieves the IE's rejection of this claim (lines 8 and 9), made in overlap with his disclaimer, and topicalizes that as a new question (line 11). At this point, the criticism has been deflected, the IE has a chance to reinforce her position, and the interview has reverted to the Q–A format. "Normality" is restored.

In (40), the IE (industrial magnate, Sir James Goldsmith) initiates a hostile Q–A sequence directed at the IR. In this example, Goldsmith's complaint (lines 1–12) concerns the coverage given to his business affairs in a previous edition of the program in which he is presently appearing. His lengthy turn at the beginning of this sequence culminates in the claim (lines 9–11) that the previous edition of the program misled the audience about his business activities. He then proceeds (at line 12) with the beginning of a question ("Why") that would demand an explanation for this coverage.

(40)   UK BBCTV *Omnibus*: 21 Apr 1981: Misleading Program
       IR: Unknown   IE: Sir James Goldsmith

```
 1   IE:     ...despite the fact there were fou:r major
 2              factories that you knew about,=despite the fact
 3              there was a two hundred and thirty million
 4              capital investment programme that you knew
 5              about,=.hhh that we dealt in companies you
 6              stated and restated toda::y, .hhh despite the
 7              fact that ninety one per cent of our companies
 8              are still there:,=and only the marginal ones
 9              which you knew were sold, .hhh and you e:ven
10              mislead people by suggesting for instance that
11              we owned the Parisian publishing house Brooke.
12              Why=
```

```
13   IR:    =s- s- s- Sir James I['m so sorry (  ) I'm=
14   IE:                     [No,=I'm asking a question=
15   IR:    =so s-]
16   IE:    =   n]ow.=
17   IR:    =It's more conventional in these programmes
18          [fo:r ]
19   IE:    [Well] I don't mind ab[out    convention.  ]=
20   IR:                           [me to ask questions,]
21   IE:    =I'm asking you why
22          (.)
23   IE:    you distorted those facts.
24          (0.2)
25   IR:    Well we didn't distort them. [ I mean   er  ]
26   IE:                                 [Well w- then] did
27          you...
```

The IE's question start is met by an interjection from the IR (line 13) who attempts to pre-empt its production. This action is, in turn, intersected by the IE (line 14) who sustains his questioning stance ("No,=I'm asking a question now."), overtly acknowledging his reversal of normal interview conduct. The IR again resists the IE's attempt to adopt a questioning role, sanctioning his conduct with an appeal to the normal conventions of news interviews (lines 17–18 and 20) already implicated in the IE's prior turn (at line 14) and this, in its turn, is resisted by the IE who rejects the appeal (line 19) and again presses for a response with a fully articulated demand for an explanation (lines 21 and 23). The IR does eventually respond (at line 25) but only after vigorously attempting to forestall and sanction the IE for asking it.[14]

The danger in this case is that, once the IE has successfully articulated an attacking question, the IR may be forced to abandon the "safety" of the questioning stance. It is not surprising therefore that the IR strenuously resists the IE's questioning (lines 17–18 and 20) and is finally brought to a response to the IE's question (line 25) only after a lengthy struggle. It is noteworthy here that the turn-taking rules for news interviews are thematized as an explicit feature of this struggle.

Attacks on interviewer questions or conduct have the potential to disrupt not only the Q–A turn-taking system for news interviews,

---

[14] The IR was not a participant in the program that Sir James Goldsmith is criticizing here and may have known little about its contents.

but the neutralism and audience orientation that are characteristics of professional conduct in the news interview. Their impact is particularly disruptive because on the one hand they cast interviewers as non-neutral and, in a troublesome double-bind, they also seem to require interviewers to abandon further the neutralistic questioning stance in order to defend themselves. Interviewers can best respond and preserve their neutralism by asserting their role as questioners (see excerpts [38] and [39]). In other cases, they can attempt to forestall the attacks during the course of their production, or assert objective or "public interest" grounds for their conduct. Only in quite unusual cases do interviewers risk flatly contradicting interviewees with an associated dangerous potential for the collapse of their professional footing.

Finally, it is not only interviewers who can lose their neutralistic stance within the interview. Interviewees can also move into fully-fledged attacks on interviewers and their employers. In the following case, a leading Labour politician, Tony Benn, who had been narrowly defeated four years earlier in a divisive election for the deputy leadership of his party, is asked whether he will stand against the new leaders of the party.

(41)   UK Central Television Central Lobby: 1985: The Labour Party
       IR: Reg Harcourt   IE: Tony Benn

```
 1  IR:    Mister Benn we're running out of time. Can I ask
 2          you th[is.
 3  IE:          [mmhm=
 4  IR:    =Have you any intention of standing against
 5          either Mister Kinnock (.) or Mister Hattersley
 6          .hhh at the party conference for either of their
 7          two jobs.
 8  IE:    No.
 9          (0.2)
10  IR:    Why not.
11          (0.6)
12  IE:    Well I've:: given you the answer.=Why should
13          I.=I mean I:'m in favour [of the=
14  IR:                               [Because=
15  IE:    =electoral college. .hhhh
16  IR:    =you disagree with them on- on a number
17          [of issues.
18  IE:    [uhr
```

```
19   IE:   You see (that) is very- you are really very
20         funny. I mean I understand why people hate the
21         media. .h[hh Because when I=
22   IR:        [hah huh hah
23   IE:   =give you a straight answer to a straight
24         question which I've given on television for
25         weeks and weeks .hhh you press, .h you
26         try to make trouble. [You're paid to make=
27   IR:                       [Do you not accept-
28   IE:   =trouble. .hh And I- I hate to say it to you,
29         .hh but your jo:b is to try and make enough
30         trouble in the Labour Party .hh to keep Mrs
31         Thatcher in power:. .hh And if you do that you
32         fail. .hh But I tell you when: Mrs Thatcher goes
33         dow:n .hh Central Television will go down with
34         it.=Because people will say they were supporting
35         the Tories throughout the whole campaign.
36         (0.2)
37   IR:   I disagree with you on the last point,=but I
38         think (0.6) you've had the last word. (.) Thank
39         you very much.
```

Here Benn, goaded by a recurrence of questions thematizing his disagreements with the leadership of his party, launches a direct attack on the questioner from line 19 onwards. Beginning with his claim to have given a "straight answer to a straight question," he criticizes the IR's follow-up questions as "pressing" and "making trouble." From here he escalates his criticism to include the IR's employing organization (Central Television) as paying the IR to "make trouble" (line 26), intimates its political motivation as anti-Labour (lines 30–31) and concludes by suggesting that electoral defeat for the Conservatives could mean that Central Television will "go down."

Just as interviewers rarely move into direct assertions, so interviewees rarely slip into the kind of generalized charges illustrated in (41). Even when attacking interviewers, interviewees rarely make generalized claims about interviewer neutrality, and instead comment on the details of particular propositions and lines of questioning. Thus, while politicians may often complain about media bias or about particular interviewers, they do not normally use the news interview itself as a context in which to voice these criticisms. In the interview context, complaints about interviewer conduct are relatively brief and rarely develop into extended exchanges. Thus, as a general rule, interviewees treat interviewer conduct, regardless of how presuppositionally weighted against their positions it may be, as part of the cut and thrust of the modern interview. Interviewers are not treated as advocates of personal or institutional positions, although interviewees may well believe them to be so on occasion.

The rarity of these examples highlights the weight of the institutional framework which underpins the news interview and, correlatively, the extent to which both interviewers and interviewees commit themselves to play "the interview game" and engage in the "facework" (Goffman 1955) that is appropriate to it. Just as interviewers are obliged to refrain from direct attacks on interviewees, so interviewees are obligated to treat aggressive or negative questioning with a kind of tact. Interviewees are obliged to treat most questioning in ways that warrant the issues raised as "fair game" and the style of questioning as appropriate for the setting. Thus the self-imposed constraints of action that we have observed in this chapter also involve parallel self-imposed constraints on how the actions of others are to be interpreted and treated within the public arena of broadcast news. An interviewer who may privately know that an interviewee is lying must still continue with questioning that will appear reasonable to the general public. And an interviewee who may be privately enraged by a line of questioning will nonetheless normally address each inquiry in a manner that validates it as reasonable and appropriate. The participants' sense of the "parameters of the permissible" in the news interview context shape not only their public actions, but also the interpretations of the actions of others that their public actions may appropriately index.

Conclusion

In this chapter, we have covered a lot of ground. We have described the basic turn-taking processes that make news interview interaction distinctive from conversation and, incidentally, from interaction in other contexts not addressed here such as classrooms or doctors' offices. We have drawn out some of the institutional significance of turn-taking procedures in the news interview by pointing to some of the specific tasks and constraints of journalism that news interview turn-taking helps to handle.

Although there is real complexity to some of the processes involved, the core of these processes can be simply stated as the rule that one party (the interviewer) will ask questions, while the other (the interviewee) will respond to them. This turn-taking system is normative in character and, on occasion, may be overtly thematized within the interview as an object in its own right. A tacit orientation to it runs – like a spine – throughout the situated management of ordinary news interview interaction. Through their detailed respect for the rule, the parties display their pervasive orientation to the context of their talk and the relevancies of their local social and discourse identities as interviewer and interviewee.

These turn-taking processes are closely associated with the basic task of the news interview – the elicitation of talk that is expressly produced for an overhearing audience by an interviewer who should properly maintain a formally neutral or "neutralistic" posture. Observance of the provisions of this turn-taking system is associated with the appropriate management of these central tasks and constraints, while departures from these provisions often render their management problematic. Thus compliance with news interview turn-taking provisions is not the fetishistic maintenance of an empty form. Rather it is the most economical means by which the parties manage the fundamental business of the interview.

These processes are basic in defining the fundamental interaction arena for the news interview. But important though they are, they only set the scene for the complex maneuvers that take place within that arena. And it is these that will occupy the next chapters of this book.

5

Defensible questioning: neutralism, credibility, legitimacy

Interviewing can be a hazardous occupation for the professional journalist. Interviewers are closely scrutinized for their conduct toward prestigious public figures, and it is not uncommon for them to become the target of criticism. As noted in chapter 1, Dan Rather's contentious encounter with presidential candidate George Bush ignited a firestorm of protest from various quarters, and even though both parties contributed to the conflictual encounter that resulted (Clayman and Whalen 1988/89), Rather bore the brunt of criticism. A fellow journalist expressed the views of many when he said that Rather "stepped over the line of what is just intelligent professionalism" by moving "outside the role of reporter and...into the role of judge."[1] A hostile reaction also befell David Frost after his adversarial interview with Emil Savundra, a businessman who had liquidated his auto insurance company leaving many claims outstanding. This interview, which preceded Savundra's trial for fraud, was criticized for its prejudicial impact on the trial, and the appeal judge later commented that such "trial by television is not to be tolerated in a civilized society" (Tracey 1977).

As members of the journalistic profession, news interviewers are expected to adhere to certain basic standards of professional conduct. Most importantly, they are obliged to be objective in their work. As noted in chapters 2 and 4, objectivity is an umbrella concept that encompasses a range of journalistic values, including factual accuracy, balance between opposing views, and neutrality in presentation. These values are deeply ingrained in the professional

---

[1] This comment was made by Hodding Carter in a discussion of the Bush–Rather encounter on the MacNeil/Lehrer *NewsHour* the following day (Sep. 26, 1988).

culture of journalism in both England and the United States, and at various points they have been codified in the regulations governing broadcasters. They have also penetrated the wider Anglo-American culture, so that public officials, professional pundits, ordinary citizens, and numerous well-financed media watchdog organizations now regularly monitor news output for the presence of "bias."[2]

For journalists who conduct interviews for broadcast, maintaining even an appearance of objectivity is a complex and vexing task. Interviews are spontaneous and unpredictable events, and yet most are broadcast without the benefit of editorial review. Moreover, the interviewer is expected to uphold diverse and often conflicting aspects of objectivity simultaneously. For instance, to promote ideological *balance*, an interviewer may be moved to act as devil's advocate by aggressively challenging an interviewee. But this adversarial approach can, in turn, threaten the ideal of *neutrality* if the interviewer is seen to be promoting his or her own political biases or the biases of the news organization's owners or sponsors. How are these divergent goals reconciled in practice? More specifically, *how do interviewers manage to assert themselves in an adversarial manner while maintaining a formally impartial or neutralistic posture?*

A partial solution to this puzzle was elaborated in the previous chapter. The turn-taking system for news interviews, which is organized around questions and answers, provides an important foundation for interviewer neutralism. As we have seen, interviewers normally restrict themselves to asking questions and hence avoid actions whose primary purpose is to express a point of view – unvarnished assertions as well as receipt tokens (*yeah, uh huh*, etc.) that might be taken to indicate approval or agreement with the interviewee. When assertions are introduced, they are normally rendered in conjunction with a subsequent question, and are treated as accomplice to the activity of questioning rather than as distinct actions in their own right. Of course, no question can be completely neutral in an absolute sense, a theme that we will explore further in chapter 6. Nevertheless, because the manifest purpose of a question is to solicit the interviewee's point of view rather than to express a viewpoint in itself, this type of speech act has an intrinsically neutralistic quality. This is undoubtedly why interviewers, when they come under attack,

---

[2] For more thorough discussions of objectivity in journalism, see Gans (1979: chapter 6), Schudson (1978), Tuchman (1972).

can and do defend themselves by pointing out that they were "only asking a question."[3]

In this chapter, we move beyond the question–answer turn-taking system to examine other supplementary practices which are implicated in the maintenance of interviewer neutralism. As we shall see, these practices not only promote neutralism, but they also provide more generally for the defensibility of a line of questioning and the professionalism of the journalist who is pursuing it (for a fuller analysis, see Clayman 1992, 2002).

Speaking on behalf of a third party

Interviewers often work to place some degree of distance between themselves and their more overtly opinionated remarks. The most straightforward way of doing this is to attribute the point of view being expressed to some third party – a maneuver that Goffman (1981) has referred to as a shift in the speaker's interactional "footing." For example, in the following the IR asserts (in lines 9–12) that nuclear waste can be readily managed, but before launching into the assertion itself he ascribes it to "Doctor Yalow" (6–8, arrowed).

(1)   US ABC *Nightline*: 6 June 1985: Nuclear Waste
       IR: Ted Koppel   IE: James Steele

      1   IE: ...And if you <u>lo</u>ok et- simply the record in
      2   the <u>low</u> level waste field over the last
      3   fifteen to twenty <u>ye</u>ars...the record is not
      4   very <u>goo</u>d (0.3) an' it doesn't give one a cause
      5   for <u>op</u>timism.=
      6   IR: →   =You heard what Doctor Yalow said earlier in
      7   →   this br<u>oa</u>dcast she'll have an opportunity to
      8   →   express her own opinions ag<u>ain</u> but she seems to
      9   feel that it is an <u>e</u>minently soluble problem,
     10   and that <u>u</u>ltimately that radioactive mat<u>e</u>rial
     11   can be red<u>u</u>ced, to manageable quantities, 'n put
     12   in the bottom of a salt mine.
     13   IE: The p- the <u>po</u>int that she was making earlier
     14   about (.) reprocessing of: the fuel rods goes
     15   <u>ri</u>ght to the heart (.) of the way a lotta
     16   people look at this particular <u>i</u>ssue...

In this case the third party is another program guest whose optimistic view of waste disposal is introduced by the IR to counter an IE's

---

[3] For illustrations of this type of defense, see chapter 4.

more critical assessment (1–5) (Olsher Forthcoming). The IR does not offer a direct quotation (cf., Holt 1994), but rather a summary characterization of Yalow's position on the waste disposal problem, and he makes a special point of indicating that this represents "her own opinions" which "she seems to feel" (lines 8–9). He also refrains from either endorsing or rejecting this viewpoint, or offering any commentary of his own on the matter. In short, the IR casts himself as disinterestedly invoking the opinions of a third party.

The cited third party need not be a specific individual. It may also be a group or category of persons, such as "Democrats," "Tories," or as in the following example, "critics" (arrowed).

(2) US PBS *NewsHour*: 22 July 1985: South Africa
      IR: Jim Lehrer   IE: Herbert Beukes

```
1  IR:      Finally Mister Ambassador as you know the
2     →     critics say that the purpose of the state of
3            emergency the real purpose of the state of
4            'mergeh- uh state of emergency is to suppress
5            political dissent. those who are opposed to the
6            apartheid goverment of South Africa. Is that so,
```

IRs may also refer to a generic and anonymous collectivity, such as "people" (arrowed).

(3) UK BBC Radio *Today*: June 1993: Bosnian Camps
      IR: John Humphrys   IE: Ian Smedley

```
1  IR:  →  .hhh People have used the phrase concentration
2            camps: and the Bosnians themselves have used
3            that phrase. Do you believe there's any
4            justification for that at all?
```

Finally, a responsible third party may be evoked without actually being named. The primary way of doing this is by using an attributive verb in the passive voice with the agent deleted – e.g., "it is said that..." or "it has been reported that..." (arrowed):

(4) UK BBCTV *Newsnight*: June 1989: Thatcher
      IR: John Cole   IE: Margaret Thatcher

```
1  IR:  →  .hhh It's been widely reported that these
2            matters 'e:re are an:d particularly have put
3            .hhh heavy strains on th- your relationship with
4            the Foreign Secretary and indeed with the
5            Chan:cellor. How would you defi: :ne that
6            relationship (  ).
```

Across these examples the effect is the same: an opinion that might otherwise be attributed to the IR is instead deflected toward a third party, and the IR is cast as one who is merely reporting that view.

Shifts of footing are recurrently used for question-preliminary assertions (as in excerpts [2]–[4] above), but they are particularly prevalent when interviewers produce assertions without an accompanying question, as in (1) above. As we noted in chapter 4 (Table 1), interviewers restrict themselves to asking questions of one form or another roughly 85 percent of the time, and more than a third of the remaining turns produced by interviewers are attributed to third parties. The association between free-standing assertions and third-party attributions is far from coincidental. Free-standing assertions pose the greatest threat to neutralism, so interviewers take particular care to distance themselves from such remarks.

Indeed, third-party attributed statements appear to function as virtual questions. Although they are not grammatically formatted as questions, like questions they topicalize matters to which the interviewees should respond, and they continue to preserve the neutralistic posture that questions otherwise provide. The virtual-question status of such statements is apparent in the following excerpt. The IR invokes the views of "a lot of people" to assert that the IE's profession – he is a canine psychiatrist – is "a bunch of poppycock" (lines 1–2, 4).

(5)   US NBC *Dateline*: 16 Dec 1997: Canine Psychiatry
      IR: Unknown   IE: Unknown

```
 1  IR:   → A lotta people would hear: (.) about your
 2         → profession.
 3  IE:     Ye:s.=
 4  IR:   → =and say that's a bunch o'poppycock.
 5  IE:     Ye:s,
 6           (0.2)
 7  IR:     And you say:?
 8           (.)
 9  IE:     I say they're entitled to their opinion. .hh
10          And I would also say to those people that
11          they'll believe that (0.9) .h right up until
12          their very favorite dog growls at them. (0.2)
13          .hh And then you'd be surprised at how quickly
14          .hh people can suddenly become a convert.
```

The IE acknowledges but does not respond substantively to this charge (line 5), thus treating it as preliminary to a question-in-progress. However, the IR makes no effort to supply an interrogative at that point; he merely prompts the IE to answer (line 7), thereby treating the statement as adequate in itself. The clash of understandings evident in this excerpt demonstrates that third-party attributed statements indeed have the status of virtual – ie., almost but not quite – questions.

The capacity to shift footings nimbly is a crucial interviewing skill, because interviewers must make opinionated assertions in order to accomplish a variety of basic journalistic tasks. Consider the goal of maintaining a balance of perspectives – as we saw in the previous chapter, interviewers are often compelled to act as devil's advocate by disagreeing with, criticizing, or otherwise challenging what an interviewee has been saying. Thus, in (1) above, the IR counterbalances an IE's pessimistic view of nuclear waste disposal by conveying a more upbeat assessment. And in (2), which occurs after the South African Ambassador to the USA defended and justified his government's decision to curtail civil liberties and impose a state of emergency (he had argued that it was necessary to curb violence), the IR challenges the legitimacy of the crackdown (arguing that it is really an attempt to suppress political dissent). By shifting footings at such moments, the interviewer can introduce a balance of perspectives while maintaining a neutralistic posture.

The need to pursue ideological balance actively is particularly acute in interviews involving a single interviewee, where the responsibility to provide such balance rests exclusively on the shoulders of the interviewer. This problem is somewhat lessened in panel interviews, where the presence of multiple interviewees ensures some diversity of opinion (see chapter 8). And yet, even then the interviewer must summarize and relay interviewees' views to one another to solicit opposing views and generally focus the course of the discussion (Olsher Forthcoming). Thus, cited third parties may be other co-present IEs, as we saw in (1) above. The following is a more elaborate example in which the IR encapsulates the previously expressed views of three IEs on civil unrest in China (see especially the arrowed lines) to solicit a contrasting view from the fourth IE on the panel.

(6)   UK BBCTV *Newsnight*: May 1989: China Civil Unrest
      IR: Peter Snow   IE: Jonathan Mirsky
1   IR: Now Jonathan Mirsky finally back to you.   .hh
2   Are you (0.2) are you as (.) opti<u>mis</u>tic I think
3   I could almost say as the three (.) statesmen
4   we've heard from (.) he:re (.) that this thing
5   can be peacefully re<u>solved</u> . . .
6   →   Th- they seem quite d- determined that there can
7   →   be a peaceful solution if- uh people are wise
8   →   and patient.   .hh Are <u>you</u> (.) <u>per</u>sonally
9   satisfi:ed that there really <u>can</u> be a peaceful
10   solution? With the students so determined (.)
11   eh and the Government apparently determined to
12   clear them away?
13   (1.2)
14 IE: Well I think that's exactly the question . . .

In short, both by playing devil's advocate and by generating disagreement among interviewees, interviewers strive to foster diversity of opinion and partisan balance. Third-party attributions enable the IR to discharge this core journalistic responsibility without abandoning a neutralistic posture.

The significance of footing for the achievement of neutralism can be seen most clearly in cases where interviewers shift footings *selectively* over the course of a questioning turn. Rather than distance themselves from everything said within a turn at talk, interviewers often do so only during remarks that might be regarded as particularly opinionated or controversial. This pattern can be seen in the following excerpt from an interview with Senator Bob Dole, then the Senate majority leader for the Republican Party.

(7)   US NBC *Meet the Press*: 8 Dec 1985: Troubled Programs
      IR: Marvin Kalb   IE: Senator Bob Dole
1   IR: 1→ Senator, (0.5) uh: <u>Pres</u>ident Reagan's elected
2   thirteen months a<u>go</u>: an en<u>or</u>mous landslide.
3   (0.8)
4   2→ It is s: :<u>aid</u> that his <u>programs</u> are in trouble,
5   though <u>he</u> seems to be terribly <u>pop</u>ular with the
6   American people.
7   (0.6)
8   3→ It is <u>said</u> by some people at the <u>White</u> House
9   we could <u>get</u> those programs <u>through</u> if only we
10   <u>ha</u>:d perh<u>aps</u> more: .hh ef<u>fec</u>tive leadership

```
11        on on the H̲ill and I [suppose] indir̲ectly=
12  IE:                      [hhhheh ]
13  IR:   =that m̲ight (0.5) relate t'you as we̲ll:. (0.6)
14        Uh wha̲t do you t̲hink the problem i̲s really.
15        Is=it (0.2) the l̲eadership as it might be
16        claimed up on the H̲ill, or is it the
17        pr̲ograms thems̲elves.
```

The initial statement beginning at arrow 1 – that Reagan was elected "thirteen months ag̲o" in "an eno̲rmous landslide" – is a relatively concrete historical fact and a matter of public record. This fact is asserted straightforwardly. In contrast, the subsequent claim that Reagan's programs are "in trouble" (beginning at arrow 2) and the suggestion that the IE is to blame for this (beginning at arrow 3) are by comparison matters of judgment and interpretation. Significantly, the IR distances himself from these last assertions ("it is said . . ."). He thus indicates that they derive from another source which remains unnamed in the first case (arrow 2), but which is loosely identified as "some people at the W̲hite House" in the second (arrow 3).

Interviewers also shift footings selectively over the course of a single sentence. Thus, a contentious word or two may be singled out for attribution to a third party. For example, although the IR begins (at lines 1–2 below) by attributing an upcoming statement of opinion in its entirety (regarding violence and negotiations in South Africa) to a third party ("the Ambassador"), this footing is later renewed within the assertion itself (line 7, arrowed) just prior to a specific loaded term ("colla̲borator") which is reattributed to that party.

(8)   US ABC *Nightline*: 22 July 1985: South Africa
      IR: Charles Gibson   IE: Reverend Allan Boesak

```
 1  IR:    Reverend Boesak lemme a- pick up a po̲int uh the
 2         Ambassador made. W̲hat- wh̲at assu̲rances can y̲ou
 3         give u̲:s.hh that (.) ta̲lks between mo̲derates
 4         in that country will take pla:ce .h when: it
 5         see̲:ms that a̲ny black leader who is
 6         wi̲lling to talk to the Government i̲s b̲randed
 7    →    as the Ambassador said a colla̲borator and is
 8         then pu̲nished.=
 9  IE:    =Eh theh- the- the Amb̲assador has it wr̲ong.
10         It's n̲ot the people who want to ta̲lk with
11         the Government that are branded collaborators . . .
```

Similarly, in the following an IR (line 1) attributes a forthcoming remark (regarding Britain's involvement in the European Economic Community) to "Michael Heseltine," but he later reintroduces and amplifies that attribution (lines 11–13, arrowed) after characterizing the IE's approach as "negative" (line 10).

(9)   UK BBCTV *Newsnight*: May 1989: European Social Policies
      IR: Peter Snow   IE: John Redwood

```
 1   IR:    ... Michael Heseltine said tonight in a speech
 2           and you know his views about Europe and ah he
 3           may not say so but he's clearly opposed to the
 4           (.).h rather strong line that you and Missus
 5           Thatcher ta:ke on this.  .hhh He said (.) we can
 6           (0.2) choose for either to influence the
 7           community's (.) form as a leading partner (0.3)
 8           or to be subjected to it by others more
 9           determined than ourselves. Isn't it a fact that
10           the rather negative approach you seem to take,
11   →       (.) uh and I:'d and and I'm using words
12   →       characterized by .hh Mister Heselti:ne Mister
13   →       Heath and o[thers .hhh uh is in fact damaging=
14   IE:                [mm
15   IR:    =(0.3) your chances of contributin[g to the=
16   IE:                                       [no
17   IR:    =future of the community.
18   IE:    What I've been saying tonight is not negative at
19           all...
```

In these examples, the attributed terms are both contentious and objectionable. As a way of characterizing black leaders who negotiate with the South African Government, "collaborator" has strong morally judgmental overtones. Similarly, to describe an approach to British involvement in the European Economic Community as "negative" is tantamount to taking sides on a highly divisive issue. In each case the IR goes to extra lengths to disavow any personal attachment to such items.

Perhaps the clearest evidence that interviewers are working to sustain a neutralistic footing comes from those cases where an interviewer *begins to launch into an assertion, but then aborts and revises it so as to invoke a responsible third party.* Such mid-course corrections (e.g., "Turn righ- uh left") are, of course, commonplace in ordinary conversation, and they have been analyzed as instances of *self-repair* (Jefferson 1974; Schegloff, Jefferson, and Sacks 1977). Speakers initiate self-repair not only to correct grammatical and factual errors, but also to replace potentially inappropriate talk with material that is more appropriate or suitable to the immediate social situation (Jefferson 1974). In the journalistic context of the news interview, it is not uncommon for interviewers to self-repair so as to shift to an appropriately neutralistic footing. Consider the following excerpt from an interview with a Reagan administration official regarding the President's decision to continue to honor the Salt II arms control treaty.

(10)   US PBS *NewsHour*: 10 June 1985: Nuclear Weapons
       IR: Robert MacNeil   IE: Kenneth Adelman

```
 1  IR:    How d'you sum up the me:ssage. that this
 2          decision is sending to the Soviets?
 3  IE:    .hhh Well as I started- to say:: it is ay- one
 4          of: warning and opportunity. The warning is (.)
 5          you'd better comply: to arms control::
 6          agreements if arms control is going to have any
 7          chance of succeeding in the future. Unilateral
 8          compliance by the United States just not in the
 9          works...
10          ((Four lines omitted))
11  IR:  → But isn't this- uh::: critics uh on the
12          conservative side of the political argument
13          have argued that this is:. abiding by the
14          treaty is:. unilateral (.) observance. (.)
15          uh:: or compliance. (.) by the United States.
```

After the official carefully distinguishes the administration's decision from "unilateral compliance" (lines 3–9), the IR presents the opposite point of view. This is foreshadowed from the very beginning of his turn (line 11, arrowed) – the contrastive preface ("But isn't this-...") clearly projects that some form of disagreement is in the works.[4] However, the IR abruptly abandons the turn at this point, pauses briefly ("uh:::"), and then restarts on a different footing such that "critics on the conservative side" are cited as responsible for the forthcoming viewpoint. This revised version is no longer formatted

---

[4] This preface is also negatively formulated. As we will see in the next chapter, this way of formatting a question is highly assertive, so much so that it straddles the boundary between what is understood to be "neutral questioning" versus "expressing opinions."

as a question, the interrogative preface having been omitted – it is now a free-standing assertion that disputes the IE's previous point, but now does so on someone else's behalf.

The following excerpt contains a more complex instance of self-repair to shift footings (arrowed). The discussion here concerns black involvement in recent violence in South Africa, and the IE is a black South African spokesperson who is arguing that the police forces are responsible for starting the most recent episode of violence.

(11)   US ABC *Nightline*: 22 July 1985: South Africa
       IR: Charles Gibson   IE: Allan Boesak

```
 1  IE:     ...what you find in the black townships it
 2           seems to me is the kind of reaction of the
 3           people to the violence of the police and this is
 4           the situation in which we find our[selves.]
 5  IR:                                     [ .hhhh] Well
 6           you- you may argue that it- that it is a
 7           result of apartheid the violence, it certainly
 8           was not s- uhhh apartheid is uh- is uh- system
 9           (.) imposed by the Government but the
10  1→      violence itself was not started by the Government,
11  2→      the violence now st- (.) the violence the
12           Goverment now says has to be stopped .hh before
13           ANything else can happen an the state of
14           emergency is necessary (0.3) to do that.
15           (.)
16  IE:     .hhh Well I don't know what they me:an you
17           see...
```

After formulating the gist of the IE's prior remarks (in lines 5–7), the IR proceeds to challenge this view. He packages the challenge in the form of a common rhetorical device: a *contrast* (Atkinson 1984; Heritage and Greatbatch 1986). The first part of the contrast begins at arrow 1 and negates the IE's view, while the second positively formatted part begins at arrow 2 with "the violence now st-." Given the parallel wording and the contrastive stress on "now," the IR appears to be moving to complete a contrast that blames the current violence on blacks rather than the Government. That is, he seems to be about to say that "the violence *now* started *because of the actions of blacks*," or words to that effect. This would have been a rather pointed accusation, but it is not brought to completion. The IR stops abruptly, pauses briefly, and then resumes with a substantially different assertion that is not only weaker and nonaccusatory, but is also ascribed to "the Government."

Across these examples, interviewers can be seen exercising marked caution when introducing matters of opinion or controversy. Such matters could in principle be quite damaging to neutralism, but interviewers are able to sustain a professional posture by taking care to attribute such views to a third party. Of course, audience members may suspect that the interviewer actually agrees (or disagrees) with what he or she is saying. Such suspicions may be founded on subtle aspects of the interviewer's demeanor (Goffman, 1959: 2ff.), background knowledge of his or her personal opinions, or even on the basis that "everyone agrees with that." But by virtue of the footing shift, the interviewer's own position is not officially "on record" in the discussion, and as a consequence the reported viewpoint is not something for which the interviewer or the employing news organization can be held responsible.

These attributional practices have a significance which extends beyond the interviewer's professional stance. Anyone who is watching the program may notice that the interviewer is taking care to disavow certain bits of talk rather than others. Such remarks may well have seemed controversial in any case, but because they are being treated so gingerly they come across as distinctly contentious or objectionable. Thus, even as the footing shift achieves neutralism for its speaker, it simultaneously portrays the attributed item as nonneutralistic or opinionated in character.

By implication, the selective deployment of attributional practices helps to establish and maintain the separation between what Hallin (1994) has referred to as the domain of consensus versus the domain of legitimate controversy in public discourse. As we saw in chapter 2, this fundamental division in the public sphere is constituted in part through the selective way in which public figures are invited to participate in news interviews (Croteau and Hoynes 1994) and the broad manner in which they are treated on the air, but it is also constituted through the differential articulation of specific elements of political discourse by interviewers obligated to remain neutral. With some elements asserted straightforwardly while others are deflected toward a third party, the boundaries between matters of fact and opinion, between domains of consensus and controversy, are thus established and reinforced.

Neutralism as a collaborative construction

How do interviewees respond to such maneuvers? Since the attributed assertions are often introduced in the spirit of devil's advocacy, interviewees generally seek to refute them. However, they typically do so in a way that does not challenge the interviewer's neutralistic posture. For the most part, interviewees accept the basic premise of the footing shift, that the interviewer is speaking on behalf of a third party rather than expressing his or her own views. Within this framework, three distinct forms of response may be distinguished. These range from responses that actively validate and reinforce the interviewer's neutralism, to those that merely avoid undermining that stance.

In the most validating type of response, the interviewee *cites the same third party* as responsible for the previously expressed viewpoint. This typically happens when the interviewee makes some reference to that viewpoint in the course of countering it. In (12) the IR's original attribution is marked at arrow 1, and the IE's parallel attribution is at arrow 2.

(12)   US ABC *Nightline*: 22 July 1985: South Africa
          IR: Charles Gibson   IE: Reverend Allan Boesak

```
 1  IR:      Reverend Boesak lemme a- pick up a point uh
 2       1→ the Ambassador made. What- what assurances can
 3           you give u:s .hh that (.) talks between
 4           moderates in that country will take pla:ce .h when:
 5           it see:ms that any black leader who is willing
 6           to talk to the Government is branded as the
 7           Ambassador said a collaborator and is then
 8           punished.=
 9  IE:   2→ =Eh theh- the- the Ambassador has it wrong.
10           It's not the people who want to talk with
11           the Government that are branded collaborators
12           it is: those people .hh who are given powers
13           by the Goverment that they use in an oppressive
14           fashion .hh within the township that are branded
15           collaborators . . .
```

The IR initially relayed the viewpoint of "the Ambassador" from South Africa (arrow 1). The IE eventually presents an elaborate rebuttal (lines 12–15), but he begins by negating the previous view (lines 9–11), and in so doing he attributes it to the same third party ("the Ambassador" in line 9), thus validating the IR's neutralistic stance.

A similar pattern may be observed in the following excerpt, from the discussion of nuclear waste with which we began this chapter.

(13) US ABC *Nightline*: 6 June 1985: Nuclear Waste
       IR: Ted Koppel   IE: James Steele

```
 1  IE:      ... And if you look et- simply the record in
 2            the low level waste field over the last
 3            fifteen to twenty years ... the record is not
 4            very good (0.3) an' it doesn't give one a cause
 5            for optimism.=
 6  IR:   1→ =You heard what Doctor Yalow said earlier in
 7        1→ this broadcast she'll have an opportunity to
 8        1→ express her own opinions again but she seems to
 9            feel that it is an eminently soluble problem,
10            and that ultimately that radioactive material
11            can be reduced, to manageable quantities, 'n put
12            in the bottom of a salt mine.
13  IE:   2→ The p- the point that she was making earlier
14            about (.) reprocessing of: the fuel rods goes
15            right to the heart (.) of the way a lotta
16            people look at this particular issue ...
```

Here the IR initially relays the pro-nuclear viewpoint of "Doctor Yalow" (arrow 1). The IE will eventually present the anti-nuclear viewpoint, but he first negates the previous view (lines 13–16) and attributes it to the same third party ("the point that she was making" at arrow 2). In both of these examples, then, the IEs present themselves as countering the views of the cited third party rather than the IR, and this type of response maximally ratifies and advances the IR's neutralistic footing.

In the second form of response, the interviewee does not go so far as to actually name a third party. Instead, he or she simply refers to the disputed viewpoint without attributing it to anyone in particular, as in the following excerpt (arrowed). Here the IE asserts disagreement with the prior view, and in so doing he refers to it as "that premise" – noticably absent here is a possessive pronoun (e.g., "your premise") that would attach it to the IR or to anyone in particular.

(14)   US PBS *NewsHour*: 22 July 1985: South Africa
       IR: Jim Lehrer   IE: Herbert Beukes

```
1   IR:    Finally Mister Ambassador as you know the
2          critics say that the purpose of the state of
3          emergency the real purpose of the state of
4          'merjuh- uh state of emergency is to suppress
5          political dissent. those who are opposed to the
6          apartheid goverment of South Africa. Is that so
7          (.)
8   IE:    I would have to: uh- take issue with
9      →   that premise. because...
```

In the next example, the attributive verb is formulated in the passive voice ("Now if that is being said") so that its agent remains unformulated.

(15)   US PBS *NewsHour*: 22 July 1985: South Africa
       IR: Robert MacNeil   IE: Herbert Beukes

```
1   IR:    But all the people around the world, the
2          Common Market foreign ministers today:, the
3          Secretary: uh General: of the forty seven
4          member: uh British Commonweal:th, uh members of
5          the af- banned African National Congress, .hhhh our-
6          our guest Doctor Motlana all say that- and the
7          American statement we've just heard, .hhh that
8          the reason for the violence that the state of
9          emergency: is designed to sto:p, the reason for
10         that violence, is the policy of apartheid.
11  IE:  → .hhhh Now if: that is being said 'n for the
12         argument it's being accepted, .hh then:...
```

In both cases the IEs cast themselves in opposition to an anonymous point of view without reference to the individuals or groups who may endorse that viewpoint. In essence, these IEs are arguing impersonally against a *viewpoint* rather than its *advocates*.

Although a responsible party is not explicitly named in the previous two examples, in the latter case it is strongly implied that responsibility does not lie with the IR. Notice that the attributive verb is formulated in the present progressive tense ("if that is being said"), thereby evoking an ongoing process of "saying" which cannot be ascribed to the IR per se. More generally, whenever an interviewee refers to the prior viewpoint but declines to attribute it to the interviewer, the effect is to reinforce – at least implicitly – the interviewer's neutralistic posture.

In the third and final form of response, interviewees may simply present a contrasting argument without referring to the prior viewpoint in any direct way. This occurs in the following excerpt from a discussion of South Africa. The IR reports a criticism to the effect that the South African Government's decision to declare a state of emergency will cause more violence in the country.

(16)   US PBS *NewsHour*: 22 July 1985: South Africa
        IR: Jim Lehrer   IE: Herbert Beukes
  1 IR: What do you say to Bishop Tutu and others who
  2   have said since the state of emergency was
  3   declared that this will cause even more
  4   violence rather than t'stop the violence
  5   that's in effect,
  6   (0.4)
  7 IE: Well- (0.2) it is pretty clear that something
  8   has to be do:ne. h.hh in order to stop the
  9   violence. .hh Now the state of emergency: uh
 10   is intended .hh to clamp down on that violence.
 11   h.hh Uh to stop it somehow . . .

Here the IE makes no reference to the prior viewpoint in the course of countering it. Unlike the response forms examined previously, this one cannot properly be characterized as validating, explicitly or implicitly, the IR's proposedly neutralistic stance. But it does not undermine that stance either, and this it shares with the other response forms. In each case IEs refrain from taking actions which would imply that the prior assertion is an expression of the IR's own point of view. They cast themselves in opposition to *the views conveyed by IRs* rather than in opposition to *the IRs themselves*.

It would seem that the neutralistic posture achieved through third-party attributions is quite literally a collaborative achievement. While interviewers initially present themselves as disinterestedly relaying the views of others, interviewees usually act in ways that validate and reinforce that stance. The resulting appearance of neutralism is thus accomplished through a process of co-construction to which both parties actively contribute. We have already registered a similar point in relation to the question–answer turn-taking system discussed in chapter 4, but it is equally true in relation to the ancillary practices of third party attribution. It is important to bear in mind that while interviewees may privately suspect that the interviewer endorses the viewpoint being invoked, they rarely act on such suspicions. Most of the time their responses serve to reinforce and extend a "definition of the situation" in which the interviewer is understood to be relaying the views of others. Of course, interviewees are not always so cooperative – their involvement in the process also enables them to subvert the appearance of neutralism, a theme to which we return at the end of this chapter.

Neutralism and credibility

Citing a third party, beyond fostering neutralism, has certain ancillary benefits from the interviewer's point of view. When third parties have recognized expertise in the subject, they can be invoked in such a way as to endow an asserted viewpoint with a modicum of credibility. Thus, even though interviewers tend to avoid *explicitly* endorsing or rejecting the views that they report, they do act in ways that have an *implicit* bearing on the credibility of such views. As we shall see, it is more common for interviewers to upgrade rather than downgrade credibility in this manner, thereby placing interviewees in the position of having to wrestle with compelling alternative points of view.

While some third parties are intrinsically authoritative, interviewers may make a special point of highlighting their authoritativeness in the course of citing them. In this connection, the specific manner in which the third party is referred to or described can be highly significant. As a general principle, any person or group may be characterized in a virtually infinite number of ways, each of which is equally "correct" (Sacks, 1972). Person characterizations thus always entail a choice between alternative formulations, and for the news interviewer seeking to play the role of devil's advocate effectively, this choice is often conditioned by the pursuit of credibility. For instance, notice how the IR refers to those responsible for the view that Bosnian prison facilities are tantamount to "concentration camps." This highly judgmental characterization is first attributed to "people" generally (arrow 1) but is subsequently specified by reference to "the Bosnians themselves" (arrow 2).

(17) UK BBC *Radio Today*: June 1993: Bosnian Camps
      IR: John Humphrys   IE: Ian Smedley

```
1  IR:   1→ .hhh People have used the phrase concentration
2        camps:
3        2→ and the Bosnians themselves have used that
4        phrase. Do you believe there's any
5        justification for that at all?
```

This latter formulation invokes a third party with first-hand knowledge of the camps in question. By shifting reference terms, the IR has subtly enhanced the credibility of the viewpoint he is conveying.

The effort to accentuate a third party's authoritativeness is perhaps most apparent when interviewers refer to that party, not by a minimal name and/or title (e.g., Senator X, Doctor Y), but through a more elaborated characterization. For instance, when an IR relays President Carter's critical assessment of the US Government's failure to join the Soviet Union's moratorium on nuclear weapons testing (lines 13–14), notice the elaborateness with which Carter is characterized (lines 8–12).

(18) US ABC *Nightline*: 6 Oct 1986: Nuclear Weapons
      IR: Ted Koppel   IE: Frank Gaffney, Defense Dept.

```
1  IE:    ... We don't like hh (.) uh (.) having: :
2         arguments made which we feel are .hh uh (.) not
3         only not (0.9) contributing to: : (0.3) positive
4         and effective arms control, .hhh uh but we of
5         course don't like having people (0.3) e-
6         misrepresenting: our view of what would
7         constitute (.) effective arms control.
8  IR:   → We:ll now when a former president of the
9        → United Sta:tes, and a man who knows a little
10       → something about nuclear weapons, having
11       → ser:ved on a nuclear submari:ne and was
12       → himself an engineer, when Jimmy Carter calls
13         it an embarrassment. .hhh to have the United
14         States not (.) match the ba:n, uh: not exactly a
15         lightweight.
16 IE:    .hhh The President of the United States today:,
17         is Ronald Reagan. and the President (0.3) has
18         seen our problem very clearly, .hh as one of
19         ensuring:, (0.4) as long as we have to rely upon
20         nuclear weapons for deterrence, .hh that we: (.)
21         can do so with confidence. and that require
22         testing them
```

In addition to referring to Carter as "a former President of the United States" (lines 8–9), the IR also provides an elaborate description of him as knowledgeable on the issue at hand (9–10), as well as a description of the credentials and experiences which form the basis of that knowledge (11–12). All of this material precedes the actual report of Carter's assessment (13–14). But the IR goes even further – after the assessment, he summarizes (in lines 14–15) the cumulative upshot of his Carter description: "not exactly a lightweight." Given the credentials enumerated just previously, this characterization stands as a transparently understated commentary on Carter's authoritativeness.

None of this escapes the notice of the IE, who as a Reagan administration official is motivated to defend the administration against criticism. As he constructs his rebuttal, he enhances its credibility by citing the current President (16–17). One president's views are thus invoked to counter another's views. Indeed, the IE engages in a bit of one-upmanship here by noting, prior to the counterassessment, that he is speaking on behalf of the president who is *currently* in office (note the emphasis on "today" in line 16). The IE's response thus constitutes a second move in a developing contest for authoritativeness and credibility.

Credibility can be further enhanced by commenting on the range of experts who believe or endorse a position. While an unpopular view may be dismissed as the idiosyncratic product of a particular person's perspective, a widely endorsed viewpoint is endowed with intersubjective validation. Thus, when an IR reports that civil disorder or violent revolution is imminent in South Africa (lines 4–6), this viewpoint is attributed to a collectivity of recent program guests (2–3, arrowed).

(19)   US PBS *NewsHour*: 25 July 1985: South Africa Sanctions
       IR: Jim Lehrer   IE: John Chettle

```
1   IR:     .hhhh Mister Chettle what d'you say to those
2       →   who: people who've said this on our program
3       →   several times now:: uh in the last uh few
4           weeks, that .hh time is running out in South
5           Africa. >that something must b- must be done:
6           (.) or the whole thing is gonna go up
7   IE:     Well- eh that's been said for the last twenty
8           five years:. and I've heard it pretty
```

9   continuously ever since then:. uh: I don't (.)
10   uh think that that's true . . .

Just prior to this extract, another IE (Sheena Duncan, a South
African critic of apartheid) made essentially the same point, so the
IR is in effect picking up on that point and re-presenting it to the
IE (John Chettle, a defender of the South African status quo) for
rebuttal. However, the IR does not attribute this point to the prior
IE alone; by indicating that this viewpoint has been expressed by
various guests "several times now in the past few weeks," he depicts that view as increasingly widespread and thus implies that it
represents an emerging consensus among knowledgeable insiders.

The IE orients to the credibility being proposed here and attempts
to undermine it (lines 7–10). He does not actually deny that there is
something of a consensus on the imminence of disorder/revolution,
but he casts doubt on that view by noting that people have been
saying that "for the last twenty five years:." The upshot, which
remains implicit, is that since revolution has plainly not occurred
during this time, such predictions have regularly been misguided,
and the more recent predictions that the IR is referring to are apt to
be misguided as well. Note that this way of casting doubt is designed
specifically to show that the sheer number of persons endorsing a
position is no guarantee of its validity.

In a more dramatic illustration of this phenomenon, the IR proposes that a viewpoint is universally held among those in positions
of authority. The following occurred in an interview concerning the
South African Government's imposition of a state of emergency (see
line 7, arrowed).

(20)   US PBS *NewsHour*: 22 July 1985: South Africa
       IR: Robert MacNeil   IE: Herbert Beukes

1   IE: . . . And that is the issue of (0.2) violence.
2   .hh And if we can get out of that cycle exactly
3   to break hh that cycle. .hh I think it'll be:-
4   uh in the interest of everybody .h to get then
5   to the point (0.3) of dealing with peaceful
6   reforms.=
7   IR: → =But all people around the world the Common
8   → Market foreign ministers today: the Secretary:
9   → uh General: of the forty seven member: uh
10   → British Commonwea:th uh members of the af-

11   → banned African National <u>Co</u>ngress, .hhhh our- our
12   → guest Doctor Mot<u>la</u>na <u>all</u> say that- and the
13   → A<u>me</u>rican statement we've just <u>heard</u> .hhh that
14   the <u>rea</u>son <u>for</u> the violence that the <u>sta</u>te of
15   eme<u>rge</u>ncy: is de<u>si</u>gned to <u>sto</u>:p, the <u>rea</u>son <u>for</u>
16   that violence, <u>is</u> the policy of ap<u>a</u>rtheid.
17   IE: .hhhh Now if: <u>that</u> is being <u>sa</u>id 'n for the
18   <u>ar</u>gument it's being ac<u>cep</u>ted .hh then: (0.3) uh-
19   to <u>do</u> so: an to <u>de</u>al with it in a <u>pea</u>ceful
20   <u>ma</u>nner. (0.4) you <u>have</u> to <u>get</u> a<u>way</u> from the
21   point of <u>vi</u>olence . . .

After Herbert Beukes, the South African Ambassador to the USA, justifies new restrictions on civil liberties as necessary to end the current cycle of violence (lines 1–6), the IR questions whether such emergency powers are truly necessary by proposing that apartheid is the primary cause of the current violence. He presents this view as held by "<u>all</u> the <u>pe</u>ople ar<u>ou</u>nd the <u>w</u>orld" (line 7), and he goes on to enumerate a list of five highly prominent parties who believe that apartheid is indeed the root cause of unrest. Notice that after producing the fourth party, the IR begins to launch into the focal assertion (line 12) but cuts off to add a fifth party before proceeding. In one sense this list works to support the initial claim of universality by providing concrete instances of its adherants, but the list also allows the IR to display each party's authoritative status. In short, this viewpoint has been greatly strengthened, and this may be why Beukes does not attempt to refute it directly – he "grudgingly" allows it (via the hypthetical "if"-clause at lines 17–18) and then resists its larger implications (by insisting that violence must be stopped before apartheid can be dealt with).

It is striking that in both of the previous examples, neutralism remains firmly intact. Despite the fact that the IR has strongly boosted the credibility of the viewpoint in question, he has not actually endorsed it as his own; and the IE in both cases responds accordingly, treating it as an anonymous point of view rather than something that belongs to the IR per se ("that's been said for the last twenty-five years" in excerpt [19]; "if that is being said" in excerpt [20]). Thus, even at a clearly adversarial juncture in these respective interviews, the interviewee continues to "play along" with the interviewer's posture of neutralism.

Tribune of the people

Just as interviewers can invoke knowledgeable experts, they can also present themselves as speaking on behalf of the general public. This type of footing was adopted by Ted Koppel in an interview with ousted Phillippine President Ferdinand Marcos. Just as Koppel broaches the issue of Marcos's wife Imelda and her enormous shoe collection (lines 1–3, 6), he makes a point of indicating that this is "what most people are interested in."

(21)   US ABC *Nightline*: 4 Apr 1986: Ferdinand Marcos
          IR: Ted Koppel   IE: Ferdinand Marcos

```
 1   IR:   → Whe:n people heard I was coming out (.) to do an
 2           → interview with you (1.0) you know what most
 3           → people are interested in?
 4   IE:     Mm mm.
 5           (0.4)
 6   IR:     Your wife's:: three thousand pairs of shoes.
 7   IE:     How many shoes
 8   IR:     How many sh[oes
 9   IE:                 [can you wear: (0.2) on (.) twenty
10           years.
11   IR:     Exactly (.) how many can you?
```

Koppel thus presents this issue, not as his own personal concern or of concern to political elites, but as a matter of general interest to the public at large. Correspondingly, he presents himself as a "tribune of the people" who relays their concerns and interests to those in public life.

References to the public operate rather differently than references to experts or other elites, and the footing achieved through this practice has different ancillary benefits for the interviewer. Recall that interviewers invoke experts mainly during contentious opinion statements (both question-preliminary and free-standing), where the benefit is enhanced credibility for the viewpoint being expressed. In contrast, interviewers invoke the public more broadly, not only during opinion statements but often for the very act of questioning itself. As the previous excerpt illustrates, the public may be presented as the primary motivation for a given question, the reason why the interviewer chose to ask that particular question at that moment. Correspondingly, the main ancillary benefit for the interviewer is not *credibility* so much as *legitimacy* – speaking on behalf of the public both neutralizes and legitimates a question by casting it as something the public either wants or needs to know. By implication, this practice also increases the pressure on interviewees to be forthcoming in response. It is more difficult for an interviewee to sidestep or evade a question that has been packaged in this way, because that could be taken as an offense not merely to the interviewer but to the broader public that he or she claims to represent.

The legitimizing import of a tribune-of-the-people stance is apparent in the selectivity with which this stance is taken up. Interviewers adopt this stance only occasionally and in a limited range of interactional environments – most often during highly probing or adversarial lines of questioning. Consider the Marcos interview excerpted above. The interview began with the IR asking comparatively open-ended and downright sympathetic questions regarding Marcos's trials and tribulations as an exiled leader (see below):

(22)   US ABC *Nightline*: 4 Apr 1986: Ferdinand Marcos
       IR: Ted Koppel   IE: Ferdinand Marcos

   IR: President Marcos, you're a very proud man. I
         think even your enemies recognize that. Tell me
         a little bit about what it has been like for you
         these past few weeks...

   IR: Where can you go? I mean, it must be a terribly
         humiliating experience. At one point you were
         thinking of going to Spain...

   IR: So what you're really saying is that in some
         fashion the American Government was helping the
         rebel forces against you...

These questions are offered straightforwardly, without any overt reference to the public. It is only with the distinctly unflattering matter of the shoe collection – which had been widely reported by the news media and treated as emblematic of the aristocratic extravagance of the Marcos regime – that the IR makes a point of emphasizing that it is a matter of broad public concern.

Interviewers invoke the public not only when broaching a sensitive issue, but also in more transparently hostile circumstances, such as when overtly criticizing an interviewee. This occurred in an interview with a convicted child molester who had served out his sentence but remains in confinement because he has been judged a

continuing threat to society. The IE, arguing for his release, makes
an impassioned claim to have been cured of his propensity to molest
(lines 1–5), and he begins to weep at this point (line 6–8).

(23)   US CBS *60 Minutes*: 12 Jan 1998: Stephanie's Law
        IR: Ed Bradley   IE: Leroy Hendricks
1   IE: Well the law was the one that brought me here.
2   (0.5) But it was me that decided that I wanted
3   to stop ( ) .hh I want to stop the molesting,
4   I want to stop the offending, I want to stop the
5   hurting? (0.2) ((sniff)) I want to heal myself.
6   ((choked up voice))
7   (2.5) ((sniff:::))
8   (2.5) ((removes eyeglasses to wipe eyes))
9   IR: → Do you know that there're people watching (0.7)
10   → who will say: that that's: part of the deal he's
11   doing=ya know.
12 IE: Oh I know. But I was an em[osh-
13 IR: [That's part of the
14   act.
15 IE: ((sniff))=Well- (0.5) .h I wish they'da known me
16   before . . .

At this emotionally charged moment, just when the IE appears to
be most distraught and vulnerable, the IR counters by proposing, in
effect, that he is merely putting on an act (lines 9–11), presumably
as a ploy to win release from prison. And when the IE attempts
to respond (line 12), the IR cuts him off to reiterate this point
(cf., Jefferson, 1981), characterizing the IE's emotional plea as "part
of the act" (lines 13–14). This disparaging retort is framed as something that "people watching . . . will say" (arrowed), and the IE treats
it accordingly – as a general sentiment rather than an expression of
the IR's point of view ("I wish they'da known me before" in lines
15–16).

   In a still more hostile variant of this practice, an IR invokes the
public when stepping back from the specifics of what has just been
said to mount a broader condemnation on the IE and the profession with which he is affiliated. Consider this excerpt (seen earlier)
from an interview with a canine psychiatrist who uses psychiatric
principles to treat dogs' behavioral and emotional problems. At the
opening of this segment, the IE is praising a dog at his side (line 1).

(24) US NBC *Dateline*: 16 Dec 1997: Canine Psychiatry
      IR: Unknown   IE: Unknown
1   IE: G<u>oo</u>:d b<u>oy</u>:.
2   IR: → A l<u>o</u>tta people would hear: (.) about your
3   → prof<u>e</u>ssion.
4   IE: Y<u>e</u>:s.=
5   IR: → =and say that's a bunch o'p<u>o</u>ppycock.
6   IE: Y<u>e</u>:s,
7   (0.2)
8   IR: And y<u>ou</u> say:?
9   (.)
10 IE: I say they're ent<u>i</u>tled to their op<u>i</u>nion. .hh
11   And I would <u>a</u>lso say to those people that
12   they'll bel<u>ie</u>ve that (0.9) .h r<u>i</u>ght up until
13   their v<u>e</u>ry f<u>a</u>vorite dog gr<u>ow</u>ls at them. (0.2)
14   .hh And then you'd be surpr<u>i</u>sed at how qu<u>i</u>ckly
15   .hh people can s<u>u</u>ddenly become a convert.

The IR bluntly asserts that the IE's profession "is a bunch of poppy-cock" (line 5). Obviously this denunciation is neither responsive to nor targeted at the previous turn at talk; it is aimed at the entire profession as it has been represented by the IE over the course of the encounter. And once again, this remark is cast as something that "a lotta people" would say (arrowed). As hostile as this question is, the IR does not align with the viewpoint it expresses, and the IE in response validates its neutralistic quality ("I say they're entitled to their opinion" in line 10).

The tribune-of-the-people stance played an important role in one of the most highly anticipated news interviews ever conducted – David Frost's famous 1977 encounter with former President Richard Nixon. This was Nixon's first major interview since resigning in scandal, and many tuned in to see what the former President would say regarding the events that drove him from office. This case nicely illustrates both the import of a tribune-of-the-people stance and the effort interviewers expend to achieve it.

The interview focused on Nixon's involvement in the Watergate affair and its aftermath, and in the course of the discussion Frost succeeded in getting Nixon to admit to having made "mistakes." At one point, however, Frost tries to induce Nixon to go further than this, pointing out that the word "mistakes" seems "not enough for people to understand" (lines 1–3). Thus, the initial push for a stronger admission of guilt is presented as being done on behalf of "people" generally.

(25a)   UK BBCTV: 1977: Watergate in Retrospect
         IR: David Frost   IE: Richard Nixon

```
 1  IR:    ... Would you go further than mistakes:: (.) the
 2          wor::d (0.9) that seems n- n- (.) not enough for
 3          people to understa:nd.
 4          (1.5)
 5  IE:    What wor::d would you:: (.) express,
 6          (3.8)
 7  IR:    My goodness that's a:: hhh (0.2) I:: think (.)
 8          that there're (.) three things. (.) since you
 9          ask me, (0.2) I:: would like to hear you sa:y
10          >I think the American people< would like to hear
11          you say ...
12          ((question continues))
```

However, when Nixon invites Frost to indicate what word he would prefer (line 5), Frost momentarily strays from the safety of a tribune-of-the-people stance. Frost begins an extended question by indicating that there are three things that "I:: would like to hear you say" (line 9), emphasizing the first-person pronoun "I" and thus framing the question-in-progress as an expression of his own personal preferences. Notice, however, that he carefully modulates this stance just as he launches into it, pointing out parenthetically that he is expressing his preferences at Nixon's request ("since you ask me") rather than on his own initiative.

Even this modulated stance is not maintained for long. Executing self-repair on the utterance in progress, Frost adds that this is what "the American people would like to hear you say" (lines 10–11). Frost seems to treat this shift of footing as something of a priority – he speeds up (denoted in the excerpt by the ">" symbol) just as he launches into the clause containing this attribution. He thus quickly retreats from the dangerously non-neutralistic footing he had previously taken up.

All of this maneuvering to achieve a tribune-of-the-people stance is explicable given the gravity of the question that is eventually delivered. Frost pointedly asks Nixon to make three extraordinary admissions of guilt – the beginning of each is arrowed below.

(25b)   UK BBCTV: 1977: Watergate in Retrospect
        IR: David Frost   IE: Richard Nixon
```
 1  IR:      ...I:: would like to hear you sa:y >I think the
 2            American people would like to hear you say. .hh
 3        1→ (.) O:ne is::, (0.7) the:re was probably mo: :re
 4            (0.2) tha: :n, (0.4) mista: :kes there was:: (0.7)
 5            wro:ngdoing (0.2) whether it was a cri: :me > or
 6            not=yes it may have been a crime< too:. (0.6)
 7        2→ Secondly:: (0.8) I did h (0.6) and I'm saying
 8            this without (.) questioning the motives
 9            all right. I di:d h (0.2) abu:se th' power I had
10            as President. (0.2) or:: ha: :ve (.) not
11            fulfilled it (.) totality, .h (0.2) (eh) the oath
12            of office that- that's the second thing, (0.2)
13        3→ And thir: :dly, (0.7) I: put the American peo-
14            people through two years of needless agony > an'
15            I apologize for that. (0.9) And I: say that- (.)
16            you've explai:ned your motives, (.) I think
17            tho:se >are the categories.< (0.7) And I kno:w
18            how >difficult it is for anyone,< and most of
19            all you: but I: think h (0.8) that (.) people
20            need to hear it, (0.4) and I think unless you
21            say it, (0.6) you're gonna be hau:nted >for the
22            rest of your life.<
```

Frost asks Nixon to admit: (i) that some of his actions were wrong and possibly criminal, (ii) that he abused the power of the presidency, and (iii) that he put the American people through two years of needless agony. Frost also asks Nixon to apologize for the last offense. Frost himself acknowledges the magnitude of what he is requesting when he subsequently notes "how difficult it is for anyone, and most of all you..." (lines 18–19). But as he completes this question, he reiterates that this is something that "people need to hear" (lines 19–20). In so doing, he strives to neutralize and legitimate what is an extremely face-threatening and incriminating set of requests, while increasing the pressure on Nixon to comply with them.

Neutralism in jeopardy

In general, as we have seen, interviewers and their guests collaborate to maintain an order of interaction that casts the interviewer as an impartial elicitor of information and opinion. Occasionally, however, this professional stance can become compromised with negative ramifications for interviewers and their employing organizations. The cautionary tales with which we began this chapter – tales involving highly aggressive interrogations by Dan Rather and David Frost – illustrate the stakes involved. When interviewers are seen as having an axe to grind, they risk damaging their journalistic reputations, alienating a segment of the audience, and incoming negative sanctions from various interested parties.

There are a variety of interactional pathways that can lead to the loss of the neutralistic posture. We provided a general overview of these pathways in chapter 4, focusing on departures from the question–answer turn-taking system and the neutralism it embodies. The practices in the present chapter add a further layer of complexity to this process, for they suggest that neutralism is founded on both the activity of questioning and the use of third-party attributions or shifts of footing – in effect, the posture of neutralism is maintained through two distinct but interlocking sets of practices. Here we focus on the footing dimension, and how threats to this aspect of neutralism are managed and dealt with.

The differential vulnerability of question prefaces

As noted in chapter 4, departures from neutralism tend to be instigated by interviewees, and one way this can occur is when interviewees respond "early" to a question-preliminary statement. Recall that interviewees usually collaborate in the maintenance of neutralism by withholding talk until the interviewer's question is completed, thus treating any preliminary statements as innocuous "background information" for the question-in-progress. Conversely, by declining to collaborate – that is, by responding immediately to such question prefaces – interviewees inhibit the completion of a question and treat the prefatory statement as an expressive action in its own right.

While question prefaces are generally vulnerable to early and hence pre-emptive responses, not all such responses are equally damaging to neutralism. When the preface consists of a straightforward assertion of opinion, a direct response can indeed cast the interviewer as a nonneutral advocate for that point of view. For example, in an interview concerning the prison system (discussed in the previous chapter) the IR makes an assertion regarding the substantial efforts made to rehabilitate criminals (lines 1–3), apparently building toward a question about what should be done to help the victims of crime (see lines 19–20 below). The IE sharply disagrees with this assertion, and he does so after only the first part of the assertion has been completed (4–5, 7, 10, 12, 14) and hence before the question is delivered. In so doing, he treats the IR as having taken up a position on rehabilitation rather than merely leading up to a question on the subject.

(26)   UK ATV *Afternoon Plus*: 7 Mar 1979: Victims' Rights
          IR: Unknown   IE: Lord Longford

```
 1  IR:    .hhhh Lord Longford erm (0.5) we- we- we do take
 2          a lot of trouble (0.8) rehabilitating (0.5)
 3          criminals. .hhh er: [and long]
 4  IE:                         [Well I d]on't- I
 5          [don't (  )-]
 6  IR:    [long term ] scheme for the criminals.
 7  IE:    No I don't agree wi[th that  at all (sir).]
 8  IR:                        [But we don't  seem ] to
 9          [Sorry.]
10  IE:    [(   )-] er [Sorry (    ) I] don't agree with=
11  IR:              [I- I see. Well-]
12  IE:    =that statement not a- no way. [We d]o very=
13  IR:                                   [Well-]
14  IE:    =little to rehabilitate criminal[ s ]
15  IR:                                    [W]ell we seem
16          to spend a lot of money on it even if we do
17          little.=
18  IE:    =Very little.=
19  IR:    =erm ((coughs)) What are your recommendations
20          to giving the victim a better deal.
```

Early responses of this sort treat the statement as a contentious action in its own right, and because the statement is asserted by the IR on his own behalf, he is indeed cast as advocating a point of view.

However, the ramifications of a pre-emptive response are much less severe when the prefatory statement has been attributed to a third party. As we pointed out earlier in this chapter, third-party attributed statements – by virtue of their intrinsic neutralism and utility in soliciting the interviewee's point of view – often function as virtual questions. Thus, when they are used to lead up to a grammatically formulated question, any pre-emptive response has no real bearing on the interviewers's neutralism. For example, Republican presidential candidate Pat Buchanan began to respond early (line 9 below) to a question-preliminary statement (lines 4–7) about the necessity of raising social security taxes. But since the viewpoint contained in that statement was portrayed as a matter of common consensus ("I don't think anyone doubts . . . " in line 4) the IR's neutralism was left essentially intact.

(27)   US ABC *This Week*: 18 Feb 1996: Social Security Taxes
          IR: George Will   IE: Pat Buchanan

```
 1   IR:     . . . Now- uh- my question about- the-
 2   IE:     Mm h[m,
 3   IR:          [the social security tax increase (was) .hh
 4            I don't think anyone doubts that by now absent a
 5            tax increase .hh social security an' all the
 6            social security recipients in this state .hh uh:
 7            would be=h de- in default?
 8            (.)
 9   IE:     tlk I don't [(agree with-)
10   IR:                 [How would you have saved it.
11   IE:     hhuh huh. .hh I would've- I would've done a
12            different approach . . .
```

IRs in this context may still strive to continue (line 10), not to preserve the posture of neutralism so much as to get the question proper out and onto the table.

Thus, question prefaces are differentially vulnerable to efforts at penetrating the interviewer's shield of neutralism. Unattributed statements of opinion are highly vulnerable to pre-emptive responses that cast the interviewer as advocating a point of view rather than behaving impartially, whereas third-party attributed statements embody a second line of defense which protects against such moves. Early responses to such statements may be uncooperative from the standpoint of the interviewer's effort to develop a question, but they have little bearing on neutralism per se.[5]

---

[5] Similarly, early responses to second-party attributed statements – that is, statements attributed to the IE – are also inconsequential in this respect. In the following extract from the infamous Bush–Rather interview, Bush responds immediately (see especially lines 12–13) to Rather's question-preliminary paraphrase of what Bush had said earlier about his involvement in the Iran-Contra affair (5, 7–8, 10–11).

The residual vulnerability of third-party statements

Although third-party attributed statements are less vulnerable (compared to unattributed assertions) to charges of bias, they are by no means invincible. Just as questions can be attacked notwithstanding their neutralistic character (as we saw in chapter 4), third-party statements can meet a similar fate. What is the basis for such attacks? While it may be literally true that a given viewpoint was indeed advocated by a third party, the interviewer is under no obligation to introduce it into the interview. The decision to invoke a given viewpoint is a voluntary choice, an exercise of agency on the interviewer's part. It is in recognition of that fact that an interviewee can raise the spectre of bias lying behind such choices.

For a mild illustration of this, consider excerpt 28 from an interview with Lord de Lisle, the Chairperson of the National Association for Freedom (NAFF), a British right-wing political pressure group. De Lisle is asked about possible foreign sources of his organization's funding (lines 3–5), and about the excessive secretiveness of the organization (lines 8–14). Both questions contain assertions which are attributed to "some people" (lines 4 and 8, respectively).

footnote 5 cont'd

US CBS *Evening News*: 25 Jan 1988: Iran-Contra
IR: Dan Rather   IE: George Bush

```
 1   IE:   ...an' I've answered every question put before me. =Now if you
 2         have a question, .hh [(what is it.)]
 3   IR:                        [I  do   ha]ve one.
 4   IE:   Ple[ase]
 5   IR:      [Ah-] I have one. .hh [hh You have said that- if yo]ud=
 6   IE:                            [Please  fire  away  heh-hah]
 7   IR:   =had know::n, you said tha' if you had known this was
 8         an arms for hostag[es sw]ap, .hh that=
 9   IE:                     [yes  ]
10   IR:   =you would've opposed it. . hhhh you
11         also [said thet-]   [that you did NOT KNOW thet y-]
12   IE:       [E x a c t]ly [(m-  may-   may  I-)   may   I  ]
13         answer that.
14         (0.4)
15   IE:   (Th[uh] right (  )-]
16   IR:      [That wasn't a] question. =it w[as a statement eh-]
17   IE:                                     [Yes  it   was   a ]
18         statement [and I'll answer it. The president]=
19   IR:             [Let me ask the question if I may first]
20   IE:   =created this program, .h has testified er s:tated
21         publicly, (.) he did not think it was arms fer hostages...
```

(28) UK BBC Radio *World at One*: July 1978: Freedom Group
      IR: Julian Mannion   IE: Lord de Lisle
1   IE: I've received <u>fa</u>:r less than I hoped I would.
2   (0.7)
3   IR: .hh What about (.) foreign sources Lord de
4   Lisle, some people have claimed that you've
5   received money from: (.) people abroad.
6   IE: We've received money fr'm everybody who shares
7   our views.
8   IR: .hhh Some people: uh: make the charge against
9   your: uh organization that it is excessively
10   secretive.=Not just about uh the sources of your
11   funding .hh but also about day to day details
12   like for example .hh your address in London.=You
13   don't publish your address on any of your
14   documents do yo[u.
15 IE: →   [You ask a number of very hostile
16   questions. (.) .hh We keep our address secret
17   because .hh we remember that Mr. Ross McWhirter
18   was murdered by the Irish. .hh We remember . . .
19   (continues)

After the second question, de Lisle characterizes the line of questioning as "very hostile" (arrowed). Thus, notwithstanding the neutralism of the "some people" attributions, he manages to imply that the
IR is being persistently antagonistic in his choice of questions. It is
notable that this is only a momentary digression from the ongoing
line of questioning – having registered his objection (at line 15), de
Lisle then proceeds to answer the question at hand (lines 16–18).

A more consequential attack occurred in a highly adversarial interview with Neil Kinnock, then leader of the British Labour Party.
In this excerpt, the IR questions Kinnock about his "authoritarian"
leadership style, and Kinnock – clearly annoyed at the line of questioning – attacks it as not newsworthy (at lines 5 and 7). To defend
the line of questioning, the IR attributes the accusation of authoritarianism to "some delegates" who were reacting to a speech given
by Kinnock's deputy, Roy Hattersley (lines 8–9, 11–14 and 16–18).
This attributed viewpoint in turn becomes the object of attack when
Kinnock strongly implies – through the accusatory question "Did
you?" (arrowed) – that the allegation of authoritarianism actually
reflects the IR's own biases.

(29)   UK BBC Radio *World at One*: 20 May 1988: Labour Policy
       IR: Chris Morgan   IE: Neil Kinnock

```
 1  IE:     ...what is it. I don't mind answering the
 2           questions, .h but really what is it whu- have
 3           you- did you get up on the wrong side of bed
 4           this morning, didn't you have a good breakfast,
 5           .hh d'you think this is news.
 6           (.)
 7  IE:     [D'you] really think this [is news.]
 8  IR:     [(   )-]                  [ We:ll  ] ye:s some-
 9           some delegates this mo[rning .hh reacte-]
10  IE:                            [I think (      )]
11  IR:     reacted strongly to mister Hattersley saying .h
12           last night at a Welsh rally .h that there would
13           be no forgiveness for tho: :se .hhhh who caused
14           division within this party. [.hhh  they] took=
15  IE:                                  [ mhm hm ]
16  IR:     =that as an indication .h=that the
17           authoritarian style of .h party leadership was
18           going to continue.
19  IE:  → Did you,
20           (.)
21  IR:     I- I:'m I'm [telling you what-]
22  IE:                 [ Well  ask  your] own questions
23           (th[en)]
24  IR:        [I- ] I'm telling you a delegate said to me
25           this morning that they thought that's enfor-
26           reinforcing an authoritarian view.
```

At a single stroke, Kinnock casts the neutralistic footing as a mere
façade. Unlike the previous example, this is not merely prefatory
to a routine answer; it is allowed to stand as an accusatory and
consequential action in its own right, prompting the IR to defend himself subsequently (lines 21 and 24–26). Plainly, the neutralism achieved through third-party attributions falls short of
invincibility.

A note on defending against attacks

Given the recurrent potential for charges of bias and other attacks on
their professionalism, how do interviewers defend themselves?[6] In
the Kinnock example above, the IR's defense involves insisting that

---

[6] A much fuller discussion of this issue can be found in chapter 4.

he was merely relaying the views of others (lines 21 and 24–26). As it turns out, this is a common line of defense, one that is remarkably similar to the "I was only asking a question" defense discussed in chapter 4. In both cases, the defense involves more or less explicitly appealing to one of the discursive practices that comprise the IR's posture of neutralism (asking a question, or speaking on behalf of a third party) to defuse an IE's attack. Accordingly, as noted in the previous chapter, these discursive practices serve dual functions in relation to journalistic professionalism – not only do they embody a first-order *display of neutralism*, but they are also invoked by interviewers to support a second-order *claim of neutralism* that can be used in responding to charges of bias and other criticisms.

Moreover, as we noted in chapter 4, this mode of defense is often associated with a resumption of the role of questioner. Recall that when interviewers justify their conduct in an explicit way, they engage in nonquestioning behavior that potentially diverges from the normative question–answer framework, and they risk losing control over the topical agenda of the interview. To avoid this, explicit defenses are often managed in a way that facilitates the interviewer's return to the safety of the questioner role. Such efforts are not always completely successful. In the previous example, the IR defended himself by insisting that he was merely relaying what "a delegate said to me this morning" (lines 21 and 24–25), and he goes on to reissue the authoritarian charge in a way that stands as a virtual question and thus calls for a response from Kinnock. However, Kinnock tries to pre-empt this move (lines 22–23), challenging the IR to "ask your own questions then" and thus implying that relaying the accusations of his political opponents is simply not legitimate. In this case, the IR's effort to defend himself and resume the role of questioner meets continued resistance.

A more effective variant on this mode of defense involves adopting a tribune-of-the-people stance. Consider the following excerpt from an interview with Pat Buchanan, who had recently become Director of Communications in the Reagan administration. Prior to the segment reproduced below, the IR asked Buchanan if his own stridently conservative ideology had begun to affect the content of Reagan's speeches. In particular, Buchanan was asked if he was responsible for Reagan's widely reported comment that the Nicaraguan Contras are "the moral equivalent" of the founding

fathers of the United States. In response, Buchanan vehemently
denies that anybody "puts words into the mouth of Ronald Reagan"
(lines 1–2 below), and he goes on to attack the IR for having
"demeaned the President" (line 5) by suggesting that "the President
doesn't know what he's saying" (lines 6–9).

(30)   US ABC *Nightline*: 3 June 1985: Pat Buchanan
        IR: Ted Koppel   IE: Pat Buchanan

```
 1  IE:      ... nobody puts wor: :ds into the mouth of Ronald
 2            Reagan he goes over every single speech he
 3            delivers. .hhh An' when 'e delivers it .hh those
 4            words are what he belie: :ves. .hh An' I think it
 5            is really uh- .hh it demea:ns the President to
 6            suggest that someone say Pat Buchanan or anyone
 7            el:se .hh is running down there at night
 8            sneaking phrases or (line:s) .hhh into speeches
 9            an' the Pres'dent doesn't know what he's
10            sayi[ng. .hhh]
11  IR: →     [No   Pat] I don't think anyone's
12            sug[ gest ]ing=
13  IE:          [(sure)]
14  IR: →     =that, I think what people are suggesting
15            is that the President of the United States
16            perhaps more than any other man or woman in
17            the country is terribly terribly busy cannot
18            pos[sibly write every speech of=
19  IE:          [Mhm
20  IR:      =his own, .hh or for that matter go over every
21            speech line by line as you suggest. [ .hhh ]
22  IE:                                            [Mhm]
23  IR:      Uh- an when that happens, then people in
24            positions such as your own, .hh can sometimes
25            get some of their own ideas across.
26  IE:      .tlkh Well sure. you can get ideas in but look.
27            every speech in the White House Ted .hh go:es
28            through a process...
```

To counter this accusation, Koppel indicates that he was merely relaying the concerns of "people" in general (arrowed). In so doing, he
not only neutralizes and legitimates the question, but he also presses
Buchanan once again for a response. Significantly, Buchanan subsequently does an about-face and proceeds to answer the objectionable
question (lines 26–28). A "normal" course of interviewing is thus
restored.

A more elaborate illustration of this line of defense occurred early
on in the infamous Bush–Rather interview. From the very first question, the agenda for that interview was Bush's involvement in the
Iran-Contra scandal, but Bush strongly objected to this agenda in
his very first response. He registered a series of complaints against
Dan Rather and the CBS *Evening News* team, accusing them among
other things of having previously misrepresented the purpose of the
interview. Specifically, he charged that he was led to believe that it
would be a broad "political profile" rather than a narrow investigation of his involvement in Iran-Contra. Following these accusations,
he calls for "fair play" (lines 1–3), and he bids to broaden the agenda
of the interview as he claims he was promised.

(31)   US CBS *Evening News*: 25 Jan 1988: Bush and Iran-Contra
       IR: Dan Rather   IE: George Bush

```
 1  IE:    .... I'm asking for: (0.3) fair play:, and I
 2          thought I was here to talk about my views on
 3          educa:tion, or on getting this deficit down=
 4  IR:    =Well Mr. Vice Preside[nt we wanna talk about=
 5  IE:                          [Yes.
 6  IR:    =the re[cord   o]n=
 7  IE:           [Well lets]
 8  IR:    =this, .hh because it-
 9  IE:    Well let's talk abo[ut the (full) record,]=
10  IR: →                     [th- the framework]=
11  IE:    =[that's what I wanna talk about] Dan,
12  IR: → =[he::re:, is that one third of-]
13  IR:    one third o'the Republicans in this
14          poll[:, one third=
15  IE:         [Yeah
16  IR: → =o'the the Republicans .hh and- and one fourth
17      → of the people who say:: that- eh y'know they
18      → rather like you:, .hh believe y[ou're hi]ding=
19  IE:                                   [(wha-) ]
20  IR: → =something.=Now if you [are: here's a ch-]
21  IE:                          [I              am]
22          hid[ing something]
23  IR:       [here's  a  ch]ance to get it out.
```

Rather simultaneously defends himself and justifies further questioning on Iran-Contra by reference to the results of an opinion
poll (arrowed) indicating that a substantial segment of Bush's own

Republican supporters believe he's "hiding something." The concerns of the citizenry are thus offered as the rationale behind the adversarial line of questioning that Rather, despite the objections, continues to pursue. (For further analysis of defensive practices, see chapter 4.)

Discussion

A shadowy presence often inhabits the exchanges between interviewers and interviewees. This presence – a third party conjured up by interviewers and oriented to by interviewees – plays an important role in the process by which questions are rendered defensible and a semblance of journalistic professionalism is maintained. Because this third party is cast as primarily responsible for interviewers' more contentious remarks, interviewers are able to express such views while preserving a posture of formal neutrality. Moreover, depending on the type of third party invoked – a knowledgeable authority or the general public – there may be further implications for the credibility of the viewpoint being expressed or the legitimacy of the underlying line of questioning being pursued. All of these happy results – neutralism, credibility, legitimacy – may on occasion be contested and even undermined by interviewees. However, to a remarkable extent interviewees "play along," simultaneously acquiescing to the line of questioning and reinforcing the interviewer's posture of professionalism.

There are still broader ramifications for the journalist–interviewer's public persona, for the specific type of professional that is portrayed through this practice. When interviewers speak on behalf of officials, experts, or other powerful individuals, they present themselves as agents of communication between societal elites. Alternatively, when the public is invoked, they acquire a more populist persona – that of a "tribune of the people" who invites elites to address the concerns of the citizenry. Although the distribution of such practices has not been examined systematically, there appears to be at least a rough correlation between persona and broadcasting environment. While elite-attributed statements are broadly distributed across programs of various stripes, public-attributed statements seem to be clustered disproportionately on certain evening programs (i.e., *Nightline* and *60 Minutes*) and are largely absent from the Sunday morning interview programs. Significantly, these programs differ sharply in the size and composition of the audience they attract – evening shows have a larger and more heterogeneous audience, whereas Sunday morning shows are watched by a smaller audience with a high proportion of politicians and opinion leaders (see chapter 9). It would seem that journalists are more inclined toward a populist stance when the overhearing audience is more closely representative of the populace.

In a pioneering study of print reporting, Gaye Tuchman (1972) long ago observed that objectivity functioned as a "strategic ritual" within the culture of journalism. Reporters equate objectivity with certain routine practices of news-writing, such as the "inverted pyramid" style of narrative, the use of quotation marks, and the segregation of editorials from straight reporting. Tuchman argued that such practices cannot guarantee objectivity in an absolute sense – Robinson and Sheehan (1983) refer to them as "objectivistic" rather than objective – but they remain important nonetheless because they solve various practical problems and they insulate the reporter and the employing news organization against assaults from various quarters.[7] Similar functions, and practices for achieving them, arise in the complex domain of the news interview. Across highly aggressive lines of questioning, such practices secure a crucial veneer of professionalism for interviewers – and a veneer of acquiescence from interviewees.

---

[7] Since Tuchman's initial study, the rituals of objectivity have been further explored in the domain of news-writing (Fishman 1980: chapter 3; Robinson and Sheehan, 1983: chapter 5) and in the construction of news photos, film, and video (Tuchman 1978: chapter 6; Altheide 1974: 85–95; Zelizer 1990).

6

Adversarial questioning: setting agendas and exerting pressure

In chapter 5, we looked at how journalists work to design their questions so as to be defensibly neutral and legitimate. In this chapter, we turn the issue around, and consider the various ways in which interviewers adopt an adversarial stance and exert pressure on their respondents. This topic is an important one: it is at the level of question design that interviewers fundamentally and necessarily handle the competing journalistic norms of impartiality and adversarialness with which we have been concerned throughout this book. In part, of course, the management of the tension between these two norms is handled by questioning itself. As chapter 4 showed, questioning is conventionally understood as a neutralistic action which does not take up a substantive position – involving either agreement or disagreement – vis-à-vis the interviewee. For this reason, interviewers work hard to package their actions as "questions," and may invoke this packaging to defeat interviewee claims that they are pursuing some kind of agenda of their own.

However, as we have suggested through the use of the term "neutralistic," news interview questioning is not, and cannot be, strictly neutral. Because questions unavoidably encode attitudes and points of view (Harris 1986), interviewers must still design their questions to strike a balance between the journalistic norms of impartiality and adversarialness. The particular balance that is achieved between these two norms can be a distinctive, or even defining, characteristic of particular interviewing styles. In turn, distinctive styles of questioning are an important element of the public personae of interviewers ranging from Walter Cronkite to Ted Koppel to Larry King in the USA, or Sir Robin Day to Jeremy Paxman to Jimmy Young in Britain. The significance of question design as a "signature" feature extends from interviewers as individuals to the news programs of which they are a part (for example PBS's *NewHour* vs. ABC's *Nightline*), and ultimately to whole periods which are characterized by what may be termed dominant styles of interviewing.

Question design then is the "cutting edge" of broadcast journalism. The limits of acceptable questioning play a significant part in defining the parameters of the permissible in mass media content, and innovations in question design often involve subtle shifts in the definition of these parameters. This chapter examines some of the resources through which interviewers design questions to manage the shifting balance between impartiality and adversarialness in this context.

A historical case

Consider the following 1951 interview of British Prime Minister Clement Attlee, who has called a general election and just returned to London to begin his election campaign. The interview is conducted at the London rail station where Mr. Attlee has just arrived. The following excerpt represents the complete interview:

(1)   UK Interview with Clement Attlee: 1951
      (British Prime Minister 1945–51)

```
 1   IR:    Good mor:ning Mister A:ttlee,=We hope (.) you've
 2          had a good journey,
 3          (0.2)
 4   IE:    Ye: :s excellent. h
 5          (0.2)
 6   IR:    Can you:- (.) now you're ba:ck hhh having cut
 7          short your: lecture tour::. (.) tell us
 8          [something of how you- (0.2) vie::w the=
 9   IE:    [°Mm.°
10   IR:    =election prospects?
11          (0.2)
12   IE:    Oh we shall go in t'give them a good fi:ght,
13          (0.2) very good, (0.4) very good cha:nce of
14          > winning,=We shall go in confidently,=We always
15          do,<
16          (0.7)
17   IR:    U:::h And- (.) on wha:t will Labour take its
18          sta:nd.
19          (0.4)
```

```
20  IE:   We:ll that we sh'll be announcing shortly.
21        (0.2)
22  IR:   What are your immediate pla:ns: Mister
23        Attlee[:.
24  IE:        [My immediate plans are < t'go do:wn> to a
25        committee t'deci:de on just that thing, .hhh (.)
26        > soon's I can get away from here.<
27        (0.2)
28  IE:   °°hheh .hh°°
29  IR:   Uhm, hh (.) Anything else you would> ca:re
30        t'sa::y about (.) th' coming election.
31        (.)
32  IE:   No:,
33        (0.6)
34  IR:   Uhm, (0.4) Uhm, ((end of interview segment))
```

The IR's questioning in this interview has a number of noticeable features. First, the IR does not materially shift topic. The context of the interview is the Prime Minister's arrival in London to strategize for national elections, and the interviewer does not diverge from that. There are no shifts to discuss Britain's relations with foreign powers, or personal disagreements within the Labour Party. The IR's questions remain tied to the immediate context of the interview – the election and Mr. Attlee's view of it.

Second, the questions are not the prefaced, multi-sentence questions that are common today, where prefatory statements are used to establish context and background for what follows. Rather Attlee is presented with simple inquiries that treat the immediate context of the interview – the impending election – as the only thing necessary to understand the questions that follow.

Third, the IR's questions are all very "open." Questions like "Can you...tell us something of how you view the election prospects" (lines 6–8 and 10) and "On what will Labour take its stand" (lines 17–18) permit the IE enormous latitude in developing responses.

Fourth, many of these questions embody "conventional indirectness" (Brown and Levinson 1987; Clayman and Heritage 2002). Questions like "Can you...tell us something of how you view the election prospects" (lines 6–8 and 10) and "Anything else you would care to say about the coming election" (lines 29–30) evidently treat Attlee's responses as optional rather than obligatory. They indicate that Attlee will not be pressed by this interviewer if he does not care to respond.

Fifth, and relatedly, even though the Prime Minister gives non-committal, if not downright evasive, replies to his questions, the IR makes no attempt to pursue more revealing responses. Rather he simply accepts whatever response he is given and moves on.

Sixth, both the openness and indirectness of these questions are fundamentally deferential to the power and status of the Prime Minister.

Finally, the deferential style embodied in the IR's questions is reciprocated in Attlee's brusquely non-committal responses. Attlee is not merely unafraid to decline the questions, he clearly feels under no obligation to respond to them. Indeed, he is quite happy to imply (line 26) that the interview itself is preventing him from getting on with more important election matters. No modern politician entering an election campaign today would dream of addressing an interviewer (or the voting public) in this way.

Interviews like this one are a valuable historical benchmark. They tell us about the extent to which present-day broadcast interviews differ from those of the past. And they are evidence of quite different relationships between broadcasters and politicians than exist today. The modern political interview differs from this one in every major respect. In this chapter, we examine some of the ways in which interviewees struggle with interviewers over the political terrain that is constructed through news interview questioning. We begin with an exploration of some of the basic features and objectives of question design in the news interview, and then consider the contribution of the more complex prefaced question designs in this context.

Analyzing question design: some preliminary observations

News interview questions are often subtle and complex constructions. They express particular aspects of the public roles of interviewer and interviewee, and they can index elements of the personal identities of both (Roth 1998a). They can be primarily geared to the concerns and preoccupations of the questioner, answerer, overhearing audience members, or all three of these to varying degrees. They can embody complex grammatical and rhetorical constructions to support or undermine the positions of public figures on issues of the moment. It is obvious therefore that they can be looked at from many different angles.

Table 1. *Dimensions of questioning and answering*

Interviewer questions:	Interviewee responses:
Set agendas: (i) Topical agendas (ii) Action agendas	Engage/Decline to engage: (i) Topical agendas (ii) Action agendas
Embody presuppositions	Confirm/Disconfirm presuppositions
Incorporate preferences	Align/Disalign with preferences

We can make a start by observing that, at minimum, interviewers' questions have the following features. First, they establish particular agendas for interviewee responses. Second, they tend to embody presuppositions and/or assert propositions about the matter under discussion. Third, they can incorporate "preferences": they are often designed so as to invite or favor one type of answer over another. Correspondingly, interviewees can formulate their responses in ways that accept or resist (or reject altogether) any or all of these. Thus interviewees' responses engage (or decline to engage) the agenda set by interviewers' questions, confirm (or disconfirm) its presuppositions, and align (or disalign) with its preferences. These possibilities are displayed in Table 1. These three dimensions are fundamental and inexorably relevant characteristics of question design and production.[1] Because it is not possible to avoid them, interviewers' questions can normally only *select* between different possibilities for agenda setting, presuppositional content, and preference design. These selections are crucial for the work that questions do, the nature of the interview that is built through them, and the interviewer and program identity that is sustained by these means.

Simple and prefaced question designs

These three dimensions of question design are enhanced by "prefaced" question designs. As we saw in chapter 4, prefaced questions contain one or more statements prior to the question proper. These prefatory statements were quite absent in our first example,

---

[1] See Boyd and Heritage (Forthcoming) for a parallel discussion of these issues in relation to questioning in medical consultations.

but they are very much a part of modern news interview questions. Their manifest function is often to "contextualize" and provide relevance – for the interviewee and the news audience – for the questions that follow. Excerpt (2) is a clear case of this:

(2) US ABC *Nightline*: 22 July 1985: South Africa
     IR: Charles Gibson   IE: Reverend Allan Boesak
1 IR: S→ .hh Two- two members of your organization (.)
2   supposedly arrested today:
3   Q→ d'you feel in some danger when you go back.

Here the prefatory statement (lines 1–2) establishes a context that gives meaning and point to the subsequent question which otherwise might seem to come "out of the blue" and indeed be incomprehensible for many members of the news audience.

A prime difference between simple and prefaced questions concerns the degree to which they embody the exercise of initiative in establishing a context for the question to follow (Clayman and Heritage 2002). Most simple questions draw on resources from the prior answer to provide for their relevance and intelligibility. The following is a case in point. Here a British Labour politician with overall responsibility for his party's defense policy explains why he walked out of the defense debate at his party's annual convention. In his first turn, he says that he was angry because the person chairing the debate did not "call" him to speak and allow him to reply to attacks on him. The IR then asks him whether the chair's action was "intentional" (line 9):

(3) UK BBCTV *Nationwide*: 30 Sep 1981: Party Conference
     IR: David Dimbleby   IE: Brynmor John
1 IE: Well I walked out because I was ang:ry at not
2   being called by the chairman after two personal
3   attacks .hhh had been launched on me from the
4   rostrum.=I don't complain about those attacks.
5   .hhh But I think that any fair chairman would
6   have given me an opportunity of replying to
7   them.
8   (0.4)
9 IR: → Was it intentional not to call you?
10 IE: .hhh Well i- (.) I don't think it was
11   mali::gn,=but it was intentional in the sense
12   that he he referred at the e:nd to the fact that

13   I had put in a note asking to be calle:d, .hh
14   and couldn't be called.=So it obviously was
15   intentional.=It wasn't .hh an o:versight on his
16   part.

This simple follow-up question raises something which is implicit
in the IE's previous answer, especially the IE's reference to what a
"fair chairman" would have done (lines 5–7), and it is explicit in
introducing the issue of the chair's "intentions" as a relevant matter
to be addressed by the IE in his next turn at talk. As a follow-up
question, it does not require any initial statements to set the context
for the question to come.

However, journalists may often find themselves in circumstances
where a simple follow-up question exploring some dimension of a
prior answer is quite undesirable. Under these circumstances, statement prefaces are an essential resource for resetting the context for
the subsequent question. In the following case, for example, a journalist uses a prefaced question design to put a topical issue raised
by the IE (about "blacks against blacks" violence in South Africa)
on hold. This requires prefatory statements:

(4)   US ABC *Nightline*: 22 July 1985: South Africa
      IR: Charles Gibson   IE: Ambassador Herbert Beukes
   1   IE: .hh The: urgent and: pressi:ng: need, h the: (.)
   2   .mlhh uh immediate one: is to stop violence.
   3   (0.2) violence perpetrated by blacks:, upon
   4   blacks. (0.4) This is what we have to end, (.)
   5   to get to: uh situation .hh u=where we can
   6   start=h (.) talking. Where we can start in uh
   7   peaceful manner_ (0.5) to have=h (.) political
   8   dialogue.
   9   IR: 1→   .mlh Arright lemme get to that blacks against
  10   1→   blacks question in uh minute b't first lemme ask
  11   1→   you=
  12   2→   =It seems to me nobody dispu:tes .hhh th't the
  13   2→   power in South Africa (.) is with the white
  14   2→   government . . h An' it seems to me that within the
  15   2→   rule of law: that could be do:ne.
  16   Why do laws hafta be suspended in order to stop
  17   the violence.
  18   IE: .hhh Uhm (.) seems to me:- uh- (eh=and) always
  19   has been: a balance between freedom, (0.5) an'
  20   disorder:....

```
21          ....
22          .... [35 lines of talk omitted]
23          ....
24   IR:  3→  =Alright lemme talk about this question then for
25          3→  a moment of violence (.) of blacks against
26          3→  blacks. (0.5)
27              We live here in the United States in a
28              country...
```

Having placed the IE's immediately preceding statements on hold
(1→), the IR uses additional prefatory statements (2→) to set up a
question about the necessity of suspending the rule of law in South
Africa, and then further prefatory statements (3→) to return to the
issue raised earlier by the IE.

Journalists may also use prefatory statements, not merely to give
"background" for a question, as in (2) above, but to provide an
experiential context for the interviewee's answer. In the following
case, discussed in Roth (1998a), dealing with proposals to arm the
British police, the personal experience of the IE – a policeman who
was shot by a criminal while unarmed – is invoked to convey to the
audience that the question has a special relevance for him:

(5) UK BBCTV *Newsnight*: 21 Oct 1993: Arming the Police
     IR: Jeremy Paxman   IE: David Brady

```
1   IR:   ...You as I say have been shot yourself in
2          the- in the line of duty, ahm let's just
3          look at the question of arming the police
4          first of all. Is it your view that the police
5          should now be armed?
6   IE:   .hhh But definitely. .hhh Ahm we: wuh- (.) we have no
7          rights as a society .hh to expect young men (.) .hh to
8          enter situations...
```

Here the question preface provides that the IE's experience of being
shot is the presumptive foundation of his perspective in answering
it, and may privilege that experience as having a special weight and
significance for the audience's understanding of the issues involved
in any decision to arm the police.

In sum, prefaced question designs give interviewers room to maneuver. Whereas simple questions leave the matters raised in the interviewee's last response as the context for the next question, prefaced questions allow interviewers to escape from this constraint,

constructing a context of their own choosing for the question they are about to put in play. The shift towards the use of complex question designs has been relatively marked in both the USA and the UK from the 1950s to the present, and it embodies a real growth in the scope, power, and autonomy of interviewer questioning. It was just this capacity to escape the immediate context of the interviewee's responses which was quite noticeably absent in the historical example with which we began the chapter. Additionally, as we shall see, the manifest function of prefaced questions – providing context for the subsequent question to "overhearing" audience members – provides justification and "cover" for very much more hostile and aggressive questioning strategies than were dreamed of in the early days of news interviewing.

Dimensions of questioning

Agenda setting

The claim that interviewer questions set agendas for interviewees involves three features of their design.

First, questions set agendas by identifying a specific topical domain as the appropriate or relevant domain of response. As the first part of an adjacency pair, they achieve this by making non-responses (e.g., silence) or failures to address the question's topical agenda noticeable and accountable (Schegloff 1972). Under such circumstances, the questioner has the right to repeat the question or to solicit an answer in other ways (Heritage 1984a: 248). Moreover, failure to respond appropriately attracts special inferences: in particular, that the answerer is being evasive, or has something to hide. This latter sanction is particularly important when there may be millions of people watching or listening to the broadcast. These constraints are quite compelling for interviewees. Silence in the face of news interview questioning is incredibly rare! When asked a question, interviewees always try to respond in some way, and most often attempt to look as if they are answering the question (see chapter 7).

Notwithstanding the fact that the term "topic" is loose and difficult to define (Sacks 1992; Jefferson 1984),[2] it is plain that interviewees are oriented to the fact that there are real boundaries to the

---

[2] See in particular Sacks's lectures of 9 March 1967 and 17 April 1968. See also Spring 1970, lecture 5; Winter 1971, 19 February and Spring 1971, 9 April.

topics set by questions. In (6) below, a British Labour politician is asked about the significance of a right-wing leadership success for the future of his party. He begins by responding to the question as put, and then adds a comment (lines 16–20) about the future actions of the losing left-wing politician.

(6) UK BBCTV *Panorama*: 28 Jan 1981: Labour Party
      IR: Robin Day   IE: Roy Hattersley

```
 1  IR:    Roy Hattersley .hhh is it right to interpret
 2          this as a move back .hh to the right.=This
 3          er victory by such a narrow marg[in of Denis=
 4  IE:                                     [ .h h h h=
 5  IR:    = Healey.]
 6  IE:    = N o  ] I don't believe it i:s. in some ways
 7          I wish I could say that . . hhhh But I don't
 8          believe it i:s. I believe it's a mo:ve back .hhh
 9          to the broad based tolerant representative
10          Labour Part (h)y, .hhh the Labour Party in which
11          Neil Kinnock and I: who disagree on a number of
12          policy issue:s .hh can argue about them .hh
13          without accusing each other of treachery:, .hhh
14          without suggesting that one or the other of us
15          is playing into the Tories' ha:nds.
16   →     .hhh And let me say something about the next
17          year because that was your original question.
18          .hhh I think Tony Benn would be personally
19          extremely foo:lish to sta:nd for the deputy
20          leadership again . . .
```

Here the IE explicitly marks his additional comment as distinct and as a departure from the question's agenda, and he goes out of his way to justify this departure by reference to an earlier question asked by the IR (see chapter 7). He thus orients to the question's topical boundary, even as he moves beyond it.

Second, questions not only identify the topical domain to be dealt with in a response, they also identify *actions* that the interviewee should perform in relation to the topical domain. For example in (7), British Prime Minister Edward Heath is asked by David Frost if he likes his main political rival of this period, Harold Wilson. Twice in this sequence, Heath responds by addressing the topic of the question – Wilson – but he does not respond in terms of the action agenda that the question called for – a yes/no response on whether he "likes" Wilson (cf. Raymond 2000). Instead he works around the issue in terms of "dealing with" or "working with" him:

(7) UK BBC *Omnibus*: Date Unknown: Harold Wilson
     IR: David Frost   IE: Edward Heath
```
 1  IR:   Do you quite li:ke him?
 2         (0.1)
 3  IE:   .hhh .h .h We:ll I th- I think in politics you
 4         see: i- it's not a ques:tion of going about (.)
 5         li:king people or not, hh It's a question of
 6         dealing with people, ° °h .h° ° a:n: :d u: :h (.)
 7         I've always been able to deal perfectly well
 8         with Mister Wilson,=as indeed: uh- he has with
 9         me,
10         (0.4)
11  IR:   <But do you like> him?
12         (0.1)
13  IE:   .hhhh Well agai:n it's not a question of uh (.)
14         li:kes or disli:kes. I: :t's a question of
15         wor:king together: : with other people who are in
16         politics,
17         (0.6)
18  IR:   But do y'like him.
19         (0.4)
20  IE:   .hhh (.) That'll have to remain t'be see:n won't
21         it.
```

Heath's avoidance of the question's action agenda licenses David Frost to renew it, and he does so in a most pointed way at line 11, and again at line 18. In each case, Frost's "But do you like him?" establishes a contrast (with the "but") between Heath's response and what the question seeks, while the repetition of his original question sets aside that response and clearly indicates (both to Heath and, more importantly, to the television audience) that Heath's response was inadequate, and that he has avoided the question.

Third, the agenda setting function of questions involves decisions about how narrowly or broadly defined the interviewee's response should be. For example, in (7) the agenda was set pretty narrowly by means of a yes/no question, and Heath was made accountable to respond accordingly (though as we saw in chapter 4, an elaboration of that response would also ordinarily be required). "Yes/no" questions are recurrent sites of conflict between interviewers and interviewees, as in (8), in which a Serbian commander who is suspected of war

crimes in the Bosnian conflict is pressed about whether he will deal
with United Nations personnel who are responsible for investigating
war crimes:

(8)   UK BBCTV *Newsnight*: 2 Nov 1993: UN Investigation
      IR: Jeremy Paxman   IE: Dragoslav Bokan

```
 1  IR:    ... Mister Bokan, are you prepared to make
 2          yourself available to UN investigators?
 3          (.)
 4  IE:    .hhhh Ah: first of all: I: just want to say that
 5          it's you know, very strange you know, to hear
 6          all those accuses.=And ah: .hhh ah: it's v(h)ery
 7          strange to be in the (passive) role:: o:f
 8          hearing, an:d ah .hh ah not to have an
 9          opportunity you know to:: say anything: uh .hhh
10          ah about yourself or: you know your: ah go:als.
11          In war. .hh An:d [ah:
12  IR:                      [I'm not interested in your
13      →  goals Mister Bokan.=The question wa:s: are you
14      →  prepared to make yourself avai:lable to UN
15      →  investigators.
16  IE:    .hhh You know uh- you know: the answer, you
17          know: uh maybe better than ah m:yself. .hhh
18          Because: o: :f >you know from the beginning of
19          war,< .hhh I: have just uh one goal an:d that's
20          t'defend you know my people: from the (lynch.)=
21  IR:  →  =Is that a yes or a n:o?
22          (0.5)
23  IE:    Uh: Is it a cour:t. (.) Or: a: interview.
24  IR:  →  So- you are: prepared to make yourself available
25      →  to UN investigators or no[:t.
26  IE:                            [Of Course.
```

Here the IE repeatedly avoids the question (lines 4–11, 16–20, 23).
As the IR's series of pursuits (arrowed) illustrates, the significance of
yes/no and alternative questions is not that IEs are necessarily forced
to say yes or no right away. Rather it is that these questions lay down
a marker, making a "yes/no" response accountably avoided if it is
not forthcoming. This in turn establishes the IR's right to re-ask
the question,[3] and IRs can and do avail themselves of this right

---

[3] In this particular instance, the IR further narrows the agenda of the question at
lines 24–25 by renewing his question as an explicitly disjunctive yes/no question.
In this way, he sharpens the degree of constraint on the IE, and further underscores
the IE's previous evasiveness as requiring this narrowing.

(Clayman 1993, Greatbatch 1986a). In a notable case, the IR in (8), Jeremy Paxman, re-asked a question fourteen times of a British Cabinet minister on network televison![4] Thus, interviewees know that visible evasions license an interviewer to press them subsequently to answer yes or no, and that this pressure may be heard as reasonable by the television audience if they seemed evasive in the first place. This kind of interviewer pressure may be heard as particularly relevant and appropriate when there is the suspicion of wrongdoing, and where there is an issue about the public accountability of the interviewee's actions.

In contrast, wh-questions – especially what, why, and how questions[5] – can set the parameters of response more broadly. For example, (9) sets up a very open range of responses from General John Vessey about his trip to Hanoi to negotiate over information about US troops missing in action from the Vietnam War:

(9)   US PBS *Newshour*: 23 Oct 1992: Hanoi MIA Trip
      IR: Jim Lehrer   IE: General John Vessey

1	IR:	.hhh with us no:w for a newsmaker interview: is
2		the delegation chairman former chairman of the
3		joint chiefs of sta:ff retired army general John
4		Vessey. General, welcome.
5	IE:	Thank you.
6	IR: →	.hhhh Sir h:ow would you descri:be the
7	→	significance of thi<u>s</u>: (.) agreement.
8	IE:	.hhhhh The Vietnamese:: uh: (0.2) <u>F</u>oreign
9		Minister and the Vietnamese <u>P</u>rime Minister
10		(0.3) de<u>s</u>cribed it to me: .hhh as a <u>turn</u>ing
11		point. (0.3) i:n (0.4) reh-resol:ving
12		the fates of our <u>missing</u>. (0.5) And I think
13		that's what it is. It- .hh in the <u>las</u>:t uh
14		fi:ve years:: ...

Here the agenda for General Vessey's response is very underspecified. Almost any on-topic response would have likely counted as a valid and appropriate answer to the question. In general, yes/no questions are more constraining on an interviewee, while wh- questions can

---

[4] This interview took place on 13 May 1997. The interviewer, Jeremy Paxman subsequently won an award from the British Academy of Film and Television Arts (BAFTA) for the interview.

[5] Not all wh- questions are equally open. In general, what, why, and how questions can require more exposition than who, when, and where questions and are, in this sense, more "open."

normally be successfully answered in a wider range of ways and using a wider range of resources.

Tightening question agendas: using prefaces

As we have already suggested, the manifest function of question prefaces normally involves giving background information to the "overhearing" audience (Heritage 1985), or managing topic shifts of various kinds. However, question prefaces can also be used to make the agenda of a question more complex, constraining, or problematic. In the following case, a British Conservative politician, Michael Heseltine, is asked about his views on closer ties with Europe, an issue that has become a source of conflict within his party:

(10)   UK BBCTV *Newsnight*: June 1989: European Ties
       IR: Donald MacCormick   IE: Michael Heseltine

```
1  IR:    .hh what Missus Thatcher has been saying: is
2          that there is a danger (.) .h of a socialist
3          superstate being imposed (0.5) from Brussels
4          (0.2) and what Mister Heath and others are
5          saying is (0.2) that is (.) is an illusory
6          fear.=Where do you: line up on that is:sue.
7  IE:    Well: (eh) technically, becaus:e (.) eh these
8          decisions are y:et to be ta:ken, it can go
9          either wa:y, . . . (continues)
```

Here Heseltine is not simply asked about his opinion on the creation of a "socialist superstate." Instead, by means of the question preface, the audience is instructed about the existence of two conflicting positions on this issue which are held by two of the most senior members of the Conservative Party. Within this framework, the question is made more pointed and newsworthy by its invitation to Heseltine to say where he "lines up" in that conflict. Here the question preface describes the parameters of the dispute and its leading participants, making the nature of his political dilemma very clear to a viewing audience which may have known little about the then-emerging dispute within the Conservative Party on this issue.

Prefatory statements may also be used to tighten the agenda being set for an interviewee by blocking certain types of answer. The following segment comes from an interview with Margaret Thatcher – also on closer ties with Europe:

(11)   UK BBCTV *Newsnight*: June 1989: Exchange-Rate Mechanism
       IR: John Cole   IE: Margaret Thatcher

1 IR: Now turning to the exchange rate mechanism you:
2   have consistently said or the Government has
3   said .hh that you will joi:n when the ti:me is
4   right but people are saying: .hh that that means
5   never. Could you defi:ne the ki:nd of
6   conditions when you think we would go in.
7 IE: Uh no I would not say it means never. For the
8   policy...

The IR's question (lines 5–6) is aimed at pinning down Thatcher to
a specification of circumstances in which she would agree to join the
exchange-rate mechanism. He establishes the agenda for this question with a preface that contrasts vaguely worded prior statements
by Thatcher concerning entry "when the time is right" with an interpretation of that statement, attributed to unidentified "people" (see
chapter 5), as "never" (lines 1–5). The preface provides a platform
from which the question itself can be launched, while blocking a
response which, like the quoted "when the time is right," would be
vague and anodyne.

Still more complex and confining is the following question preface
to then Senate majority leader Bob Dole. Here three main prefatory
statements, all attributed to Dole, are used to set problems for Dole's
stated objectives as a tax-cutter:

(12)   US NBC *Meet the Press*: 8 Dec 1985: Federal Budget
       IR: Al Hunt   IE: Senator Bob Dole

1   IR: You can't have it both ways either.=>On this
2   program< you have said that you don't think,
3   .hhh that you'll eliminate thirty to fifty
4   programs, [an'] Senator Packwood=
5   IE: [( )]
6   IR: =says you have to, .hh Number two you say you
7   hope you will not have uh tax increase,
8   [.hhhh And]=
9   IE: [But I do.]
10 IR: =number- and number three you say you h:ope you
11   can have a:l[m o s t] three percent on: .hhh=
12 ( ):   [(   )]
13 IR: =on: on defe:nse, .hh And yet you hafta cut
14   fifty billion next year. Now which o'those
15   three's gonna give Senator,

In this case, the IR uses a series of prefatory statements to create a complex dilemma for Dole. The statements describe three aspects of Dole's position – his inability to eliminate programs (lines 2–4 and 6), his desire to avoid a tax increase (lines 6–7), and his hope to increase the defense budget (lines 10–11 and 13). All three are incompatible with Dole's objective of cutting $50 billion from the federal budget. Moreover, they are prepared for with an initial statement ("You can't have it both ways either.") which, among other things, projects (to Dole and the news audience) that the subsequent statements will identify contradictions that are problematic for his position. Here the combination of the three difficulties with Dole's stated position, together with a final question that presupposes that he must backdown from one of them, is highly constraining. This confining agenda could not be constructed without the use of a question preface.

Questions and presuppositions

In addition to setting agendas, questions often assert propositions and embody presuppositions with varying degrees of explicitness. This is so for both simple and prefaced questions.

Most prefaced questions incorporate explicit contextualizing propositions. With these in place, the subsequent question can build from it and can embody additional embedded presuppositions (Harris 1986; Wilson 1990). Both of these features are illustrated in the next case which concerns an election in progress in which Labour politician Tony Benn was ultimately the loser. Here the prefatory statement (arrow 1) guardedly asserts (with the evidential verb "seems" (Chafe 1986)) two propositions: the likely result of the election is (i) close, and (ii) against Tony Benn.

(13)   UK BBCTV *Panorama*: 27 Sep 1979: Tony Benn Loss
       IR: Vincent Hanna   IE: Jon Lansman
1 IR: 1→ The result seems t' be very close but (.) on th'
2   1→ who:le it (0.2) doesn't look very good for:: (.)
3   1→ Tony Benn.
4   2→ Who do you bla:me for this?

Subsequently, the question "Who do you blame for this?" builds from this platform to project "blame" and its allocation as the primary agenda for the IE's response. Quite clearly, this question

embodies the presupposition that Benn will be defeated, that a name-
able set of persons can be held responsible for this, and that it is
appropriate for the IE to allocate blame.[6]

Presuppositions vary in the "depth" to which they are embedded
within a question. A measure of their embeddedness can be gained
by considering whether the respondent can address a question's presupposition while still responding to the question's agenda. In (13)
above, the respondent could have directly answered the question by
responding that no one was to blame. Here he would have responded
to the question's overt agenda, while also denying the question's
basic presupposition. In this case, then, the presupposition that persons are responsible and blameable for Benn's defeat is relatively
close to the "surface" of the question's design. This contrasts with
other more embedded cases in which, if respondents wish to contest a question's presuppositions, they must depart from directly
"answering" the question as put.

In (14), this more embedded form of presupposition is present.
This interview took place during a period when health care reform
was on the US congressional legislative agenda. Here an advertising
professional who ran a TV campaign against the Clinton proposals
is questioned about its timing. Embedded in the question "Why
so early in this debate" is the presupposition that the advertising
campaign has been initiated "early" relative to the timing of the
legislative program for health care reform:

(14)   US PBS *Newshour*: 21 Oct 1993: Health Care
         IR: Margaret Warner   IE: Linda Jenckes

```
1   IR:    =Mizz Jenckes, let me start with you. Ah:
2          y:ou've started all (of) this I think, the
3          health industry association.>Health insurance
4          association. .hhh Why:: so early in this debate
5          when there's not gonna be:: a vote on it ih- f'r
6          maybe a year?
7   IE:    Margaret (.) health care reform is well under
8          way. ...
```

---

[6] The IE, Jon Lansman, was a left-wing supporter of Tony Benn. Thus the perjorative
term "blame" also indexes his affiliation with Benn as the losing party in the
election. As a matter of historical record, the question likely invites the IE to name
Neil Kinnock, at that time a left-inclined Labour Party figure whose "treacherous"
vote againt Benn (together with those of a few supporters) may have tipped the
balance against Benn, who lost by a wafer-thin margin. After these events, Kinnock
rapidly moved to the center of the Labour Party, later becoming its leader.

In this case the presupposition is buried a little deeper than in (13): the IE begins her response by ignoring its "why" agenda, which calls for an account of some kind, in favor of an initial move to deny the question's presupposition that the campaign was started "early." Subsequently, she develops this response into an answer that justifies the timing of the campaign (data not shown).

A similar form of embedding is found in the following case – also involving a wh- question:

(15)   US PBS *Newshour*: 21 Oct 1993: Health Care
         IR: Margaret Warner   IE: Mandy Grunwald

```
 1   IR:   (Let me- Let me (just) ask Mandy Grunwald one
 2         other question.=How do you explain: that (.)
 3         public support for the President's plan has
 4         dropped off rather sharply since he announced it
 5         a month ago?=
 6   IE:   =We haven't seen those sharp drops, at all.  In
 7         fact we've[e seen
 8   IR:             [So your internal p[olling doesn't
 9   IE:                                [Our- our internal=
10         =polling has seen sustain:ed ah: support for the
11         plan,
```

In this case, a presupposition about a drop in public support for the President's plan is embedded in the question's design and treated as "given information." It is contested by the IE who, as a result, does not so much "answer" the question as "respond" to it. It is noticeable that the IR pursues the discrepancy between her assumed information and that of the IE by asking about the interviewee's alternative source of information ("internal polling").

More deeply embedded still is the following question put to vice-presidential candidate Dan Quayle:

(16)   US Bentsen–Quayle Vice-Presidential Debate: 5 Oct 1988
         IR: Judy Woodruff   IE: Dan Quayle AU: Audience

```
 1   IR:   hhhh Senator you have been criticized as we
 2         all know:: for your decision to stay out of
 3         the Vietnam War::, (0.3) for your poor
 4         academic record, .hhhhhh but mo:re troubling
 5         to so::me are some o'the comments that've
 6         been made by people in your own party. tch
 7         .hhh Just last week former Secretary of
 8         State Hai::g. .hh said that your pi:ck. (0.2)
 9         was the dumbest call George Bush could've
```

```
10            ma[:de.
11   AU:      [h-h-hhxhxhx[hxxXXXXXXXXXXXXX= ]
12   IR:                [ Your leader in the Senate]
13   AU:      =XXXXXXXXXXXXXXXXXXXX[XXXXXXXxxxxxxx
              (5.8) ]
14   IR:                           [Your leader in the Senate]
15            Bob Do:le said that a better qualified person
16            could have been chosen. .hhh Other Republicans
17            have been far more critical in private. .hhhh
18      →     Why d'you think that you have not made a more
19            substantial impression on some of these people
20            who have been able to observe you up clo:se.
21            (1.5)
22   IE:      .hhhhhh The question goe::s (1.0) to whether
23            I'm qualified (1.1) to be Vice President, (0.8)
```

The truth of the criticisms of Quayle is again presuppositionally embedded in the IR's "why" question at line 18. But here the formulation "Why d'you think you have not made a more substantial impression...," in contrast to the simpler "Why haven't you made a more substantial impression...," distances these presuppositions from the surface of the question. The focus of the question is pushed away from the criticisms themselves, and instead invites Quayle's reflections on aspects of his conduct that may have given rise to them. In the way that the question invites Quayle to reflect on his own behavior in relation to the criticisms, it makes the criticisms more difficult to address directly. Quayle's response is to evade the question (see chapter 7).

Deeply embedded presuppositions can be put to damaging effect in what have been usefully termed "quandary" questions (Nevin 1994). In these questions, epitomized by "When did you stop beating your wife?," the presuppositions are both deeply embedded and substantively very hostile to the recipient. Wh- questions are generally the most hospitable environment for the deeply embedded propositions of the "quandary" type. Thus in (17) below, the terms of the question actively discourage the IE from focusing on the damaging presupposition that he is a Marxist.

(17)   UK BBC Radio *World at One*: 13 Mar 1979: NUM Election
       IR: Robin Day   IE: Arthur Scargill

```
1    IR:     .hhh er What's the difference between your
2            Marxism and Mister McGahey's communism.
```

```
3   IE:      er The difference is that it's the press that
4            call me a Ma:rxist when I do not, (.) and never
5            have (.) er er given that description of myself.
6            . . .
```

Here any response by the IE, left-wing miners' leader Arthur Scargill, which addresses "the difference" between his views and those of McGahey would confirm the embedded presupposition of the question that he is a Marxist. It is noticeable that, although Scargill starts his response within the frame of the question ("The difference is"), he subsequently moves to undercut that presupposition. However, he can only do so by failing to respond to the agenda of the question, which concerns differences between himself and his rival (see chapter 7).

Yes/no or polar alternative questions, although they offer specific propositions for direct response, still normally contain embedded presuppositions. For example, (18) presupposes that Clinton's character is problematic – something which the IE explicitly contests in his response:

```
(18)   US ABC Nightline: 15 Oct 1992: Presidential Campaign
       IR: Chris Wallace   IE: James Carville

1   IR:   → =.hhh Mister Carville: should Governor Clinton's
2         → character now be off: limits somehow?
3   IE:     Well I don't know anything about his character
4           being off limits the man has magnificent
5           character...
```

And in the following case, which concerns an out-of-court settlement on charges that Texaco systematically discriminated against its African-American employees, the IR presents two distinct motivations for the settlement: either the company was discriminating, or it feared economic losses from the pending court case (arrowed "a" and "b"). These two options are presented as exhaustive of the possibilities:

```
(19)   US NBC Nightly News: 15 Nov 1996: Texaco Settlement
       IR: Tom Brokaw   IE: Peter Bijur

1   IR:     .h Mister Bijur what's pro:- what prompted this
2           settlement? .hh
3        a→ The fact that you concluded your company was
4        a→ in fact discrimina:ting¿
5        b→ or the prospects of: (.) more economic losses.
```

6   IE: To:m it was that we wanted to be f:air: to
7   ah all of the employees involved, we're a:
8   wonderful: gr:oup of people and family in this
9   company, and we wanta be equitable with
10   everybody.

Here, as Roth (1998b) has noted, the or-construction proposes the correctness of one of the candidate answers, simply leaving it to the IE to confirm whichever explanation is appropriate – something which the IE, Texaco's CEO, understandably resists. It is notable in this example that the IE begins his response at line 6 by addressing the IR by name ("To:m"), "summoning" him into recipiency (see Schegloff 1968; see also excerpt [14]. By this means, he projects that his subsequent action will be a "volunteered" first action, reducing its status as a "second" action that should properly fall within the terms of the prior question.[7]

In sum, all news interview questions embody presuppositions of some kind. For the most part, these presuppositions are clearly shared between interviewer and interviewee and, quite commonly, they have been established in earlier interview talk. Because of this, the presuppositional basis of many interviewer questions can easily be overlooked and taken for granted. Interviewer presuppositions are most visible when, as in most of the cases examined above, they are rejected by interviewees. In these incidents – and especially in quandary questions – the "difficulty' or "hostility" of the presuppositional content of news interview questions emerges quite clearly.[8]

The adversarial nature of interviewer questioning can be further shaped by aspects of question design which favor one type of response over another, and it is this aspect of question design to which we now turn.

Questions and "preference"

The third way in which a question can be designed to exert pressure on a respondent is through its facilitation of one response over

---

[7] See Clayman (1998) for a general account of the use of address terms in news interviews, Clayman (2001) for discussion of the use of address terms in evasive answers, and Heritage (Forthcoming b) for other practices for reducing the "responsiveness" of second position actions.

[8] See also Maynard (1985) for a discussion of how presuppositions become progressively disembedded in argument sequences involving children.

another. While many news interview questions are not designed to facilitate a particular answer, some evidently are. This is important because the more strongly interviewers design questions to favor one response over another, the more nearly their neutralistic stance may be compromised. A number of practices of question design – largely associated with "yes/no" questions – can achieve this outcome. What these practices have in common is some procedure for designing questions so as to invite – or, in conversation analytic terms, "prefer" (Pomerantz 1984; Sacks 1987, Schegloff 1988; Heritage 1988) – particular responses. They treat alternative interviewee responses as non-equivalent, and thus establish a higher threshold of accountability if the interviewee chooses to respond with the dispreferred option. When preference organization is mobilized against the likely position of interviewees, the latter may find themselves responding in a more "defensive" or self-justifying way than might otherwise be the case.

Questions can be shaped to prefer particular responses through the interrogative design of the question itself, or through prefatory statements, or by a combination of the two.

Conveying preference through interrogatives
Various aspects of questions can be designed to favor or facilitate particular interviewee responses. Some of these involve features of interrogative syntax itself. Although it might be thought that interrogatives are "safe" and "neutral" because they do not express positions, this is not always the case. For example, questions that are framed using negative interrogative syntax – e.g., Won't you . . . Isn't this . . . etc. – are routinely treated as embodying a very strong preference for a "yes" answer. Indeed interviewees recurrently respond to such designs as opinion statements to be agreed or disagreed with (Heritage Forthcoming b). The following is a case in point. Here the IE is the Deputy Assistant Secretary of State:

(20)   US PBS *Newshour*: 22 July 1985: State of Emergency
       IR: Judy Woodruff   IE: Frank Wisner

1   IR: → But isn't this (.) d- declaration of the state
2   of emergency:: (.) an admission: that the
3   eh=South African: (.) Gover'ment's policies have
4   not worked, an' in fact that the um- United
5   States (0.2) administration's policy of

6   constructive engagement (.) has not worked.
7   IE: → I do <u>not</u> agree with you .hhhh that the approach
8   <u>we</u> have taken (.) toward South Africa is- a- is
9   an incorrect app<u>ro</u>ach...

The IR's negative formulation "Isn't this..." is clearly treated by the IE as asserting an opinion when he replies "I do *not* agree with you..." And, in (21), President Clinton responds in a similar way to a negatively formulated question, from UPI's Helen Thomas, in a televised press conference:

(21)   US Presidential Press Conference: 7 Mar 1997: Campaign
       IR: Helen Thomas   IE: Bill Clinton

1   IR: W'l Mister President in your <u>zea:</u>l (.) for funds
2   → during the last campaign .hh didn't you put the
3   Vice President (.) an' Maggie and all the others
4   in your (0.4) administration top side .hh in a
5   very vulnerable position, hh
6   (0.5)
7   IR: → I disagree with that.hh u- How are we vulnerable
8   because...

These negatively formed interrogatives are the only type of interrogative to which interviewees respond in this way.

   Other aspects of interrogative syntax can also be designed to prefer particular responses. Statements followed by tag questions (e.g., "Is it?," "Hasn't it?," etc.) clearly do so. In this format, the statement describes a state of affairs and the tag invites confirmation of the statement. The use of this format is designed to promote the interviewee's acceptance of the statement. Excerpt (22) exemplifies this construction. Here the affirmative statement with the negative tag question promotes acceptance with a confirming "yes" response:

(22)   UK BBC Radio *World at One*: 3 Mar 1979: NUM Election
       IR: Robin Day IE: Arthur Scargill

1   IR: =Do you a<u>scri:</u>be to Marxist economic
2   philosophy.=
3   IE: =I would say that there: er: the: (.) <u>phi</u>losophy
4   of <u>M</u>arx as far as the eco<u>no</u>mics of <u>Bri</u>tain is
5   concerned is <u>o</u>ne with which I find <u>sym</u>pathy.=and
6   would sup<u>port</u> it.=Yes.
7   (.)
8   IR: → Well <u>that</u> makes you a <u>Mar</u>xist
9   doe[sn't it.]

10   IE: [Not= nece]ssarily makes me a Marxist in the
11   descriptive sense, .hhh er in the same way that
12   you do not describe many Labour Members of
13   Parliament as Marxist,=and equally .hhh you
14   wouldn't describe many other people who are
15   leading Christians .hhh as (.) Christian Members
16   of Parliament...

Excerpt (23) below similarly illustrates the device in reverse form.
Here the negative statement with a positive tag question promotes
acceptance with a confirming "no" response:

(23)   UK BBC Radio *Today*: June 1993: South Africa Amnesty
       IR: John Humphrys   IE: Yanni Momberg

1   IR: Now there's talk that the Cabinet will announce
2   some sort of am:nesty for people who've
3   committed crimes: ah racially motivated crimes
4   presumably. .hh Uhm under the ah over the last
5   few years.
6   →   That wouldn't be acceptable to the ANC. would
7   it?
8   IE: .hhh Question of amnesty's a very difficult
9   situation. ...

Although the polarity as between positive and negative statements
is different in (22) and (23), confirmation of the state of affairs
proposed by the interviewer is strongly favored in both cases.

The significance of these forms of question design are obvious
when we recognize that they are entirely optional. The substance of
the question in (23) could have been equally well presented in a less
tilted fashion as "Would that be unacceptable to the ANC?" Or as
the more tilted "Wouldn't that be unacceptable to the ANC?" It is
for the interviewer to determine just how much "tilt" will be built
into the question and, hence, how much pressure will be exerted on
the interviewee for a confirming response.

Other aspects of question design can also embody preferences of
this kind. For example, negative polarity items (Horn 1989) such as
"any" embody a preference for a "no" answer. In the following case,
the journalist represents other people's descriptions of prison camps
in Bosnia as "concentration camps," and then asks the IE, a representative of the International Society for Human Rights (ISHR),
"Do you believe there's any justification for that at all?"

(24)   UK BBC Radio *Today*: June 1993: Bosnia Camps
       IR: John Humphrys   IE: Ian Smedley
1   IR: .hhh People have u: :sed the phrase
2   concentration camps: and the Bosnians
3   themselves have used that phrase.
4   →   Do you believe there's any justification
5   for that at all?

Here the final segment of the IR's turn incorporates the negative
polarity terms "any justification" and "at all," inviting a "no" response. This question, asked early in the Bosnia conflict and before
Serbian war crimes had been confirmed and publicized, and directed
to a representative of an organization noted for its caution and pro-
bity in making partisan accusations,[9] is cautiously designed for a
negative answer.

Finally, incorporation of terms like "seriously" or "really" also
embody preferences for negative responses. When they are used, as
they normally are, in questions that prefer responses that contrast
with the interviewee's known position, they strongly "challenge"
them to defend those positions. For example, in the following case,
Ross Perot is interviewed about his candidacy in the 1992 US

---

[9] Earlier in the interview, the IR and IE collaborate in establishing the organization
that the interviewee represents as aiming at independence and impartiality in the
way it deals with human rights issues:

IR: 1→   Do you <u>work</u> like Amnesty International wor: :ks? I
         mean are you comp<u>le</u>tely <u>a</u>political in the way that
         Amnesty International is for in[stance.
IE: [.hhh That's right
         we're ha-a human rights organization. .hh ah that's
         simply concerned with human rights and humanitarian
         issues.
IR: 2→   .hhh And the sort of people who've been (.) looking
         at the camps, are they local people? Because if they
         are then they might be suspect might they not? (An')
         that is to say they mi- they might have views of
         their own.
IE: .hhh That's right it's very <u>d</u>ifficult to insure
         complete impartiality .hh but we have had observers
         .hh from a number of ISHR international sections
         .hh an' including myself, I went over to Croatia .hhh
         a couple of months ago .hh and talked first hand to
         people in a number of refugee camps the<u>re</u> .hh ah so
         wherever possible we have tried to also use .h
         independent ah sources from outside Yugoslavia.
IR: 3→   .hh And what sort of reports are you getting back?
IE: .hh Well we're getting s-some quite terrible reports.
         . . .

presidential election, and his position on the growing US federal budget deficit. Earlier in the interview he had justified his candidacy as a means of getting the main political parties to take the deficit seriously.

(25) US PBS *Newshour*: 18 Sep 1992: Presidential Election
        IR: Judy Woodruff   IE: Ross Perot

```
 1   IR:    Alright n-, let's talk about some of the things
 2           you propose. R:aising the tax on gasoline ten
 3           cents a yea:r for the next five y[ears fifty=
 4   IE:                                      [Yes
 5   IR:    =cents.
 6   IE:    Yes.
 7   IR:    A::h a gallon after five y[ears.
 8   IE:                              [A:fter five years.
 9   IR:    Eh: taxing all but fifteen percent of the social
10           security benefits of recipients that e:arn over
11           twenty five thousand dollars a year.
12   IE:    Exactly.=
13   IR:    =Now you're endorsing that.
14   IE:    Yes.
15   IR:  → Do you (.) s:eriously believe that President
16        → Bush, or Bill Clinton again is going to endorse
17        → either [one of those.
18   IE:           [(I thought) they feel the American
19           people don't have the stomach for fair (0.2)
20           shared (.) sacrifice. (1.2) The facts are the
21           American people do=That's the point we're trying
22           to make.
```

Here, after listing two potentially unpopular tax measures, the incorporation of the word "seriously" into the IR's question is designed for a "no" answer, and is thus hostile to Perot's political position. If he is to be consistent with his earlier stated position, his answer to this question must be "yes," must be accounted for, and must do so in a way that effectively competes with the skepticism that the IR's question conveys.

Conveying preference through question prefaces
In addition to the interrogative component of question design, prefatory statements in prefaced questions can also be built to prefer particular responses.

As we saw in chapter 5, one straightforward method for conveying preference is to invoke others who take a particular view of the issue (Clayman 1992). In (26), for example, the IE (who works for a human rights organization) is asked whether he would describe prison camps in Bosnia as "concentration camps."

(26) UK BBC Radio *Today*: June 1993: Bosnia Camps
      IR: John Humphrys   IE: Ian Smedley
 1 IR: → .hhh People have u::sed the phrase
 2   → concentration camps: and the Bosnians
 3   → themselves have used that phrase.
 4   Do you believe there's any justification
 5   for that at all?
 6 IE: .hh I think in the case of some of the larger
 7   camps there are, that's certainly accurate .hh
 8   ah if you count .h torture and execution as
 9   hallmarks .h of concentration camps .h then the
10   reports we've received ah would seem to suggest
11   that is an accurate description for some of
12   them.

This is obviously a delicate question for a human rights worker to answer. As noted above, in an earlier part of the interview, the IE had been at pains to stress the apolitical and non-partisan nature of his organization. The design of the IR's question is very cautious, reflecting an orientation to this issue. First, the IR introduces the question by referring to anonymous "people" who have used the term "concentration camp," and then augments this with the assertion that the "Bosnians themselves" have used the same term. These aspects of the question favor a "yes" answer. However the final segment of the question asks if there is "any justification...at all" for this term which, as we have seen, favors a "no" answer. The question is thus cautiously balanced between the two possible responses. Thus, regardless of how the IE responds, he will be seen to have responded to a carefully and judiciously formulated question, and can match it with an equally careful answer. It is just such a response that the question receives (lines 6–12).

A stronger mobilization of preference is exhibited in (27). Here the interview concerns pending legislation to narrow the time limit for legal abortions. The IE – British Conservative MP, Jill Knight – is in favor of the proposed legislation.

(27)   UK ATV *Afternoon Plus*: 22 Jan 1980: Abortion Limits
        IR: Unknown   IE: Jill Knight

```
 1   IR:      ... Can we now take up then the main issues of
 2            that bill which r- (.) remain substantially the
 3            same. (.) and indeed (0.2) have caused a great
 4            deal of concern. (0.4) But first you'll note
 5            .hhh is the clause about (.) time limits h in
 6            which h abortions can be .h legally=
 7   IE :     =°(yes)°=
 8   IR:      =ha:d. And the time limit h (.) according to the
 9            bill has now dropped .h from twenty eight weeks
10            .h (.) to twenty wee[ks.
11   IE:                          [Yes.=
12   IR:   →  =Now< a lot of people are very concerned about
13         →  this. [.hh How concerned are you.
14   IE:             [°Yeh°
15   IE:      .hhh uh: (.) I think this is right. I think that
16            um: .hh again one's had a lot of e:uh
17            conflicting evidence on this but .hh what has
18            come ou: :t h an' I think that .h the public have
19            been concerned about this. .hhh is that there
20            have been th'most distressing cases ...
```

The IR's lengthy question preface (1–10) shifts topic (lines 1–4) and
describes the proposed reduction of the period within which abortion can be legally obtained (from twenty-eight weeks to twenty
weeks). It culminates in the observation that "a lot of people are
very concerned about this" (lines 12–13). With this statement, the
IR clearly suggests widespread concern about curtailing the time period, mobilizing a sense of support for that point of view which the IE
must deal with. The IR's final question ("How concerned are you?")
invites, or challenges, the IE to address that concern. But here the
IE is invited to address the "concern" of people about the *reduction*
in the time limit for abortions – something that this IE favors. The
compelling power of this hostile question preface is shown by the
IE's rather convoluted effort to harness the term "concern" to issues
on her – anti-abortion – side of the argument: the "distressing cases"
she goes on to describe involve the destruction of well-formed fe-
tuses. In this way, the IE establishes a superficial lexical connection
between her comments and the agenda set by the IR's question, and
thus the terms of the question are managed in a fashion which is
more helpful to her position.

In these cases, preference is established by a statement prior to the IR's question. A similar effect can be achieved by a statement positioned after the question as in (28), where a member of the governing Conservative Party is questioned about the upshot of his disagreements with the Thatcher administration:

(28)   UK BBCTV *Newsnight*: 14 Oct 1981: Conservative Splits
         IR: John Tusa   IE: Sir Ian Gilmour

```
1  IR:    But won't you have to consider threatening to
2         vote against the Government,=That's surely what
3         (.) what all the critics now have to face.
4  IE:    We::ll I don't know, no I- I think the: the
5         we're still at the (.) stage of the intellectual
6         argument which I think .hh we're winning,=
7         because what they've put forward is just the
8         same old stuff.=Which nobody believes and it
9         hasn't worked.
```

Here the initial question component of the IR's turn, a negative interrogative which is itself strongly weighted to expect an affirmative answer (see the discussion of [21] above), is further supported by a statement that asserts that all the (internal) government critics "now" have to consider threatening to vote against the Government.

The practice of prefacing questions with statements that are designed to favor particular responses can be developed to the point that interviewers present positions as effectively incontrovertible, and then invite interviewees to deny them. This practice is common in cases where interviewees are "stonewalling" positions which they are mandated to defend. The following is a case in point. Here then-US Defense Deputy Secretary, John Deutch, is interviewed about "Gulf War Syndrome" and its possible origin in seron gas use during the conflict. The syndrome is now the focus for claims for compensation by war veterans:

(29)   US CBS *60 Minutes*: 12 Mar 1995: Seron Gas in Kuwait
         IR: Ed Bradley   IE: John Deutch

```
1  IR:    Secretary Deutch you say there is no evidence.
2         .hh You've got ca:ses where: khh theh- Czechs:
3         say: that they ↑foun:d seron. You say they
4         didn't, th:ey say: (.) that they did. .hh You
5         have soldiers say:ing: that they experienced
```

```
 6            burning sensations after explosions in the air.
 7            That they became nauseous, that they got .hh
 8            headaches. .hh You have two hundred fifty
 9            gallons of chemical agents that were found
10            in:si:de Kuwait. .hh You had scuds that had
11            seron in the warheads.
12            (1.0)
13    IR:     If that's not evidence what is it.
```

Deutch is, of course, defending the federal government against medical and other damages claims which could be very extensive. Here
Deutch's position is contrasted with the statements of Czechs, the
reported symptoms of soldiers, and with other observations that
are presented as "fact." The final interrogative simply challenges
the IE to deny the status of these various reported statements and
assertions as evidence.

Hostile questioning

So far we have examined a range of resources which interviewers can
deploy to exert pressure on interviewees. In the remaining part of
this chapter, we turn to deal with questions that are quite markedly
hostile and, in a number of instances push the boundaries of hostile
questioning to their limits.

Chapters 4 and 5 showed that interviewers are very cautious
about making free-standing assertions. They make them infrequently and when they do so it is often in guarded fashion
(chapter 5). We have also seen that interviewees may attempt to
maneuver interviewers into unguarded assertions and that interviewers generally strongly resist these maneuvers. In the remainder
of this chapter, we examine some relatively unusual cases in which
interviewers seem voluntarily to slip outside the boundaries of the
permissible and clearly start to take an advocacy role. We begin with
interrogatives that do not really "question."

Negative formulation as a "coercive" feature of question design

So far, we have argued that interviewers can use any interrogatively formed utterance and be clearly understood as engaged
in "questioning" rather than stating an opinion. However, there
are some interrogatives that are so severely framed in favor of a

particular kind of answer that they are routinely treated as asserting
a position. The most prominent of these are the negatively formed
questions discussed earlier, of which the following are typical:

(30)   UK BBCTV *Newsnight*: 14 Oct 1981: Conservative Splits
       IR: John Tusa   IE: Sir Ian Gilmour
1 IR: But won't you have to consider threatening to
2   vote against the Government,=That's surely what
3   (.) what all the critics now have to face.

(31)   UK ATV Central Lobby: 1985: Labour Party
       IR: Reg Harcourt   IE: Tony Benn
1 IR: But shouldn't you be preaching unity now instead
2   of this class warfare which you: which you: talk
3   about.

The negative question in (30) very strongly projects a "yes" response to the proposition that follows it, i.e., that he will have to
"consider theatening to vote against the Government"; and in (31), it
projects that the IE will respond that he should be "preaching unity."
So strong is this projection that questions formatted in this way are,
as noted earlier, frequently treated by IEs as expressing an opinion.
This is particularly marked when, as is most often the case, the format is used to propose a position that counters or challenges the
IE's stated position, or otherwise runs contrary to the IE's political
interests.

    Thus, in (32), the IE – British Liberal Democrat leader Paddy
Ashdown – responds by treating the IR as having made an assertion
that he can be challenged to "prove" and, subsequently, by asserting
that the IR made a "proposition":

(32)   UK BBCTV *Newsnight*: Sep 1993: Liberal Party
       IR: Jeremy Paxman   IE: Paddy Ashdown
1 IR: .hh Right. (.) Okay. S:o (0.2) you have
2   loose cannon:s. (0.2) on your deck jus:t (.)
3   as you rightly say a:ll parties have. .hh
4   But if we generously put this do:wn to (.)
5   over exuberance. (0.2) tch .hh (.)
6   → doesn't that suggest that your party is still:
7   (0.2) immatur:e. (0.3) irresponsible (.)
8   undisciplin:ed h (0.2) unserious.
9 IE: ⇒ Well, (0.2) prove tha:t.

```
10          (0.6)
11   IE:   ⇒ <You made th'proposition,> (0.2) propose it to
12          me.=
```

And in (33), the IE – a senior British Labour Party figure – comments that the IR's prior turn was "good trade union bashing stuff" while the IE responds by claiming that, on the contrary, "it's just describing the way things are."

(33)   UK BBCTV *Panorama*: 28 Jan 1981: Trade Unions
       IR: Donald MacCormick   IE: Neil Kinnock

```
 1   IR:   → ... Isn't the overall impa:ct of this whole
 2             procedure we've seen .hhh to: remind the country
 3             that the Labour Party is very largely in the
 4             grip of trade unions whose procedures are both
 5             .h ramshackle and undemocratic, .hh and to call
 6             what's just happened .hh an election of a deputy
 7             leader .h is actually a farce:. [And has just]=
 8   IE:                                       [But-    But-]
 9   IR:   = demonstrated .hh to the country at large how
10        the [Labour Party's affairs are conducted]
11   IE:   ⇒ [Yeah. tha- tha- tha- that']s
12         ⇒ good trade union bashing stuff but it's
13         ⇒ absolutely irr[elevant (           )]
14   IR:   →              [It's not trade union] bashing at
15        all,=it's just describing the way things are.
```

These data suggest that "negative" questions are a very strong way for an IR to project an expected answer – strong enough, when produced in association with question content that contests an IE's position, to be disagreed with and hence treated as having made an assertion. In this context, it is clear that IE Sam Donaldson was cutting it fine when he claims – in (34), lines 13–14 – "to be asking a question" and not "expressing my personal views."

(34)   US ABC *This Week*: Oct 1989: Savings & Loan Bailout
       IR: Sam Donaldson   IE: Richard Darman

```
 1   IR:   → Isn't it a fact, Mr. Darman, that the taxpayers
 2             will pay more in interest than if they just paid
 3             it out of general revenues?
 4   IE:   No, not necessarily. That's a technical
 5             argument –
 6   IR:   It's not a – may I, sir? It's not a technical
 7             argument.
```

8   → Isn't it a fact?
9   IE: No, it's definitely not a fact. Because first
10   of all, twenty billion of the fifty billion is
11   ⇒ being handled in just the way you want –
12   ⇒ through treasury financing. The remaining –
13   IR: → I'm just asking you a question. I'm not
14   → expressing my personal views.
15   IE: I understand.

Not only is Donaldson's first question a negative interrogative of the type that is frequently treated as an opinion statement, but also at lines 6–7, Donaldson directly disagrees with the IE (with "It's not a technical argument."), and then effectively reasserts that opinion a second time with a further negative question "Isn't it a fact?" (line 8). Under these circumstances, it is hardly surprising that the IE treats him as having "taken a position" on the issue with his response that "twenty billion of the fifty billion is being handled in just the way you want – through treasury financing." Thus Donaldson's response, that he was "just asking... a question" is distinctly disingenuous! For it relies on the fact that his turn deployed interrogative syntax, while ignoring its highly argumentative tilt.

The fact that negative questions are among the most directive – and coercive – forms of question design that an interviewer can deploy, gives us a way to understand the fact that the IR in (30), for example, did not allow his turn to rest with this construction, but rather proceeded with a further unit that somewhat mitigated its impact. It also allows us to see that in the following case (from chapter 5), the IR's move from a negatively formulated question to the "weaker" third-party attributed statement as a means of soliciting IE response is a form of "retreat":

(35)   US PBS *Newshour*: 10 June 1985: Arms Control Agreement
        IR: Robert MacNeil   IE: Ken Adelman
1   IR: <u>How</u> d'you sum up the <u>me</u>:ssage. that this
2   decision is <u>s</u>ending to the Soviets?
3   IE: .hhh <u>W</u>ell as I started- to <u>say</u>::it is a- one of:
4   <u>war</u>ning and opport<u>u</u>nity. The <u>war</u>ning is (.)
5   you'd <u>better</u> comply: to arms control::
6   agreements if arms control is going to have any
7   <u>ch</u>ance of succ<u>ee</u>ding in the <u>fu</u>ture. <u>U</u>nilateral
8   compliance by the United States is just <u>not</u> in
9   the works...

```
10          ((Four lines omitted))
11   IR:  → But isn't this- uh::: critics uh on the
12          conservative side of the political argument
13          have argued that this is:. Abiding by the
14          treaty is: unilateral (.) observance. (.) uh::
15          or compliance. (.) by the United States.
```

And relatedly, reviewing (38) from chapter 4, we can see that the IR – faced with an IE's interjective resistance to his question preface (arrow 1) – in fact responds with one of the most coercive forms of question design (arrow 2):

(36)   UK BBCTV *Newsnight*: 16 Oct 1981: Conservative Splits
       IR: Peter Snow   IE: Francis Pym

```
 1   IR:        ... I couldn't help notici:ng when uh .hhh Sir
 2              Geoffrey Howe was speaking this afternoon how
 3              while all your other ministerial colleagues were
 4              clapping uh .hh during his speech in between
 5              many of the things he was saying .hh you hardly
 6              clapped at all.=You hardly applauded at all.
 7              =Sitting as you were beside Mister Heath.
 8              .hhh [Do you:]
 9   IE:  1→        [Come o]ff it.
10   IR:  2→   d- (.) Well is it not true.=
11   IE:       =cu- Come off it.=( ) I clapped ... ((continues))
```

Negative questions are a relatively extreme form of question design that is used sparingly in the news interview. Nonetheless they are part of an array of question design practices with which interviewers can display a strong expectation in favor of a particular answer. Since such expectations are also conveyed to an "overhearing" news audience, negative questions can involve a real erosion of the neutralism that interviewers generally claim through the use of interrogatives in questioning public figures.

Accusatory questions

Negative questions are not the only ones that can fail to "question." Another type of non-questioning interrogative is a variant on "accountability" questions. These normally take the form "Why did you X." However, they can also take a more damaging form: "How can you X" or "How could you X." In contrast, to the "Why did you X," the "How could you X" format is clearly confrontational.

When it is used to question the past activities of the interviewee, it implies the unanswerability of the "question," and is virtually specialized for the delivery of accusations. Noticeably, this question format is often followed by statements that consolidate the interviewer's accusatory role with hostile remarks directly asserting a position as the interviewer's own.

   The following is a case in point. Here Spartak Beglov, a Moscow press agency official is questioned about a letter he had published in the London *Times*. The letter attacked Margaret Thatcher's suggestion that human rights violations in the then-USSR should be met by a boycott of the 1980 Olympic Games in Moscow. In this excerpt, the IR increasingly drifts towards the role of an advocate for the "Western" position. He begins at line 1 with an "accusatory" form of question design ("How could you talk about human rights...").
He justifies this question (lines 2–4) by referring to the banishment of the noted Soviet physicist and dissenter Andrei Sakharov, stating that it is not a product of "just process."

(37)   UK BBC Radio *World at One*: 24 Jan 1980: Human Rights
         IR: Robin Day   IE: Spartak Beglov
   1   IR: → How could you talk about human rights when
   2   Doctor Sakharov has been banished .hhh without
   3   (.) tria::l (.) .hh er and without as we can see
   4   any form of just (.) process.
   5   IE: Well we can say about an- er uhm any of the
   6   administrative actions taken by the British
   7   government [in   Ulster   or   North]ern=
   8   IR: [Well I'm talking about the-]
   9   IE: =Ireland or in other parts. But this has
   10   [had nothing to do with] the human rights of=
   11 IR: [Well if you'd like to-]
   12 IE: =sportsman.=
   13 IR: → =If you'd like to give- if you'd like to give me
   14   → an example I'll deal with it.

Subsequently, after Beglov has countered by referring to British "administrative actions" in Northern Ireland, the IR explicitly begins to represent the British position by proposing to "deal with" any "examples" that Beglov can offer (lines 13–14). Here, where the IR could have challenged the IE to justify his position with a question, he instead elects to take a more antagonistic position and offers to defend the British Government's conduct directly.

And in the following case, an IR slips into advocacy on behalf of a studio audience against his IE. In this notorious British interview, briefly described in chapters 2 and 5, David Frost confronts a businessman, Emil Savundra, who had sold his auto insurance company – effectively liquidating it – leaving many claims outstanding. Savundra was subsequently tried and convicted for fraud. The interview took place before his trial and was conducted in front of a studio audience composed of individuals who had claims outstanding against the company. Savundra sat facing the audience, which was highly animated, while Frost addressed him from a standing position – frequently standing over him. Under the pressure of audience reaction and the abrasive questioning techniques employed, Savundra intermittently comes to abandon the interview footing. For example, the video-recording shows that his remark at line 11 is directed to the audience rather than David Frost, and he acknowledges Frost's question prefaces on several occasions (lines 14, 29 and 31).

(38)   UK BBCTV *Omnibus*: 21 Apr 1981: Insurance Fraud
       IR: David Frost   IE: Emil Savundra AU: Studio Audience

```
 1   IE:       By selling out (0.7) I have no legal
 2             responsibility,(0.2) and no moral
 3             responsibility.
 4   AU:       Rubbish
 5   AU:       No moral responsibility?
 6   IR:  1→   You have- (0.5) you have total moral
 7        1→   respons[ibility for ALL th]ese people.
 8   IE:             [I beg your pardo:n]
 9   IE:       I beg your PARDON Mister Frost.
10   AU:       You have.
11   IE:       I have not.
12   IR:  2→   How can you s- You say you're a Roman Catholic
13        2→   and [it's ] the will of God. .hh How can you be=
14   IE:           [Yes]
15   IR:  2→   =responsible and head of company when all these
16        2→   things happen. .hh And you think by some fake
17        2→   deal with Quincey Walker (.) four thousand
18        2→   pou[nds (.) on June twenty third   ]
19   IE:          [ You have already assume: :d ]
20   IE:       You have already assumed [a     fake     dea:l ]
21   IR:  3→                            [ How d'you get rid ]
22        3→   of moral responsibility.
23   AU:       Yeah                                          ]
```

24 AU: You can't
25 AU: You can't
26 IE: How- you have already assumed (0.6) you've- one
27   thing: the fake dea:l
28 IR: 4→ Well forget the fake deal.   [How] do you sign=
29 IE: [Right]
30 IR: 4→ =a bit of paper [.hh] that gets rid of past=
31 IE: [Yes]
32 IR: 4→ =moral responsibility.
33 IR: 5→ =Tell me that.
34 IE: By i- =
35 IR: 6→ ='Cause we'd all love to know.

This excerpt begins with the IE's denial of "legal responsibility" and
"moral responsibility" for his dealings. This is immediately countered by the IR with the flat assertion that the IE has "total moral
responsibility for all these people" (arrow 1). Here the IR has completely departed from any semblance of a neutralistic stance. Further,
each of the three following "questions" – which are formatted as
"How can you X" or "How do you X" and address the IE's "moral
responsibility" for past actions – push the limits of news interview
questioning. Indeed, these questions in this sequential context can
be heard – and indeed are treated by the IE and the audience – as
rhetorical in character, and not in search of an answer so much as
designed to directly *accuse* the IE. This is particularly apparent in
the second formulation of Frost's question "How d'you get rid of
moral responsibility" (arrowed 3) which overlaps and interdicts the
IE's attempt to correct an earlier assertion. Notably the audience
affiliates with this question, thereby treating it as an assertion to
be agreed with. At the third attempt (arrowed 4) the IR particular-
izes his previous question by reference to signing "a bit of paper"
thereby further undermining the credibility of the business transac-
tion that the IE argues has relieved him of his responsibilities. The
IR subsequently pursues a response with a question substitute ("Tell
me that.") and, after the IE initiates a response, further pursues by
aligning himself directly with the audience (" 'Cause we'd all love to
know."). This remark, which is articulated in a deeply ironic fashion, abruptly cuts the IE off even as it directly intimates that the
question it refers to is unanswerable.
    This interview was widely regarded as a form of "trial by televi-
sion" and indeed was cited by Savundra, in his appeal against his

subsequent conviction for fraud, as having prejudiced a fair trial. In a summing up, the appeal judge – commenting on this interview– concluded that:

The court has no doubt that the television authorities and all those producing and appearing in televised programmes are conscious of their public
responsibility and know also of the peril in which they would all stand if
any such interview were ever to be televised in future. Trial by television is
not to be tolerated in a civilised society.

These remarks, as Michael Tracey (1977) has observed, strongly in-
fluenced the subsequent outlooks of UK news and current affairs
producers, and contributed to a progressive chilling of their preparedness to seek controversy in news shows.

A third, and highly problematic instance of an interviewer going
beyond "the parameters of the permissible" emerged in the Bush–
Rather interview that occurred before the primaries for the US presidential elections in 1991. The focus of this interview concerned
Bush's involvement in the Iran-Contra scandal, and the extent of his
knowledge and culpability in that matter. In the following segment,
CBS interviewer Dan Rather is questioning Vice President Bush
about a meeting in which Secretary of State George Schultz was
alleged to have expressed fury when he learned of the arms-for-
hostages deal with Iran (data not shown). At line 1, Rather begins
a next question ("Can you explain how-") which he then abandons
in favor of an additional background element concerning Bush's
anti-terrorism expertise (lines 12–16):

```
(39)  US CBS Evening News: 25 Jan 1988: Iran-Contra
       IR: Dan Rather   IE: George Bush
 1  IR:    =.hhh Can you explain how- (.) you were supposed
 2          to be the- eh- you are:. you're an anti
 3          terrorist expert. .hhh we- (0.2) Iran was
 4          officially a terrorist state. .hh you went
 5          a[round telling eh::- eh- ehr-        ]
 6  IE:      [I've already explained that Dan, I] wanted
 7          those [hostages- I wanted  Mister ]=
 8  IR:            [( ) Mist' Vice President (the ]=
 9  IE:    =[ Buckley    ] outta there.
10  IR:    =[question is)]
11  IR:    But-
12          (0.3)
13  IE:    [before 'e was killed. ] [which he)]=
```

14 IR: ⇒ [You've- you've made us <u>hyp</u>]oc[rites in]=
15 IE: =[(   )]=
16 IR: ⇒ =[the <u>face</u> o' the <u>world</u>.]=
17 IR: ⇒ =<u>How</u> couldja [gr- <u>how</u> couldja-] (.) <u>sign</u> <u>on</u>=
18 IE: [(That was ba:d)]
19 IR: ⇒ =to such a policy. .hh[h And the <u>question</u>]=
20 IE: [Well   (half-)   the]=
21 IR: =[is, what does that tell us about your]=
22 IE: =[same   reason   the   <u>President</u>]=
23 IR: =[<u>record</u>.]
24 IE: =[si]gned on to it. (0.2) The same reason
25   the <u>President</u> signed on to it. .hh When a CIA
26   agent is being <u>tor</u>tured to <u>death</u>, .h maybe ya
27   <u>err</u> on the side of a <u>human</u> <u>life</u>.

These background remarks are intersected, however, by Bush's repetition of his reasons for negotiating with Iran (saving the life of
a senior CIA operative – Mister Buckley – lines 6–7, 9 and 13).
In response, and in overlap with the continuation of Bush's explanation, Rather expostulates "You've-you've made us hypocrites
in the face o' the world" (lines 14/16). And he continues with an
utterance – "How couldja gr- how couldja- (.) sign on to such a
policy."(lines 17/19) – embodying the format "How could you X"
that, as we have seen, is explicitly accusatory.[10] In overlap with this
interrogative, Bush can be heard to remark "That was bad." Rather
subsequently attempts to retreat to the safety of a question with
"And the question is, what does that tell us about your record,"
reconnecting with an earlier Bush demand to be interviewed about
"the record," and providing that his earlier assertion and accusatory
question were to be heard as merely prefatory, rather than stand-
alone accusations. However the damage has been done.

Splits, forks and contrasts

Perhaps the most elaborately hostile questioning that news interviewers can engage in involves constructing interviewees as en-
meshed in some form of disagreement or self-contradiction. This
can take two main forms: (i) interviewees can be presented as in

---

[10] Significantly, "How do you X," "How can you X" and, most strongly, "How could
you X," when applied to *past* actions of a *recipient*, all accomplish accusations.

disagreement with their political allies, or (ii) as in a situation of inconsistency or self-contradiction in their own positions.

We have already seen the first of these maneuvers in earlier examples (e.g., [10]). It is very common in Britain, where the parliamentary process places a premium on party loyalty and consistency in voting with the party leadership. It is less common in the United States where congressional voting is less constrained by party loyalties. British journalists sometimes refer to this style of questioning as "split-hunting." A very overt case is the following. The context of this interview is a developing disagreement within the Conservative Party over Britain's relations with the European Common Market. The Conservative right, led by then Prime Minister Margaret Thatcher, was hostile to closer relations. Her position was opposed by ex-Prime Minister Edward Heath who led a faction favoring closer ties to the community. The conflict seemed likely to impact the political succession to Thatcher – if the left prevailed, the interviewee in the following example, Michael Heseltine, would have been the likely next leader of the party. In this case, the IR attempts to induce Heseltine to take up a public position that is opposed to Thatcher's (and aligned to Heath's) on three successive occasions and, in the subsequent parts of the interview, the same topic is pursued in more subtle ways. In fact, the entire seven-minute interview is devoted to "split hunting." We begin at the beginning of the interview, where the IR's first question refers to a filmed report that had just been shown:

(40)   UK BBCTV *Newsnight*: June 1989: European Common Market
       IR: Donald MacCormick   IE: Michael Heseltine

```
 1  IR:    Well Michael Heseltine let's begin: with one of
 2          the comments towards the end of Margaret
 3          Gilmore's report.
 4     →    Was Philip Stevens of the Financial Ti:mes right
 5     →    (.) to place you: (.) in this argument closer to
 6     →    Mister Heath(.) than to Missus Thatcher.=
 7  IE:     =.hhh Well you know one of the reasons that I:
 8          wanted to (.) come on you:r pro:gra:m .hh is
 9          precisely to refu:se to invo:lve the
10          personalities: in this issue. I think Mister
11          Heath has done his own cause a disservice .hh
12          in: EU: the way in which he has spoken. This is
13          not a matter of personalities and the
```

14   Conservative Party is <u>not</u> going to have th- the
15   sort of row that the media will enjoy:. .Hhh
16   but it <u>is</u> impo:rtant .h that (.) the
17   Conservative Party <u>and</u> the country (.) discuss
18   the id<u>ea</u>s. And I <u>wholl</u>y reject the analysis that
19   this will do us harm in the po:lls. <u>I</u> believe
20   it'll do us good (.) because we shall be <u>telling</u>
21   the British people what the <u>op</u>tions are, (.)
22   what the al<u>ter</u>natives are, (.) and there will be
23   no doubt in my mi:nd they will want
24   Conservatives to pursue: whichever one we
25   select.
26   IR: → But <u>on:</u> the <u>sub</u>stance of the ar:gument are you
27   → <u>clos</u>er to: to Mister Heath=
28   IE: =No you're [back on the [sa:me si[tuation and
29   IR: [b-   [No   [I'm ah-
30   IE: what you're gonna try and do and you're <u>not</u>
31   gonna succ<u>eed</u> if we sit here all <u>night</u>, you are
32   <u>not</u> going to <u>get</u> me into a <u>per</u>sonality
33   [divisive process. .hh I will ta:lk about=
34   IR: [hm
35   IE: =the <u>id</u>eas of Europe. My:- my- I <u>can</u>not
36   over<u>stress(f)</u> to you (.) the European issue is
37   going to dominate the next deca:de, and if we
38   try to con<u>duct</u> it on a sort of <u>per</u>sonality
39   divisive basis .h we will di<u>vert</u> the
40   ind<u>us</u>trial'n commercial companies away from
41   the real cha:llenges they face.
42   IR: → Well of<u>ten</u> uh (.) politics <u>reach:</u> the public uh
43   → (.) <u>through</u> personality, .hh what Missus
44   → <u>Thatch</u>er has been saying: is that there is a
45   → <u>danger</u> (.) .h of a <u>social</u>ist <u>superstate</u> being
46   → imp<u>os</u>ed (0.5) from <u>Brus</u>sels (0.2) and what
47   → Mister Heath and <u>others</u> are saying is (0.2) that
48   → is (.) is an il<u>lus</u>ory fear.=Where do you: line
49   → up on that is:sue.
50   IE: Well: (eh) <u>technically</u>, becaus:e (.) eh these
51   de<u>cis</u>ions are y:et to be ta:ken, . . .

In the first yes/no question (lines 4–6), the IR constructs an agenda
for Heseltine's response that presupposes the conflict between
Thatcher and Heath as its primary reference point. When Heseltine
attempts to reformulate the issue in terms of "discussing the ideas"
and "options" (lines 17–18 and 20–22), the IR's subsequent question pursues the original issue of Heseltine's alignment. He does so,

with the "but" preface, and the virtual repeat of the terms of his earlier question at line 5, in such a way as to formulate Heseltine's previous response as an evasion (see the discussion of [7] above). Finally, after Heseltine again declines to respond in terms of "personalities" as a "diversion" (line 38–39), the IR reinstates the issue for a third time in terms of a substantive disagreement between Heath and Thatcher. Although this is an extreme case, it embodies characteristic features of British political interviewing that are applied to senior figures in all three political parties.

A close relative of "split hunting" questions are those which place the interviewee in a dilemma or "fork." Mainly shaped as "disjunctive" questions, these invite interviewees to select among alternatives that are all undesirable, and that they cannot endorse. For example in (41), a British Labour politician is discussing his party's defense policy: across a number of earlier turns, the IR has been pressing his respondent on the issue that the party would like to be rid of nuclear weapons:

(41)   UK BBCTV *Newsnight*: May 1989: Labour Defense Policy
       IR: Donald MacCormick   IE: David Blunkett

```
 1  IR:     So what will you be pushing for tomorrow, what
 2          is your: bottom line as you said earlier?
 3  IE:     Well I think there'll be a number of (0.2)
 4          proposals put by different colleagues, but the
 5          bottom line has to be that if things go well and
 6          talks procee:d w- uh, as we would want them to,
 7          over the first two or three years, both on
 8          strategic arm:s, and on the question of a
 9          nuclear free Europe...then, of course, we'd
10          have achieved our objective slightly more slowly
11          than we used to deba:te, but (.) as part of a:
12          an international change, which would be welcome
13          and would contribute to the safety of the world.
14          .hh if we don't get that, then I think some of
15          us have to sa:y in- in all credibility .hh that
16          we would want Britain to be able to remove those
17          weapons .hhh independently, unilateral [ly if=
18  IR:                                           [In uh-
19  IE:     =tha[t's the way you'd like to put it.=
20  IR:         [In uh-
21  IR:     =In other words, I don't understand the logic of
22     a→   this:, uh Mr. Blunkett, if things are going
23     a→   well, and the, the atmosphere of international
```

24   a→ detente continues (.) you're quite happy
25   a→ to negotiate the weapons away,
26   b→ but if things (.) go <u>badly</u>, and I assume by that
27   b→ you mean some <u>kind</u> of return, to some kind of
28   b→ cold <u>war</u> atmosphere, then you'll (.) give them
29   b→ away [anyway.
30 IE: [Well I: I I'm not talking about <u>giving</u>
31   anything away, I'm talking 'bout not being tied
32   in to the foreign policy and the internal
33   politics say of the United Sta:tes . . .

Here the IE's lengthy statement about nuclear weapons policy
(lines 3–17) straddles policy conflicts within his party between those
who wish to remove nuclear weapons as part of a negotiation, and
those who would prefer to remove them unilaterally. The IR's summary formulation (Heritage 1985), simply sharpens this into an explicit contradiction (highlighted by arrows A and B) suggesting that
the party will remove nuclear weapons under any conditions – implying either that the party has no coherent policy or negotiating
position or, worse, that it remains committed to the politically unpopular policy of unilateral nuclear disarmament.

A rather different kind of fork is manifested in (42). Here the
IE – then Senate leader Bob Dole – is invited to explain the fact the
President Reagan's political programs are "in trouble." In the question preface, the IR offers two – anonymous third-party attributed –
formulations of the situation. The first is that Reagan's programs,
though not the President himself, are "in trouble." The second offers
an explanation for that trouble in terms of ineffective legislative leadership. The latter explanation, which engenders a little laugh from
Dole, is explicitly offered as implicating Dole himself.

(42)   US NBC *Meet the Press*: Dec 1985: Reagan's Programs
       IR: Marvin Kalb   IE: Senator Bob Dole

1 IR: Senator (0.5) uh Pre<u>si</u>dent Reagan's elected
2   thirteen months a<u>go</u>: an en<u>or</u>mous landslide.
3   (0.8)
4 IR: a→ It is s: :<u>aid</u> that his <u>programs</u> are in trouble,
5   a→ though <u>he</u> seems to be terribly <u>popular</u> with the
6   a→ American people.
7   (0.6)
8 IR: b→ It is <u>said</u> by some people at the <u>White</u> House we
9   b→ could <u>get</u> those programs th<u>rough</u> if only we

```
10        b→   ha:d perhaps more: .hh effective leadership up
11        b→   on on the Hill and I [suppose] indirectly =
12   IE:                       [hhhheh ]
13   IR:  b→   =that might (0.5) relate t'you as well:.
14             (0.6)
15   IR:       Uh what do you think the problem is really. Is=it
16             (0.2) the leadership as it might be claimed up
17             on the Hill, or is it the programs themselves.
```

In the final formulation of the question (lines 15–17), the IR draws on this extensive question preface and explicitly invites Dole to identify "the problem" in terms either of the intrinsic weaknesses of the programs, or ineffective legislative leadership. These are presented as exhausting the possible explanations for Reagan's legislative difficulties. As in (19) above, neither option can possibly commend itself to a Republican senate leader, and Dole's response avoids these options in favor of a response that cites the weakness of his majority in the Senate (see chapter 7).

In a variant of this procedure, an interviewer may seek to show that an interviewee's statements are self-contradictory, incorrect, or at least incompatible with evidence. A return to (12) illustrates this kind of effort.

(12)   US NBC *Meet the Press*: 8 Dec 1985: Federal Budget
       IR: Al Hunt   IE: Senator Bob Dole

```
1    IR:       You can't have it both ways either.=>On this
2              program< you have said that you don't think,
3              .hhh that you'll eliminate thirty to fifty
4              programs, [an'] Senator Packwood=
5    IE:                 [( )]
6    IR:       =says you have to, .hh Number two you say you
7              hope you will not have uh tax increase,
8              [.hhhh And]=
9    IE:       [But I do.]
10   IR:       =number- and number three you say you h:ope you
11             can have a:l[m o s t ] three percent on: .hhh=
12   ( ):                  [(      )]
13   IR:       =on: on defe:nse, .hh And yet you hafta cut
14             fifty billion next year. Now which o'those
15             three's gonna give Senator,
```

Here, as noted earlier, the question preface describes three of the IE's stated policy objectives, prefacing these with a remark – "*You* can't have it both ways either." – that clearly suggests their incompatibility. The final question "Now which o'those three's gunna give Senator," underscores the policy contradiction underlying the IE's position.

Finally, in a convergence of the "split" and the "contrast" formats, interviewers may contrast the conduct of the interviewee with the conduct of an ally. In these kinds of contrasts, the conduct of one of the parties is normally used as a kind of "moral template" or benchmark for appropriate conduct (Smith 1978). In (43) Pat Buchanan, whose populist run for the presidency had gathered momentum at the time of the interview, is subjected to this procedure. The question concerns one of Buchanan's close campaign associates (initially identified as "your man Pratt") who has close ties with ultra-right groups in the USA. In the opening part of the question preface, the IR describes Buchanan's own conduct in immediately objecting to the use of his writings by an anti-semitic newspaper (a→):

(43) US ABC *This Week*: 18 Feb 1996: Presidential Candidacy
       IR: George Will   IE: Pat Buchanan

```
 1  IR:        I wanta ask you about your man Pratt.
 2      a→     In nineteen ninety [your [column was=
 3  IE:                          [(tl)  [i-
 4  IR: a→     =picked up by an anti semitic newspaper.
 5      a→     As soon as you learned about thi[s=
 6  IE:                                        [mm.
 7      a'→    =you demanded your column be outta there.
 8  IE:        Sure:.
 9  IR: b→     .hhh Now Mister Pratt (.) was present when
10      b→     a man said the following.=h "Your enemies
11      b→     are pumping all the (Talmudic) filth that they
12      b→     can vomit and:=defecate into your living
13      b→     room that they can."
14  IE:        (°Mm h[m.° )
15  IR: b'→          [Your man didn't leave.
16  IR:        .h[h
17  IE:          [Mm [hm,
18  IR: q→          [What kinda man is he.
19  IE:        tlk=.hh Well- #o-#=obviously George he
20             shoulda left there but lemme say this about
21             Larry Pra:tt. .mhh The man's reputation's
22             on the line, his career's on the line, his
23             life is on the line, . . .
```

These observations form the basis for a contrast with the conduct of Buchanan's associate, who is described as present in a meeting that was the venue for highly anti-semitic statements. The morally contrastive behavior of Buchanan and his political associate is highlighted in the verbal contrast between "you demanded your column *be outta there.*" (line 7), and "Your man *didn't leave.*" which in turn sets up the final question (line 18): "What kinda man is he." Here Buchanan is left to deal (i) with the morally repugnant behavior of his associate, and (ii) the inconsistency between his own behavior and that of a man with whom he has a close political association. Given that the morally correct template for this inconsistency is Buchanan himself, this is particularly difficult for him to contest. Moreover, more darkly, (iii) by contrasting Buchanan's *past* actions in 1990, with those of his *present* associate, there is a further implication that Buchanan himself may have moved to the far right, indeed to a point that is beyond the political pale. Shortly afterwards, the IR relays accusations from senior Republican figures that Buchanan is anti-Semitic, has flirted with fascism, and is reactionary rather than Republican.

A similar pattern emerges in the following segment from the Bush–Rather interview. This segment was preceded by a film report focusing heavily on the Iran-Contra scandal, and ending with a description of contacts between Bush's long-serving national security aide Donald Gregg and "Contra" middleman Felix Rodriguez. Rather's opening question took up this topic:

(44)   US CBS *Evening News*: 25 Jan 1988: Iran-Contra
       IR: Dan Rather   IE: George Bush

```
 1  IR:   Mister Vice President, thank you for being with
 2         us tonigh:t, .hh Donald Gregg still serves as
 3         your trusted advisor, He was deeply involved in
 4         running arms to the Contras, 'n 'e didn't inform
 5         you. .hhh Now when President Reagan's (0.3)
 6         trusted advisor: Admiral Poindexter: (0.5)
 7         failed to inform him: :, (0.7) the President
 8         (0.4) fired 'im.
 9         (0.5)
10         Why is Mister Gregg still:: (0.2) inside the
11         White House 'n still a trusted advisor.
12  IE:   Because I have confidence in him, .hh 'n because
13         this matter Dan:, as you well know:, . . .
```

Here the IR, building from the film report, begins by asserting that Gregg "still serves" Bush as a "trusted advisor." He continues by depicting Gregg's conduct as untrustworthy: running arms to the Contras without informing Bush. This state of affairs is then contrasted with the morally appropriate action that President Reagan took when his "trusted advisor" Admiral Poindexter engaged in actions that breached that trust (lines 5–8). The contrast between Reagan and Bush's conduct is clearly drawn out. The similarities between the advisors are established point for point, while Bush's conduct is presented as clearly differing from Reagan's. This contrast is particularly pointed. Not only is Reagan Bush's political ally and superior, he is also President of the United States, and a role model for the position which Bush is currently campaigning for. Bush can thus be directly asked to explain the contrast between his conduct and that of his superior – the occupant of the supreme position to which he aspires. This is, of course, what the IR's question (lines 10–11) proceeds to do.

Conclusion

This chapter has argued that, while "questioning" may generally be understood as a neutralistic activity in the news interview context, neutralism is not to be confused with neutrality. News interview questioning is very far from being a neutral activity. As we have seen, the interviewer holds the initiative when it comes to the topics that the interviewee will be questioned on. There can be no "neutrality" in the selection of these topics and contexts: rather the selection will be more or less favorable (or, which is not the same, more or less desirable) from the interviewee's point of view. Further, the interviewer can manage questioning so that particular presuppositions are embedded in the design of questions and at varying levels of embeddedness. These presuppositions may be more or less problematic for an interviewee's position, and their degree of embeddedness may create greater or lesser difficulties for the interviewee in formulating a response. Finally, the interviewer can manage questions so that particular audience expectations for the interviewee's response are established: expectations that the interviewee may need to resist, and where such resistance may incur an additional burden of explanation than might otherwise be the case.

News interview questioning, then, cannot be neutral but only neutralistic. It can be more or less pointed, more or less fair, more or less balanced in its approach to its subject matter. Much of the evaluation – by the interviewee and, especially, by the news audience – of these characteristics of interviewer questioning is likely to be shaped by perceptions of the relevance of particular questions. For both the interviewee and the news audience, the prevailing consideration in relation to each question is "why that now" (Sacks 1992). Although news interviewees may find aspects of interviewer questions problematic or objectionable at all three levels – why *that* topical agenda, why *that* presupposition, why design the question to prefer *that* answer – these sentiments rarely eventuate in challenges to the objectivity, impartiality, or neutrality of questioners. In this way, interviewees collude in a fiction that questioning is objective, impartial, and neutral in its import and that, as long as they stick to questioning, journalists cannot be criticized as biased promoters of a particular political or social agenda. The conclusions which are drawn by the interviewees (and, just as important, the news audience) about the "why that now" issue will shape how the questioner's purpose is understood and, relatedly, whether a question is judged to be appropriate or fair even when it is sharply or even aggressively formulated.

Question design evidently has a significant impact on the conduct of interviewees. It is fundamental in setting the parameters of response and in laying down the markers of acceptability in response. Particularly when the parameters are set relatively narrowly, as in yes/no questions, it provides the basis for interviewers to follow up and exert pressure for response on evasive interviewees (see chapter 7). The development of prefaced questions has permitted journalists to escape the immediate confines set by the occasion of the interview, to range widely over topics, to inform the news audience of the background relevant to a question, and under cover of this, to create real difficulties for interviewees. In their different ways, the deployment of presupposition and preference can be used to exert significant pressure on interviewee positions, widening the scope of their public accountability to a significant extent. Indeed it may fairly be claimed that the *interactional* accountability of answering questions is the fundamental basis for the *public* accountability of public figures.

This chapter has aimed at laying out some basic features of question design in the news interview context and to describe their deployment in a range of instances. Underlying some of these observations is the suggestion that innovation in question design can be an important element of social change in the news interview context, and broadcast journalism more generally. In particular the emergence and growth of the prefaced question design, while initially designed, and commonly used, to inform the news audience about important contextual details, represents a formidable extension of the interviewer's initiative and power. Many of the more hostile questions discussed in this paper simply could not be launched without it.

In a non-random, but wide-ranging, sample of 639 questions from British and American interview data, Heritage and Roth (1995) found that nearly half of the total questions asked were prefaced questions. In a recent study of presidential press conferences, Clayman and Heritage (2002) have also found that simple questions fell from 44 percent of the total during Eisenhower's first term to 12 percent during Reagan's first term. During the same period "hostile" question prefaces multiplied by a factor of 450 percent. Although the relative absence of follow-up opportunities may encourage journalists to produce more complex questions in the press conference context, the figures are nonetheless striking, and may index a parallel underlying growth in the deployment of prefaced questions in the interview context as well. If this is so, it is clear that journalistic initiative has expanded considerably during the past forty years and, in all probability, that this is directly associated with a growth in adversarialness which, by common consent, has also grown significantly during this period.

The growth of prefaced questioning may, however, have different institutional histories in Britain and America. As noted in chapter 2, legislative regulation and oversight of broadcast journalism has historically been more intense in Britain than in the United States. Moreover, until 1955 when the BBC's monopoly position in broadcasting was replaced by a duopoly, there were no competitive pressures which might fuel a reduction on deference and a rise in adversarialness. In the United States, by contrast, FCC oversight and regulation of news program content has been minimal, and competitive pressures have impacted broadcast journalism from the outset.

It may be conjectured then that in Britain there was a more dramatic growth in prefaced questions, beginning in the 1960s, whereas in the United States growth was more steady and gradual and began from a higher baseline. This in turn suggests that news interview questioning may never have been as deferential in the United States as it was in Britain during the 1950s, and hence that the example with which this chapter began truly represents one of the more extreme cases of deferential interviewing that one could find in the anglophone broadcasting context.

7

Answers and evasions

When Albert Gore was Bill Clinton's running mate in 1992, his position on abortion became the focus of controversy. As a legislator, Gore had opposed federal funding for most abortions, but now he was expressing support for it as part of Clinton's health care reform plan. In an aggressive interview conducted by Sam Donaldson, Gore received a barrage of tough questions exposing this apparent contradiction. He was momentarily rescued by a commercial break, during which he was urged by his media advisor to sidestep the abortion issue altogether: "Don't be afraid to turn their questions. If they ask you about [abortion], just say ... 'I want to talk today about the new direction that Governor Clinton and I want to take the country.'" The media advisor to presidential candidate Pat Robertson was even more blunt when Robertson appeared on *Larry King Live* and faced tough questions – from King and members of the audience – about his divisive and controversial speech at the 1992 Republican Convention. During a commercial break, Robertson's advisor launched into a pep talk: "<u>You</u>'re answering the questions. You can talk about anything you <u>want</u> to."[1]

There is a widespread perception that politicians are often evasive under questioning from members of the news media, and this perception is not without merit (Harris 1991). The impetus toward evasiveness is understandable in the context of the contemporary news interview, which is so often adversarial in character. Hostile questions, if answered straightforwardly, can inflict real damage on an interviewee's policy objectives and career prospects. When 1996

---

[1] These incidents were discussed in a documentary by Brian Springer entitled *Spin*.

presidential candidate Bob Dole was questioned about the addictiveness of tobacco, his equivocal response was roundly attacked by the Clinton campaign and received weeks of unfavorable media coverage. On the other side of the Atlantic, a question about the Labour Party's opposition to nuclear weapons prompted party leader Neil Kinnock to give a seemingly cavalier response that was subsequently exploited by the Tories and helped ensure Thatcher's re-election in 1987. And it is not only politicians who face such dangers; no interviewee is immune. In response to a question about the absence of blacks at the managerial level in professional baseball, Al Campanis (vice president of the Los Angeles Dodgers) made some racially insensitive remarks which caused such an uproar that he was fired the next day. To avoid consequences like these, interviewees may be motivated to be less than forthcoming, or even downright evasive, in the face of hostile questioning.

However, evasiveness has a downside. Given the normative ground rules of the interview (chapter 4) and the interview contract to which they are responsive (chapter 2), interviewees are obliged to answer questions posed by interviewers and thus deal with whatever agendas they raise in the way in which they raise them (chapter 6). Attempts to resist, sidestep, or evade are thus accountable actions that usurp the interviewer's role and prerogatives in the encounter. Such maneuvers can be costly. Interviewers themselves monitor for evasiveness and respond to such moves with probing follow-up questions and, at times, explicitly negative sanctions (Greatbatch 1986b). When Senator Bob Dole failed to give a straightforward answer to a question about the prospects for a tax increase, the interviewer pointedly accused him of "ducking that question" and then pressed him again for an answer. The reaction was even harsher when Treasury Secretary Robert Rubin dealt with a question about the gasoline tax by launching into a rosy analysis of the Clinton administration's general economic successes. The interviewer reprimanded Rubin at length for his slipperiness: "When we ask people like you [a simple question], you do the light fantastic instead of giving us a direct answer." Responses like these underscore that the interviewee was evasive, making it available to all audience members, and thereby increasing the pressure for a full-fledged answer.

The ability to counter evasiveness is fundamental to the interviewer's professional reputation. The most highly regarded and successful interviewers are generally adversarial in their conduct toward public figures, and are adept at pursuing recalcitrant interviewees. Interviewers pride themselves on this skill, which they take pains to highlight in their autobiographies (e.g., Day 1989, 1993; Donaldson 1987; Koppel and Gibson 1996). Consider the choice of book titles such as . . . *But With Respect* by Robin Day (1993) and *Hold On Mr. President!* by Sam Donaldson (1987). Although the former is phrased with ritual politeness, both titles are common prefaces to pointed follow-up questions, and they evoke images of persistent interviewers doggedly pursuing their elusive prey. In the Donaldson autobiography, this image is further on display in the dust jacket photograph, which depicts Donaldson in a confrontational posture, speaking and gesticulating toward a cornered President Reagan.

Monitoring by journalists can extend beyond the occasion of the interview itself. Subsequent news stories about interviews and press conferences often contain excerpts that show public figures to be refusing to answer questions, or initially resisting questions, or answering only after being repeatedly pressed to do so (Clayman 1990). Correspondingly, political commentary also tends to focus on moments when the politician has been less than forthcoming. Bill Clinton's responses to questions about the draft, marijuana use, and extramarital affairs – responses that appeared evasive upon analysis – would come back to haunt him as they became recurrent grist for the news mill. Similarly, during the 2000 presidential campaign, questions to George W. Bush about drug use triggered a feeding frenzy of stories dissecting the ramifications of his carefully worded responses. An act of evasion can thus become a newsworthy event in its own right, generating further media exposure with negative ramifications for the politician who produced it.

Even when journalists allow such acts to pass without comment, there still may be consequences for the broadcast audience and for public opinion. Some audience members may not notice when an act of evasion has occurred, but others might. When one catches a public figure in the act of sidestepping a question, it is only natural to try to account for the breach of conduct, resulting in inferences that are apt to be unflattering or incriminating. Audience members may infer that the interviewee has some ulterior motive for avoiding the question, or that he or she has something to hide. American citizens have a constitutionally protected right to remain silent in the face of police questioning, so that silence cannot be treated as incriminating in courts of law. But public figures have no such protection in the court of public opinion constituted by the news interview.

In a nutshell, then, interviewees face a dilemma. There are various pressures – from interviewers, the audience, and subsequent media exposure – to "just answer the question." But when the question is adversarial, there are cross-cutting pressures to take precisely the opposite course of action.

How do interviewees manage these conflicting pressures? How do they reap the benefits of an evasive response while minimizing the various costs associated with this risky course of action? More generally, how do interview participants discriminate between responses that "evade" and those that genuinely "answer"? These puzzles guide our examination of the dynamics of answering and evading questions.

Conceptual preliminaries

Evasiveness is an elusive phenomenon, and its analysis is fraught with conceptual pitfalls. The concept is a familiar part of our ordinary language for characterizing interactional conduct, and yet its meaning is curiously difficult to pin down.

A major source of difficulty concerns the perspective from which evasiveness is assessed. One approach treats the *analyst's perspective* as primary – here the boundary between "answering" and "evading" is something that the analyst determines by formulating a clear-cut operational definition, which can then serve as a benchmark from which to assess particular responses. This approach can generate informative results (e.g., Harris 1991; Bull 1994; Bull and Mayer 1993), but it becomes problematic when the analyst's assessment diverges from that of the interview participants themselves. It is, after all, the participants' own understandings of their conduct, and not the analyst's, that are consequential for the way an interaction develops. In light of these considerations, and consistent with the conversation analytic tradition that informs this book, we treat the *participants' perspective* as of primary importance in the analysis of answers and evasions.

This ideal can be difficult to achieve in practice. One problem is that the participants may not necessarily agree on the import of a particular response. While an interviewer may treat a given response as improperly evasive, the interviewee who produced it may treat it as an essentially valid way of dealing with a difficult and perhaps flawed question. In this connection, the very terms used by the analyst to characterize responses can become problematic. "Evasion" connotes moral impropriety and thus may be seen as embodying a contestable perspective on the action under analysis.

A more fundamental difficulty is the fact that the participants' understandings are not always transparent, and they may at times be designedly opaque. Consider that when interviewees sidestep a question, they may strive to conceal that fact in an effort both to avoid prompting a hostile follow-up question and to forestall negative inferences from the viewing audience. Correspondingly, even if interviewers recognize that an evasion has occurred, they may decide to "let it pass" in the interest of moving the interview forward. Thus, it is possible for an act of evasion to occur, one that is fully apparent to both participants, and yet have neither party register that fact in any demonstrable way.

Given this, well-grounded analytic judgments must draw on resources internal to single instances of the phenomenon as well as patterns of conduct that cut across numerous cases. To maintain analytic clarity, we will reserve the term "evade/evasive" for actions that are treated as inadequately responsive by at least one of the participants. Other terms – e.g., resist, sidestep, agenda-shift – will be used more broadly to encompass responses that depart from the agenda of the question, but that the participants may not necessarily overtly register as inadequate on that occasion.

Doing "answering"

Any analysis of answers and evasions must begin by considering the fundamental nature of *answering* as a type of social action. This may seem obvious at first glance – an answer is an action that addresses the agenda of topics and tasks posed by a previous question. What is less obvious is precisely how such responsiveness is displayed by interviewees, and recognized by interviewers and audience members, in actual practice. This puzzle is complicated by the fact that, as we observed in chapter 4, there is no primary indicator or marker of "answering" (unlike questioning, which typically is marked by interrogative syntax). How then do interviewees indicate that they are indeed being responsive to the question at hand? In other words, how do they *accomplish or do "answering"*?

As a point of departure, consider that there are different paths or trajectories that answers may follow. Some answers take a *roundabout trajectory* – they begin with a unit of talk which does not in itself answer the question, but is part of a larger stretch of talk which can be seen in its entirety as answering. For instance, when a Conservative politician is asked (lines 1–2 below) about the attractions of a new workfare proposal – which would require those receiving unemployment benefits to work for them – his initial remarks (lines 3–10) do not, by themselves, answer the question. Instead of talking about the advantages of workfare, he begins by attacking the current unemployment program as "ludicrous" (lines 3–7), and he then goes on to say that reducing benefits is not a viable solution (lines 7–10). Only after he has in effect ruled out these other courses of action, taking three full sentences to do so, does he speak directly to the issue of the advantages of workfare (lines 11–14).

(1)   UK BBC Radio *Today*: June 1993: Social Security Cuts
       IR: John Humphrys   IE: David Howell
1   IR: ... Mister Howell what are the attractions as you
2   see them: uh- of this workfare idea?
3   IE: .hh Well (.) hh it seems to me to be ludicrous
4   that we are <u>spen</u>ding according to the Governmen<u>t</u>
5   more than eight <u>bil</u>lion pounds: in support of
6   the unemploy:ed on condition that they do
7   nothing whatsoever .hhh to(r) help society. .hh
8   And <u>I</u> believe the time has come when- when we've
9   got to recognize: that (.) par::ing down
10   benefits is not the an:swer. That isn't how
11   savings can be made. .hhh Savings ku- <u>huge</u>
12   savings could be made: if ahm (.) <u>one</u> the
13   unemployed people were offered the right to work
14   and given an opportunity to work...

Although the initial remarks could not by themselves stand as an answer, they are not irrelevant to the question at hand. Indeed, the initial assessment of alternatives to workfare can be seen as a relevant prelude to rendering a comparative assessment of workfare itself. Thus, considered holistically, this entire turn can be seen as occupied with the task of answering the question. And interviewers generally treat such roundabout answers, once completed, as adequate.

However, interviewers do not only enounter *completed* turns; they monitor and evaluate turns *incrementally*, while they are unfolding. From that internal vantage point, the subsequent trajectory of a response may be decidedly uncertain. In the previous example, the IE could have simply attacked the alternatives without ever advancing an affirmative argument for workfare. To hear an unfolding roundabout response as building toward a genuine answer to the question thus requires an interpretive leap of sorts. And this is a leap that interviewers may not be willing to make.

Thus, roundabout answers are initially vulnerable to being heard as evasive, and are subject to countermeasures from the interviewer. This is illustrated in the following excerpt from a 1985 interview with Pat Buchanan, shortly after he began serving as Reagan's second-term director of communications. The IR rather delicately makes the point (in lines 2–5) that other administration officials do not seem to like Buchanan very much, and have leaked that view to the press, and he goes on to ask Buchanan (lines 8–9) how that can happen. Buchanan responds (lines 11–13) by noting that "there was a lotta that in the first term," and he begins to explain why. This could be the first component of a roundabout answer which will eventually deal with the current situation, but it could also be a move to shift the agenda. The IR takes the skeptical view, analyzing it as an incipient evasion – he interjects at line 14 (arrowed), pointing out that "you weren't in in the first term," thereby treating Buchanan's turn-thus-far as irrelevant and unresponsive.

(2) US ABC *Nightline*: 3 June 1985: Buchanan as Com. Director
     IR: Ted Koppel   IE: Pat Buchanan

```
1  IR:   Continuing our: conversation now with Pat
2         Buchanan, Pat- uh:- (0.2) to put it as gently as
3         I can there're some people: fairly high up in
4         this administration who seem to be able to
5         contain their enthusiasm for you, .hhh An' every
6         once in a while stories crop up in the press
7         that one can only assume come from some o' those
8         folk. (0.2) How does that sort of thing happen.
```

```
9                in an administration.
10               (.)
11   IE:         tch .hhh Well I think there was a lotta that 'n
12               the first term Ted, an' uh: >I think one o'the
13               reasons< was you had-=
14   IR:  →      =Well you weren't in in the firs' [term.
15   IE:                                          [Right, but
16               you had three chiefs of- (.) ehsta: ff virtually,
17               you had Baker (.) Deaver and Meese .hhhh An'
18               there was it seemed to me from the outsi:de an
19               awful lot of leaking on one er against one er
20               another, from secondary an' tertiary personnel
21               .hhhhh A:n' since Don Regan came in we've been
22               goin' through a bit of a transition, there was
23               some o'that I think back in April, .hhhh but
24               since the transition's been complete I haven't
25               seen any of it an' we don't expect to see as
26               much in the:: uh .hhh in the second term . . .
```

It's possible that the design of the final question (lines 8–9) unintentionally encourages Buchanan to begin his response as he does. Perhaps to soften what is plainly a face-threatening subject, the IR depersonalizes the question somewhat by asking how "that sort of thing" can happen, and this may license Buchanan's decision to talk initially about the larger history of Reagan administration leaks. Notwithstanding this veneer of politeness, the question is plainly concerned with current leaks pertaining to Buchanan himself, and his initial response specifically avoids that subject, although he eventually comes around to addressing it (lines 22–26). The basic point is that this kind of circuitous trajectory is vulnerable to being heard as evasive, and may be pursued as such. This may in part explain why roundabout answers are relatively uncommon.

A more common type of trajectory establishes the "answering" character of the talk early on. This trajectory – which may be termed *minimal answer plus elaboration* – begins with a first unit of talk that minimally provides the information targeted by the question, followed by subsequent talk that clarifies and elaborates. For instance, a yes/no question can prompt an initial one-sentence expression of affirmation or negation before that answer is elaborated. An explicit "yes" or "no" may be included in the initial response, which is the normative way of answering a yes/no-question (Raymond 2000). For example:

(3)   US ABC *Nightline*: 22 Feb 1985: State of Emergency
      IR: Charles Gibson   IE: Reverend Allan Boesak

```
1  IR:    tch .hh Are you willing (0.2) personally to
2         renounce the violence (.) in that country.
3         (0.5)
4  IE:  → .hh Yes I will. I mean I have said so on
5         Saturday I was on a platform ...
```

Similarly, a wh-type question ("how long" below) can prompt an initial one-sentence provision of the requested information (arrowed) prior to further elaboration.

(4)   UK BBCTV *Newsnight*: May 1989: China Crisis
      IR: Peter Snow   IE: Zsu Zsa Ming

```
1  IR:    And how long how long will that take and how
2         long has he got to prove he can do it?
3  IE:  → .hhhh Ah:: (0.2) it ti- (0.2) maybe it take uh
4       → one or two years (.) to to do that. (0.7)
5         And I think ah that ...
```

This trajectory of answering is analogous to a standard written paragraph. Like the topic sentence in a paragraph, the first utterance in a response is a rather general statement which minimally fills the information gap targeted by the question, while subsequent talk furnishes details which clarify, support, or elaborate.

Furthermore, the initial remark's relevance to the question is often highlighted by various surface features of the remark's design. Perhaps the most obvious way of marking question-relevance is to incorporate some of the wording of the question into the initial response.[2] The repetition may involve a single key word – "confrontation" in the following (arrowed):

(5)   UK BBCTV *Newsnight*: May 1989: Tiananmen Square Uprisings
      IR: Peter Snow   IE: Jonathan Mirsky

```
1  IR:    Jonathan first (.) let me ask you:, uh what is
2         the latest situation are we any nearer: the
3       → actual (.) straight confrontation between the
4         troops and the students (.) in the square.
5  IE:    Well I think we've already had this
6       → confrontation. The: uh citizens of Peking .hhhh
7         and of course ...
```

---

[2] On this point we are indebted to Roth (1996) and Schegloff (1998).

A larger phrase may also be repeated, such as "side effects" below (arrowed):

(6) US CBS *Face The Nation*: 8 Dec 1985: Cancer Treatment
        IR: Lesley Stahl   IE: Dr. Steven Rosemberg
1 IR: → .hhh Now <u>tell</u> us about uh=the s<u>i</u>de effects. .hhh
2   IS it as <u>tox</u>ic (.) as chemotherapy <u>is</u> it as
3   poisonous: un- (.) to the s<u>y</u>stem an' wh<u>at</u>'re the
4   → other side effects.
5 IE: → The s<u>i</u>de effects could be quite seve:re, but
6   they're somewhat <u>d</u>ifferent than the kinds of
7   → side effects 'at one s<u>ee</u>s with- uh with
8   → chemoth<u>e</u>rapy. .hhh The m<u>a</u>jor s<u>i</u>de effect is a
9   buildup of fl<u>u</u>id in the body . . .

An IE may go still further, incorporating the entire framework of the question into the initial response, thereby matching his response word for word to the question at hand:

(7) UK BBC Radio *World At One*: 13 Mar 1979: NUM Election
        IR: Robin Day   IE: Arthur Scargill
1 IR: → And what do you think the re<u>s</u>ult of the ballot
2   will be.
3 IE: → I::: <u>th</u>ink that the result of the ballot will
4   most <u>prob</u>ably be ac<u>cep</u>tance of the deal:, (.)
5   but it <u>c</u>ould be: er closer than most people
6   ex<u>p</u>ect.

This last mode of response can seem exaggerated or hypercorrect, and may be indicative of an undercurrent of resistance or hostility to the question. Indeed, by repeating the framework of the question, rather than building on it, the IE asserts some independence from the question as he responds to it (cf., Schegloff 1996). But the general import of repeating lexical items from the question remains much the same across these examples. Through this practice, interviewees can propose that they are attending to the question in detail, and are thus properly reponsive to the issues that it raises.

   The significance of lexical repetition is apparent in the fact that such repetitions also appear quite often as the interviewee is winding down a lengthy turn at talk, and just before the interviewer takes the floor (as we saw in chapter 4; see also Roth 1996; Schegloff 1998). For example (arrowed):

(8)   UK BBCTV *Newsnight*: 21 Oct 1993: Arming the Police
        IR: Jeremy Paxman   IE: David Brady

```
 1   IR:   → ...Is: it your: view that the police should now
 2         → be armed?
 3   IE:    .hhh But definitely. .hhh Ahm we: wuh- (.) we
 4          have no rights as a society .hh to expect young
 5          men (.) .hh to enter situations wh:ere (.) the
 6          there is a fair: percentage, (.) of: arm:ed (.)
 7          people against them. It's- it's wrong: that they
 8          should- we should ask them .hhh to risk their
 9          lives, and to risk being shot, .hhh and the
10          chances of th- of them meeting an armed: uh:m
11          assailant is so much in- increase: .hh (.) that
12         → police should definitely be ar[med.
13   IR:                                    [And you don't
14          worry that arming the police might actually...
```

This conjunction of events is not coincidental. The return to the actual terms of the original question signals that the spate of talk which had been unfolding now constitutes a possibly complete answer, thus prompting the transfer of speakership. At both the beginning and ending of the interviewee's turn, repeating words from the prior question is a way of doing "answering" that question.

The practices we have examined thus far mostly involve similarities in phrasing, but other practices for doing "answering" work quite differently. Certain *indexical expressions*, namely *anaphoric indexicals*, have meanings which are inextricably linked to the prior question. The simplest type involves the use of a pronoun that refers back to the issue raised by the question, as in "that" below (arrowed).

(9)   US PBS *Newshour*: 22 July 1985: South Africa
        IR: Jim Lehrer   IE: Ambassador Herbert Beukes

```
 1   IR:   .hhhhh Reports today: are: of course that the
 2          violence has continued uh what have you heard
 3          tha- whether er not the state of emergency is in
 4          fact working.
 5          (0.4)
 6   IE:    tch .hhhhh It is perhaps too soon:: to make make
 7         → a judgment on that...
```

Here the IR asks whether the South African Government's imposition of a state of emergency is working to stop the violence in that

country. The IE's response – "It is perhaps too soon to make a judgment on *that*" – ends with a pronoun that acquires its meaning by
referring back to the matter raised by the previous question.

It is not only pronouns that have this back-referencing character.
For example, certain verbs are also heavily context-dependent for
their meaning, such as "was" below (arrowed).

(10)   UK ATV *Afternoon Plus*: 5 Nov 1979: Innocent Man
       IR: Unknown   IE: Tony Stocks

1 IR: .hh Were you surpris:ed when you: w- <u>w</u>ent to
2   court, an- and indeed went <u>d</u>own,
3   (0.2)
4 IE: → hhhh .hhh I was mos- I- I <u>cert</u>ainly was, in fact
5   I- I .hh all the way up to the- to the court . . .

In the context of the prior question ("Were you surprised"), the
response ("I certainly was") can readily be understood as meaning
was surprised.

Units of talk which are shorter than a sentence also tend to be
parasitic on the question for their meaning. For example, the initial
phrasal response below – "Child support offices" – can be understood in context as advancing a claim that *child support offices will
be the judge of good cause.*

(11)   UK BBC Radio *Today*: May 1993: Child Support
       IR: John Humphrys   IE: Roz Hepplewhite

1 IR: .hh But who's going to be the judge of that, the
2   judge of good <u>cau</u>se:.
3 IE: → .hhhh Child support offices. Ahm in the local
4   offices and in our regional centers .hh ah we'll
5   look at <u>e</u>ach case <u>v</u>ery very carefully . . .

Finally, certain turn-initial discourse markers also refer back to
the previous question. Answers to <u>why</u>-type questions may be prefaced by *because*, which identifies what follows as an explanation
fitted to the question. For example:

(12)   US PBS *Newshour*: 18 Sep 1992: Candidacy
       IR: Judy Woodruff   IE: Ross Perot

1 IR: So <u>why</u> don't you go ahead and (.) say: I'm (.) a
2   candidate for Pr[esident?

3 IE: →   [Because that's not (.) where
4   the organization is now. Our organization (.)
5   is <u>to</u>:tally focused on try:ing to get both
6   parties to do the job. (0.7) That's why.

In all of these cases, the sense of the initial remark is, by itself, indeterminate at least to some extent. Observers must refer back to the question to disambiguate the remark, and in so doing its meaning is "filled in" in a way that is thoroughly question-relevant.

In analyzing these various practices for doing "answering," it may seem that we are expending a great deal of energy for a modest payoff. However, these practices are far more significant than the analysis thus far suggests. As we shall see, not only do they figure in genuine efforts to answer the question, but interviewees can also use them subversively in maneuvers that are less than fully responsive.

Dimensions of resistance

Resisting a question is, like answering, a complex and multifaceted course of action. We can begin to dissect this phenomenon by drawing some basic conceptual distinctions between the different levels of magnitude at which it can occur. Resistance to a question has two distinguishable dimensions or aspects.

The negative dimension

The *negative* aspect is manifest to the degree that an interviewee fails to produce an adequate answer to the question. In the strongest variation on this theme, the interviewee declines to provide any information at all bearing on the question. For example, when a member of the Labour Party is asked about his willingness to serve in a Cabinet committed to unilateral nuclear disarmament, he flatly refuses to answer (arrowed).[3]

---

[3] Notice that the IE refers to the IR by name ("Mister Day") as he launches his resistant response. It turns out that this is a highly recurrent practice across various forms of resistance. It appears to be related to the pragmatics of address term usage in interaction generally – speakers often address their recipients by name when expressing deeply felt opinions and personal feelings (Clayman 1998), particularly when such opinions/feelings are oppositional in character.

(13)   UK Greatbatch 1986: 451: Unilateral Nuclear Disarmament
       IR: Robin Day   IE: Peter Shore
```
 1   IR:        You wouldn't serve in a Cabinet committed to lu-
 2              unilateral nuclear disarmament of Britain would
 3              you Mister Shore?
 4   IE:        .hh What I do believe:: er: Mister Day (which)
 5       →      I will not a:nswer that question, I'm not (.)
 6       →      deliberately answering that question. What I do
 7              believe is thi:s. I do actually genuinely
 8              believe lo:ng believe: (d) .hhh that unilateral
 9              initiatives: (.) can assist (.) multilateral
10              disarmament...
```

In a less extreme form of negative resistance, the interviewee provides an answer that is partial or incomplete. For instance, in the
face of a complex question with multiple components, he or she
may address one part while leaving the others unanswered. In the
following discussion of nuclear power, the IR first asks why those in
charge at Three Mile Island did such a poor job of informing the
public about the accident (lines 1–5). He then unpacks this rather
general question in terms of two more specific questions (lines 5–9),
one concerning the magnitude of the problem ("was it indeed a major problem") and the other concerning the viability of informing
the public ("could it have been simply passed off immediately to the
public...").

(14)   US ABC *Nightline*: 6 June 1985: Nuclear Waste
       IR: Ted Koppel   IE: Dr. Jacob Fabricant
```
 1   IR:        tch Doctor Fabricant I- I realize it is not your
 2              problem nor your responsibility but could you
 3              explain to me why such (0.5) a ba:d job was done
 4              at Three Mile Island of kinda fessing up to what
 5              had gone wrong. (0.4) And was it indeed a major
 6              problem, or could it have been .hh could it've
 7              been: simply passed off immediately to the
 8              public .hh revealing all and thereby: (.)
 9              diminishing some of the aftereffect(s).
10              (0.8)
11   IE:        Well Mister Koppel I:: don't want to (0.5) in
12              any way defend or protect the industry. .hh But
13              let's go back to the first part of your
14              question. .hhh Uh the: uh the accident was a
15              major accident there's no question about it. (.)
```

```
16          A great deal of the fuel was damaged very
17          seriously damaged. .hh In fact we're just
18          learning now the extent of that damage. .hh
19          But of importance is that the: containment held.
20          (.) Even to the extent that there's a
21          considerable amount of fuel in the bottom of
22          the containment .hh it turns out in fact it did
23          not escape. So the very first thing we've
24          lear:ned .hhh is even tha- though the accident
25          was a very major one .hh with considerable core
26          damage. .hh we've learned that our safeguards
27          built into the system .hh even in a routine: or
28          in a typical reactor in the United States .h
29          does hold.
30   IR:    Are you prepared to conclude from that that
31          there:fore: under similar circumstances it would
32          always hold in other plants?
```

However, the IE addresses only the first of these questions
(lines 11–29) – he discusses the magnitude of the accident while
sidestepping entirely the issue about informing the public.

Another type of incomplete answer is a simple yes-or-no reply to
a yes/no question. As we saw in chapter 4, normally interviewees
are expected to produce elaborated answers. Against this backdrop,
minimal responses (arrow 1 below) can be seen as inadequate and
are indicative of tacit resistance to the broader agenda of the question. Accordingly, they regularly lead interviewers to probe for further elaboration (arrow 2).

(15)   US NBC *Meet the Press*: 24 Oct 1993: Television Violence
       IR: Tim Russert   IE: Janet Reno

```
1    IR:        ... .hh Madam Attorney General you've testified
2               this week- u- in front of Congress abou:t .h
3               violence and television. .hhh And said that if
4               the TV industry didn't in effect clean itself
5               up, clean its act up, .hhh there may be
6               government intervention. Government regulation.
7               (0.4) The New York Ti:mes in an editorial said
8               that (.) you embarked ona quote <dangerous
9               embrace of censorship.> (0.3) Did you?
10   IE:   1→  No.
11              (0.2)
12   IR:   2→  .hhhh Wha:t kind of government intervention are
13              you thinking about? Would you ban: programs
```

```
14          like NYPD: Law and Order, would you [uh:
15   IE:  1→                                        [No.
16          (.)
17   IR:  2→  W- Wh:at are we talking about.
18   IE:      We're talking about (.) asking the media to stop
19          talking (.) about what it promises to do, and do
20          it.
```

In any case, to the extent that interviewees avoid coming forth with an adequate answer, they have exhibited resistance in its negative aspect.

The positive dimension

Resistance has a positive dimension as well. This is manifest to the degree that an interviewee moves beyond the parameters of the question, saying and doing things that were not specifically called for. These departures vary greatly in magnitude and in kind (see also chapter 6). The most dramatic form of departure involves a substantial change of topic. In a discussion of nuclear waste, a physicist first refuses to answer a question about nuclear waste disposal (lines 6–7 below), and then goes on to refute allegations made much earlier in the program that the Three Mile Island accident brought about higher cancer rates in the surrounding area (lines 8–12). Although this response lies within the general area of nuclear energy, the issue of power plant accidents is rather far removed from the issue of routine waste disposal efforts.

(16)   US ABC *Nightline*: 6 June 1985: Nuclear Waste
        IR: Ted Koppel   IE: Dr. Rosalyn Yalow

```
 1   IR:   Continuing our conversation now with Doctor
 2          Rosalyn Yalow. Doctor Yalow uh- ehh lemme put
 3          it in very simple terms. If it's doable, if it
 4          is: easily disposable, why don't we.
 5          (1.0)
 6   IE:   Well frankly I cannot- (.) answer all these
 7          scientific questions in one minute given to me.
 8          On the other hand there was one horrible thing
 9          that happened tonight that you have- .h in
10          addition extended. .hh And that is the notion
11          that there is an increased incidence of cancer
12          associated with the Three Mile Island accident.
```

Here, then, the IE veers sharply away from the topical agenda of the question and toward a substantially different topic. She plainly treats this as an accountable matter that requires an explanation (a theme that will be developed later in the chapter).

Alternatively, a response may lie within the question's topical parameters, but perform a task or action other than what was specifically requested by the question. Thus, when Senator Bob Dole is asked whether he would support the reappointment of the Federal Reserve Board Chairman (lines 1–3), Dole offers only a generally favorable assessment of the Chairman's past performance (line 4), but he does not specifically endorse his reappointment (presumably in deference to the political independence traditionally granted to the Federal Reserve). This evasive maneuver does not escape the notice of the IR, who presses again for an explicit endorsement (line 5).

(17)   US ABC *This Week*: March 1986: Federal Reserve chair
        IR: Sam Donaldson   IE: Senator Bob Dole

1 IR: Talking about money, what about Paul Volcker,
2   whose term is up next year? Would you like to
3   see him reappointed to the Fed?
4 IE: I, I think he's been very effective.
5 IR: Well, would you like to see him reappointed?

Here the response is, broadly speaking, within the topical parameters of the question, but it performs a somewhat different task than the question originally called for.

A still more subtle form of resistance is embodied in those responses which alter the terms of the question ever so slightly. Consider the following excerpt from an interview with the Deputy Secretary of Defense, John Deutch, on the subject of Gulf War Syndrome.[4] Across this excerpt, the IR tries to get Deutch to either confirm or deny reports that US troops were exposed to chemical weapons during the Gulf War. However, Deutch will not be pinned down and repeatedly offers denials that are partial or qualified.

(18)   US CBS *60 Minutes*: 12 Mar 1995: Gulf War Syndrome
        IR: Ed Bradley   IE: John Deutch

1 IE: hh Our most th:orough (0.2) and careful efforts
2   to determine (.) whether chemical agents were
3   us:ed in the Gulf, (.) .hh lead us to conclu:de
4   that there was no: (.) w:idespread use of

---

[4] This taped interview appears to have been edited to highlight the IE's evasiveness.

```
5              chemicals against US troops.=
6  IR:         =Was there any use.=Forget w[idespread. Was]=
7  IE:                             [I-    I    do ]=
8  IR:         =[there any use.]
9  IE:         =[ not belie:ve] I do not believe there was
10             any: o:ffensive use of chemical agents by:
11             .hh uh- Iraqi: (0.2) uh military: (.) troops.
12             Ther[e was not-
13  IR:             [Was there any- any accidental use. Were our
14             troops exposed in any way:.
15             (0.4)
16  IE:         .hhh Uh- I do not believe that our troops
17             were: expo:sed in any widespread way to:
18             u[h: chemical
19  IR:          [In any narrow way.=In any way.
20  IE:         hh .hh The defense science board did an
21             independent study of this matter: .hh [and=
22  IR:                                               [( )
23  IE:         =fou:nd in their judgment that there was no::
24             confirmation .hh of chemical: (0.2) weapon (0.2)
25             widespread use: in the Gulf.
```

The Deputy Secretary first denies that our troops were exposed to any "*widespread* use" of chemical weapons (lines 1–5). The IR seeks to disallow this qualifying adjective and asks about *any* use whatsoever (line 6, 8), but the IE again qualifies his response (lines 7, 9–11), this time denying only that there was "*offensive* use." When the IR tries to disallow that qualification (lines 13–14), the IE switches back to his previous qualifying adjective, restricting his denial to "*widespread*" exposure (16–18). This maneuver is countered more aggressively by the IR, who interjects his next pursuit just after the qualifying adjective is introduced (19). He makes one last attempt to elicit a blanket denial, but the IE holds fast to his more cautious position (20–21, 23–25). The Deputy Secretary's caution is not difficult to understand – any confirmation would presumably expose the Government to numerous costly lawsuits, while a flat denial may be unsupportable by current or future evidence. He manages to avoid both of these alternatives repeatedly and in a rather subtle way. He comes across as if he were dutifully answering the question, but in each case he winds up denying a proposition that is slightly more narrow in scope than the one originally posed by the question.

A similar round of resistance and pursuit occurred in Jeremy Paxman's interview with Michael Howard on BBC's *Newsnight*.

This interview was discussed in chapter 1 as a landmark of aggressive questioning. Recall that Howard – a former Home Secretary and candidate for the Conservative Party leadership – was asked whether he had instructed the Director General of Prisons (Derek Lewis) to fire a prison official and whether he had threatened to overrule him if he did not carry out the instruction. Howard had previously testified before the House of Commons that he had no operational involvement in the prison service (presumably to insulate himself from blame for a recent escape), but several authoritative sources claimed otherwise. Accordingly, a simple negative answer to this question would directly contradict those other sources, while an affirmative answer would be self-contradictory and would show Howard to have willfully misled the House. Not suprisingly, Howard avoids giving either response, prompting Paxman to reissue essentially the question no less than thirteen times. The following excerpt contains the first few rounds in this remarkable line of questioning.

(19)   US BBC *Newsnight* 13 May 1997: Michael Howard
       IR: Jeremy Paxman   IE: Michael Howard

```
 1  IR:    Did you threaten [to overrule
 2  IE:                     [I- I was not entitled
 3         to instruct Derek Lewis and I did not instruct
 4         him .hh [an the
 5  IR:            [Did you threaten to overrule [ (him)
 6  IE:                                          [>The<
 7         the truth of the matter i:s thet (.) Mister
 8         Marriott was not suspende[d. I did not-
 9  IR:                             [Did you threaten to
10         overrule him.
11  IE:    I did not overrule Der[ek (Lewis).
12  IR:                          [Did you threaten to
13         overrule h[im.
14  IE:              [I took advice on what I could or
15         could not d[o::
16  IR:               [Did you threat[en to overrule him=
17  IE:                              [and I acted=
18  IR:    =Mister Howard.
19  IE:    =scrupulously in accordance with that advice=I
20         did not overrule D[erek
21  IR:                      [Did you threaten to
22         overrule him
```

When first asked whether he "threatened to overrule" Derek Lewis (line 1), Howard neither confirms nor denies this charge, but talks instead about what he was legally entitled to do (lines 2–4). When the IR presses the issue by repeating his original question essentially verbatim (5), Howard again sidesteps the question but in a different way, this time by shifting away from the process and toward the final outcome of the personnel incident – he asserts that the official (Marriott) "was not suspended. I did not overule him" (6–9, 10). The IR pursues the question yet again, first in overlap with Howard's unfolding response (9–10) and again in the clear (12–13). Notice that this time around (at line 13) while the question is still repeated verbatim, it is articulated differently – the IR places marked emphasis on the word "threaten," thereby seeking to disallow Howard's previous maneuver by highlighting the fact that the question concerns the bureaucratic process rather than the outcome. But Howard still will not be pinned down, shifting this time to the (presumably legal) advice he received (14–15), and ending with another remark about the outcome (19–20). And Paxman, for his part, is not deterred from continuing his pursuit (21–22).

Finally, it should be noted that even responses that initially address the agenda of the question, but subsequently shift away from that agenda (see below), are treated as problematic in the news interview context (Greatbatch 1986b). This is a product of the distinctive turn-taking system that organizes news interview talk, which as we saw in chapter 4 obligates interviewees to restrict themselves to answering interviewers' questions. Given this normative constraint on interviewees' talk, any attempt to produce something other than an answer – even as a supplement to an otherwise responsive answer – may be regarded as an improper diversion from the agenda at hand.

By changing the topic of a question, or the task that it poses, or the specific terms in which it is framed, interviewees can loosen the strictures inherent in being on the receiving end of an interrogation. They can, in other words, exert some independent influence on the course of the interview, thereby usurping the interviewer's role as agenda setter. Any such maneuver is resistant in the affirmative sense, and constitutes an effort to *shift the agenda* of the question.

Overt practices

Having identified the various dimensions of evasiveness, we turn now to consider how such maneuvers are actually managed by interviewees. Once an interviewee has decided to sidestep a question to some degree or another, he or she must then determine how to go about it. As we shall see, the various practices that interviewees recurrently use in such situations serve to reduce the risks associated with a resistant course of action.

One alternative is to be up-front and explicit about what is taking place. The strategy of resisting a question *overtly* has, from the interviewee's point of view, an obvious disadvantage: it renders the resistance conspicuous and hence unlikely to escape the notice of the interviewer or the media audience. However, this disadvantage is offset by an equally important advantage: having admitted the evasion, an interviewee can take steps to minimize the damage that it might otherwise cause. We will examine these forms of damage control as they are employed in efforts to shift away from the agenda of the question, after which we will consider the special case of outright refusals to answer.

Deference to the interviewer

Interviewees often preface their agenda shifts with remarks that display some degree of deference to the interviewer. Perhaps the greatest deference is conveyed when the interviewee actually *requests permission from the interviewer* to shift the agenda (Greatbatch 1986b).[5] For example, in a debate interview concerning health care reform, the IE – a health insurance industry executive who opposes President Clinton's health care reform plan – is asked whether anti-reform television ads disclose the fact that they were paid for by the insurance industry (lines 1–4 below). She answers this question in the affirmative (lines 5–9), but then goes on (arrow 1) to ask the IR for permission to comment on an issue raised earlier in the program by a reform proponent ("Ron"). When the IR grants permission (arrow 2), she proceeds to address this other issue (which has to do with whether the so-called "Coalition for Health Insurance Choices" is actually an association of insurance companies masquerading as a grass-roots public interest group).

---

[5] In chapter 4 it was noted that similar requests for permission and token requests are used by IEs when speaking out of turn. Such practices generally serve to mitigate violations of the normative turn-taking arrangements in the news interview, and agenda shifts represent a specific type of violation that is mitigated in this way.

(20)   US PBS *Newshour*: 21 Oct 1993: Health Care
       IR: Margaret Warner   IE: Linda Jenckes

```
 1   IR:        .hhh Well Miss Jenckes he raises an interesting
 2               question.=Again just as a matter of stra:tegy
 3               your ad doesn't say:: that it's sponsored by the
 4               heal:th (.) in[surance companies]
 5   IE:                       [Margaret that's abs]olutely
 6               incorrect. .hh Our a:ds (.) whether they're
 7               on TV, .h our print a-advertisements, that
 8               appear in newspapers .hh even radio spots
 9               indicate that we have paid for it.=
10        1→    Let me may- just make one
11               comm[ent in [terms of wha[t Ron: says.
12   IR:             [.hhh [wh-      [ih-
13   IR:  2→    Al[l right.]
14   IE:         [.h h h ] Of course. any coalition, I don't
15               care whether it's Save: the Whal:es .hh I mean
16               Common Cause you always start with like minded
17               people. But whether you're an agent or a
18               broker, .hh you have legitimate health care
19               concerns youself...
```

Requests for permission openly acknowledge that a shift of the agenda is in the works. In the preceding example, the IE specifically indicates (lines 10–11) that she wishes to respond, not to the IR's question, but to a point made earlier by another IE. At the same time, however, such requests defer to the IR as the one who is properly in charge of the discussion agenda.

The interviewee may also offer what might be termed a *token request for permission* to shift the agenda – this resembles an actual request, but is not treated as requiring a response from the interviewer. Thus, in a discussion of newly proposed legislation to restrict access to abortion, an anti-abortion advocate answers a legalistic question about the wording of legislation, but she then goes on to argue that current law is too permissive. She prefaces this agenda shift with a request-like object: "can I also point out..." (arrowed).

(21)   UK ATV *Afternoon Plus*: 22 Jan 1980: Abortion Limits
       IR: Unknown   IE: Jill Knight

```
 1   IR:        Jill Knight may I ask you how far that's going
 2               to be put into practice and [what- who: is=
```

```
 3  IE:                          [°Ye::s°
 4  IR:     =going to deci:de what i[s serious and what=
 5  IE:                          [°Ye:s°
 6  IR:     =[is a substantial-
 7  IE:      [.hh uh
 8  IE:     Well of course the doctor:: and u::h the-
 9          [in other a:reas wh(h)ere medical- th'medical=
10  ():     [(                          )
11  IE:     =profession is practiced .hhh doctors've been
12          quite capable of deciding what's serious. (.)
13          and what substantial means,
14    →     .hhh And can I also point out, .hh that u::h
15          Professor Huntingford whom you had on .hh your
16          program in December:: .hh supporting the
17          abortion act .hhh u::h eh said (.) really (.)
18          again quite recently there's no do (h)ubt
19          abo (h) ut it=we have got abortion on ↑ request,
20          .hhh and thi[s is what Parliament did NOT ask
21          for . . .
```

Notice that the IR makes no attempt either to grant or refuse permission, and the IE does not seem to expect a response. Indeed,
she actively discourages a response by building her token request as
an incomplete clausal unit ("can I also point out that . . .") which
projects further talk to come. Because they provide so little opportunity for response, token requests are somewhat less deferential than
their full-fledged counterparts. Nevertheless, they do show the interviewee to be "going through the motions" of seeking permission,
thereby continuing to honor the principle that it is the interviewer
who normally sets the agenda.

As we saw in chapter 4, both genuine and token requests for
permission are used more generally in moves that violate the underlying turn-taking system for the news interview. Whether they are
"genuine" or "pro forma," such requests openly acknowledge the
fact that an agenda shift is being contemplated. At the same time,
they alleviate some of the damage that an agenda shift can cause.
Given that agenda shifts threaten to usurp the interviewer's role as
agenda-setter, any effort to seek permission mitigates that threat
by deferring to the interviewer and sustaining a sense in which the
interviewer remains at least formally in charge.

Requests for permission have an additional mitigating feature.
Many requests are designed in such a way as to downplay the agenda

shift by portraying it as insignificant in character. Requests often contain minimizing characterizations, such as reference to a "very quick" or "just one" point (see below).

(22)   UK BBCTV *Newsnight*: May 1989: Civil Unrest in China
           IR: Peter Snow   IE: Dennis Healey

1   DH: But I would like to make <u>two</u> very quick points

(23)   US PBS *Newshour*: 21 Oct 1993: Health Care Ad War
           IR: Margaret Warmer   IE: Linda Jenkes

1   LJ: Let me may- just make one comment in terms of
2   what Ron says . . .

The divergence may be further downgraded by including the adverb "just," as in the preceding example and again in the following:

(24)   UK BBC Radio *Today*: May 1993: Child Support
           IR: John Humphrys   IE: Roz Hepplewhite

1   RH: Can I say just to (set) the context . . .

Thus, in the course of deferring to the interviewer, interviewees often take steps to portray what is to follow as a minor digression from the framework of the question, and by implication an insignificant encroachment on the interviewer's prerogatives.

Justifying the shift

Finally, interviewees may also take steps to *explain and justify* their efforts to divert the discussion. A justification of sorts may be embedded within requests for permission. For example, in a discussion of the 1992 vice-presidential debate, a Republican strategist first responds to a question about the performance of Ross Perot's vice-presidential candidate, Admiral Stockdale, but he then shifts the agenda (lines 17–19) to defend George Bush's flip-flop on abortion, and he prefaces this shift with a token request for permission (arrowed).

(25)   US ABC *Nightline*: 13 Oct 1992: Presidential Debate
           IR: Chris Wallace   IE: William Kristol

1   IR: .hhhh Uh Bill Kristol, does: <u>S</u>tockdale's
2   performance tonigh:t take some of the air:: (.)

```
3            out of the thuh Pe[rot balloo]n:: just as it=
4   IE:                [p H H Hhhh]
5   IR:     =was getting bl:own up again.
6            (0.6)
7   IE:     Uh:: I'm not sure about that Chris. I think
8            the: ah: two things were remember- we'll
9            remember about Admirable Stock- Admiral
10           Stockdale tonight ah: are his: very strong
11           denunciation of Al Gore:'s extreme
12           environmentalism .hh and his statement about
13           the important of cah- 'portance of character.
14           .h to leadership. Both of those statements
15           will: (reboun:d) to the benefit of President
16           Bush. .hh Ah and on that last point
17   →  >if I could just speak to Molly's point: uh
18           before the break, uhm President Bush changed
19           his mind about abortion an:d said so...
```

This token request contains a justificatory element embodied in how the requested action is characterized. Instead of asking generically to "say one more thing" or "make an additional point," this IE asks specifically to address "Molly's point before the break." This way of characterizing what he wants to do is not technically necessary for the token request to be intelligible; it is a strategic choice which provides an implicit rationale for the agenda shift. In the context of a debate interview involving partisan interviewees, portraying the shift as a response to a point made earlier by another interviewee tacitly justifies the shift on the grounds of fairness and the principle that partisan accusations should not be permitted to stand unanswered. In addition, the shift is characterized in relation to an impending commercial break, which further justifies the move by explaining why it is being launched at this particular point in time.

Justifications can also appear outside of permission requests, where they tend to be more explicit and elaborate. An example is highlighted below. The IR asks whether corporate mergers are creating monopolistic entities, and the IE briefly addresses this issue, but he then raises other concerns about mergers. Before doing so, however, he justifies this shift (arrowed) on the basis that it will address "the real concern" with corporate mergers, but one that has not yet been addressed in the interview.

(26) US ABC *Nightline*: 5 June 1985: Corporate Mergers
      IR: Ted Koppel   IE: Senator Howard Metzenbaum

```
 1  IR:      .hhhh Senator Metzenbaum take me back to the- to
 2            that difference: that uh Mister Forbes made a
 3            moment ago, between monopolies and what we have
 4            today:, which it seems in- in some instances is
 5            moving .hh at least (0.2) gr:adually in the
 6            direction of a monopoly. is it not?
 7            (0.4)
 8  IE:       Well I think thet some mergers (.) don't have
 9            any element of monopoly in them at all. .hh (.)
10            Uh for example General Motors buying Hughes
11            Aircraft (I'm) not at all certain that there's
12            any monopoly (.) issues there. (0.5)
13  →        On the other hand I think the real concern that
14  →        h:asn't been addressed (.) previously (.) in
15            this program (0.7) HAS to do with the fact
16            that . . . ((parenthetical comment omitted))
17            . . . secondly you have to be concerned as to the
18            impact (.) on the shareholders, (0.4) and third
19            but certainly not least of the three, (.)
20            is the impact upon the community . . .
```

The rationales offered for agenda shifts tend to fall into either of two basic categories. One argument is based on the principle of fairness and the need to respond to points raised by other interviewees. This argument is particularly common in debate interviews where interviewees represent opposing points of view on some controversial issue (see chapter 8). Excerpt (25) above typifies this rationale, but other examples are commonplace:

(27) US PBS *Newshour*: 3 Feb 1992: Haitian Refugees
      IR: Unknown   IE: Bernard Aronson

```
 1  BA:      Ahm: let me just respond to a few things that
 2            (.) Congressman Rangel said . . .
```

(28) US PBS *Newshour*: 21 Oct 1993: Health Care
      IR: Margaret Warner   IE: Linda Jenckes

```
 1  LJ:      Let me may- just make one comment in terms of
 2            what Ron: says
```

Alternatively, unsolicited material may be justified on the basis that it has a significant bearing on the overarching subject at hand. This is exemplified in (26) above, and in the following:

(29)   UK BBC Radio *Today*: May 1993: Child Support
       IR: John Humphrys   IE: Roz Hepplewhite
1   RH: Can I say just to (set) the context...

(30)   US ABC *This Week*: 5 May 1996: Gas Tax
       IR: David Brinkley   IE: Robert Rubin
1   RR: But I think there's really a- a mu:ch b:igger
2   (0.4) this is part of a much bigger picture...

Whatever specific grounds may be offered, the import of such a
move remains much the same. Interviewees acknowledge the fact
that a digression is being launched, while seeking to forestall unflattering inferences that interviewers and audience members might
otherwise draw (e.g., "they must be hiding something") by portraying the shift as legitimate and properly motivated.

The special case of refusing to answer

Justificatory accounts become particularly elaborate and strenuous
when the interviewee overtly refuses to answer the question altogether. Among the various forms of resistance, blanket refusals to
answer constitute perhaps the strongest "breach of contract." It is
one thing to make some effort to be responsive before proceeding to
shift the agenda; it is quite another to refuse to speak to the question
in any way (Greatbatch 1986a). The latter course of action violates
not only the normative ground rules for the news interview, but also
much more basic and fundamental norms governing interactional
conduct per se (Schegloff 1968; 1972). Accordingly, justificatory
accounts become crucial in this context, and they are an important
locus for delicate facework and relationship management between
interviewees and interviewers.

    Various rationales may be offered to account for a refusal to
answer, but they tend to have one element in common: they deflect
responsibility for the refusal away from the interviewee and onto
some external circumstance. For instance, one common rationale is
to claim that the information necessary to answer the question is
unavailable. Thus, when a medical researcher is asked whether a
new cancer treatment may have other applications, he suggests that
the relevant research has not yet been done.

(31) US CBS *Face the Nation*: 8 Dec 1985: Cancer Treatment
      IR: Lesley Stahl   IE: Dr. Steven Rosenberg
1 IR: Uh <u>two</u> final qu<u>e</u>stions. Doctor Rosenberg. d'y<u>ou</u>
2   see this h<u>a</u>ving application for <u>oth</u>er diseases,
3   like multiple sclerosis or even <u>A</u>:IDS,
4   (0.4)
5 IE: We h<u>a</u>ven't y<u>e</u>t. beg<u>un</u>: to explore th<u>a</u>t, although
6   I think possibilities ex<u>i</u>st 'at need to be
7   investigated 'n I think <u>oth</u>er:: sc<u>i</u>entists will
8   be l<u>oo</u>king at those questions.

Notice that the IE does not merely assert that he *doesn't know* the
answer, which might damage his reputation as a medical expert. In
general, *don't know* accounts in the news interview usually contain
some further explanation for the interviewee's lack of information,
thereby preserving the interviewee's expert status.

Alternatively, the interviewee may suggest that an answer is available but cannot be provided under current circumstances. The temporal limitations of the broadcast interview are often cited – as when
a nuclear physicist asserts that she cannot answer "all these scientific
questions in one minute given to me" (arrowed).

(32) US ABC *Nightline*: 6 June 1985: Nuclear Waste
      IR: Unknown   IE: Dr. Rosalyn Yalow
1 IR: Cont<u>i</u>nuing our conversati<u>o</u>n now with Doctor
2   Rosalyn <u>Ya</u>low. Doctor Yalow uh- ehh l<u>emm</u>e put
3   it in very simple terms. If it's doable, if it
4   is: <u>ea</u>sily disposable, <u>why</u> <u>don't</u> we.
5   (1.0)
6 IE: → Well frankly I cannot- (.) <u>answer</u> <u>all</u> these
7   scient<u>i</u>fic questions in one minute given to
8   me . . .

An interviewee may also refuse to answer on the basis that to
do so would be somehow inappropriate under the circumstances.
When public officials are being interviewed, they often invoke the
delicacies of official negotiations to deflect questions. In a discussion
of the federal budget (examined in chapter 6), Senate majority leader
Bob Dole is asked whether it will be necessary to cut social programs,
raise taxes, or reduce defense spending, but Dole declines to answer
(arrowed), arguing that it would be premature to do so in advance
of formal negotiations.

(33)   US NBC *Meet the Press*: 8 Dec 1985: Federal Budget
       IR: Albert Hunt   IE: Senator Bob Dole

```
 1  IR:      You can't have it both ways either. =>On this
 2            program< you have said that you don't think,
 3            .hhh that you'll eliminate thirty to fifty
 4            programs, [an'] Senator Packwood=
 5  IE:               [( )]
 6  IR:      =says ya have to, .hh Number two you say
 7            you hope you will not have a tax increase,
 8            [.hhhh And]=
 9  IE:      [But I do.]
10  IR:      =number- and number three you say ya h:ope you
11            can have a:l [m o s t] three percent on: .hhh=
12  ():                   [(   )]
13  IR:      =on: on defe:nse, .hh And yet you hafta cut
14            fifty billion next year. Now which o 'those
15            three's gonna give Senator,
16            (0.4)
17  IE:   →  I think that's going to happen sometime next
18        →  year when those of us:: uh in- leadership
19        →  positions=set=down with the President and make
20        →  the hard choice. I don' think I'd make it today:
21        →  .hhhhh ih=in December of 1985.
```

Here the IE justifies his refusal by proposing that *to answer* would be inappropriate. Such accounts could also be taken to imply that *the question* was inappropriate, although in the previous example this remains an unstated implication of an account that remains primarily focused on the inappropriateness of answering.

Occasionally, however, an interviewee will go one step further and assert that the question itself was somehow improper and hence unworthy of an answer – in effect, deflecting the question by attacking it. For example, when a Serbian spokesperson is asked if recent prisoners of war are being beaten (lines 1–3), he asserts that the line of questioning is biased, hostile, and provocative (lines 6–13).

(34)   US NPR *All Things Considered*: 15 July 1995: Serbia
       IR: Alex Chadwick   IE: Jovan Zametica

```
 1  IR:      Are they being beaten? Or will you be: are you
 2            treating them (u-) humanely according to
 3            inter[national conventions.
```

```
 4  IE:        [hhh!
 5             (.)
 6  IE:        Well I mean your line of questioning really
 7             suggests that we are the most awful creatures on
 8             earth. That we a:re beating the prisoners,
 9             raping women, and so on and so forth. .hh
10             Please I think I have been very: uh: uh correct
11             in my answers, an' I would expect you to: .hh be
12             more correct in your line of question=because
13             it's extremely provocative...
```

By attacking the question in this way, he both justifies his failure to provide an answer and deflects the discussion away from the substance of the question and toward the propriety of the IR having raised it.

It is rare for an interviewee to refuse a question flatly, without providing a rationale of some sort. When that does happen, it comes across as an extremely hostile gesture. For example, consider how a Labour politician flatly refuses a question concerning his willingness to serve in an administration committed to unilateral nuclear disarmament.

(35)   UK Greatbatch 1986: 451: Nuclear Disarmament
       IR: Robin Day   IE: Peter Shore

```
 1  IR:        You wouldn't serve in a Cabinet committed to lu-
 2             unilateral nuclear disarmament of Britain would
 3             you Mister Shore?
 4  IE:        .hh What I do believe:: er: Mister Day (which)
 5        →    I will not a:nswer that question, I'm not (.)
 6        →    deliberately answering that question. What I do
 7             believe is thi:s. I do actually genuinely
 8             believe lo:ng believe: (d) .hhh that unilateral
 9             initiatives: (.) can assist (.) multilateral
10             disarmament...
```

Here the IE declines to offer any justification, and he characterizes his refusal as a deliberate, willful choice (arrowed). This can be taken to imply that the question is unworthy of an answer, so transparently unworthy that his refusal to answer requires no explicit justification. This amounts to a powerful attack on the legitimacy of the question and, perhaps indirectly, on the judgment and character of the IR who asked it.

One type of account is distinctly equivocal in terms of its hostility toward the interviewer. An interviewee may refuse to answer as a matter of general policy, asserting, in effect, that he or she never answers questions of that sort. For example, when Arthur Scargill is asked if he is planning to run for the presidency of the National Union of Mineworkers (lines 1–2), he refuses to say at this point, and he prefaces his refusal by noting that he's given the same response to "every other pressman over the past forty-eight hours" (lines 3–5).

(36)   UK BBC Radio *World at One*: 13 Mar 1979: NUM Election
         IR: Robin Day   IE: Arthur Scargill

```
 1   IR:    M:ister Scargill will you run for the presidency
 2           of the National Union of Mineworkers.
 3   IE:    .hhh er Mister Day: I must give you the same
 4           answer that I've been giving every other
 5           pressman over the past forty-eight hours. .hhh
 6           If and when Mister Gormley officially (.) hands
 7           in his resignation and that's by no means
 8           certain .hhhh er during: this year or at any
 9           time during the next three years .hh then I will
10           give (.) serious consideration to the matter...
```

Treasury Secretary Robert Rubin does something very similar when asked about the direction of future interest rates. He characterizes his refusal as part of a three-and-a-half-year-old policy of not commenting on the future course of the financial markets (lines 2–4).

(37)   US ABC *This Week*: 5 May 1996: Interest Rates
         IR: Sam Donaldson   IE: Robert Rubin

```
 1   IR:    But which way are they going now?=
 2   IE:    =>For three and a half years.< .hhh Sa:m. I have
 3           had for three and a half years a policy of >not
 4           commenting on what markets are gonna do...
```

This type of account can have the effect of *depersonalizing* the refusal, casting it not as an idiosyncratic response to a particular question from a particular interviewer, but as a general policy applied to all questions of that sort. This can in turn be disarming in its import, helping to ensure that the refusal will not be taken as an act of aggression against the interviewer per se. However, if it is implied that the interviewer should have known of the policy, as in (37), the import is rather more hostile. In any case, insofar as it suggests that any further efforts to elicit an answer will prove fruitless, this type of account inhibits follow-up questions and represents a strong bid to close down the entire line of inquiry.

Covert practices

Overt practices have their counterpart in strategies for resisting a question *covertly*. Covert practices are mainly used in the context of positive resistance, or talk that departs from the agenda of the question. What makes them covert is that the interviewees avoid any explicit acknowledgment of the fact that they are shifting the agenda, and they may go so far as to actively conceal that fact. For the interviewee, the obvious advantage of a surreptitious strategy is the possibility of "getting away with it" – if done with enough subtlety, it may escape the notice of the interviewer and audience members. On the other hand, if the evasive maneuver *is* noticed, it can be particularly costly. Those who evade questions while pretending to answer them risk being seen as devious and manipulative, and this is over and above all of the negative attributions that stem from having evaded the question in the first place. Furthermore, such inferences cannot be forestalled via forms of "damage control," because the covert nature of the practice precludes any explicit remedial measures. Interviewees can, however, reduce the likelihood that the resistance will be noticed by taking steps to render it less conspicuous.

Unmarked transitions beyond answering

To get an initial sense of just how inconspicuous and elusive an agenda shift can be, let's examine a remarkable interview with Peter Bijur, chairman and chief executive officer of Texaco, conducted just after Texaco had agreed to settle a large racial discrimination lawsuit. Bijur is asked a series of questions about discrimination at Texaco and the events leading up to the settlement; in each response, he eventually departs from the agenda of the question through a subtle shift in the verbal tense through which the talk is expressed.

The very first question–answer sequence in the interview (examined in chapter 6) embodies this type of maneuver. Bijur is asked to explain what prompted the decision to settle the lawsuit (lines 1–2), and this open-ended question is subsequently specified in terms of two thoroughly undesirable alternatives: either the discrimination was found to be genuine (lines 2–3), or the company wanted to avoid more economic losses (line 4).

(38)   US NBC *Nightly News*: 15 Nov 1996: Texaco Lawsuit
       IR: Tom Brokaw   IE: Peter Bijur

```
1   IR:     .h Mister Bijur what's pro: what prompted this
2           settlement. .hh The fact that you concluded
3           your company was in fact discrimina:ting¿
4           or the prospects of: (.) more economic losses.
5   IE:     T:o:m it was that we wanted to be f:air: to ah
6           all of the employees involved,
7    →      we're a:wonderful: gr:oup of people
8           and family in this company, and
9    →      we wanta be equitable with everybody.
```

Bijur initially chooses neither of these alternatives, explaining instead that "we wanted to be fair" to those involved (lines 5–6). In avoiding the proferred explanations, this response is already manifestly resistant, but insofar as it deals with the past decision-making process it remains consistent with the time frame targeted by the original question. However, at the first arrow Bijur alters the verbal tense of his talk – he shifts from past to present tense as he proceeds to characterize the company as a "wonderful group of people" and "family" who "want to be equitable with everybody." This transition is inconspicuous but nonetheless significant and plainly advantageous to the Texaco chairman. It has the effect of pushing the problematic incident into the past and refocusing the discussion toward the company's current state, which is presented as entirely fair and equitable.

Virtually all of Bijur's responses sidestep the question in a similar manner. The very next question concerns the import of new evidence that had emerged just prior to the settlement – audiotaped conversations of Texaco executives expressing racist attitudes. Countering Bijur's prior claim to have been motivated purely out of a desire to be fair, the IR asks whether the surfacing of those tapes is what actually prompted the settlement. He does so by conjuring up a hypothetical situation ("if those tapes had not surfaced..." at line 1) and asking whether in that situation the discrimination "would still be going on." Notice that the question ends in a conditional form of the present progressive tense.

(39) US NBC *Nightly News*: 15 Nov 1996: Texaco Lawsuit
      IR: Tom Brokaw   IE: Peter Bijur

```
1  IR:    Bu: t in f:a:ct if those ta:pes had not surfaced,
2         (.) This ah: (.) c:ase after all >has been going
3         on< for two years, .hhh is there any doubt in
4         your mi:nd that it would still be going on?
5  IE:  → .Pthh Ah it mi:ght very well have been going on.
6         Those tapes were hor: ren:dous.and we needed to
7         get this behind us as quickly as possible.
```

Bijur's initial response (line 5), while otherwise on-topic, shifts from present progressive to a conditional form of past tense – from "it would still be going on" to "it might very well have been going on." His subsequent expression of Texaco's desire to deal with the problem as quickly as possible is in the simple past tense ("we needed to get this behind us" in 6–7) and thus embodies, in its very form, what the remark substantively expresses and what his prior tense shift accomplishes: pushing the troublesome incident into the past.

Two questions later, the IR cites outside observers to propose that more needs to be done "to get Texaco up to speed here." By deploying various forms of the present tense, Texaco's problems are portrayed as a current and continuing concern.

(40) US NBC *Nightly News*: 15 Nov 1996: Texaco Lawsuit
      IR: Tom Brokaw   IE: Peter Bijur

```
1  IR:    B:ut in fa:ct outside observers inclu::ding:
2         Andrew Young looking at this program whi-on this
3         program last night said a lot of other companies
4         are doing a lo::t better, .hhh we just need to
5         get Texaco up to spee:d h:ere:.
6  IE:  → We've been doing really w:ell:.=But we
7       → haven't been doing well enough, O:bviously.
8       → And we're gonna do better in the future.
```

Bijur, however, shifts to a form of the past tense as he admits that "we haven't been doing well enough" (lines 6–7), and he proceeds immediately to a future-oriented promise to do better (line 8). Taken together, Bijur's answers all fall broadly within the topical domain targeted by the prior question, but they exploit tense shifts and allied practices to alter the temporal orientation of the talk in a way that relegates Texaco's problems to the past and refocuses the discussion to the corporation's current state and future prospects.

As inexplicit and subtle as these practices are, the interviewee does not attempt to disguise or conceal what is taking place. In other instances, however, outright concealment is the order of the day. One way of actively blurring the boundary between answer and unsolicited material involves linking the two as part of a common project (cf., Heritage and Sorjonen 1994; Jefferson 1986). To illustrate, consider this excerpt from an interview with conservative commentator and presidential candidate Pat Buchanan, conducted when Buchanan was rising in the polls to become a contender for the 1996 Republican nomination. Much of the questioning was aimed at positioning Buchanan ideologically to the right of frontrunner Bob Dole. Just before the excerpt begins, the IR reads a quotation from one of Buchanan's newspaper commentaries, and notes that when referring to discrimination against women Buchanan had put the word *discrimination* in quotation marks. She then asks if Buchanan's view is that women have *not* been discriminated against (lines 1–3).

(41)   US ABC *This Week*: 18 Feb 1996: Pat Buchanan
          IR: Cokie Roberts   IE: Pat Buchanan

```
 1  IR:      Now first of all discrimination in quotation
 2            marks does that mean .hh women have not been
 3            discrimi[nated against (in [your           )
 4  IE:  1→        [.hh              [Women have
 5       1→indeed been discriminated against,
 6       2→an:d quite frankly it was wro:ng,
 7       3→an' it oughta e:nd,
 8       4→an' it will end in the Buchanan administration,
 9       5→.hh An' without women in my campaign I wouldn't
10       5→be where I wa:s. It's not (simply) my campaign
11       5→chairman, .hh My finance chairman is a woman,
12       5→.hh an:d the individual that put together
13       5→Geor:ge that Louisiana (triumph) is a woman
14       5→Sandy Mc(Day:d) who would never put up: with
15       5→the ki:nd of garbage .hh that's being ascribed
16       5→t'that campaign in Louisiana,
```

Buchanan first answers the question in the way in which it was framed (arrow 1), countering the preference built into the question to assert that women "have indeed been discriminated against." This becomes the first in a list of items, each prefaced with *and*, that move beyond the question in stages. The next three items in the list (arrows 2–4) move away from the literal question to address what might be regarded as its broader objective – namely, to reveal where Buchanan stands on the politics of gender equality and what policies he would pursue as president. Thus, with items 2 and 3, Buchanan shifts from the factual question of extant gender discrimination to a moral condemnation of such discrimination, and with item 4 he promises to end discrimination if elected. Item 5, however, which occupies the bulk of the response, embodies a more substantial shift. Here Buchanan enumerates the various women who have worked on his campaign. This is revealing of Buchanan's own individual professional relationships with women, but it is no longer in the realm of public policy and it reveals nothing about what he would do as president. Buchanan thus moves from answering the literal question, to addressing its broader objective, to addressing matters which reflect favorably on his character but which have little bearing on the question per se.

Across this stepwise agenda shift, the components are all *and*-prefaced and are thus constructed as co-members of a single overarching activity with almost a list-like quality. As Jefferson (1986) has demonstrated, when items are grouped together in this way, their differences are minimized and they are presented as if they somehow "belong together" (see also Heritage and Sorjonen 1994). This generic interactional practice is exploited by interviewees in a way that obscures the transition from answer to unsolicited material. This same practice was deployed by George Bush in the infamous Bush–Rather interview from 1988 (discussed in chapter 1), and here it blurs the boundary of a much more substantial departure. In the very first question of the interview (discussed in chapter 6), Bush is asked to explain why Donald Gregg, who was implicated in the Iran-Contra scandal, remains "inside the White House and still a trusted advisor" (lines 1–10).

(42)   US CBS *Evening News* 25 Jan 1988: Iran-Contra
        IR: Dan Rather   IE: George Bush

```
1  DR:    Mister Vice President, thank you for being with
2         us tonigh:t, .hh Donald Gregg still serves as
3         your trusted advisor, he was deeply involved in
4         running arms to the Contras, 'n 'e didn't inform
5         you. .hhh Now when President Reagan's (0.3)
```

```
 6              trusted advisor: Admiral Poindexter: (0.5)
 7              failed to inform him::, (0.7) the President
 8              (0.4) fired 'im. (0.5) Why is Mister Gregg
 9              still:: (0.2) inside the White House 'n still
10              a trusted advisor.
11   GB:   1→Because I have confidence in him, .hh
12         2→'n because this matter Dan:, as yow well know:,
13              'n your editors know:, has been looked at by .hh
14              the ten millon dollar study by the: (.) Senate
15              'n the Hou:se, .hh it's been looked at by the
16              Tower commission, .hh the Rodriguez testimony
17              that you put on here, I jus' think it's
18              outrageous, because he was totally vindicated,
19              .hh swore under oath thet 'e never talked to me
20              about .hh the Contras, 'n yet : this:(.) report
21              you're making which you told me:: er your people
22              did, you have a Mister Cohen thet works for you,
23              .hh was gonna be a political profile. .hh now if
24              this is a political profile for an election, .hh
25              uh: I have a very different opinion as to what
26              one should be:... ((ten lines omitted))
27              ...And so I find this to be a: rehash .hh and a
28              li:ttle bit (.) if you'll excuse me a
29              misrepresented- tation on thuh part of CBS who
30              said you're doin' political profiles .hh on all
31              the candidates, .h and then you- (0.2) come up
32              with something thet 'as been exhaustively looked
33              into.
```

Bush's initial remark ("Because I have confidence in him" at arrow 1) is fully responsive to the question and is constructed as such. In the context of the IR's *why* question, this *because*-prefaced clause ties back to the question and is built as an explanation for what the question was seeking. Bush's next remark ("and because..." at arrow 2) is linked to the prior via the *and*-preface, and is framed more specifically as the second component of an explanation (via the *because*-preface). By all indications, Bush at this point seems to be about to elaborate on his explanation for retaining Donald Gregg as his advisor. However, notwithstanding the framing of this remark, what Bush actually does is very different. He proceeds at this point to attack Dan Rather and the CBS News team for various misdeeds, including raising accusations for which he had already been vindicated (lines 12–20), and misleading him into thinking that the interview would be a broad political profile rather than a narrow investigation of the Iran-Contra scandal (lines 20–33). Here, then, a rather dramatic shift of direction – from answering the question to attacking the questioner – is initially packaged as if it entailed no shift at all.

Subverting the trappings of "answering"

Earlier in this chapter, we considered how a stretch of talk becomes recognizable as an "answer," and we described a variety of practices – including word repeats, anaphoric pronouns, and so on – that are implicated in this process. While these practices are important in the construction of answers, they provide no guarantee that a genuine answer has been given. Indeed, interviewees can use these same practices subversively, to provide a kind of surface camouflage for maneuvers that are substantively resistant. We've already caught a glimpse of this practice with Bush's *because* prefaced shift in the preceding example; now we explore how the various accoutrements of "answering" can be similarly subverted.

Word repeats – preserving some of the exact wording of the question in the initial response – are exploited in this way. A straightforward example occurred in the interview (examined in chapter 6) with Arthur Scargill of Britain's National Union of Mineworkers. The interview took place just as the mineworkers were preparing to elect a new president, and Scargill was discussed as a likely candidate representing the left wing of the union. In a question seeking to distinguish the candidates on the left, the IR (in lines 1–2) asks Scargill to explain "the difference between your Marxism and Mr. McGahey's Communism." Scargill launches his response (line 3) with a repeat of a key word from the question: "The difference is... " By virtue of this literal repetition, he appears to be moving straightforwardly to answer the question.

(43)   UK BBC Radio *World at One*: 13 Mar 1979: NUM Election
          IR: Robin Day   IE: Arthur Scargill

```
1  IR:     .hhh er What's the difference between your
2          Marxism and Mister McGahey's communism.
3  IE:  → er The difference is that it's the press that
4          constantly call me Ma:rxist when I do not, (.)
5          and never have (.) er er given that description
6          of myself ...
```

But appearances can be deceiving – Scargill uses the word to mean something other than what it meant in the IR's original question. In that question, "the difference" referred to a distinction between two candidates – Scargill vs. McGahey – and their ideologies. In the response, "the difference" refers to a distinction between two interpretations – by the press vs. by Scargill – of Scargill's ideology in particular. This semantic shift in the meaning and reference of "the difference" is part and parcel of a more encompassing shift in the topical agenda. Scargill veers away from the question as it is framed, deals instead with a presupposition that was embedded in the question – that he is in fact a Marxist – and counters that presupposition in his response.

To be sure, this is a relatively mild readjustment of the agenda. What Scargill has to say is not irrelevant to the question at hand – indeed, he suggests that the question was inaccurately and unfairly presumptive. Nevertheless, he does not, strictly speaking, answer the question in the way in which it was framed. And yet he presents himself as if he were being dutifully responsive. By repeating a key lexical item from the question ("What's the difference...?" → "The difference is..."), he packages his response as if it were straightforwardly filling the information gap created by the question.

Like word repeats, anaphoric pronouns also can be used subversively. Consider the following exchange with a spokesperson for presidential candidate Ross Perot. The IR prefaces his question with a comment on the amount of money Perot is planning to spend on television advertising during the final weeks of the campaign (lines 1–4), and he goes on to ask whether Perot is "actually gonna get out and meet with the voters..." (lines 4–6). The IE begins to respond by saying "Let's talk about this" (line 7), using a pronoun that refers back to the questioning turn in a way that promises a bona fide answer.

(44)   US ABC *Nightline*: 15 Oct 1992: Presidential Debate
       IR: Chris Wallace   IE: Clay Mulford

```
1  IR:   .hh Mister Mulfor:d ah r- your man Ross Perot is
2         gonna spen:d at lea::st ten mill:ion dollars .hh
3         in TV advertising in the final two and a half
4         weeks of this campaign.< .hhh Is he actually
5         gonna get out and- and meet with voters,
6         campai:gn like the other candidates?
```

```
 7   IE:    Yeh, well l- let's: (.) talk about this: for a
 8          second. Ah- the- the other two: (.) candidates
 9          recei:ve over fifty five point two million
10          dollars directly from the taxpay:ers. .hh
11          Mister Perot is spending his own money. In
12          addition to the fifty five million dollars that
13          they get from the federal government, .hh they
14          get over a hundred million dollars in so::ft
15          money. The whole way the (.) political
16          process is financed is something we objec:t
17          to::. .hhhh I- I imagine he will spend ten
18          million dollars on media 'cause what we see is
19          something very extraordinary in Amer:ican
20          politics. .hh Usually, with the passage of
21          ti:me independent candidates go down: in the
22          polls:. .hh Since we have entered the race
23          according to the polls, we've gone from seven
24          to fifteen percent ... And we think Perot is
25          gonna win ...
26                 .
27                 . ((Some 20 lines of transcript omitted))
28                 .
29   IR:    ... You : you gave a good answer. = You never
30          answered my question, how:ever. .hh>Part of
31          the political process< is for candidates
32          actually to get out and mee:t with voters.
33          (0.3)>Is he gonna do tha:t?
```

However, rather than answer the question about meeting with the voters, the IE responds instead to the prefatory comment – he offers a lengthy justification for Perot's advertising expenditures (lines 8–17). He then goes on to comment on Perot's rise in the polls and his chances of winning (lines 18–25). This shift is obscured by the initial back-referencing statement, but it is not exactly invisible. The IR pursues the matter, pointing out that the IE "never answered my question" (lines 29–30), and then reissuing that question (line 33).

Subversive word repeats and pronouns can also be used in combination. In a discussion of former President Clinton's health care reform plan, the IR asks a Republican media consultant about the strategy behind the television advertising campaign opposing the Clinton reform plan. More specifically, he asks what the advertising campaign "has to do ... what does it have to tap in the American

public to be successful." The IE, in his initial response, seems to be
moving to answer straightforwardly – he refers back to the question
and repeats some of its key words: "that's what we're trying to
do..."

(45) US PBS *NewsHour*: 21 Oct 1993: Health Care
      IR: Margaret Warner   IE: Alex Castellanos

```
 1  IR:      Let me turn now to our (.) two professionals
 2           here: in media- in media wars. Mister
 3           Castellanos. .hhh Ah you of course produced the
 4           Republican National Committee ad. = If you were
 5           de:signing the entire: ad campaign for
 6           opposition to this plan .hhh what would you
 7           say are the two or three most important things
 8           it has to do. What does it have to tap in the
 9           American public (.) to be successful.
10           (0.5)
11  IE:  →   I think we'r- that's what we're try:ing to do in
12           the: ah: in the Republican ad Margaret. .hh We
13           ah: we want people to read the pla:n. And when
14           they do, I think ah: they'll understand that
15           this is not a plan for better health care .hhh
16           we just want them to know that this is a plan
17           for bigger government.
18  IR:      And you think that's an effective argument.
```

However, this initial remark masks what is in fact a very subtle shift
in the framing of the subject at hand. The IR's question emphasizes
the arts of rhetoric and persuasion. She prefaces her question by
noting that the IE is a professional in "media wars," and that he
"produced the Republican National Committee ad." The question
itself asks if the IE were designing the advertising campaign for the
opposition, what does the campaign "have to tap in the American
public to be successful." The thrust of the question is that the ads will
exploit attitudes and anxieties in the public to mobilize opposition
to health care reform. However, in his response, the IE characterizes
his approach as one that would let the facts speak for themselves. As
he puts it, the Republicans simply "want people to read the plan."
He makes no reference to rhetorical tactics, or strategies for striking
a responsive chord in the American people. This subtle shift in the
framing of the issue is obscured by the initial remark that launched
his response, which refers back to the questioning turn, repeats some
of its key words, and thus seems to promise a fully responsive answer.

A more complicated example is from a British debate interview concerning a proposal to revise abortion law so as to narrow the circumstances under which abortions would be legal. The excerpt begins with the IR asking Jill Knight, an outspoken opponent of abortion, about one aspect of the legislation, which would shorten the time period for legal abortions.

(46)   UK ATV *Afternoon Plus*: 22 Jan 1980: Abortion Limits
         IR: Unknown   IE: Jill Knight

```
 1  IR:     .hhh (Oh) can we now take up then the main
 2           issues of that bill which r- (0.1) remain
 3           substantially the same. (.) and indeed (0.1)
 4           have caused great deal of concern. (0.4) But
 5           first you'll note .hhh is the clause about (.)
 6           time limits h in which h abortions can be .h
 7           legally =
 8  (IE):    =*(yes)*=
 9  IR:      =ha:d. And the time limit h (.) according to the
10           bill has now dropped .h from twenty eight weeks
11           .h (.) to twenty wee[ks.
12  (IE):                       [Yes.=
13  IR:      =Now< a lot of people are very concerned about
14           this. [.hh How concerned are you.
15  (IE):          [*Yeh*
16  IE:      .hhh Uh: (.) I think this is right. I think that
17           um: .hh again one's had a lot of e:uh
18           conflicting evidence on this but .hh what has
19     →     come ou::t h an' I think that .h the public
20     →     have been concerned about this. .hhh is that
21           there have been th'most distressing cases. .hhh
22           of (.) live (.) kicking babies who have been
23           destroyed. .hh I've had nurses come to me in
24           great distress (0.2) about this .hh and uh there
25           was undoubtedly (0.1) throughout the whole
26     →     (ambit) of public opinion .hh very great concern
27     →     .h on this whole question . . .
```

A key word here is, obviously, "concern." As we saw in chapter 6, it is central to the final question (line 14), which asks about the IE's level of "concern" regarding the more restricted time frame. It's also central to the preceding statement (line 13) and to the earlier lead-in (line 4), both of which make reference to widespread public "concern" about the new restrictions.

In her initial response, the IE appears to be moving to answer the question straightforwardly. Her first remark ("I think this is right") refers back to the IR's prior talk, and seems to be expressing some form of confirmation or agreement. And when she begins to elaborate, she twice uses that same key word: "concern" (arrowed). She says at lines 19–20 that "the public have been concerned about this," and she refers in line 26–27 to "very great concern on this whole question." However, this comes to mean something very different here than it did originally. She uses "concern" to mean *concern about late-term abortions*; but in the original question it meant *concern about the more restricted time frame*, and at least by implication the more restricted access to abortion that this entails. This semantic reversal is intertwined with a more encompassing shift in the topical focus of the response vis-à-vis the original question.

Now this shift could in principle have been done much more explicitly. The IE could have said something like "I'm not the least bit concerned about a shorter time frame; what worries me is the destruction of live and kicking babies!" But that would place her in direct disagreement with the viewpoint embedded in the question, and would show her to be insensitive to the plight of those seeking abortion services. Her actual course of action avoids all of that. She presents herself as if she were straightfowardly answering, and agreeably expressing "concern," while surreptitiously veering away from the question in the way in which it has been framed. The cover for this maneuver is provided by the back-referencing assessment and the lexical repetition. The latter serves as a kind of pivot between the question's agenda and the somewhat different direction pursued subsequently, and thus provides the ensuing talk with at least a veneer of continuity.

Operating on the question

Agenda shifts can be obscured in other ways. Before "answering" a given question, an interviewee may first refer to, characterize, or paraphrase the question at hand. These various operations can modify the question in a way that both facilitates and conceals a shift of the agenda. Thus, not only can interviewees adjust the surface form of a response to fit the question, but they can in effect adjust the question to fit the response that they intend to give.

To illustrate, consider this excerpt from an interview with
Senator Gary Hart when he was a candidate during the 1988 presidential campaign. The interview took place after evidence surfaced
suggesting that Hart had had an extramarital affair with a young
woman named Donna Rice. In an effort to salvage his candidacy,
Hart appeared on Ted Koppel's *Nightline*. At one point he was asked
specifically if he had had an affair with Miss Rice (arrow 1 below).
Before answering, Hart comments (not shown) on the difficulty of
responding to this type of question, and he then reformulates the
question (starting at arrow 2) – he broadens it so that it is made
to concern his marital fidelity over the past twenty-nine years, including periods during which he and his wife were publicly known
to have been separated. Only after he completes this reformulation
does he provide an "answer" (arrow 3), an admission of infidelity.
But the parameters of his admission have been set, not by the original
question, but by the reformulation.

(47)   US ABC *Nightline*: 8 Sep 1987: Gary Hart & Donna Rice
       IR: Ted Koppel IE: Senator Gary Hart
 1   IR: Uh- (0.5) I told you::. (0.4) some days ago when
 2   we spo:ke, and I told our audience this evening
 3   that I would ask you both questions. I will ask
 4   you the first now: just before we take a brea:k
 5   because I think I know what your answer's gonna
 6   be.=
 7   1→   = Did you have an affair with Miss Rice?
 8   IE: 2→   ... If the question: (.) is in the twenty nine
 9   y:ear:s of my marriage, including two public
10   separations have I been absolutely and totally
11   faithful: to my wife .hhh
12   3→   I regret to say the answer is no:...

The advantages of such a transformation should be obvious. It enables Hart to appear "forthcoming," but in response to a question
that, by virtue of its generality, is much less pointed. Consequently,
his admission is less politically damaging than it might otherwise
have been. In effect, Hart manages to "steer the question" in a more
desirable direction.

In this particular example, Hart seems to acknowledge the fact
that the question has been modified. Notice that his reformulation is
offered tentatively within an *if-clause* ("Mister Koppel, if the question is ... "). This case is thus comparatively overt in the way in
which it shifts the agenda.

Other question reformulations are asserted more forcefully, as if they faithfully preserve the essence of the original question. The next example comes from the 1988 vice-presidential debate – although this was not a news interview in the usual sense, the candidates did respond to questions from a panel of journalists. In the first question to Dan Quayle, a journalist enumerates several prominent Republicans who had been highly critical of Bush's decision to choose Quayle as his running mate (lines 4–17); the journalist then asks Quayle why he hasn't made "a more substantial impression" on his own Republican colleagues (18–20). Quayle begins his response (arrowed) by reformulating the question in terms of his general qualifications for the presidency.

(48)   US Bentsen–Quayle Vice-Presidential Debate: 5 Oct 1988
          IR: Judy Woodruff   IE: Dan Quayle AU: Audience

```
 1   IR:      hhhh Senator you have been criticized as we
 2            all know:: for your decision to stay out of
 3            the Vietnam War::, (0.3) for your poor
 4            academic record, .hhhhhh but mo:re troubling
 5            to so::me are some o'the comments that've
 6            been made by people in your own party. tch
 7            .hhh Just last week former Secretary of
 8            State Hai::g. .hh said that your pi:ck. (0.2)
 9            was the dumbest call George Bush could've
10            ma[:de.
11   AU:         [h-h-hhxhxhx[hxxXXXXXXXXXXXXX= ]
12   IR:                     [Your leader in the Senate]
13   AU:      =XXXXXXXXXXXXXXXXXXXX[XXXXXXXxxxxxxx (5.8) ]
14   IR:                          [Your leader in the Senate]
15            Bob Do:le said that a better qualified person
16            could have been chosen. .hhh Other Republicans
17            have been far more critical in private. .hhhh
18            Why d'you think that you have not made a more
19            substantial impression on some of these people
20            who have been able to observe you up clo:se.
21            (1.5)
22   IE:  →   .hhhhhh The question goe::s (1.0) to whether
23            I'm qualified (1.1) to be vice President, (0.8)
24            .hhh and in the case of a:: (.) tragedy whether
25            I'm qualified to be President. (0.6) .hhhh (0.7)
26            Qualifications for:: (0.2) thee office of vice
27            president 'r president (1.0) are not age alo:ne.
28            (1.5) you must look at accomplishments: (1.0)
29            and you must look at experience . . .
```

This is a substantial transformation. On one level, it moves from subjective impressions of Quayle – which may be difficult to explain or refute – to his qualifications considered as an objective matter. There is also a change in the presuppositional loading of the question. The original question is presuppositionally negative – it presumes that Quayle did not in fact make a good impression, and asked why this was so. That negative presumption is encoded in the preliminary background information (1–17) and in the wording of the question itself ("Why do you think you have not made a more substantial impression ... "). In contrast, the reformulated version is presumptively neutral ("whether I'm qualified"), and is thus conducive to a more upbeat response. Despite the magnitude of this transformation, it is asserted affirmatively and without qualification ("The question goes to ... "). Quayle thus proposes that his reformulation successfully captures what the question comes down to in its essence.

To appreciate the significance of this practice for managing an agenda shift, it might be useful to consider what the preceding exchange would look like without the reformulation:

(49) Invented
1 IR: ... Why do you think that you have not made a
2   more substantial impression on some of these
3   people who have been able to observe you up
4   close?
5 IE: Qualifications for the office of Vice President
6   or President are not age alone. You must look
7   at accomplishments and you must look at
8   experience.

When the "answer" is made to follow the question without any preparatory work, it is manifestly disjunctive. Against this backdrop, the importance of the reformulation is that it affiliates the matter-to-be-pursued with the matter-that-was-inquired-about, thereby minimizing any discrepancy between the two which might otherwise be obvious. In effect, the reformulation provides a version of the question that the subsequent response can be seen as "answering."

In the previous example, the IE operates on the question as a whole object. But interviewees also may operate on a component of the question – a phrase, a prefatory statement, or even an embedded presupposition. In the next example, from a Nixon press conference during the Watergate period, Nixon targets the first part of a two-part question for reformulation. The journalist first asks (beginning at arrow 1) whether Nixon is personally investigating charges that his campaign funds were mishandled, and he then asks (arrow 2) whether the charges will hurt his bid for re-election. After a prefatory remark, Nixon produces a reformulation (arrow 3) that highlights the first part of the question.

(50)   US Nixon Press Conference: 29 Aug 1972
          IR: Unknown   IE: Richard Nixon

```
 1  IR:  1→  Mr. President, are you personally investigating
 2              the mishandling of some of your campaign funds,
 3         2→  and do you agree with Secretary Connolly that
 4              these charges are harmful to your re-election?
 5  IE:       Well, I commented upon this on other occasions,
 6              and I will repeat my position now.
 7         3→  With regard to the matter of the handling of
 8              campaign funds, we have a new law here in which
 9              technical violations have occurred and are
10              occurring, apparently, on both sides. As far as
11              we are concerned, we have in charge, in
12              Secretary Stans, a man who is an honest man and
13              one who is very meticulous – as I have learned
14              from having him as my treasurer and finance
15              chairman in two previous campaigns – in the
16              handling of matters of this sort. Whatever
17              technical violations have occurred, certainly he
18              will correct them and will thoroughly comply
19              with the law. He is conducting any
20              investigation on this matter, and conducting it
21              very, very thoroughly, because he doesn't want
22              any evidence at all to be outstanding,
23              indicating that we have not complied with the
24              law.
```

This reformulation is subversive in two respects. First of all, it replaces a key term from the question that implied wrongdoing ("mishandling") with a more favorable term ("handling"). Furthermore, the ensuing response refers to "technical violations ... on both sides", and deals exclusively with the matter of the investigation – Nixon never gets around to answering the second part of the question regarding the consequences for his re-election campaign. This omission may not have been accidental. Nixon may well prefer to answer the first question because by talking about the investigation he can show himself to be "doing something" about a scandal within his administration, and thus cast himself as independent of the morally tainted forces which brought it about. In contrast, the issue of whether the scandal will hurt his campaign seems, at least from his standpoint, less advantageous.

While this omission is clear in retrospect, it was not evident at the outset that some form of evasion was in progress. Nixon could have gone on to answer the second question. Indeed, it is standard practice for interviewees, when "reaching back" to deal with something other than the last component of the questioning turn, to indicate as much by referring to or reformulating that aspect of the question. This is because interviewees normally address the final component of a question (Sacks, 1987), so they take steps to warn listeners when an atypical response trajectory is in the works. Thus, Nixon's operation was initially accountable as an effort to manage an atypical response trajectory, rather than shift the agenda.

There are still more subtle variations on the practice of operating on the question. In the cases examined thus far, the operation is performed quite openly, but it may also be lodged within some other activity – assertions of agreement or disagreement, for example. In the course of claiming to agree/disagree with some aspect of the question, an interviewee can embeddedly reformulate that question. For instance (arrowed):

(51)   US PBS *Newshour*: 22 July 1985: South Africa
      IR: Judy Woodruff   IE: Frank Wisner

```
 1  IR:     But isn't this (.) d- declaration of the state
 2          of emergency:: (.) an admission that the eh
 3          South African Government's policies have not
 4          worked, an' in fact that the um-United States
 5          (0.2) administration's policy of constructive
 6          engagement (.) has not worked.
 7  IE:  →  I do not agree with you .hhhh that the approach
 8       →  we have taken (.) toward South Africa is- ay-
 9       →  is an incorrect approach. .hhhhh We _want (0.5)
10          to see that s- system change. We want to see
11          South Africa end apartheid. We wanta see basic
12          rights established for all South Africans. .hhhh
13          We wanta see peace and stability in that
14          country. .hhh An' that's a perfectly respectable
15          goal. Second. (.) The way we have pursued _it
```

16   .hhh I <u>a</u>lso believe .hhh is the most <u>sen</u>sible
17   way in dealing with a dangerous situation.
18   .hhh U:Sing our <u>in</u>fluence. .hh to ch<u>ange</u>
19   government's th<u>in</u>king...

Here the IE first asserts disagreement ("I do not agree with you"),
and then characterizes the object of his disagreement ("that the approach we have taken...") in a manner that transforms the terms of
the original question. The transformation is subtle yet advantageous
for the IE, who at the time was the US Ambassador to South Africa
during the Reagan administration and is defending the administration's policy of "constructive engagement." The original question
had asked (after some preliminary talk) whether the US policy of
constructive engagement "has not worked." This is reformulated
in the statement of disagreement as a question about whether US
policy "is an incorrect approach." The latter version is much easier
for the IE to refute. It is difficult to argue with the original assertion that US policy "has not worked," since at the time of the interview apartheid remained intact. But one can assert the essential
"correctness" of US policy even in the face of its manifest failure to
bring about an end to apartheid, and this is precisely what the IE
does in his ensuing response.

Two case studies

We have examined various practices as they are employed across a
wide range of interview circumstances; now it is time to synthesize
and apply what we have learned to some singular noteworthy cases.
One objective of these extended case studies is to illustrate the power
of the analytic framework developed thus far to elucidate just how it
is that particularly slippery interviewees manage to elude the grasp
of an advancing line of questioning. Moreover, while a systematic
analysis of audience reactions is beyond the scope of this book, these
case studies are suggestive of the impact that such practices can have
on subsequent media commentary and on pubic opinion.

Dan Quayle and the succession question

During the 1988 US presidential campaign, the two main
vice-presidential candidates – Senators Lloyd Bentsen and Dan

Quayle – squared off in a nationally televised debate. Although the event was not, strictly speaking, a news interview, the format had the candidates responding to questions from a panel of four journalists, making it not unlike a multi-interviewer interview or small press conference. Opportunities to follow up and pursue evasive answers were more limited than in ordinary news interviews, because here each journalist could ask only one question at a time and the order of questioners was predetermined. Nevertheless, processes of resistance and pursuit were both very much in play.

An extended tug-of-war developed around the issue of presidential succession. It started when Dan Quayle – a youthful senator and George Bush's running mate – was asked what he would do if the President died or became incapacitated for some reason. The purpose of this question was to test Quayle's readiness for assuming the presidency in an emergency – what would be his plan of action? Quayle sidestepped this issue when it was first raised, prompting several follow-up questions and rounds of evasion and pursuit.

The first journalist to raise this question was Brit Hume of ABC News. Noting the apprehensions people may feel about Quayle being "a heartbeat away from the presidency" (lines 1–4), he asks Quayle to describe, in the event of his sudden succession to power, "the first steps that you'd take and why" (lines 5–11).

(52) US Bentsen-Quayle Vice-Presidential Debate: 5 Oct 1988
      IR: Brit Hume   IE: Dan Quayle

```
 1  IR:   Senator I wan- I wanna take you back if I can to
 2         the question Judy as:- asked you about some
 3         o'the apprehensions people may feel about your
 4         being a heartbeat away from the presidency.
 5         .hhhh And let us assume if we can for the sake
 6         of this question that you become Vice President-
 7         an:d the President is incapacitated for one
 8         reason or another and you hafta take the reigns
 9         of power. .hhhh When that moment ca::me, w-
10         what would be the first steps that you'd take
11         (0.2) and why::.
12         (3.2)
13  IE:    .hh First I'd- first I'd say a prayer (1.1) tch
14         for myself (2.3) and for the country I'm about
15         to lead, (2.4) And then I would (1.1) assemble
16         his (1.1) people and talk (0.8) .hhh And
17  →      I think this question keeps going ba:ck to:
```

```
18          (1.0) the qualifications and what kind of (1.1)
19          of vice president 'n (0.7) in this hypothetical
20          situation (1.0) if I had to assume:: (0.8) the
21          responsibilities of: (0.3) President what I
22          would be. (1.0) .hhh And as I have said (1.2)
23          tch age alo:ne. (0.3) .hh although I can tell
24          you h.h after the experience of: these last few
25          weeks 'n the campaign I've added ten years to
26          my a[ge,
27  AU:          [x-x-x-x-x-x[-x (1.7)
28  IE:                      [Age alone. (1.0) is not (0.2)
29          the only (0.5) qualification. .hhhh You've got
30          to look at ex:perience. (.) And you've got to
31          look at accomplishments. And ca:n you make a
32          difference. .hhh Have I made a difference in the
33          United States Senate where I've served fer eight
34          years, (1.2) Yes I have. (0.7) Have I made a
35          difference in the Con:gress that I've served
36          for twelve years, .hh (0.5) Yes I have . . .
```

Quayle makes an initial stab at answering the question (lines 13–
16), but it is rather half-hearted and insubstantial. He says only that
he'd "say a prayer," and would "assemble his people and talk."
He then proceeds to reformulate the question (arrowed, lines 17–
22), veering away from the issue of his plan of action for assuming
the presidency in an emergency, and toward the more general issue
of his overall qualifications for the presidency. He then goes on to
discuss his qualifications at length, ruling out age as a qualification
and focusing on experience and accomplishments (lines 28–36). In
the end, talk about qualifications dominates his response.

Although this shift is managed covertly and is obscured by the use
of a question reformulation, Brit Hume is not oblivious to what has
transpired. After a full round of questioning from the other panelists, Hume regains the floor and pointedly pursues the question
(line 6). Before doing so, however, he carefully justifies this move by
calling attention to the inadequacy of Quayle's previous response,
summarizing it in a way that highlights its feebleness: "You said
you'd say a prayer, and you said something about a meeting" (lines
4–6). He then presses Quayle to elaborate (line 6). Notice that some
audience members in the hall begin to laugh at this point (line 8), displaying appreciation of Hume's rather withering characterization,
and aligning with him in his pursuit of an answer.

(53)   US Bentsen-Quayle Vice-Presidential Debate: 5 Oct 1988
       IR: Brit Hume   IE: Dan Quayle   AU: Audience

```
 1  IR:     Senator I wanna take you back to the question
 2          that I asked you earlier about what would happen
 3          if you were to: take over in an emergency and
 4          what you would do first and why:: .hhhh You said
 5          you'd say a prayer:: and you said something
 6          about a meeting, (.) What would you do next.
 7          (.)
 8  AU:     ((laught[er))
 9  IE:             [I don't believe that it's
10          (0.6) proper for me:: to: .hh get into
11          the specifics: (0.5) of a hypothetical (.)
12          situation like tha:t (1.2)
13    →     The situation is: (0.8) that if (0.8) I was
14          called upon (0.7) to ser:ve (0.7) as the
15          President (0.4) of this country, or the
16          responsibilities of the President of this
17          country, (1.0) would I be capable and qualified
18          (0.2) to do that. (0.5) .hh and I've tried (0.4)
19          to list the qualifications. (1.0) of twel:ve
20          year:s in the United States Congress...
```

But that answer remains elusive – Quayle again sidesteps the question, although his method of doing so here is rather different. Given that his prior covert maneuver has been exposed by Hume's pursuit, Quayle now chooses a more overt means of resistance. He justifies his failure to provide a more substantial answer by characterizing the focus of inquiry as "a hypothetical situation" and suggesting that it would be improper to answer in specifics (lines 9–12). He then proceeds to shift the agenda (lines 13–17) in precisely the same direction as before – away from his plan of action and toward his overall qualifications for the presidency. Thus, while Quayle's resistance is now overt and on record, it is also justified and accounted for.

Unfortunately for Quayle, justificatory accounts do not necessarily bring the line of questioning to a halt; such accounts can be argued with and contested. This is what the very next questioner on the panel – Tom Brokaw of NBC News – does, relinquishing whatever question he had planned to ask in order to pursue the succession question yet again. Brokaw begins with a disclaimer to the effect that he does not mean to "beat this drum until it has no

more sound left in it" (lines 1–2 below). He then takes issue with
Quayle's account for not answering (that it is a hypothetical situation), pointing out that "it is Sir after all the reason that we're here
tonight..." (lines 4–6). He concludes, not with an interrogatively
formatted question, but with a pointed assertion (lines 13–17) that
"surely you must have some plan in mind" for presidential succession, since it has happened to "so many vice presidents" in recent
years. By rejecting Quayle's previous account for not answering, and
by pressing the issue in a more pointed way, Brokaw has upped the
ante for a genuine response.

(54) US Bentsen-Quayle Vice-Presidential Debate: 5 Oct 1988
        IR: Tom Brokaw   IE: Dan Quayle   AU: Audience

```
 1  IR:      Senator Quayle I don't mean to beat this drum
 2            until it has no more sound left in it but to
 3            follow up on Brit Hume's question w:hen you said
 4            that it was a hypothetical situation, .hhhh it
 5            is Sir after: all: the reason that we're here
 6            tonight. .hh[h because you are=
 7  IE:                  [Mhm
 8  IR:      =[running [not just for Vice President,]
 9  AU:       [x x    [x-x-x-xxxxxxxxxxx=        ]
10            =xxxxxxxxxxxxxxxxxxxxxxx[xx-x-x-x-x (4.4)   ]
11  IR:                              [And if you cite the]
12            experience that you had in Congress, (0.2)
13            surely you must have some plan in mind about
14            what you would do: if it fell to you to become
15            >President of the United States< as it ha:s to
16            so many vice presidents .hh just in the last
17            twenty five years er so.
18            (0.3)
19  IE:      tch .hhh Lemme try to answer the question one
20            more ti:me. I think this is the fourth ti:me,
21            (1.0) [that I have had this question, .h=
22  IR:            [(this is-)
23  IE:      =[and I think=
24  IR:       [Third time
25  IE:      =that- .hh three times, (0.8) that I have had
26            this question, and I'll try to answer it again
27            for you. (0.3) as clearly as I can. (0.7) .hh
28       1→  Because the question you're asking. (1.3) is
29            what (.) kind (.) of qualifications .hhhhhh does
30            Dan Quayle have to be President. (1.0) tch
31       2→  What kind of qualifications do I have and
32       3→  what would I do: (1.0) in this kind of a
```

33	situation. (0.4) And <u>wh</u>at would I do in this
34	situation, .hh I would (1.9) make <u>su</u>re. (2.1)
35	that the <u>pe</u>ople in the <u>C</u>abinet, (0.9) 'n the
36	<u>pe</u>ople 'n the ad<u>vi</u>sors to the <u>P</u>resident, (.) are
37	<u>c</u>alled in, (0.2) an I'll <u>ta</u>lk to 'em, (0.5) an
38	I'll <u>work</u> with 'em . . .

After commenting on the number of times he's had this question (at lines 19–21, 25–26), Quayle promises to "try to answer it again for you as clearly as I can" (lines 26–27). Quayle then does something which is very puzzling on its face. He launches into yet another question reformulation (beginning at arrow 1) that begins to reframe the issue once again as a matter of qualifications. However, in the course of this reformulation, he backtracks a bit (arrow 2), and then returns to the original subject of inquiry (arrow 3) – his plan of action for taking charge of the presidency, which he subsequently elaborates (lines 34–38). Why does Quayle start to veer away from the agenda of the question, only to return to it subsequently?

The solution to this puzzle lies at the nonvocal level. After Quayle launches into his reformulation (at line 3 below), and completes the focal word "qualifications" (line 5), Brokaw begins shaking his head (line 6) and he continues to do so until the reformulation reaches a first possible completion point. In this way, Brokaw nonvocally rejects Quayle's bid to shift the agenda.

(55)   US Bentsen-Quayle Vice-Presidential Debate: 5 Oct 1988
          IR: Tom Brokaw   IE: Dan Quayle

1	IE:	. . . and I'll <u>tr</u>y to answer it ag<u>ai</u>n for
2		you. (0.3) as <u>c</u>learly as I <u>c</u>an. (0.7)
3		.hh Because the <u>qu</u>estion you're <u>as</u>king.
4		(1.3) is <u>wh</u>at (.) <u>ki</u>nd (.) of
5		<u>qualifi</u>cations .hh[hhhh does <u>D</u>an Quayle=
6	IR:	[((Headshaking)) =
7	IE:	=<u>ha</u>ve to be <u>P</u>resident. (0.5)] (0.5)
8	IR:	=((Headshaking))]
9	IE:	tch <u>Wh</u>at kind of qualifications do I have and
10		<u>wh</u>at would I <u>do</u>: (1.0) in <u>t</u>his kind of a
11		situat[ion. (0.4)]
12	IR:	[((Nodding))]
13	IE:	And <u>wh</u>at would I do in this situation, .hh I
14		would (1.9) make <u>su</u>re. (2.1) that the <u>pe</u>ople in
15		the <u>C</u>abinet, (0.9) 'n the <u>pe</u>ople 'n the ad<u>vi</u>sors
16		to the <u>P</u>resident, (.) are <u>c</u>alled in, (0.2) an
17		I'll <u>ta</u>lk to 'em . . .

This rejection is consequential, for Quayle subsequently abandons the incipient agenda shift and returns to the original agenda (lines 10–11). Brokaw nods approvingly (line 12), and Quayle proceeds to elaborate on his emergency plan. Thus, while Quayle initially steers the question in a different direction, Brokaw steers him right back.

However, Quayle's return to the original agenda is made to appear as if it is unrelated to what Brokaw has done. Notice that Quayle does not respond immediately to the headshakes – he continues to speak through the headshaking until the reformulation is possibly complete (line 7). He also places some distance between the completion of the headshakes and the start of his continuation, allowing some silence to elapse, and then backtracking a bit when he continues (line 9). Furthermore, when he finally gets to the plan-of-action component of the reformulation, he links it to the previous component with *and* – it is thus introduced as a supplementary rather than a contrastive matter. By these various means, Quayle constructs his reformulation so that it can be seen as a single continuous action rather than an "about face" in response to Brokaw's prompting. In other words, he presents himself as if he were headed in this direction all along.

One implication of this case study has to do with the consequentiality of response behavior. In the aftermath of this debate, most observers declared Lloyd Bentsen the decisive winner, and extensive media commentary focused on Quayle's performance and its shortcomings. A common criticism was that he came across as overly "rehearsed" or "programmed" in his remarks. This widespread impression is undoubtedly rooted in patterns of response such as those analyzed above. He repeatedly returns to the same basic theme – qualifications and experience – as a favored response to various kinds of questions (see also excerpt 48 above). Moreover, he repeatedly uses variations on the same basic practice – which we have termed operating on the question – to "fit" that favored response to whatever question is at hand. This recurrent mode of evasion was first managed covertly, but it was subsequently exposed by persistent follow-up questions from the panel of journalists, at which point it became transparently manipulative. Here, then, patterns of response within the event appear to have been consequential for subsequent media commentary, and perhaps also for public opinion more generally, both of which tended to reinforce

Dan Quayle's emerging reputation as a less than imposing political figure.

The affairs of Bill Clinton

Perhaps more than any other American president, Bill Clinton's conduct in answering questions – not only in news interviews and press conferences, but in courtroom interrogations as well – has had far-reaching ramifications for his political fortunes and public image. He is a notoriously skilled interrogatee, adept at turning questions to his advantage while appearing to be dutifully responsive. This ability has gotten him through some difficult situations, but it has also come back to haunt him. We will focus our analysis on two interviews concerning the delicate subject of extramarital affairs.

Early in the 1992 presidential campaign, allegations surfaced about an extended affair between then-Governor Bill Clinton and Gennifer Flowers. These allegations emerged just as Clinton was breaking from the pack of Democratic candidates to become the frontrunner in the primary campaign, placing his buoyant candidacy in serious jeopardy. In an effort to confront the issue and put it to rest, both Bill and Hillary Clinton appeared on the venerable *60 Minutes* program. That interview has been called one of the great performances in American presidential politics, and it was widely credited with rescuing the Clinton candidacy.

Many factors undoubtedly contributed to this outcome, but at least part of the success can be attributed to the manner in which Governor Clinton dealt with core questions concerning his relationship with Gennifer Flowers. Although he admits in a general way to having had "problems" and "difficulties" in his marriage, specific questions about the alleged affair with Ms. Flowers are met with what seem at first glance to be straightfoward denials. However, upon analysis it becomes apparent each response falls at least a hair's-breadth shy of a full-fledged denial. Within our framework, Clinton's responses are covertly resistant and extremely nuanced in the manner in which they elude the agenda of the question.

Consider the first question of this kind, in which the IR – Steve Kroft – raises Ms. Flowers' allegation of a twelve-year affair with Clinton (lines 1–3).

(56)   US CBS *60 Minutes*: Jan 1992: The Clintons
          IR: Steve Kroft   IE: Bill Clinton

1 IR: She's alleging (0.2) and has described in some
2   detail in the supermarket tabloid .hh what she
3   calls a twelve year affair with you.
4   (1.5)
5 IE: It- That allegation is false.

Clinton responds to this allegation (line 5) with a simple assertion to
the effect that it is false. This assertion is squarely on-topic, but it is
nonetheless only minimally responsive. As we demonstrated earlier,
given that elaborated answers are the norm, minimal responses involving a single word, phrase, or sentence are tacitly resistant to the
agenda of the question. In the present case, Clinton's unelaborated
denial – "That allegation is false" – is not particularly informative
about his relationship with Ms. Flowers. Is he denying any extramarital affair whatsoever? Or is he merely denying an affair that
lasted twelve years? By responding minimally, Clinton is able to issue a denial in a way that avoids specificity regarding what, exactly,
is being denied.

The IR notices the ambiguity in Clinton's denial, and he pursues
the question in a way that seeks to resolve it (lines 1–5 below). He
tries to pin Clinton down to an absolute denial, reformulating the
prior response as "categorically denying that you ever had an affair
with Gennifer Flowers."

(57)   US CBS *60 Minutes*: Jan 1992: The Clintons
          IR: Steve Kroft   IE1/IE2: Bill/Hillary Clinton

1 IR: I'm assuming from your answer (0.4) that you're
2   (.) categorically denying (.) that=you ever had
3   an affair.
4   (1.0)
5 IR: with Gennifer Flowers.
6 IE1:   .hh I said that before. (.) .hh °uh°
7   An' so has she
8 IE2:   (hmh hmh hmh)
9   (.)
10 IE1:   hh=huh Wh(h)en these st(h)ories came out (0.5)
11   she an' thee other people invol:ved, (0.2) uh:
12   denied them, (.) An' denied them (.) repeatedly,
13   (.) An' she changed her story when she was paid.

Once again, Clinton seems at first glance to be cooperating with the agenda of the question by confirming this version of his denial. However, he avoids a straightforward "yes" or "that's right," asserting instead that he had already denied the affair on some prior occasion (line 6), an occasion which remains unspecified in his response. He then proceeds to talk at greater length about Flowers' own previous denials of the affair (lines 7, 10–12) – a lateral move that is *and*-prefaced and thus affiliated with the prior talk as part of a single coherent activity (Heritage and Sorjonen 1994; Jefferson 1986) – and he suggests that the recent change in her story was motivated by the money she received from the tabloid that first published it (line 13). Thus, while he fosters the impression of having categorically denied an affair, on closer analysis it becomes apparent that he never quite does so in the here-and-now, on his own accord. He adopts an interactional footing in which he is merely relaying denials previously expressed by himself and others.

This interview went over well at the time, and Clinton would go on to win both the nomination and the election decisively. But his performance would eventually boomerang. Early in 1998, when Clinton was called to give a deposition in the Paula Jones lawsuit, he admitted under questioning that he did indeed have an affair with Ms. Flowers. Shortly thereafter, the interview was rebroadcast on *60 Minutes*, placing his slipperiness in answering on display for the entire nation.

Around the same time, allegations about another affair surfaced, this time involving a young White House intern named Monica Lewinsky. Shortly thereafter, Clinton was questioned about the affair in an interview on *The NewsHour*. Once again, what initially appear to be forthright denials of the affair are in fact covertly resistant. In this case the specific mode of resistance is a subtle shift in the terms of the question, a shift involving the verbal tense in which it is expressed.

(58)   US PBS *Newshour*: 21 Jan 1998: Monica Lewinsky
       IR: Jim Lehrer   IE: Bill Clinton

```
1  IR:   You had no sexual relationship with this
2        [young wo[man.]
3  IE:   [ml      [Th- ]
4  IE:   There is not a sexual relationship. That
5        is accurate.
```

The IR asks Clinton to confirm that he "had no sexual relationship with this young woman." Clinton eventually issues a confirmation ("That is accurate"), but only after reformulating the issue from past to present tense ("There is not a sexual relationship.") This response does not necessarily rule out an affair that is over and done with, but to the casual listener it might seem that Clinton has denied the affair. This type of tense shift would later become notorious when it was exposed as a strategy employed by Clinton in the Paula Jones deposition.

The Clinton case is a powerful illustration of the unique attractions and dangers associated with a covert mode of resistance. Throughout these examples, Clinton never owns up to the fact that he is not answering the question fully or straightforwardly. To the extent that resistance occurs, it remains unacknowledged and subtle. This approach to answering questions has gotten Clinton past many difficult moments in his original presidential campaign and his tenure in office, enabling him to give socially acceptable responses to questions on a range of unflattering and incriminating topics. But because so many of these responses have been exposed as evasive through subsequent events, he has paid a price over the long term in the form of damage to his personal reputation and his relations with Congress and the American public. The criticism leveled against him by his detractors is not merely that he sidesteps questions – many politicians are guilty of that – but that he is less forthcoming about it. The so-called "slick Willie" factor should stand as a cautionary note to public figures contemplating a covert mode of resistance.

Conclusion

In this age of political cynicism coupled with anxiety about the decline of civility in public life, it is tempting to assume that virtual anomie now characterizes mediated political communication. Politicians, in such a world, would no longer be bound by traditional norms and could ignore with impunity the questions they receive in journalistic interviews and press conferences. This viewpoint was aptly expressed by Pat Robertson's media advisor in an incident recounted at the beginning of this chapter. During a commercial break following a particularly adversarial exchange, Robertson's media advisor gave his client a pep talk of sorts: "*You*'re answering the questions. You can talk about anything you *want* to." Implicit in this remark is the assumption that answering journalists' questions is now wholly optional, that the normal practice in news interviews is for public figures to pursue their own agendas.

But is it? The sheer commonality or frequency of resistance is not necessarily indicative of its normativity. The fact that Robertson's advisor had to give him a pep talk on the acceptability of ignoring questions suggests that the norm of answering has not exactly disappeared. Indeed, the present analysis suggests that, in the contemporary news interview, answering questions remains a formidable social convention imbued with a powerful normative force. Resistant or evasive responses, while frequent, are done cautiously and are managed with an elaborate array of remedial practices that work to ameliorate the breach of conduct. Our analysis of these remedial practices has been far from exhaustive, and yet the practices we have examined are only explicable by reference to a norm of answering that remains very much in force.

On the other hand, this norm can be danced around, tested, and manipulated by interviewees seeking to gain some "wiggle room" within the interview framework. The amount of wiggle room can be increased through the practices we have described. By obscuring the evasion, or by casting it in a favorable light, such practices reduce some of the risks associated with an evasive course of action.

It is possible that such practices have evolved over time in relation to the changing culture of the journalistic profession. As noted in chapter 2, in both England and the USA, journalistic questioning has become less deferential and more adversarial since the 1950s. This could prompt interviewees to become more resistant and/or to develop more sophisticated methods for dealing with difficult questions, just as they have developed other strategies for managing adversarial encounters with journalists (see Jones 1992). Alternatively, increasingly adversarial questioning could have precisely the opposite effect – insofar as adversarialness includes a greater propensity to ask follow-up questions that pursue evasive responses (Clayman and Heritage 2002), it could encourage interviewees to adhere more closely to the question agenda. Whether there actually has

been a systematic change in public figures' responsive conduct –
in either the propensity toward resistance or in the practices for
managing resistance – must await further research.

Whatever the long-term historical trend, it seems clear that the
remedial practices examined in this chapter, while significant, do not
make interviewees immune to probing follow-up questions, negative media commentary, or the vagaries of public opinion. Thus, for
contemporary public figures who find themselves cornered by a particularly pointed question, the decision about whether to answer or
to resist continues to have serious and far-reaching ramifications.

8

The panel interview: discussion and debate among interviewees

Thus far we have concentrated on the dynamics of interplay between interviewers and interviewees, which is the essence of the news interview in its classic form. However, the contemporary form frequently involves a panel of participating interviewees offering a variety of perspectives on some newsworthy topic. Often such panels are comprised of just two ideologically opposed interviewees who informally debate the issue. In the panel interview format, there is interplay not only between interviewers and interviewees, but also – directly or indirectly – between the interviewees themselves.

The typical panel interview attracts a less distinguished cadre of participants. While presidents, prime ministers, and senior cabinet officials are periodically interviewed solo, they rarely participate in panel discussions or debates. This selectivity is not difficult to understand. If one is sufficiently newsworthy to be the exclusive focus of attention in an interview (or better yet in a press conference involving dozens of reporters), then why share the spotlight with – and by implication lower oneself to the level of – one's political opponents? Thus, legislators, certified experts of various stripes, and representatives of advocacy groups are the mainstay of the panel interview. Consequently, rather than featuring the first-hand reflections of prominent movers and shakers, such interviews often consist of expert analysis and commentary on current events.

This variant has grown steadily over the years. Panel interviews were rare in the 1950s and 1960s, occasional through much of the 1970s, and commonplace from the 1980s onward. In the USA, they have been ubiquitous since the advent of Ted Koppel's *Nightline* program, which was initially promoted under the auspices of the slogan, "Bringing people together who are worlds apart."

299

The proliferation of the panel format stems from its utility to broadcast journalists – it helps to solve certain practical problems associated with interviewing as a journalistic activity. Earlier in this book we discussed the twin professional ideals of neutrality and adversarialness, and we also noted how difficult it is for interviewers to reconcile these ideals in practice. When interviewing a single public figure, interviewers are motivated to be suitably adversarial in an effort to hold public figures accountable for their words and deeds and to introduce a fair balance of viewpoints (see chapter 6). However, adversarialness can conflict with the equally venerated ideal of journalistic neutrality (see chapter 5), in that an interviewer who is persistently adversarial can be seen as having a partisan axe to grind. Against this backdrop, the attractions of the panel format should be obvious – it creates a division of labor that reconciles the divergent ideals of neutralism and adversarialness. With partisan interviewees playing the role of adversary vis-à-vis one another, the interviewer is removed from the heat of battle and is free to act as an impartial moderator and catalyst.

In addition to its import for professionalism, the panel format also serves the practical interests of broadcasters in attracting an audience and holding its interest. By "bringing people together who are worlds apart," the panel format provides fertile ground for cultivating lively and dramatic conflict. What might otherwise be a boring succession of "talking heads" – one of whom is professionally constrained to a neutralistic posture – can become a lively sparring match between thoroughly committed adversaries.

Our analysis of the panel interview format is heavily indebted to previous research by Greatbatch (1992) and Olsher (Forthcoming). Drawing on their work, we will show that while panel interviews exhibit considerable variation in terms of the degree to which restrained discussion or acrimonious conflict predominates, the contemporary panel interview tends toward the conflictual. This is so in part because of the manner in which guests are assembled – producers typically select interviewees precisely because they represent divergent interests and ideologies. However, the selection process only partly explains the combative nature of the ensuing interview. Various processes and practices internal to the interview itself have the effect of facilitating and encouraging expressions of disagreement and conflict. We will also consider how the interviewer, while mediating such conflict, can occasionally become embroiled within it.

Setting the scene

Consider, first, the very beginning of the interview – interviewers can create an atmosphere of impending conflict even before the questioning begins via the manner in which the interview is opened. As we saw in chapter 3, interviews typically begin with the interviewer announcing the topic of discussion and introducing the interviewees, thus foreshadowing both the content and form of the discussion to follow. When a panel of interviewees is involved, such openings can portray the ensuing interview in any number of ways, but they often project a polarized debate between partisan advocates on opposing sides of the issue. To illustrate, consider this opening to an interview on legislation aimed at detecting discriminatory housing practices.

(1)   US PBS *NewsHour*: 13 June 1985: Housing Discrimination
       IR: Robert MacNeil   IE: Phyllis Spiro, William North

1	IR:	How do authorities catch landlords or realtors
2		who discriminate against minorities? There's an
3		interesting proposal before Congress and it's
4		what we look at first tonight. The idea is to
5		stage tests by sending people with similar
6		incomes but different racial or ethnic
7		backgrounds to buy or rent housing...
8		The Reagan administration is pushing a new fund
9		of some four million dollars to help community
10		groups set up such tests. But the move is being
11		fought by the National Association of Realtors...
12		We have both sides of the argument now.
13		Phyllis Spiro of the Open Housing Council
14		here in New York City supports federally funded
15		testing. William North, general counsel of the
16		National Association of Realtors, opposes it.

From the outset, this topic is framed as controversial. After the IR initially describes the proposed legislation (lines 2–7), he goes on to outline the clash between political factions that support it and others who oppose it (lines 8–11). Correspondingly, he introduces the IEs (lines 12–16) in such a way as to align them as representatives of these factions and hence as advocates for "both sides of

the argument" (line 12). Although they could in principle be characterized in any number of ways (e.g., real estate attorney, housing
policy expert, etc.), these IEs are characterized in terms of their opposing institutional affiliations (the Open Housing Council versus
the National Association of Realtors), as well as their opposing positions on the issue under discussion (the first IE is said to "support
federally funded testing" while the second is said to "oppose it").[1]

By way of contrast, consider the launching of an interview about
a summit meeting between US and Soviet leaders. Here the opening
projects a harmonious discussion rather than a polarized debate,
but this is by no means determined by the "objective" nature of the
subject matter or the panelists.

(2)   US PBS *NewsHour*: 4 Dec 1989: US–USSR Summit
       IR: Jim Lehrer   IE: Robert McNamara

   1   IR: Now to some analysis of the summit and its
   2   accomplishmen[ts it comes from
   3   ( ):   [mm:.
   4   IR: Kennedy Johnson Defense Secretary Robert
   5   McNamera. .hh Reagan Secretary of Sta:te and
   6   former NATO commander Alexander Hai:g .hhh
   7   senate majority leader George Mitchell of Ma:ine
   8   who joins us from Portland, Maine, .hh Nixon
   9   Ford Secretary of State Henry Kissinger .hh and
  10   Egan Barr a member of the West German
  11   Parliament and the opposition's Social
  12   Democratic Party's leading East West policy ma:n
  13   .hh Mister Barr and Secretary Kissinger are with
  14   us tonight from Bonn. hhh Mister McNamera was
  15   this a successful summit for President Bush?

Although two of the IEs are Democrats (Robert McNamara and
George Mitchell) and two are Republicans (Alexander Haig and
Henry Kissinger), the IR makes no mention of this fact. Nor does
he provide any indication as to the IEs' respective attitudes toward
this particular summit or to summit meetings in general. Moreover,
the entire encounter is characterized as a detached "analysis" of the
summit (line 1).

Both of these openings set up an expectation – for interviewees and for the audience – about the type of interview to follow,

---

[1] For a very similar example, see excerpt (9) in chapter 3.

although the precise nature of that expectation varies dramatically. The second projects a *discussion* between relatively disinterested experts, while the first projects an informal *debate* between committed advocates on opposing sides of the issue. Does this have any bearing on what transpires within the interview itself? It may. As a general principle, ordinary conversational interaction exhibits a systematic bias that favors expressions of agreement over disagreement (Pomerantz 1984), and more generally approving and affiliative actions over hostile and disaffiliative ones (Heritage 1984a: 265–80). Against this backdrop, the significance of the news interview opening stems from the way in which it operates on the default preference for agreement (Greatbatch 1992), informing both the interviewees and the audience that, contrary to what might be expected in ordinary conversation, the panelists are there to disagree. A debate-framed opening thus sets an agenda that licenses and encourages expressions of disagreement for the occasion of the interview.

Inviting disagreement

Disagreement is also fostered within the body of the interview itself via the manner in which the interviewer solicits contributions from interviewees on the panel. As Olsher (Forthcoming) has demonstrated, interviewers can invite interplay in a great many ways, and these vary in the degree to which they promote disagreement and confrontation among the panelists.

One axis of variation has to do with how the interviewer positions the contributions of interviewees vis-à-vis one another. At the non-conflictual end of the spectrum are those interviews wherein each member of the panel is questioned separately, with the interviewer interrogating first one interviewee at length before turning to the next. In this serial interview arrangement, interviewees are in effect kept at arm's length from one another. This plainly minimizes the occurrence of disagreement, and renders what disagreement does occur as distal, indirect, and nonconfrontational. However, even within this framework the interviewer can take steps to heighten the clash between panelists. The primary way of doing this is by paraphrasing remarks expressed previously by one panelist and deploying them to counter the remarks of another. For example, when a critic of nuclear energy offers a gloomy assessment of the waste disposal situation (lines 1–7), the IR invokes contrary views expressed much earlier in the program by a defender of the nuclear industry (lines 8–14).

(3)   US ABC *Nightline*: 6 June 1985: Nuclear Power
      IR: Ted Koppel   IE: James Steel

```
 1  IE:      ...An:d if you look at: simply the record in
 2            the low level waste field. over the last
 3            fifteen to twenty years. 'n low level waste is
 4            admittedly .hh far less hazardous than the
 5            high level waste from power plants. .hh The
 6            record is not very good. (.) an' it doesn't give
 7            one a cause for optimism.=
 8  IR:  →   =You heard what Doctor Yalow said earlier in
 9       →   this broadcast she'll have an opportunity to
10       →   express her own opinions again but she seems to
11            feel thet it is an EMinently soluble problem,
12            an:d that ultimately that radioactive material
13            can be reduced to manageable quantities, 'n put
14            in the bottom of a salt mine.
15  IE:      The p- the point that she was making earlier
16            about: reprocessi:ng of: the fuel rods goes
17            right to the heart (.) of the way a lotta
18            people look't this particular issue...
```

The IR here serves, in effect, as a proxy for the views of a previous IE, thereby manufacturing a disagreement that was not overtly expressed by the panelists themselves. Thus, even within the serial interview arrangement an interviewer can take steps to accentuate the clash between interviewees.

At the other end of the spectrum are those interviews in which each successive question is asked of a different interviewee on the panel, an arrangement with much greater potential for generating disagreement and confrontation. Whether or not this potential will be realized, however, depends heavily on the design of the questions themselves, which differ in what might be thought of as their disagreement-implicativeness. While some questions merely provide interviewees with an *opportunity* to express disagreement with one another, others actively *encourage* it, and in other ways contribute to the antagonistic atmosphere found in many panel interviews (Olsher Forthcoming).

The least antagonistic question forms are those that merely invite successive interviewees to present their views on the same subject matter. To illustrate, consider the round of questioning that begins a panel discussion of a summit meeting between the USA and USSR.

(4) US PBS *NewsHour*: 4 Dec 1989: US–USSR Summit
      IR: Jim Lehrer   IE1: Robert McNamara
      IE2: Alexander Haig   IE3: George Mitchell

```
 1  IR:   → hhh Mister McNamara was this a successful
 2          summit for President Bush?
 3  IE1:   Indeed it was. One of our columnists in the US
 4          today reported it as a miserable performance by
 5          President Bush. As a Democrat I thought it was
 6          a very successful one. .hhh It was a further
 7          step toward ending the cold war. . hhh it didn't
 8          end the cold war, but it was a major step in
 9          that direction.
10  IR:   → Secretary Haig?
11  IE2:   Well I think I said it was a h .hh non-summit
12          doomed to succeed and it di:d except for
13          weather . . . ((16 lines omitted)) . . . an' I think
14          this was a very constructive outcome probably
15          of the consultations in Brussels.
16  IR:   → .hhhh Senator Mitchell, what's your overview of
17          the summit from President Bush's point of view.
18          (.)
19  IE3:   It was positive uh the:: eh significant
20          improvement in the uh economic relationship
21          between the two countries that I think will
22          result . . .
```

Although the IR's questions (arrowed) differ in specifics, each invites a particular IE to perform the same basic speech act (give an evaluation) about the same subject matter (the summit meeting). The resulting evaluations may stand in a relationship of agreement or disagreement with one another, but the crucial point is that such a relationship is not the primary focus of any of these questions. In essence, the IR asks each IE to produce an independent assessment of the summit meeting, and this is indeed the spirit in which the IEs build their subsequent remarks, which make no reference to prior IEs.

At the next level are questions that directly solicit expressions of agreement or disagreement with a prior interviewee. Questions such as "How do you respond to Senator X" or "Do you agree with Congressman Y" or "Is he right about that" have this character. In the next example (examined in chapter 5), when a nuclear expert (IE1) offers a particularly optimistic assessment of the nuclear waste problem, the IR (arrowed) asks a second expert (IE2) whether he "accepts" that assessment.

(5)   US ABC *Nightline*: 6 June 1985: Nuclear Power
      IR: Ted Koppel   IE1: Dr. Rosalyn Yalow   IE2: James Steel

```
 1  IE1:      ... As a result of this type of testimony from me
 2             an the input from the scientific community .hh
 3             in fac the Nuclear Regulatory Commission .hh now
 4             permits disposal of- radioactive carbon (an
 5             tritium) [.hh a t      [   cer]tain=
 6  ( ):              [#hmh        [hmh#]
 7  IE1:       =very low levels as if they were not
 8             radioactive. .h so that in fact there's no
 9             longer uh nee:d to- ship across (.) to Hanford
10             .hh this .h organic fluids .h containing very
11             low amounts of (.) radioacti[vity.   ]
12  IR:   →                                [Mister] Steel,
13        → d'you accept that?
14             (.)
15  IE2:       Ted could I interject one point on that 'ticular
16             point .hh uh: the question on low level waste.
17             uh (0.2) the problem with low level waste is
18             the way it's defined. As Doctor Yalow is
19             saying (.) much low level waste which is medical
20             waste_ .hh hospital waste_ .h genuinely doesn't
21             pose .h that much of uh problem to the society.
22             The problem with low level waste is .h is that
23             there's a lotta material lumped into that
24             general category. .h that is hazardous. The
25             [low level wa]ste from power plants. .hh does=
26  ( ):       [(            )]
27  IE2:       =pose .hh uh- a serious long term problem...
```

Rather than being asked to speak to the same issue, here IE2 is asked to respond to IE1's viewpoint, and specifically to indicate whether or not he concurs with that viewpoint. Correspondingly, Steel builds his subsequent remarks explicitly as a counter to hers, referring to her in the process (see line 18).

   Taking this one step further, an interviewer can go beyond merely inviting a *response* to the prior interviewee – which could in principle be either agreement or disagreement – to inviting *disagreement per se*. Using the terminology introduced in chapter 6, such turns are tilted in favor of disagreement as the preferred type of response. For example, notice how this IR invites a response (arrowed) to IE1's argument in support of economic sanctions against the apartheid regime of South Africa:

(6) US PBS *NewsHour*: 25 July 1985: South Africa Sanctions
    IR: Jim Lehrer   IE1: Sheena Duncan   IE2: John Chettle

```
 1  IE1:    ... and if: one can: .hh put sufficient pressure.
 2           .hhh on them to re:ally in- int=hh=end. (.) .h
 3           uh: to::: pursua:de the Government to change,
 4           .h and if that pressure is also coming from
 5           the West at the same time .hh then:
 6           <our: Government is faced with: very real::
 7           .h real pursuasive forces.>
 8           (0.4)
 9  IR:   →  You don't think the Government would react
10        →  that [way,] [(Mister Chettle,)]
11  IE2:        [tch ] [ N o :. ] every time the:
12           Government has been pressured in a crass way.=
13           =For example in the arms embargo. .h They
14           promptly set about, (e)=stablishing: a major
15           arms industry, and in fact it's the tenth
16           largest ar:ms industry in the world today:.
17           .hh An' the same has been true of a whole
18           number of issue:s. If anybody thought th't
19           they were going to lie down an' play dead, .h I
20           think it's unlikely that that will happen...
```

This is not a neutral solicitation – it strongly anticipates that a disagreement will be forthcoming. That expectation is manifest in the design of the solicitation, which takes the form of a statement outlining IE2's probable disagreement and offering it up for confirmation.[2] As it turns out, the practice of paraphrasing or formulating an IE's as-yet-unexpressed objection is a rather standard method for inviting that IE to disagree with a predecessor. Indeed, by anticipatorily formulating the crux of the IE's objection, the IR even assists in launching the IE down the path of disagreement.

---

[2] This is what is known as a B-event statement, which functions as a question. See chapter 4.

A somewhat more subtle method of inviting disagreement involves a different kind of paraphrase or formulation of interviewee talk. Instead of *prospectively* formulating the next interviewee's reaction, the interviewer can *retrospectively* reformulate the prior interviewee's remarks. Such reformulations are never purely neutral summaries of what has been said; they are usually designed in such a way as to sharpen the interviewee's point (Heritage 1985; Olsher Forthcoming). That is, they omit hedges and qualifying remarks, as well as other extraneous details, thus boiling down the argument to a more compact and boldly stated point. For a striking example of this practice, consider this excerpt from the discussion of nuclear power.

(7)   US ABC *Nightline*: 6 June 1985: Nuclear Power
      IR: Ted Koppel   IE1: Sen Jim McClure   IE2: James Steel

```
 1  IE1:      . . . But remember that the p- uh- that these
 2             plants that were designed by what we would say
 3             now are <inadequate safety standards.> .hh
 4             nevertheless have operated without incident.
 5             .hh Uh=nobody:=has yet been injured or: killed
 6             b- as uh result of ay .h the operation of ay-
 7             (.) nuclear k- k-uh power plant, .hh in spite
 8             of the fact that we do: now do better than we
 9             did be [fore we do] (it) in many instances.=
10  IR:               [ .m l h h  ]
11  IE1:      =[I   ] think the same thing's true of (.) .hh=
12  IR:       [We-]
13  IE1:      =uh:=m:edical techniques?, uh: in: terms of many
14             things we do in life. We do uh better, safer,
15             .hh more thorough job today than we did=uh (.)
16             two er three decades [ago.    ]
17  IR:                            [Alright.]
18        →   (.) Mister Steel:, there's the classic li:ne.
19        →   Uh: what's all the fuss about, no one's been
20        →   killed.
21  IE2:      .hhh Well I think one of the problems with:
22             the whole notion of- that no one 'as been
23             killed is that while people will say that: on
24             that particular .hh uh- side of the issue the
25             fact of the matter is=uh: we don't often: (.)
26             know the answer to that . . .
```

At the beginning of the excerpt, Idaho Senator Jim McClure is defending the safety of nuclear power plants. His argument is rather nuanced – although he points out that they have operated "without incident" and without deaths or injuries (lines 4–5), he also admits at the outset that older plants were designed with inferior safety standards (lines 1–3), and he ends by noting the superiority of more recent power plants over their admittedly inferior predecessors (lines 8–16). At this point the IR turns to a noted critic of nuclear power, James Steele, to solicit his reaction (arrowed, lines 18–20). He does so by characterizing the previous pro-nuclear argument as "the classic line," and then reducing it to a flat assertion: "What's all the fuss about, no one's been killed."

This type of turn invites the interviewee not just to *respond* to what has been said, but to *dispute* it. The preference for disagreement here is encoded in the design of the reformulation, which recasts the prior argument in more extreme, provocative, and hence disagreeable terms. Beyond encouraging the expression of disagreement, this type of turn also contributes more generally to the polarization of the ensuing discussion, casting the participants into positions of diametric opposition.

In summary, interviewers have various resources for generating disagreement and conflict in panel interviews. Although there are also ways of inviting interplay without conflict, the tendency to push for and to anticipate conflict is quite strong. Indeed, it is so strong that when the panelists unexpectedly express agreement rather than disagreement, interviewers can be quite taken aback!

Expressing disagreement

The distinctiveness of interviewee disagreements

How, then, do interviewees actually articulate their disagreements? To gain some perspective on this, it is useful to consider how disagreements here differ from parallel actions that occur in ordinary conversation. As Greatbatch (1992) has demonstrated, disagreements between interviewees are, in a variety of ways, highly distinctive. Perhaps the most obvious difference stems from the specialized turn-taking system that organizes news interview talk. Within this framework, interviewees normally refrain from expressing disagreement on their own initiative, waiting instead to be asked to do so by the interviewer. Correspondingly, such disagreements are packaged

as answers-to-questions and are thus addressed to the interviewer
rather than the person whose views are being disputed.

Disagreeing in this manner requires a substantial amount of self-
restraint, and this is powerfully illustrated in the following excerpt from a discussion of South Africa under apartheid. Herbert
Beukes, the South African Ambassador to the USA, is defending his
Government's suspension of civil liberties on the grounds that it is
necessary to quell violent unrest in the country. Winding down his
argument, he asserts that "people are using forms of democracy or
freedom to destroy democracy" (lines 6–8).

(8)   US PBS *NewsHour*: 22 July 1985: South Africa
      IR: Charles Gibson   IE1: Herbert Beukes
      IE2: Ntatho Motlana

```
 1   IE1:    .hhhhh Well it's clear when we look at the:
 2            pictures: obviously hh uh something is wrong
 3            there.    It's violence. occurring. .hh Now how
 4            d'you DEal: (0.2) in uh v- in a democratic form
 5            (.) with the: situation of that kind of (.)
 6            violence. .hh Uh when people are using: (.)
 7            forms of democracy. or freedom (.) in order to
 8            destroy democracy.
 9      →    (0.3)
10      →    That is not the way to go about it.
11      →    (0.7)
12   IR:     tch .hhh Doctor?
13            (1.1)
14   IE2:    It is interesting to hear Mister Ambassador
15            say:: that people are using democracy to destroy
16            democracy. .hhhh The protests tha:t (.) are
17            seen all over South Africa today (.) arise
18            mainly from the fact that blacks .hhh have (.)
19            no representation at any level at all:...
```

This particular assertion will eventually be disputed by the other
IE – Ntatho Motlana, a black South African civil rights leader –
but the crucial point is that his counterargument is not articulated
when the objectionable assertion is first completed at line 8. Indeed,
he passes over a series of opportunities to respond (arrowed) – he
allows a silence to elapse (line 9), and then a recompletion by Beukes
(line 10), and yet another silence (line 11). Only when the IR invites
him to respond (line 12) does he come forth with his disagreement,
and at that point it is so delayed that he must first indicate what in the

previous turn he finds objectionable (lines 14–16) before proceeding
to refute it (lines 16–19). Correspondingly, although Beukes is the
object of his disagreement, he addresses his remarks to the IR and
refers to Beukes in the third person ("It is interesting to hear Mister
Ambassador say . . . ").

Plainly a considerable amount of self-restraint is required to allow contentious assertions by other panelists to stand unchallenged.
On the other hand, interviewees are undoubtedly aware of the fact
that they need not restrain themselves for very long – they can be
reasonably confident that the interviewer will provide them with
opportunities to articulate their disagreements in due course.

Beyond their character as answers-to-questions, such disagreements are distinctive in yet another way. In ordinary conversation,
interactants normally strive to minimize the occurrence of disagreement, and when disagreement does arise it tends to be softened in
a variety of ways (Pomerantz 1984). Thus, following a contentious
assertion by a first speaker, the onset of disagreement by a second
speaker tends to be delayed either by silence or by some preliminary
talk or both. The systematic occurrence of pre-disagreement delay
has a dual significance. On the one hand, it portrays the second
speaker as "hesitant" or "reluctant" to disagree, and hence reduces
the force of the disagreement. Correspondingly, when disagreement
is delayed by talk, such talk very often consists of a brief token
of agreement (e.g., "That's true, but . . .") that counterbalances the
disagreement and further reduces its force. On the other hand, the
delayed onset of disagreement foreshadows what is to come and provides the first speaker with an opportunity to step in and back away
from the objectionable assertion, thereby forestalling the incipient
disagreement before it can be fully realized. Finally, on those occasions when disagreement is eventually expressed, it rarely leads to
a full-fledged argument. Conversationalists generally strive to limit
the intensity and duration of argument by subsequently moderat-
ing their positions or by deploying other de-escalatory techniques
(Greatbatch and Dingwall 1997). Taken together, these practices
treat conversational disagreement as a dispreferred activity.

Turning now to the news interview environment, disagreement
here is prosecuted rather differently. Interviewee disagreements are,
for the most part, offered straightforwardly and vigorously. That
is, they tend to begin as soon as the interviewer solicits them, and

they almost never contain mitigating agreement prefaces that are
so characteristic of conversational disagreements. This pattern is
most apparent in excerpts (5), (6), and (7) above. Excerpt (8) is
slightly more complicated – although the disagreement is delayed
by a substantial silence and by an item of talk that indicates what
is being disagreed with, it is not softened by any form of agreement
and is otherwise boldly stated.

Several factors converge to explain this pattern of straightforward
disagreement. First, in the news interview context, expressions of
disagreement are "automatically" mitigated by the routine operation of the question–answer turn-taking system (Greatbatch 1992).
Within that system, interviewee disagreements are delayed by the
intervention of the interviewers' questions, and panelists address
their disagreements to the interviewer rather than to one another.
In effect, the interviewer functions as a mediating third party who
intervenes between each successive expression of disagreement and
ensures that it will be expressed indirectly in relation to its target.
Given this, the mitigating features associated with conversational
disagreements become redundant and are dispensed with.

Secondly, as we argued earlier, the preference for agreement can
be weakened in a situation that has been constructed from the outset as an informal debate between ideologically opposed panelists.
Where disagreement rather than agreement is projected as the expected course of action, this naturally reduces the impetus to "pull
punches" and encourages more vigorously stated disagreements.

A third factor has to do with the design of the questions that actually elicit disagreement. Earlier we demonstrated that some of these
questions are built in such a way as to favor disagreement as the
preferred response. This amounts to a preference for disagreement
encoded in the design of the question itself. This type of question
should encourage prompt unmitigated disagreement, and indeed responses following such questions are strikingly blunt. To illustrate,
we will take a second look at the exchange in (6):

(6)   US PBS *NewsHour*: 25 July 1985: South Africa Sanctions
      IR: Jim Lehrer   IE1: Sheena Duncan   IE2: John Chettle

1   IE1:   ... and i<u>f:</u> one can: .hh put suff<u>i</u>cient
2   pr<u>e</u>ssure. .hhh on them to <u>re</u>:ally in-
3   int=<u>hh</u>=<u>e</u>nd. (.) .h uh: to::: pursu<u>a</u>:de the
4   Government to change, .h and <u>if</u> that pressure

```
 5              is also coming from the West at the same time
 6              .hh then: <our: Government is faced with: very
 7              real:: .h real pursuasive forces.>
 8              (0.4)
 9   IR:   1→  You don't think the Government would react
10              that [way, ]  [(Mister Chettle,)]
11   IE2:  2→       [tch  ] [ N o : .          ] every time the:
12              Government has been pressured in a crass way.=
13              =For example in the arms embargo. .h They
14              promptly set about, (e)=stablishing: ay major
15              arms industry, and in fact it's the tenth
16              largest ar:ms industry in the world today:.
17              .hh An' the same has been true of a whole
18              number of issue:s. If anybody thought th't
19              they were going to lie down an' play dead,
20              .h I think it's unlikely that that will happen.
```

The IR's question (beginning at arrow 1) anticipates IE2's disagreement and thus plainly prefers a "no" answer. Correspondingly, IE2 provides that answer promptly and straightforwardly (arrow 2), overlapping the end of the question and avoiding any mitigating preface. Thus, interviewees can be moved to vigorous disagreement not only because of compensatory mitigation built into the turn-taking system, and because of generalized expectations created at the outset, but also because the prior question has specifically invited just that course of action.

Escalation: from disagreement to confrontation

Just as disagreements between panelists are organized differently than are disagreements in ordinary conversation, they are also escalated in distinctive ways (Greatbatch 1992). In conversation, disagreements become intensified when the standard forms of mitigation (such as preliminary silences and token agreement prefaces) are withheld, resulting in more vigorous and boldly stated expressions of conflict. It is at such points that one can say that what began as a "polite disagreement" has escalated into a "hostile argument" (Kotthoff 1993). Obviously this method of escalation is not available in the news interview context, where disagreements normally lack such mitigating features. Instead, panelists escalate their disagreements by departing from the question–answer turn-taking system, with its mediated pattern of interaction, so as to deliver their objections with greater immediacy and directness. As panelists move from addressing the interviewer to addressing one another, disagreement is plainly intensified and becomes more confrontational.

Varying degrees of escalation may be distinguished (Greatbatch 1992).[3] At the mild end of the continuum, an interviewee may choose to launch a disagreement without waiting for a question to intervene, but still address that disagreement to the interviewer rather than to the co-interviewee who is being disagreed with. An example of such an escalated disagreement begins at the arrowed point below.

(9) US PBS *NewsHour*: 19 July 1993: Gays in the Military
     IR: Jim Lehrer   IE1: Duncan Hunter   IE2: Barney Frank

```
 1  IE1:   ... So I think that we're .hh embarking on (u)
 2          something to accommodate President Clinton
 3          political promise that is going to damage the
 4          military.
 5  IR:     How do you respond to tha::t uh Congressman
 6          Frank that even with your reservations about it
 7          if it goes forwar:d in the form the President
 8          .hhh has proposed at least according to
 9          Congressman Hunter it's going to hurt the
10          military.
11  IE2:    tch Oh I think (.) people like Congressman
12          Hunter: rah (.) greatly exaggerate the amount of
13          prejudices out there.>At the same time they-
14          they try- it's a self fulfilling prophecy for
15          them. They whip up the prejudice at the same
16          time as they: uh as they decry it...
17          ((16 lines omitted))
18          ... And what we're told is is:: (.) the very
19          knowledge: that someone else is gay (0.3) not
20          having s:een::: or hear:::d or been the victim
21          of any kind of advance .hh but the simple
22          knowledge that there is a gay person .hh in the
23          room with you .h will somehow ah: drive people
24          to distraction. Fortunately I think that is a
25          gross exa[ggera]tion of the amount of=
```

---

[3] The following represents only a partial sketch of the various levels of intensity that characterize IE/IE disagreements. For a more thorough discussion, see Greatbatch (1992).

```
26  ():                [(      )]
27  IE2:        =prejudice that exists in this so[ciety.  ]
28  IE1: →                                    [Well J]im I
29           think the one- I think the one I think the
30           one th'group that the President should've
31           listened to are the young men and women who
32           ser:ve in unifor:m. And most of them have
33           responded .hhh that they don't want to have to
34           serve in close quarters with homosexuals for
35           long periods of time. .hh That's the one group
36           the President (.) didn't listen.=
```

This is from a discussion of President Clinton's "don't ask don't tell" policy for dealing with homosexuals in the military. At the beginning of the excerpt, Congressman Duncan Hunter – an opponent of allowing gays in the military – asserts that tolerance of gays and lesbians will "damage the military" (lines 1–4). Congressman Barney Frank – an outspoken supporter of gay rights – eventually disagrees (beginning at line 11), but only after waiting for the IR to invite him to do so (lines 5–10). Hunter will in turn disagree with Frank (beginning at line 28), but he launches his disagreement much earlier, before the IR can intervene, and in overlap with the end of Frank's turn. Thus, in contrast to the self-restraint manifest in Frank's mode of disagreement, Hunter presents himself as comparatively "eager" to begin his rebuttal. In this respect, the intensity of the disagreement has indeed increased.

But in other ways it remains remarkably restrained. Notice that Hunter still allows Frank to talk for an extended period before coming in with his disagreement. So while he pre-empts the IR's question, he does not interfere with Frank's capacity to take the type of extended turn that is so characteristic of news interview talk (see chapter 4). Moreover, he delivers his remarks to the IR Jim Lehrer, addressing him by name (at line 28) as he begins to disagree. He thus comports himself as if he were answering the IR's questions, and he thereby avoids confronting his co-IE directly. When the interviewees are co-present in the television studio, this indirect mode of disagreement can extend to the nonvocal level as well. That is, through body posture and gaze direction, interviewees may continue to orient themselves toward the interviewer and studiously avoid gazing at one another, even though from a substantive point of view they are locked in disagreement. In short, while disagreements of this sort are discernibly stronger than those delayed by the interviewer's question, they remain markedly nonconfrontational.

A further increment of escalation occurs when disagreement is offered with greater immediacy and directness. The discussion of gays in the military soon escalates in just this fashion. This extract begins where the previous one left off.

(10)   US PBS *NewsHour*: 19 July 1993: Gays in the Military
       IR: Jim Lehrer   IE1: Duncan Hunter   IE2: Barney Frank

```
 1   IE1:      ... And most of them have responded .hhh that
 2              they don't want to have to serve in close
 3              quarters with homosexuals for long periods of
 4              time. .hh That's the one group the President
 5              (.) didn't listen.=
 6   IE2:      =Well h:ere:[::. N]o we have not ha:d the=
 7   ():                   [ (eh)]
 8   IE2:      =military run:: by: uh >and I'm not sure exactly
 9              what the overall: numbers were: rah:: but uh a
10              majority would probably come out that way. But
11              uh: not ah:: everybody .hhh But that criterion
12              (.) would have kept the military from being
13              racially integrated. .hhh If you had as::ked (.)
14              and the policies are different in some ways.
15              But if you had asked the:: existing:: white
16              soldiery: and the sailors in 1948 what do you
17              want, they would have said don't integrate. .h
18              If you had asked the: all male military (.)
19              years ago you want women involved .h they would
20              have said no. No we haven't decided that we will
21              r:un American military policy .hhh by polling
22              the enlisted people. And I hope we don't. I
23              don't think that['s   a   g]ood way >to run=
24   (IE1):                      [ °yeh ]
25   IE2:      =mil[itary po[licy-
26   (IE1):          [. h h h [But a- but a majority of young
27              black people who are enlisted have said that
28              they don't want to be [ forced ] to=
29   IE2:                             [ Oh-kay ]
30   IE1:      =ser[ve   w   i ] [th homosexuals.]
31   IE2:          [>I know<] [but'chur already] have white
32              people in nineteenf[orty    eight]=
33   IE1:                          [And     that']s
34   IE2:      =would have said that they wouldn't of
35              i[nte]grated at al[ l :  (       )]
36   IE1:      [ih- ]             [I don't th]ink that you
```

```
37            can call those young black people ah bigoted
38            Ba[rney.=And] I don't=
39    IE2:       [Who   did?]
40    IE1:    =think yo[u        [ (ca:n)  ]
41    IE2:                [No, I [      call]ed you bigoted Duncan
42            H[u nter.]
43    IE1:       [Well   I-] I: don't think you can say that.
```

In this extended clash between Frank and Hunter, the first exchange (lines 1–25) is unmediated by a question, but the turns at talk remain extended and nonconfrontational. In contrast, from line 26 on the participants begin to respond to one another on a sentence-by-sentence basis, often overlapping the end of one another's talk. Moreover, the talk becomes increasingly confrontational as they address one another directly and eventually progress from impersonal disagreement to personal attack. Hunter (at lines 36–38) is the first to refer to his co-participant in the second person in the course of disagreeing ("I don't think you can call those young black people bigoted Barney"), and Frank retaliates (lines 41–42) with a direct and sharply personal assault on Hunter's character ("No, I called you bigoted Duncan Hunter"), which is itself responded to directly (line 43). Thus, what began as a restrained disagreement expressed to the IR has become, by this point, an unmediated and highly confrontational argument between the IEs themselves.

When interviewees are co-present, escalation from indirect disagreement to direct confrontation can be dramatically embodied in the participants' nonvocal conduct. It was noted earlier that interviewees normally orient to the interviewer through body posture and gaze direction, not only when responding to questions but also when no actual question has intervened. Given this regularity, disagreement is visibly intensified when an interviewee turns away from the interviewer to express objections directly to the co-interviewee's face. This trajectory of escalation occurs in the discussion of economic sanctions against South Africa. Here the IEs (John Chettle who opposes sanctions, and Sheena Duncan who favors them) are seated with the IR around a table. When either IE has the floor, they systematically restrict themselves to gazing at the IR rather than at each other. This pattern is most striking when it is maintained even in the absence of an intervening question from the IR. For example, in the following extract, Chettle's argument against sanctions (lines 4–12) is promptly countered by Duncan (beginning at line 14), but she continues to gaze unflinchingly toward the IR throughout her rebuttal. When she refers to him in the third person ("I don't agree with John" in line 18), she does lean slightly in his direction, posturally acknowledging him as the relevant target of her remarks, but her gaze remains squarely focused on the IR.

(11)   US PBS *NewsHour*: 25 July 1985: South Africa Sanctions
       IR: Jim Lehrer   IE1: Sheena Duncan   IE2: John Chettle

```
 1  IR:                [You mean apart]heid would get worse:?
 2                 The Goverment would (ge:-)
 3                 be e[ven more] repressive [against blacks?]
 4  IE2:            [I- I-   ]              [I think that   ] in
 5                 fact it could we:ll: ↑ lead in that direction.
 6                 Because eh if they feel themselves
 7                 increasingly beleaguered, .h if they feel
 8                 themselves increasingly under attack, .hh if
 9                 they feel that- .h uh there is absolutely no
10                 comprehension that they are tryin to reform, (.)
11                 then what:=uh: (.) advantage is it: for them to
12                 continue to reform.
13                 (0.2)
14  IE1:           Well:: nuh- uh:: the: arms embargo is uh very
15                 good example of uh sanction that has actually
16                 created thousands of jobs inside South Africa.
17                 .hhh A:nd uh=that's the first thing. .hhh
18       →         Uh:::: I: don't agree with John: that=that:=uh:m
19       →         our Government it's not any longer: .hh >eh<the:
20                 nationalist Afrikaner nationalism that would
21                 rahther die with its back to the wall: an' shed
22                 the last drop of blood . . .
```

In marked contrast, when Duncan again counters Chettle somewhat later in the interview (beginnning at line 19 below), she turns away from the IR to present her rebuttal directly to Chettle's face.

(12)   US PBS *NewsHour*: 25 July 1985: South Africa
       IR: Jim Lehrer   IE1: Sheena Duncan   IE2: John Chettle

```
 1  IR:     =D'you think that people like=uh Sheena Duncan
 2          are doing more harm than good=uh: to
 3          [t=resolve the pro- this=
 4  IE2:    [.tlkh
 5  IR:     =[problem]
```

```
 6  IE2:    [I- I'm ] afraid that they are::. that they've
 7           done great things inside South Africa but I
 8           think she's doing something that is deeply
 9           deeply damaging to the very people that she
10           wants to help, .hh and- .h if the seht- action
11           is ineffective. an' I believe that it will be
12           ineffective.
13  IR:     The san[ction ac[tion,
14  IE2:            [(thi-)  [The sanction action. .h It is
15           going deeply to hurt (.) thousands of- of black
16           people. An' I'm afraid Sheena's gonna hafta take
17           the respon[sibility for ur:ging that.=
18  IE1:              [.hhh
19  IE1:  →  =Well:: I: will take that responsibility if YOU
20           will take responsibility for the fact that all
21           the money that has been invested in South
22           Africa .h since diamonds were discovered in
23           eighteen fifty two::, .hhhhas not- .h has
24           br:ought the black people into uh state .h of
25           total dispossess:ion?, .hh from their la:nd, .h
26           their citizenship, and everything that
27       →  matters.=an' if YOU will take responsibility for
28           that_ .h I am prepar:ed .hh if::: the::
29       →  sanctions don't wor:k, .hh and go the way YOU
30           think, I'm prepared to take my share of the
31           responsibility.
32  IR:     .nlhh Miz Duncan_ Mister Chettle, thank you
33           both.
```

Here, then, the escalation of the dispute is quite literally embodied
in the visible postural orientations of the IEs.

The trajectory of escalation in the preceding examples is in fact a
recurrent pattern in panel interviews. Although this is only a rough
generalization, it is accurate to say that disputes between interviewees often start out as restrained, mediated, and indirect, but as the
interview progresses they tend to become increasingly intense, unmediated, and direct. This pattern of escalation can be explained in
part by the same factors that encourage the expression of disagreement in the first place. Of particular importance are the interviewer's
questions – as we have seen, such questions can invite the panelists
to respond to one another rather than to the issue at hand, can invite
expressions of disagreement in particular, and can thus nudge the
panelists toward an argumentative confrontation.

The IR's role in instigating confrontation is stikingly apparent in the preceding example. As the interview is winding down, the IR asks Chettle if in calling for sanctions "people like Sheena Duncan are doing more harm than good" (lines 1–5). This question not only invites commentary on another IE's conduct, and anticipates an argumentative response, but it invites more specifically a criticism of her conduct. That is, it personalizes the dispute by making Duncan's role in supporting economic sanctions, rather than the sactions themselves, the primary target of evaluation. Chettle responds accordingly (lines 6–17), asserting that sanctions will hurt thousands of people and that Duncan will be partly to blame. It is that accusatory prediction, invited and encouraged by the IR's original question, that prompts Duncan to retaliate with an unmediated and in-your-face rebuttal. Clearly, then, interviewees do not necessarily become confrontational of their own accord; they may be, and often are, encouraged in that direction by the interviewer.

One additional factor that facilitates escalation has to do with how such disputes are brought to a close (Greatbatch 1992). Here again the news interview environment is highly distinctive. In informal contexts, conversationalists must extricate themselves from the disputes in which they are involved (cf. Greatbatch and Dingwall 1997). Recognition of this eventuality may lead conversationalists to be rather cautious about launching into highly argumentative confrontations and to avoid such confrontations when possible. In the news interview, however, responsibility for de-escalating and ending disputes does not lie solely with the interviewees. Interviewers normally manage this process, typically by interjecting to ask a question, thereby restoring the mediated turn-taking system and de-escalating the conflict. Consider this debate interview concerning proposed abortion legislation.

(13)   UK ATV *Afternoon Plus*: 22 Jan 1980: Abortion Limits
       IR: Unknown   IE1: Jill Knight   IE2: Oonagh Macdonald

1 IE1:   . . . They must have <u>no</u> interest at a:ll in the woman
2   .hhh auto<u>ma</u>tically going ahead and having an
3   a[bo:rtion.
4 IE2:   [.hh But Jill I mean how do you explain the fact that
5   women approaching the NHS:: .hhh in:: a senior
6   gynecologist's experience=we don't have complete

```
 7              figures on this except that if it says that ninety
 8              five percent of the women: in his experience who
 9              approach their doctors for an abortion go ahead and
10              have one? .hhh The point is: that by and la:rge when
11              when people seek out an agency like that they have
12              made up their mi:nds[:,
13   IE1:                       [Not necessarily because .hh
14   IE2:       [Unless they come under heavy p[ressure from the [kind=
15   IE1:       [Certainly the ones-          [ye-             [no-
16   IE2:       =of  counseling  organization that  you:
17              [have in mind such as=
18   IE1:       [No I- I have- I'm not-
19   IE2:       =Life, which tries to make a woman feel guilty
20              and takes
21   IE1:       this is no- there's no pressure::. at all= ↑ no .hhh uh-
22   IE2:       no respon[sibility for the ( )    ( )- (        )   (really).
23   IE1:                [no::, (.)   (        [                      )
24   IR:    →                            [Now can I put one point
25          →  to you ( ) ( ) that I- I- as I hear
26          →  you arguing yet ag[ain
27   ?:                           [Yes.
28   IR:        hhh Wouldn't the ide:al situation Jill be: that we
29              ha:ve more national he[alth ser:vice clinics an-
30   IE1:                             [Oh cer::tainly.
31   IR:        [an- (then we) uh A:re there an[y plans to o::pe[n=
32   IE1:       [Certainly.                    [°Mm mm°       [Yes.
33   IR:        =more hh to perhaps take o:ver for the private sector.
```

After the debate has become directly confrontational, the IR intervenes (at line 24). The IR first sanctions the participants for being argumentative (lines 24–26, arrowed), and he then proceeds to ask a question that eventually restores the turn-taking system and the mediated pattern of IE/IE disagreement that it entails.

Interviewees thus need not be quite so concerned about the consequences of dispute escalation, because they can be reasonably confident that, eventually, the interiewer will step in and restore a semblance of harmony. The presence of a third party who is both formally impartial and formally "in charge" makes the news interview a comparatively safe environment for the expression of disagreement. Ironically, then, the very arrangements and practices that are deployed to dampen disputes can, at least indirectly, encourage them to flower.

Neutralism redux: the problem of balanced treatment

Earlier we pointed out that, for broadcast journalists, one of the attractions of the panel interview format is that it promotes adversarialness without necessarily compromising neutralism. With interviewees taking on the adversarial role vis-à-vis one another, the interviewer is removed from the heat of battle and is free to act as a disinterested catalyst.

However, the problem of neutralism re-emerges here in a different form – namely, balanced treatment of the panelists. Since the interviewer is seen questioning different interviewees who represent divergent interests and ideologies, treatment of one panelist can be compared and contrasted with treatment of another, and variations can make the interviewer vulnerable to charges of partiality or favoritism.

How serious is this problem? It is difficult to say. There is as yet no systematic analysis of the extent to which interviewers are unbalanced in their conduct toward panelists.[4] The lack of comparative research undoubtedly stems from the formidable methodological difficulties that surround this issue. Consider, for example, that a pattern of differential treatment is not necessarily indicative of favoritism. If one interviewee receives tougher questions than another, this may be because the remarks of the former contain more factual errors, are more evasive, or are otherwise faulty and hence deserving of adversarial treatment. There may, in other words, be good reasons for an interviewer to treat the panelists differently, and these must be ruled out in order to demonstrate convincingly that ideological favoritism is at work. Further complicating matters is the fact (as noted in chapter 2) that journalistic norms may require neutralism only within certain broad ideological boundaries, permitting more unabashedly hostile treatment of those who are regarded as "beyond the pale."

Nevertheless, *any* pattern of differential treatment may be significant from a public relations point of view. To the ordinary audience member, it can make an interviewer appear to be "playing favorites"

---

[4] Several researchers have compared treatment of different IEs and categories of IE across different interviews. For quantitative analyses, see Bull and Elliott (1998); Bull and Mayer (1988); Clayman and Heritage (2002); Elliott and Bull (1996). For qualitative analyses, see Hall (1973); Schlesinger, Murdock and Elliot (1983); Jucker (1986).

in a manner that is anything but neutral. This is something that interviewers generally try to avoid – consistent with the general tendency
to maintain a neutralistic posture (chapter 5), interviewers strive to
treat panelists in a roughly similar manner.

There is, however, one interview in our data set in which asym-
metrical treatment was massive and highly conspicuous. Whatever
considerations may have contributed to this asymmetry, and however it may be justified *post hoc*, it can be taken by the casual ob-
server to be a manifestation of unprofessional favoritism. Accordingly, we shall examine this interview in some detail as a case study
in the pitfalls of mediating a debate interview.

Preliminaries and introductions

The interview in question was conducted by Lesley Stahl for the
Sunday public affairs program *Face the Nation*. The interview concerned the topic of genetic engineering, and it was set up as a debate
between two panelists, one a supporter of genetic engineering and
the other an opponent. A tilt toward the "pro" side can be detected
throughout the program and is apparent even before the focal interview begins. The program opened with news about a promising new
application of genetic engineering in the fight against cancer. This
good news is discussed in a taped segment, and in an initial interview
with two medical doctors involved in that research. In documenting
the life-saving potential of genetic engineering, this first part of the
program is at least implicitly favorable toward its development.

When the debate interview itself begins, the participants are introduced in divergent ways that can be taken as favoring the supporter of genetic engineering (Alexander Capron) over the opponent
(Jeremy Rifkin).

(14)   US CBS *Face the Nation*: 8 Dec 1985: Genetic Engineering
         IR: Lesley Stahl   IE1: Jeremy Rifkin
         IE2: Alexander Capron
1 IR: Joining us now::, Jeremy Rifkin. author, (.)
2   and opponent of genetic engineering, .hh
3   And on the other si:de, Alexander Capron, former
4   Director of the President's Commission on
5   Bioethics.

Notice that the introduction of Rifkin (lines 1–2) makes no
mention of his relevant credentials or institutional affiliations.
Although he has degrees from the Wharton School of Finance and
the Fletcher School of Law and Diplomacy at Tufts University, and
established the Foundation on Economic Trends,[5] he is characterized only as an "author and opponent of genetic engineering."
By contrast, Capron's introduction highlights his relevant institutional affiliation – "former Director of the President's Commission
on Bioethics" – despite the fact that he no longer holds that position. Moreover, Capron's attitude toward genetic engineering is
never stated outright (although it is implied by the lead-in: "on the
other side . . . "). Thus, Rifkin is portrayed as a free-floating political activist who is committed to a particular point of view, whereas
Capron is portrayed as a bioethics specialist with a legitimated track
record of service in his specialty.

The first round of questioning

This pattern of apparent favoritism toward Capron over Rifkin continues as the questioning begins. Consider how their initial contributions to the interview are subsequently dealt with.

The very first question (lines 1–6 below) is directed toward
Rifkin – it asks whether he is opposed to genetic engineering for
medical purposes as discussed previously in the program. Rifkin,
in response, denies that he is flatly opposed to such research (lines
7–10), but he then goes on to argue for careful consideration of the
long-range ethical implications of genetic engineering (lines 10–21).

(15) US CBS *Face the Nation*: 8 Dec 1985: Genetic Engineering
       IR: Lesley Stahl   IE1: Jeremy Rifkin
       IE2: Alexander Capron

1 IR: Mister Rifkin you are an opponent=h of genetic
2   >engineering,=.hhh< D'you oppo:se h the kind of
3   work that Doctor Rosenberg is doing with
4   interluken two<which is de[veloped through=
5 IE1:   [.hh

---

[5] This background information was obtained from the Biography Online Database
(www.biography.com), which itself incorporates the Cambridge Encyclopedia
Database.

```
 6  IR:     =genetic engineering,=
 7  IE1:    =No I don't.=I- I think that=uh: (.) that work
 8          is very exciting, there are some (0.4)
 9          obvious:=uh breakthroughs happening: with
10          genetic engineering technology. .hh (Ya know)
11          like: with every technology: ih- there are
12          benefits an' cost(s). .h And=uh- with genetic
13          engineering we have thee ultimate technology . . .
14          ((nine lines omitted))
15          . . . But I think we owe it to ourselves >as
16          a species.< to begi:n to look at some o' the
17          lo:ng term questions. .h uh- (0.2) what ge:nes
18          are permissable to engineer. (.) Which genes
19          are no:t. (0.2) Who should make the decisions
20          of- as to which ki:nd of: genetic engineering
21          should be: (0.4) taken an' what should no:t.
22  IR:     (Well) let me stop you >for one minute.<
23          Didn't=you:: uh:- e=sponsor, .hh uh: uh
24          program duh s:top all of this research?
25          <I mean it isn't just that you think we oughta
26          (f- think) it you want it sto↑pped.
```

The IR responds to Rifkin's opening statement by forcefully challenging its veracity. She proposes that, contrary to his denial, he
is indeed seeking to stop genetic engineering research altogether.
Although her initial proposal (lines 23–24) is built as an interrogative and thus might be thought to be epistemically cautious, it uses a
linguistic form that is in fact highly assertive – it is negatively formulated ("*Didn't you* sponsor a program to stop all of this research").
As we saw in chapter 6, negative interrogatives are tilted in favor
of a "yes" answer, so much so that they are treated as if they were
asserting a position rather than merely asking a question. Furthermore, after completing this interrogatively formatted challenge, the
IR goes on to make the same point once again via an unvarnished
declarative assertion (lines 25–26). In all of these ways, she counters
the position Rifkin has taken.

   Capron's first contribution to the interview is treated very differently by the IR. Capron launches an unmediated disagreement with
Rifkin (the last part of which is reproduced below), and he concludes (lines 1–5) by pointing out that the cancer-fighting benefits of
a new drug – interluken two – would be impossible without genetic
engineering.

(16)   US CBS *Face the Nation*: 8 Dec 1985: Genetic Engineering
       IR: Lesley Stahl   IE1: Jeremy Rifkin
       IE2: Alexander Capron

```
 1  IE2:    ... after all the interluken two that's being
 2           used here is a result of genetic engineering.
 3           (.) Without genetic engineering, (.) this
 4           wouldn't be possible. <It was a very ra:re .h
 5           protein to have,=it can now be produced easily.
 6  IR:     .h Yeah (b- ehI-) I- that's what I wanna ask
 7           you.=if you stop the research_ uh- in any
 8           phase of this aren't=you cutting us o:ff?, from
 9           finding cu:res, <not only for cancer, but for
10           these .h horrible genetic diseases that- people
11           are born with, 'n: die young from or .h sickle
12           cell anemia, some of these other- (0.5) horrible
13           dis[eases.]
14  IE1:     [.hh  ] Well I think >this is something
15           (that's)< been brought up quite a few ti:mes at
16           the National Institute of He:alth ...
```

In response, the IR first acknowledges Capron's final point via a
token – "Yeah" in line 6. As we saw in chapter 4, interviewers very
rarely use receipt tokens of any kind, in part because such tokens
can be taken as expressing at least a modicum of agreement with the
interviewee and are thus incompatible with a neutralistic posture.
The supportive import of this particular token foreshadows what
immediately follows (lines 6–13) – the IR subsequently takes up
and uses Capron's argument as the basis for yet another challenging
question directed toward Rifkin, one that portrays Rifkin as un-
reasonably hindering the progress of medical research that might
otherwise find cures for various "horrible genetic deseases." As she
launches the question, she explicitly indicates that it is touched off
by Capron's remarks ("that's what I wanna ask you" at lines 6–7).
Moreover, this question is again negatively formatted ("aren't you
cutting us off ..." in line 8) and thus highly assertive in its unflattering portrayal of Rifkin.

   In short, the panelists' initial contributions are subject to very different interactional fates. Whereas Rifkin's remarks are challenged
(excerpt 15), Capron's remarks are accepted and used as a resource
with which to challenge Rifkin once again (excerpt 16).

Inviting interplay between panelists

The next four question–answer sequences follow a consistent pattern – the IR begins each line of inquiry by asking a question of Rifkin, after which she solicits a reaction from Capron, and then shifts to a new topic with the next question put to Rifkin. In this phase of the interview, the tilt toward Capron is further apparent in the design of the questions that solicit his responses to Rifkin – questions that Olsher (Forthcoming) has aptly characterized as *inviting interplay* between IEs. As we have seen, questions of this sort can in principle take a variety of forms, including open invitations to address the same issue (e.g., "What's your view of the Summit?"), invitations to agree or disagree (e.g., "How do you respond to the Senator?"), and invitations that solicit disagreement in particular (e.g., "You don't agree with the Senator, do you?").[6] However, these alternatives do not all figure in the present context. The IR's inviting-interplay questions most closely resemble the third category, albeit a markedly strong variant thereof. Beyond merely inviting Capron to *disagree* with Rifkin, these questions invite a response that *undercuts the relevance* of Rifkin's point. Moreover, by virtue of their design, these questions provide resources for Capron to mount such a rebuttal, and in that way they can be seen as collaborating with his side in the dispute.

The first instance of this sort occurred immediately after Rifkin answered the IR's challenge in (16) above. Rifkin argues that although some forms of genetic engineering may be less hazardous (i.e., somatic gene therapy, which does not affect offspring), nevertheless "we owe it to ourselves to begin the process of studying the long-term effects" and the implications for "our relationship to our children and future generations" (lines 1–23).

(17)   US CBS *Face the Nation*: 8 Dec 1985: Genetic Engineering
       IR: Lesley Stahl   IE1: Jeremy Rifkin
       IE2: Alexander Capron

1 IE1:   [.hh] Well I think >this is something
2   (that's)< been brought up quite uh few ti:mes at

---

[6] A much fuller discussion of alternative forms of inviting-interplay questions can be found in Olsher (Forthcoming).

```
 3              the National Institute of He:alth. At thee:=uh
 4              last uh:- uh- (.) meeting at the National
 5              Institute on this .hh they were discussing the
 6              first gene therapy. somatic gene therapy:, an'
 7              the kind of guidelines that oughta be
 8              established. An' the point I made at that time
 9              is .hh even though thee ethical considerations
10              for somatic therapy .h are not a:s uh- as
11              profou:nd as the ethical implications for germ
12              line, .hh we owe it to ourse:lves to begin the
13              process of studying the long term effe:cts. of
14              bringing in a wi::de range of disciplines
15              (that) can loo:k .h at thee: long term eugenics
16              implications. .hh Certainly when we talk about
17              engineering changes in the genetic co:de.
18              regardless of the tremendous benefits
19              available_ .hh we've gotta a:lso -be aware of
20              (the) responsibility_ (.) that this kind of
21              genetic engineering:=uh: e-e- really me:ans,
22              in terms of our relationship to our children.
23              (in)/(an') future generati[ons.   ]
24  IE2:                                 [Owe-] [I: :  see-]
25  IR:   →                                     [Does any]body
26        → disagree [with that,
27  IE2:             [No no one disagrees with=that Jeremy
28              as you know- we've been talking about this: .h
29              for fifteen yea:rs . . .
```

As Rifkin winds down his argument, the IR invites Capron to respond with the question "Does anybody disagree with that" (arrowed). Considered as a strictly grammatical object, this yes/no
question is formulated in such a way – via the stressed negative polarity item "anybody" – as to prefer a "no" answer. Consistent with
this preference, Capron produces just that type of answer forcefully
and at the first grammatical completion point (line 27). In terms
of the action it accomplishes, this question treats Rifkin's point
as banal, something that no one could possibly disagree with and
hence of no real consequence to the issue under discussion. It thus
provides grounds for a dismissive response, which Capron subsequently provides – launching his response with almost the very same
terms as were used in the antecedent question.

In the very next round of questioning, the IR again aligns with
Capron as she invites him to respond to Rifkin. When Rifkin is asked

about his effort to block the use of a genetically engineered microbe in agriculture (lines 1–8), he argues that such organisms should not be released without first considering the long-term environmental consequences (lines 9–19).

(18)   US CBS *Face the Nation*: 8 Dec 1985: Genetic Engineering
          IR: Lesley Stahl   IE1: Jeremy Rifkin
          IE2: Alexander Capron

```
 1  IR:     =But we're getting onto a pha:se where (.)
 2           th-uh products of some of this: research .h are
 3           now being (.) uh allowed to get out into the
 4           environment=>an' I understand< .h Mister=Rifkin
 5           you're going to c(h)ourt this week to try an'
 6           prevent .h- (h)one of these microbes from
 7           being introduced into the agricultural process.
 8           What is that issue.
 9  IE1:    Well that's the issue of uh- releasing
10           genetically engineered organisms into the
11           biosphere. .hh And the fact i:s we haven't
12           taken a look at the long term (.)
13           environmental consequences of introducing: (.)
14           genetically modified for:ms into our
15           environment...((eight lines omitted))
16           ...<perhaps we: could ask> the hard questions
17           at the beginning_ .h an' have a more realistic
18           appra:isal (.) of the context in which this
19           technology's going=to be introduced.=
20  IR:   → =Have we not °done that, °
21  IE2:    We have done that.=>I mean< the <scientists
22           themselves> back in nineteen seventy five called
23           a moratorium on their work...
```

Following this argument, the IR turns to solicit Capron's response via the question, "Have we not done that" (arrowed). Much like the previous example, this question invites a counterargument from Capron and implicitly aligns with that as-yet-unexpressed counter-argument. How is this accomplished? Notice first that the question is negatively formulated and thus strongly favors a *yes* answer. Substantively, the question is tilted toward an answer that would render Rifkin's point moot, and it anticipatorily formulates what might be the crux of Capron's rebuttal ("we have done that" – i.e., we have already considered the environmental consequences). In effect, the question assists Capron in making his point, and Capron

incorporates much of the wording of the question into the beginning
of his response (line 21), thereby asserting it "independently" while
simultaneously borrowing its phraseology.

In summary, both of the IR's inviting-interplay questions display
a preference for Capron's side of the debate, and they do so through
a common set of design features. Both questions (i) are highly assertive in character, (ii) undercut the relevance of Rifkin's point, (iii)
invite a rebuttal from Capron, and (iv) provide grounds for rebuttal
that are subsequently taken up and used by Capron in his ensuing
response. In all of these ways, the IR can be seen as partial toward
and subtly collaborating with Capron in the debate. Further con-
tributing to the sense of partiality is the fact that the grounds for
rebuttal are not attributed to Capron or to a third party (cf., "Your
position is that we have already done that"), and are thus offered
on the IR's own behalf (cf., chapter 5).

A note on facial expressions

The IR's apparent partiality can also be discerned at the nonvocal
level. In the previous exchange ([18] above), she exhibits clearly
different facial expressions as she delivers questions to Rifkin and
Capron respectively. Throughout her question to Rifkin (lines 1–8
above), she remains largely expressionless, except for brief eyebrow
flashes at points of emphasis.

However, when she turns to Capron to invite an oppositional response (line 20 above), she smiles broadly. The smile's point of onset
cannot be determined, because the camera does not cut to the IR
until the final word of the question ("that"). At that point, the smile
is in full bloom, and it remains – albeit fading slowly – for about one
full second into Capron's response. Smiles can, of course, convey a
range of meanings, not only when blended with other facial expressions (Ekman and Friesen 1975), but also when produced in association with a particular spate of talk. In the environment of a question that so clearly favors Capron's side in the debate, this particular
smile can be taken as a further display of affiliation with that side.

Throughout the body of the interview, the IR is shown smiling
broadly at only one other juncture – during another "friendly" question directed to Capron (in [20] below). Rifkin never receives such
a nonvocal display of affiliation.

Cross-examining one panelist

Following the preceding exchange, the IR subsequently shifts gears,
so to speak, in her management of the interview. Instead of inviting
Capron to counter Rifkin, she enters the fray and begins challenging
Rifkin on her own initiative. By assuming the role of cross-examiner,
she becomes more directly adversarial toward, and thus more clearly
aligned against, Rifkin in the dispute.

The cross-examination phase begins with the IR asking Rifkin to
talk about "what some of these microbes can do" (line 1) – she elaborates on this query by noting their "enormous benefits" (lines 2–3)
and referring to one microbe that "prevents frost from forming"
(lines 6–7). Rifkin begins to respond at this point (line 8), taking
up the issue of the anti-frost microbe and pointing out that it could
negatively affect worldwide rainfall patterns.

(19)   US CBS *Face the Nation*: 8 Dec 1985: Genetic Engineering
       IR: Lesley Stahl   IE1: Jeremy Rifkin
       IE2: Alexander Capron

```
 1  IR:       Tell us what some (of) these microbes can ↑ do
 2            though.=It-it all=we:(m)- talked about the
 3            benefi[ts   ] they're en:ormous.
 4  (IE1):          [Yes.]
 5  ():       .h [h-
 6  IR:          [You c'n-] (w-) the one you're tryin' to
 7            sto:p_ (.) prevents frost from forming,=
 8  IE1:      =Well let's- let's take a look at this
 9            particular microbe. (.) In nature this
10            genetically engineered microbe also is- (.)
11            plays a major role in rainfall patterns.
12            .h The genetically enginee:red counterpart,
13            (.) uh does not make ice for- uh- rai:n
14            nucleation. .h So: you could have uh
15            si[t u a t i o n        h e r e-]
16  IR:        [*Whatever that means* .hh] huh [huh
17  IE1:                                        [Could
18            have a situation here where yo[u('re) putting=
19  IR:                                      [Mm hm,
20  IE1:      =out a bacteria in the environment, .h an' in
21            the long run it could develop a niche, an'
22            prevent uh=s- uh: effective rainfall patterns on
23            the planet. .hh an i[t-  ]
24  IR:                           [But]=you don't know that.
```

```
25   IE1:   .h But you see the other side [ doesn't ] know=
26   IR:                                   [Do you?]
27   IE1:   =either until: we devel[op (uh s-)]
28   IR:                            [But they s]ay it won't.
29           (.)
30   IE1:   .h Well thee interesting thing i:s we've never
31           developed a science to judge the risk of
32           placing these experiments in the environment.
```

The IR's initial reaction to Rifkin's argument is striking. Midway through his argument, just after he uses a bit of technical terminology ("rain nucleation" at lines 13–14), she makes a dismissive remark ("Whatever that means" in line 16) followed by derisive laughter. This remark does not appear to be directed toward Rifkin. It begins in overlap with Rifkin's talk, midway through the turn constructional unit following the focal term. Moreover, it is delivered *sotto voce*, and can be interpreted as an aside aimed at Capron or the audience or perhaps both. Correspondingly, Rifkin does not respond to it overtly, although he does abort (line 15) and then restart (line 17) the overlapped unit in progress. Substantively, the remark is entirely out of character in the news interview context. Not only does it depart from the norm that IRs should restrict themselves to asking questions, but it is clearly nonneutral in its treatment of Rifkin. To be sure, interviewers are generally alert to technical terminology that the audience may not understand, but they normally deal with it by asking the interviewee to clarify; they do not dismiss it altogether, nor as a rule do they laugh at the interviewee who produced it![7]

Perhaps even more striking is how the IR deals with Rifkin's argument once it is completed. When Rifkin arrives at a possible completion point (at line 23), asserting that the microbe could "prevent effective rainfall patterns on the planet," the IR directly and forcefully challenges him ("But you don't know that" at line 24) on the grounds that he does not know for certain that this dire consequence will follow. A delayed tag question – "Do you" in line 26 – adds a veneer of epistemic caution to this otherwise assertive challenge, while at the same time disrupting his response-in-progress (cf., Jefferson 1981). In contrast, when Rifkin points out that his

---

[7] On the distinction between "laughing at" versus "laughing with," see Clayman (1992) and Glenn (1995).

opponents cannot be certain that this *won't* happen (lines 25, 27), the IR counters with "But they s<u>ay</u> it won't" (line 28). Across this exchange, the parties are held to dramatically different epistemic standards – Rifkin to a standard of absolute certainty ("But you don't k<u>now</u> that" at line 24), but the opposition to a standard of mere assertion ("But they s<u>ay</u> it won't" at line 28).

The closing

The final question of the interview is a fitting coda to what has transpired. Capron is given the last word when the IR addresses him with this question (arrowed):

(20)   US CBS *Face the Nation*: 8 Dec 1985: Genetic Engineering
       IR: Lesley Stahl   IE1: Jeremy Rifkin
       IE2: Alexander Capron

```
 1  IR:       Mister Capron one final quick h question.
 2  IE1:      [#Yes,]
 3  IR:    → [.hh   ] Can: we stop this trai:n,
 4  IE2:      .mlh I don't think we c(h)a::n stop it but I do
 5            think_ (.) there are mechanisms_ (.) to control
 6            it.  an'  to make sure it's gonnu_ (0.2) go as
 7            well as (we) ca:n.
 8  IR:       Gentlemen, (.) Thank you very much, .hh This is
 9            a discussion I'd like to have (.) a[gai:n on=
10  ():                                         [mm hm,
11  IR:       =Face the Nation.
```

Stepping back from the details of the preceding discussion, she asks whether it's possible to halt the progress of genetic engineering. As it is designed, this question is far from neutral with respect to the issue that it raises. By metaphorically characterizing the enterprise as a "train," she evokes the image of something that would be both difficult and disruptive to stop. Correspondingly, as she completes this question, she shakes her head laterally. Thus, through both discursive and gestural resources, she tilts the question strongly in favor of a *no* answer – which is just the sort of answer that Capron, who has argued for genetic engineering all along, can be expected to give. Another broad smile caps off and accentuates the affiliative character of this final question.

Conclusion

In the panel interview format, the interviewer's substantive journal-istic role is to some extent diminished. As the interactional center of gravity shifts toward the interplay between interviewees, the inter-viewer inevitably becomes a less central player in the discussion.

While interviewers are in effect marginalized within this format, they are by no means irrelevant. They continue to play an important role as catalysts of conflict. Through opening remarks that set the tone for the overall occasion, and through the design of specific questions, interviewers often encourage interviewees to build their remarks in opposition to one another. Moreover, the impetus to-ward disagreement and its escalation is also facilitated by the larger system of interaction in which all parties are embedded – i.e., the question–answer turn-taking system, which embodies a mediated participation framework that provides a relatively "safe" environ-ment for the expression of interviewee/interviewee disagreement.[8]

The interviewer's diminished but continued involvement in the panel interview is not without pitfalls. The questioning of multiple interviewees provides a new basis on which observers can detect bias. Of course, interviewers can always be monitored for their con-duct toward different public figures, but in one-on-one interviews any such monitoring must extend across separate and temporally distant events. Differential treatment is clearly much easier to detect when interviewees are being questioned in close proximity, although within a given panel interview, avenues for the differential treatment of interviewees vary in their conspicuousness. Particularly notewor-thy in this regard are inviting-interplay questions, wherein a single action pivots between the panelists and can be scrutinized for signs that the interviewer is "leaning" this way or that. The launching of an inviting-interplay question is a distinctly sensitive moment for the journalist, a moment when his or her professionalism is perhaps most vulnerable to critical scrutiny.

Of course, the broader ramifications of differential treatment are by no means predetermined. Such conduct may be entirely justifi-able in context, given the trajectory of the interaction prior to that

---

[8] This system of interaction bears a striking resemblance to that which organizes formal mediation hearings. In that context, as Garcia (1991) has demonstrated, it facilitates "dispute resolution without disputing."

point, and given where the panelists stand along the ideological spectrum. Indeed, hostile treatment of one panelist may encourage audience members to view that panelist as outside the political mainstream and hence "beyond the pale" (see chapter 2). Alternatively, differential treatment may also be taken as a manifestation of the interviewer's own personal biases or the biases of the news organization. For this reason, gross patterns of differential treatment as exhibited in the *Face the Nation* case remain extremely rare on elite news interview programs.

As we noted at the beginning of this chapter, the panel format emerged somewhat late in the history of the news interview, but it it has gained momentum in recent years. In the USA, the long-running Sunday morning interview programs initially featured a single public figure at a time, and they did not begin to include panels with any frequency until the 1970s and then only sporadically. The panel format rose to prominence at the end of the 1970s, when the interview moved outside of its Sunday morning niche via nightly news programs such as *Nightline* and *The MacNeil/Lehrer NewsHour*. Given the more desirable time slot and the potential of attracting a much larger audience, news producers have been drawn to the panel format as a way of generating more lively discussions with greater audience appeal. It has now become the most common form of news interview across a range of broadcasting contexts.

This development has been a mixed blessing. On the one hand, it has given audience members direct access to the clash between public figures and the enduring political factions that they represent. Such conflicts have long been a staple of the traditional news story, but there they are necessarily edited and framed by the journalist's narrative. With the panel interview, factional conflict is played out before the direct scrutiny of the public.

On the other hand, with the marginalization of the journalist and the emphasis on conflict and confrontation, there is a danger of generating more heat than light. When disagreement intensifies to the level of a shouting match, when the participants become unable to develop their points without interruption, when they have difficulty being heard above the din, then it can be said that entertainment value has overwhelmed informational substance. In this respect, the debate interview can come to resemble other less prestigious forms of broadcast talk that exploit the spectacle of interactional conflict – programs such as CNN's *Crossfire* and *The McLaughlin Group*. Notwithstanding their entertainment value, such programs contribute to an argument culture that inhibits thoughtful debate and does little to advance mutual understanding or an informed public (Tannen 1998).

Fortunately, this is not a necessary or inevitable consequence of the panel interview format; it all depends on how that format is implemented. Programs vary greatly in their permissiveness and tolerance of unmediated conflict. While *Nightline*'s Ted Koppel permits a certain amount of direct disagreement, when it becomes excessive he is quick to step in and restore order. The interviewers on PBS's *NewsHour* tend to keep their panelists on an even shorter leash. In the final analysis, when properly managed by a journalist who permits lively debate but does not hesitate to rein in the panelists when the conflict becomes counterproductive, this format can accomplish the elusive objective – always difficult in the world of broadcast talk – of being *both* entertaining *and* informative.

9

Conclusion

Over the course of this book, we have examined a number of fundamental practices through which interaction in the modern news interview is conducted. These practices are shaped by the basic institutional conditions of broadcast journalism in Western democracies, and they constitute a set of ground rules that effectively define the playing field within which, sometimes cooperatively and sometimes competitively, journalists and public figures make the news.

Our description and analyses of these practices have drawn extensively from both American and British news interviews. This reflects our conclusion that there are no fundamental differences between the two countries in the overall palette of practices through which news interviews are realized. As we have suggested, though there are important differences in the methods by which broadcast journalism is legally regulated in the two countries, there are no significant differences in the basic institutional constraints which shape the news interview. In both countries, there is a need to balance objectivity with adversarialness in the news interview context. And most of the practices we have examined connected with turn-taking, neutralism, question design, the management of answers, and debate interviews represent systematic solutions to the practical management of this balance. Thus a mix of legal regulation, economic pressures, and the mutual needs (and sanctions) of journalists and public figures have combined to create a remarkably similar "fingerprint" of basic communication practices in the broadcast interview in both countries.

The main differences in news interview practice, then, are not between countries but rather between program and interviewing styles that effectively transcend national boundaries. There are more similarities in the relatively adversarial interviewing styles of ABC's

Nightline and BBC Televisions *Newsnight*, than either has with PBS's more sedate *NewsHour*. The "Sunday morning" interview shows in both countries also embody remarkable similarities. The differences between the various types of news programs are a matter of tone and style, of the predominant manner of questioning interviewees and countering intervewees' positions, rather than of basic ground rules for interview conduct.

If there is a clear convergence in the fundamental character of the news interview in both countries, they have nonetheless arrived at this convergence through different pathways. The dominant American news interview shows of the 1950s and 1960s – the "Sunday morning" shows – were always relatively adversarial in their treatment of interviewees. Writing in 1967, sometime CBS news chief Fred Friendly (1967: 147) commented that "A live interview with the man in office usually results in a *Face the Nation–Meet the Press* verbal fencing bout, in which a wary but nimble politician spends the half-hour trying to prevent his interrogators from getting him to put his foot in his mouth." This conclusion seems to have been almost as true of interviews in the 1950s as it was in the more rebellious 1960s when Walter Cronkite would be criticized for handling Chicago Mayor Richard Daley with kid gloves in the aftermath of the tumultuous 1968 Democratic Party National Convention. The significant development in the USA over the past thirty years has been the growth of news interview shows and their movement into more regular daily programming slots. These shows are by no means mainstream and the audiences they attract are far from huge, but their growth has involved a significant convergence with Britain in both the type and frequency of news interview programming available to the viewing audience.

In Britain, the story has been rather more complicated. The kind of interviewing that was characteristic of *Meet the Press* in the 1950s was unthinkable during the comparable period of the BBC's monopoly. The rapid development of probing, investigative interviewing after the BBC's monopoly was broken offers support for the American view that the public's right to be informed is best secured in the context of competition in broadcasting. In the 1970s and 1980s, British broadcasters (especially at the BBC) found themselves in conflict with the government of the day. There seems to be little doubt that, at least at the margin and probably substantially more than that, news and current affairs programming – and with it news interviewing – was inhibited by various forms of pressure from politicians and administration officials. More recently, news programming in Britain has become constrained in both budgetary and scheduling terms by the burgeoning ratings wars of the 1990s. These have been exacerbated by the advent of broadband, satellite and Internet competition, which has intensified competition for a declining television audience. The extent and scheduling of news programming containing "heavyweight" news interview content seems unlikely to expand in this context, and indeed there is now significant convergence between British and American schedules in the extent and timing of news interview shows.

While news interview programming per se has ceased expanding and has stabilized, broadcast talk more generally has grown and diversified over the course of the past decade. This growth embodies two trends that have been identified by others: the "conversation-alization" of the mass media that is sometimes argued to create a kind of pseudo-democratization of political discourse (Fairclough 1992), and the growth of what Tannen (1998) calls the "argument culture." Both these trends are apparent in the evolution of the news interview itself. The last thirty years have witnessed a kind of communication arms race in which innovations in journalists' questions have been matched by politicians' increasing skills in the medium and in the arts of evasion and agenda setting. While some of the verbal fencing is indeed mere shadow play, there can be no doubt that the modern news interview has become more "conversational." One consequence of this has been a massive reduction in the social distance between politicians and journalists and, through them, the general public (cf. Clayman and Heritage 2002). Insofar as politicians and others are increasingly made accountable to the public by these means, the result can only be an extension of democratic accountability, at least some of the time.

These developments have been driven by competitive pressures in broadcasting, and have been given further shape by the rise of twenty-four hour cable news channels – particularly in the USA – which has led to a plethora of new interaction-based program formats. Some of these are quasi-news interview formats that more or less resemble the prototypical news interview but with a twist of one sort or another. One important format combines interview-style questioning of public figures with various forms of audience participation, as occurs on CNN's *Larry King Live* and some daytime talk shows such as *Oprah*. Also resembling the news interview are those programs (e.g., CNBC's *Rivera Live* and MSNBC's *Hardball* with Chris Matthews) involving highly opinionated hosts who are not bound by the norm of neutralism. Farther afield are the numerous panel discussion and debate formats such as *Crossfire*, *Capital Gang*, *The McLaughlin Group*, and *Washington Week in Review*, celebrity talk shows that run in the daytime and late evening hours, and radio call-in programs of various stripes. The news interview now co-exists alongside, and in competition with, these other formats. Moreover, it exists within a context that is shaped by these formats, in particular the decline in deference and reduction in social distance between journalists and interviewees, and the intermingling of journalists and political elites within a general ambiance of money and celebrity (Fallows 1996).

One consequence of the diversification of broadcast talk is that the elite journalistic interview has seemed to become less central as a medium for politicians and others to communicate with the electorate. The audience for such programs has declined somewhat with increasing competition from other formats. Moreover, politicians can now pick and choose among programs and the media markets they offer. In the 1992 presidential campaign, Bill Clinton appeared on the *Phil Donahue Show* while Ross Perot appeared numerous times on *Larry King Live*, and in 2000 both George W. Bush and Al Gore appeared on *Oprah*. Similar trends were visible in British politics from the mid-1980s, culminating in town-meeting style shows in which members of the public, with some assistance from professional interviewers, put questions directly to prime ministerial candidates. Like their counterparts in the USA, prime ministerial candidates have clearly favored the more relaxed and audience-participatory environment afforded by these programs over the traditional news interview.

Given these developments – the fragmentation of the media market, diversification of media appearances by politicians and others, and the relatively small audiences for news interview shows – it is certainly relevant to ask whether the traditional "heavyweight" interview has lost its significance as a means of communicating information and opinion to the news audience. Put bluntly, is the news interview dead?

There are several reasons for suggesting that the news interview is robustly alive and likely to remain so. While politicians and other newsmakers have been appearing more frequently on the more relaxed and "feel good" alternatives to the news interview, they tend to do so primarily in the context of elections. During elections, politicians face an imperative need to reach segments of the electorate that do not normally watch news and current affairs programming: the less challenging daytime and late-night talk shows are an ideal vehicle for this purpose, and one which politicians have increasingly turned to during the past twenty years. However, their participation in such shows is typically limited to the election context, and it is unlikely that participation will be extended any time soon. From the perspective of talk show programmers, politicians are not the most exciting of guests outside of the "horserace" context of the election. From the perspective of the politician, participation in such shows is a necessary evil, mandated to be sure by the election context, but not to be extended far outside the election context lest the gains from appearing as a "regular person" diminish and the risks of over-exposure multiply. For these reasons, outside of election time politicians and other public figures tend to stick to the more elite news interview, and in the USA to the quasi-interview press conference. Just as skill in public oratory was an important asset to aspiring politicians in the pre-television era, so today being "good on television" remains a vital skill in the present television-saturated age. Politicians rarely rise to national prominence without this vital skill, and this is most often evaluated, as Al Gore found to his cost in the 2000 presidential debates, in terms of performances in news interview-type contexts.

Outside of the election context, politicians who do not participate in "heavyweight" interviews and press conferences attract sanctions from the news media. For example, in the aftermath of his successful 1992 presidential campaign, Bill Clinton continued with "town hall" meetings with the public using the successful *Phil Donahue Show* as the basic format. Though these events drew big television ratings and were perceived as successful by the public, Clinton was swiftly rebuked by the Washington Press Corps, and many commentators speculated that this mode of presidential communication could not last. The sceptics were right. By midsummer 1993, Clinton was corralled into the regular formats of news interviews and press conferences. The "town hall" meetings were over until the 1996 election.

It is sometimes suggested that the news interview is insignificant because audiences for news interview shows are small relative to sports and entertainment programming. While it is true that the audience for shows outside the network news (itself declining) is indeed small, this argument overlooks the nature of the news interview audience. This audience includes other politicians, journalists, and business and community leaders. These people are interested in politics at a professional or amateur level, and because of that interest they often serve as opinion leaders in the community. The most obvious example of this are the Sunday morning news interview shows. In both Britain and America these are extensively monitored by other news organizations and their content is frequently reported in later television news programming and in Monday morning newspapers. Here the coverage of particular pronouncements from public figures can vastly exceed the initial audience that tuned in for the show. Even where this is not the case, however, the opinion leadership exercised by political and civic elites can exert a multiplier effect on the popularity of particular participants on news shows, and on the value attached to their ideas. Ross Perot, for example, a 1992 presidential candidate whose participation in that election had a significant influence on its tone and outcome, had earlier become well known to the news audience. A series of appearances on *60 Minutes, The MacNeil-Lehrer Newshour*, and other heavyweight news shows reaching back into the late 1980s established him as a trenchant critic of budget deficits long before he announced as a candidate.

Another argument for the demise of the news interview focuses less on its audience than its content. According to this argument, the news interview has become a form of ritualized swordplay in which the politician dodges questions, and substitutes various prepared statements for the kind of reasoned thoughtful responses that are being sought by the interviewer. No less an authority than Robin Day argued that during the 1980s interviews "have tended to become a series of statements, planned for delivery irrespective of the question which had been put. This technique has gradually brought about the decline of the major television interview. It is now rarely a dialogue which could be helpful to the viewer" (Day 1989: 245). Day once joked of beginning an interview with Margaret Thatcher with: "Prime Minister, what is your answer to my first question?" (*ibid.*), and elsewhere he has commented on the negative effect of media advisors and trainers on the art of news interview performance (Day 1987). Thirty years earlier, however, during the meteoric emergence of the news interview in Britain, Day had a different perspective: "You cannot 'groom' people into giving effective answers in a TV interview, any more than you can 'groom' them into being persuasive platform orators. There is no special magic about television. It is an instrument of communication, which shows what it sees. If what it sees is uninteresting, that is that" (Day 1961: 101). It is almost certain that the truth lies somewhere between these two extremes. Politicians can be, and are, groomed to be effective evaders of questions and to substitute their own agendas and presuppositions for those which the interviewer is seeking to examine. But it is unlikely that they are systematically better at these "black arts" than were their predecessors forty years ago (Jones 1992). It is more likely that politicians can get away with uninformative answers and set-piece statements during periods of political consensus, or when a particular party or ideological position dominates the political agenda. However, during times of intense debate or discussion, or when a political party or administration or policy is in disarray, the balance of opportunity tends to favor the interviewer, and a medium that previously seemed played out renews itself as an instrument of journalistic inquiry.

In suggesting that the news interview remains a relevant form of political communication, we do not intend to downplay the range of alternative media outlets and modes of communication – some of which are even now emerging in the new broadband environment of cable and Internet communication. Yet it can also be suggested with some confidence that, to adapt Mark Twain's famous aphorism, stories of its demise are much exaggerated. The news interview continues to occupy a prominent place in both American and British broadcasting, and barring a dramatic decline in the institution of journalism in either country, it will remain a force to be reckoned with.

The findings reported in this book can provide a foundation for subsequent research on the dynamic relationship between journalists and public figures. Our primary objective has been to characterize the fundamental ground rules that organize conduct within the news interview, as these are revealed through the repertoire of practices that interviewers and interviewees draw from in their dealings with one another. Taken together, these practices comprise the basic building blocks of the news interview, the elementary components out of which news interview interaction is constructed. Now that these elementary components have been identified and understood, it is relevant to ask how they combine to form persistent styles of interview conduct that are characteristic of different broadcasting environments. Thus, systematic comparative research – which would be premature without a foundational understanding of the basic building blocks of interview conduct – can now proceed in a defensible way. It becomes possible to explore how the components of news interview conduct are differentially distributed across interviewers and interviewees, across different programs and communication media, and across national and historical boundaries. The practices described in this book can thus provide a detailed and sensitive "fingerprint" of the state of journalism and politics as they constitute themselves through different practitioners and in different social environments.

We have already launched one research project along these lines (Clayman and Heritage 2002). Building on the forms of question design analyzed in chapter 6, and supplementing that analysis with new observations, we have developed a system for measuring the level of deference/adversarialness in the questions that journalists ask of public figures. The system encompasses twelve features of question design that serve as indicators of four basic dimensions of adversarialness: (i) initiative, (ii) bluntness, (iii) assertiveness, and (iv) hostility. We have applied this system in a comparative study of the questions asked of Presidents Dwight Eisenhower and Ronald Reagan in their respective press conferences. The results reveal substantial and significant differences for eleven out of twelve indicators, all in the direction of declining deference and increasing adversarialness. This pattern provides powerful evidence that different presidents have had to function in dramatically different journalistic environments, and that journalists in the postwar era have become much more aggressive in their treatment of the president. Recognizing that the tenor of relations between journalists and public figures is "not something easy to measure" (Schudson 1995: 151; see also Kernell 1986:76; Smith 1990: 10–11), a focus on the design of journalists' questions can introduce a measure of precision into such research.

Future research can shed light on the factors that might have contributed to this trend – the rise of television and the proliferation of television journalists at press conferences, the decline of the postwar political consensus and growing social unrest of the 1960s, the impact of the Watergate affair on American journalism, etc. It would also be interesting to explore whether the long-term rise of adversarialness extends beyond presidential press conferences to other environments of journalistic questioning, to the treatment of other public figures, and to other national contexts. Given that journalism is widely believed to have become more independent and vigorous in recent decades in countries ranging from Russia and Taiwan to Brazil and Colombia (Waisbord 2000), journalistic questioning offers a precise way of charting these cross-cultural trends.

Numerous other issues can also be explored via comparative analysis of journalists' questions. To what extent is questioning sensitive to short-term fluctuations in economic, political, and social conditions and to a public figure's standing in the polls? What styles of questioning are favored by different journalists operating within different programming and media environments, and what is the relationship between such styles and journalists' public personae? What about varying treatment given to public figures at different levels of status and power and at different points along the ideological spectrum, and the import of such variations in constituting the boundaries of legitimate opinion in the public sphere? Turning to the interviewee side of the equation, research might build on the observations in chapter 7 by examining predominant ways of answering, resisting, or evading questions as an index of the extent to which public figures of various stripes and in various contexts are bound by the questions they receive. This in turn can shed light on the shifting balance of power between journalists and public figures in times of peace and war, prosperity and hardship, stability and unrest. Finally, the impact that all of this may or may not have on audiences and on the course of public opinion also remains to be explored.

It is our hope that this book will provide an impetus for research along the lines outlined above. We have placed the news interview under the equivalent of a microscope. We have examined the inner workings of this interactional form with an eye toward understanding what makes it "tick." Much has been revealed about its cellular composition, and much undoubtedly remains to be learned at deeper molecular, atomic, and subatomic levels. These findings in turn provide a resource for surveying the larger population of news interviews – and allied forms of broadcast talk – that inhabit diverse environments of broadcasting around the world.

Appendix

Transcript symbols

Transcripts in this book employ the notational conventions used in conversation analysis. The transcripts are designed to capture the details of talk and interaction as it naturally occurs. This page provides a brief guide to the most commonly used transcript symbols; a more thorough and detailed exposition appears on subsequent pages.

IE: <u>Th</u>at's our <u>po</u>licy. Underlined items were hearably stessed.

IE: That's our po::licy. Colon(s) indicate the prior sound was prolonged.

IE: THAT'S our policy. Capital letters indicate increased volume.

IE: That's our- our policy. A hyphen denotes a glottal stop or "cur-off" of sound.

IE: .hhh That's our policy.
IR: But should it be? hhhh String of "h" mark audible breathing. The longer the string, the longer the breath. A period preceding denotes inbreath; no period denotes outbreath.

IE: That's (.) our policy.
(1.3) Numbers in parentheses denote elapsed silence in tenths of seconds;
IR: But should it be? a period denotes a micropause of less than 0.2 seconds.

IE: That's our policy.=
IR: =But should it be? Equal signs indicate that one sound followed the other with no intervening silence.

IE: That['s our policy]   Brackets mark the onset and termi-
IR: [But should it] be?   nation of simultaneous speech.
IE: That's our policy,   Punctuation marks denote intona-
IR: But should it be.   tion rather than grammar at turn
IE: I think so?   constructional unit boundaries.
                                Periods indicate falling intonation,
                                question marks indicate rising
                                intonation, and commas indicate
                                "continuing" or slightly rising
                                intonation.
IE: That's our ( )   Open parentheses indicate
IR: But (should it) be.?   transcriber's uncertainty.
                                Words in parentheses represent a
                                best guess as to what was said.

Temporal and sequential relationships

(a) Overlapping or simultaneous talk is indicated in a variety of
ways.

[Separate left square brackets, one above the other on two succes-
[sive lines with utterances by different speakers, indicate a point
     of overlap onset, whether at the start of an utterance or later.

]   Separate right square brackets, one above the other on two suc-
     cessive lines with utterances by different speakers, indicate a
     point at which two overlapping utterances both end, where one
     ends while the other continues, or simultaneous moments in
     overlaps which continue.

//   In some older transcripts or where graphic arrangement of the
     transcript requires it, a double slash indicates the point at which
     a current speaker's utterance is overlapped by the talk of another,
     which appears on the next line attributed to another speaker.
     If there is more than one double slash in an utterance, then the
     second indicates where a second overlap begins, the overlapping
     talk appearing on the next line attributed to another speaker, etc.
     In transcripts using the // notation for overlap onset, the end of
     the overlap may be marked by a right bracket (as above) or by
*   an asterisk.

So, the following are alternative ways of representing the same event: Bee's "Uh really?" overlaps Ava's talk starting at "a" and ending at the "t" of "tough."

Ava: I 'av [a lotta   t]ough cou:rses.
Bee: [Uh really?]

Ava: I 'av // a lotta t*ough cou:rses.
Bee: Uh really?

=   (b) Equal signs ordinarily come in pairs – one at the end of a line and another at the start of the next line or one shortly thereafter. They are used to indicate two things:

(i) If the two lines connected by the equal signs are by the same speaker, then there was a single, continuous utterance with no break or pause, which was broken up in order to accommodate the placement of overlapping talk. For example, TG, 02:18–23:

Bee: In the gy:m? [(hh)
Ava: [Yea:h. Like grou(h)p therapy.
                            Yuh know
                    [half the grou]p thet we had la:s' term wz
                        there en we=
Bee: [O h :: : .]·hh
Ava: =[jus' playing arou:nd.
Bee: =[. hh

Ava's talk is continuous, but room has been made for Bee's overlapping talk (the "Oh").

(ii) If the lines connected by two equal signs are by different speakers, then the second followed the first with no discernible silence between them, or was "latched" to it.

(0.5)   (c) Numbers in parentheses indicate silence, represented in tenths of a second; what is given here in the left margin indicates 5/10 seconds of silence. Silences may be marked either within an utterance or between utterances, as in the two excerpts below:

Bee: .hhh Uh::, (0.3) I don'know I guess she's aw- she's
         awright she went to thee uh:: hhospital again
         tihda:y,
Bee: Tch! .hh So uh I don't kno:w,
         (0.3)
Bee: En:=

(.)   (d) A dot in parentheses indicates a "micropause," hear-
           able but not readily measurable; ordinarily less than
           2/10 of a second.

((pause)) (e) In some older or less carefully prepared transcripts,
           untimed silences may be indicated by the word "pause"
           in double parentheses.

Aspects of speech delivery, including aspects of intonation

.   (a) The punctuation marks are not used grammatically, but
       to indicate intonation. The period indicates a falling, or final,
       intonation contour, not necessarily the end of a sentence.
?   Similarly, a question mark indicates rising intonation, not nec-
       essarily a question, and a comma indicates "continuing" into-
,   nation, not necessarily a clause boundary. In some transcript
       fragments in your readings you may see a combined ques-
       tion mark and comma, which indicates a rise stronger than a
       comma
?,   but weaker than a question mark. Because this symbol cannot
¿   be produced by the computer, the inverted question mark (¿) is
       used for this purpose.

: :   (b) Colons are used to indicate the prolongation or stretching
       of the sound just preceding them. The more colons, the longer
       the stretching. On the other hand, graphically stretching a word
       on the page by inserting blank spaces between the letters does
       not necessarily indicate how it was pronounced; it is used to
       allow alignment with overlapping talk. Thus,

Bee: Tch! (M'n)/(En) they can't delay much lo:nguh they
         [jus' wannid] uh- ·hhh=
Ava: [O h   :   .]
Bee: =yihknow have anothuh consulta:tion,

Ava: Ri::ght.
Bee: En then deci::de.

The word "ri::ght" in Ava's second turn, or "deci::de" in Bee's third are more stretched than "oh:" in Ava's first turn, even though "oh:" appears to occupy more space. But "oh" has only one colon, and the others have two; "oh:" has been spaced out so that its brackets will align with the talk in Bee's ("jus' wannid") turn with which it is in overlap.

-           (c) A hyphen after a word or part of a word indicates a cut-off or self-interruption, often done with a glottal or dental stop.

word   (d) Underlining is used to indicate some form of stress or emphasis, either by increased loudness or higher pitch. The more underlining, the greater the emphasis. Therefore,
word   underlining sometimes is placed under the first letter or two of a word, rather than under the letters which are actually raised in pitch or volume. Especially loud talk may
WOrd   be indicated by upper case; again, the louder, the more letters in upper case. And in extreme cases, upper case may be underlined.

°   (e) The degree sign indicates that the talk following it was markedly quiet or soft. When there are two degree
° °   signs, the talk beween them is markedly softer than the talk around it.

            (f) Combinations of underlining and colons are used to indicate intonation contours, as follows:
_: If the letter(s) preceding a colon is underlined, then there is an "inflected" falling intonation contour (you can hear the pitch turn downward).
:   If a colon is itself underlined, then there is an inflected rising intonation contour (i.e., you can hear the pitch turn upward).
            So, in

Bee: In the gy:m? [(hh)
Ava: [Yea:h. Like grou(h)p
                     therapy. Yuh know

        [half the grou]p thet we had la:s' term wz there

        en we=

Bee: [O h ː ː ː .]·hh

Ava: =[jus' playing arou:nd.

Bee: =[.hh

Bee: Uh-fo[oling around.

Ava: [·hhh

Ava: Eh-yeah so, some a' the guys who were bedder

        y'know wen' off by themselves so it wz two

        girls against this one guy

        en he's ta:ll.Y'know? [·hh

Bee: [Mm hm?

the "Oh:::." in Bee's second turn has an upward inflection while it is being stretched (even though it ends with falling intonation, as indicated by the period). On the other hand, "ta:ll" at the end of Ava's last turn is inflected downward ("bends downward," so to speak) over and above its "period intonation."

(g) The up and down arrows mark sharper rises or falls in pitch than would be indicated by combinations of colons and underlining, or may mark a whole shift, or resetting, of the pitch register at which the talk is being produced.

(h) The combination of "more than" and "less than" symbols indicates that the talk between them is compressed or rushed. Used in the reverse order, they can indicate that a stretch of talk is markedly slowed or drawn out. The "less than" symbol by itself indicates that the immediately following talk is "jump-started," i.e., sounds like it starts with a rush.

(i) Hearable aspiration is shown where it occurs in the talk by the letter "h" – the more hs, the more aspiration. The aspiration may represent breathing, laughter, etc. If it occurs

(hh) inside the boundaries of a word, it may be enclosed in parentheses in order to set it apart from the sounds of the word (as in TG, 02:12–13 below). If the aspiration is an inhalation,

.hh   it is shown with a dot before it (usually a raised dot).

Bee: [Ba::]sk(h)etb(h)a(h)ll?   (h) (°Whe(h)re.)

Other markings

(( ))   (a) Double parentheses are used to mark transcriber's descriptions of events, rather than representations of them. Thus ((cough)), ((sniff)), ((telephone rings)), ((footsteps)), ((whispered)), ((pause)) and the like.

(word)   (b) When all or part of an utterance is in parentheses, or the speaker identification is, this indicates uncertainty on the transcriber's part, but represents a likely possibility.

( )   Empty parentheses indicate that something is being said, but no hearing (or, in some cases, speaker identification) can be achieved.

(try 1)   (c) In some transcript excerpts, two parentheses may be printed, one above the other; these represent alternative
(try 2)   hearings of the same strip of talk. In some instances this format cannot be printed, and is replaced by putting the alternative hearings in parentheses, separated by a single oblique or slash, as in

Bee: °(Bu::t.)=/°(Goo:d.)=

Here, the degree marks show that the utterance is very soft. The transcript remains indeterminate between "Bu::t." and "Goo:d." Each is in parentheses and they are separated by a slash.

The core of this set of notational conventions was first developed by Gail Jefferson. It continues to evolve and adapt both to the work of analysis, the developing skill of transcribers, and changes in technology. Not all symbols have been included here, and some symbols in some data sources are not used systematically or consistently. Other papers may introduce additional conventions, especially for registering body behavior in relation to the talk.

References

Adkins, Barbara. 1992. Arguing the point: the management and context of disputacious challenges in radio current affairs interviews. *Australian Journalism Review*, 14 (1): 37–49.

Albert, Ethel M. 1972. Culture patterning of speech behavior in Borundi. In J. Gumperz and D. Hymes (eds.) *Directions in Sociolinguistics: The Ethnography of Communication*. New York: Basil Blackwell, pp. 72–105.

Altheide, David L. 1974. *Creating Reality: How TV News Distorts Events*. Thousand Oaks, CA: Sage.

Atkinson, J. Maxwell. 1982. Understanding formality: notes on the categorisation and production of "formal" interaction. *British Journal of Sociology*, 33: 86–117.

1984. *Our Masters' Voices*. London: Routledge.

Atkinson, J. Maxwell and P. Drew. 1979. *Order in Court: the Organisation of Verbal Interaction in Judicial Settings*. London: Macmillan.

Aufderheide, Patricia (ed.). 1999. *Communications Policy and the Public Interest*. New York: Guilford Press.

Auletta, Ken. 1991. *Three Blind Mice: How the TV Networks Lost Their Way*. New York: Random House.

Bavelas, Janet B., A. Black, L. Bryson, and J. Mullett. 1988. Political equivocation: a situational explanation. *Journal of Language and Social Psychology*, 7 (2): 137–46.

Beach, Wayne A. 1993. Transitional regularities for casual "okay" usages. *Journal of Pragmatics*, 19: 325–52.

Bell, Allan. 1991. *The Language of News Media*. Oxford: Blackwell.

Bell, Allan and Peter Garrett. 1998. *Approaches to Media Discourse*. Oxford: Blackwell.

Blumler, Jay G. and Michael Gurevitch. 1981. Politicians and the press: an essay on role relationships. In Dan Nimmo and Keith Sanders (eds.) *Handbook of Political Communication*. Thousand Oaks, CA: Sage, pp. 467–93.

Boyd, Elizabeth and John Heritage. Forthcoming. Taking the patient's personal history: questioning during verbal examination. In John Heritage and Douglas Maynard (eds.) *Practising Medicine: Structure and Process in Primary Care Encounters.* Cambridge University Press.

Brown, Penelope and Stephen Levinson. 1987. *Politeness: Some Universals in Language Usage.* Cambridge University Press.

Bull, Peter. 1994. On identifying questions, replies, and non-replies in political interviews. *Journal of Language and Social Psychology,* 13 (2): 115–31.

1998. Equivocation theory and news interviews. *Journal of Language and Social Psychology,* 17 (1): 36–51.

Bull, Peter and Judy Elliott. 1998. Level of threat: a means of assessing interviewer toughness and neutrality. *Journal of Language and Social Psychology,* 17 (2): 220–44.

Bull, Peter, Judy Elliott, Derrol Palmer, and Libby Walker. 1996. Why politicians are three-faced: the face model of political interviews. *British Journal of Social Psychology,* 35: 267–84.

Bull, Peter and Kate Mayer. 1988. Interruptions in political interviews: a study of Margaret Thatcher and Neil Kinnock. *Journal of Language and Social Psychology,* 7 (1): 35–45.

1993. How not to answer questions in political interviews. *Political Psychology,* 14 (4): 651–66.

Chafe, Wallace. 1986. Evidentiality in English conversation and academic writing. In Wallace Chafe and Johanna Nichols (eds.) *Evidentiality: The Linguistic Coding of Epistemology.* Norwood NJ: Ablex, pp. 261–72.

Clayman, Steven E. 1988. Displaying neutrality in television news interviews. *Social Problems,* 35 (4): 474–92.

1989. The production of punctuality: social interaction, temporal organization, and social structure. *American Journal of Sociology,* 95 (3): 659–91.

1990. From talk to text: newspaper accounts of reporter-source interactions. *Media, Culture and Society,* 12 (1): 79–104.

1991. News interview openings: aspects of sequential organization. In P. Scannell (ed.) *Broadcast Talk: A Reader.* Thousand Oaks, CA: Sage, pp. 48–75.

1992. Footing in the achievement of neutrality: the case of news interview discourse. In P. Drew and J. Heritage (eds.) *Talk at Work.* Cambridge University Press, pp. 163–98.

1993. Reformulating the question: a device for answering / not answering questions in news interviews and press conferences. *Text,* 13 (2): 159–88.

1998. Some uses of address terms in news interviews. Paper presented at the annual meetings of the National Communication Association, San Francisco, November, 1998.

2001. Answers and evasions. *Language in Society*, 30: 403–42.

2002. Tribune of the people: maintaining the legitimacy of adversarial journalism. *Media, Culture and Society*, 24: 191–210.

Forthcoming. Disagreements and third parties: the problem of neutralism in panel news interviews. *Journal of Pragmatics*.

Clayman, Steven E. and Virginia Teas Gill. Forthcoming. Conversation analysis. In Alan Bryman and Melissa Hardy (eds.) *Handbook of Data Analysis*. Thousand Oaks, CA: Sage.

Clayman, Steven E. and John Heritage. 2002. Questioning presidents: journalistic deference and adversarialness in the press conferences of Eisenhower and Reagan. *Journal of Communication*, 52: in press.

Clayman, Steven E. and Douglas W. Maynard. 1995. Ethnomethodology and conversation analysis. In P. ten Have and G. Psathas (eds.) *Situated order: Studies in the Social Organization of Talk and Embodied Activities*. Washington DC: University Press of America, pp. 1–30.

Clayman, Steven E. and Jack Whalen. 1988/89. When the medium becomes the message: the case of the Rather–Bush encounter. *Research on Language and Social Interaction*, 22: 241–72.

Cockerell, M. 1988. *Live from Number 10: The Inside Story of Prime Ministers and TV*. London: Faber and Faber.

Cordon, Gavin. 1997. Home news. Press Association Ltd., 14 May.

Croteau, David and William Hoynes. 1994. *By Invitation Only: How the Media Limit Political Debate*. Monroe, ME: Common Courage.

Curran, James, Michael Gurevitch, and Janet Woollacott (eds.). 1977. *Mass Communication and Society*. London: Edward Arnold.

Davidson, Judy. 1984. Subsequent versions of invitations, offers, requests, and proposals dealing with potential or actual rejection. In J. M. Atkinson and J. Heritage (eds.) *Structures of Social Action*. Cambridge University Press, pp. 102–28.

Day, Robin. 1961. *Television: A Personal Report*. London: Hutchinson.

1975. *Day by Day*. London: William Kimber.

1989. *Grand Inquisitor*. London: Weidenfeld and Nicholson.

1993. . . . *But With Respect: Memorable Interviews With Statesmen and Politicians*. London: Trafalgar Square.

Dimbleby, Jonathan. 1975. *Richard Dimbleby: A Biography*. London: Hodder and Stoughton.

Donaldson, Sam. 1987. *Hold On, Mr. President!* New York: Random House.

Drew, Paul and John Heritage. 1992. Analyzing talk at work: an introduction. In P. Drew and J. Heritage (eds.) *Talk at Work*. Cambridge University Press, pp. 3–65.

Du Brow, Rick. 1990. Did Rather–Bush tiff help sink CBS anchor? *Los Angeles Times*, 6 Jan: sec. F, p. 1.

Duranti, Alessandro and Elinor Ochs. 1979. Left-dislocation in Italian conversation. *Syntax and Semantics Vol. 12: Discourse and Syntax*, pp. 377–416.

Efron, Edith. 1971. *The News Twisters*. Los Angeles: Nash.

Ekman, Paul and Wallace V. Friesen. 1975. *Unmasking the Face*. Englewood Cliffs: Prentice-Hall.

Elliott, Judy and Peter Bull. 1996. A question of threat: face threats in questions posed during televised political interviews. *Journal of Community and Applied Social Psychology*, 6: 49–72.

Elliott, Philip. 1972. *The Making of a Television Series: A Case Study in the Production of Culture*. London: Constable.

Epstein, Edward Jay. 1973. *News From Nowhere*. New York: Random House.

Fairclough, Norman. 1992. *Discourse and Social Change*. Cambridge, MA: Polity Press.

1995. *Media Discourse*. London: Edward Arnold.

Fallows, James M. 1996. *Breaking the News: How the Media Undermine American Democracy*. New York: Vintage Books.

Fishman, Mark. 1980. *Manufacturing the News*. Austin: University of Texas Press.

Fowler, M. and D. Brenner. 1982. A marketplace approach to broadcast regulation. *Texas Law Review*, 60: 207–57.

Fowler, Roger. 1991. *Language in the News: Discourse and Ideology in the Press*. London: Routledge.

Franklin, Marc A. 1981. *The First Amendment and the Fourth Estate*. Second edition. Mineola, NY: Foundation Press.

Friendly, Fred. 1967. *Due to Circumstances Beyond Our Control...* New York: Random House.

Gans, Herbert. 1972. The famine in American mass communications research: comments on Hirsch, Tuchman, and Gecas. *American Journal of Sociology*, 77: 697–705.

1979. *Deciding What's News*. New York: Random House.

Garcia, Angela. 1991. Dispute resolution without disputing: how the interactional organization of mediation hearings minimizes argumentative talk. *American Sociological Review*, 56: 818–35.

Gerbner, George and Larry Gross. 1976. Living with television: the violence profile. *Journal of Communication*, 26: 172–99.

Gibson, Janine. 1999. Now Mr. Howard, I want to ask you one more time... *The Guardian*, 8 Dec: Home Pages, p. 2.

Gitlin, Todd. 1980. *The Whole World is Watching: Mass Media in the Making and Unmaking of the New Left*. Berkeley: University of California Press.

Glasgow Media Group. 1976. *Bad News*. London: Routledge.

Glenn, Phillip J. 1995. Laughing *at* and laughing *with*: negotiations of participant alignments through conversational laughter. In P. ten Have and G. Psathas (eds.) *Interaction competence*. Washington DC: University Press of America, pp. 43–56.

Goffmen, Erving. 1955. On face work. *Psychiatry*, 18: 213–31.

1959. *The Presentation of Self in Everyday Life*. Garden City, NY: Doubleday.

1971. *Relations in Public: Microstudies of the Public Order*. New York: Harper and Row.

1981. Footing. In E. Goffman (ed.) *Forms of Talk*. Philadelphia: University of Pennsylvania Press.

Goldberg, Robert and Gerald Jay Goldberg. 1990. *Anchors: Brokaw, Jennings, Rather and the Evening News*. Secaucus, NJ: Birch Lane Press.

Goodwin, Charles. 1996. Transparent vision. In E. Ochs, E. Schegloff, and S. Thompson (eds.) *Interaction and Grammar*. Cambridge University Press, pp. 370–404.

Greatbatch, David L. 1986a. Aspects of topical organisation in news interviews: the use of agenda shifting procedures by interviewees. *Media, Culture and Society*, 8: 441–55.

1986b. Some standard uses of supplementary questions in news interviews. In *Belfast Working Papers in Language and Linguistics*, Vol. 8, ed. J. Wilson and B. Crow, Jordanstown: University of Ulster, pp. 86–123.

1988. A turn-taking system for British news interviews. *Language in Society*, 17 (3): 401–30.

1992. The management of disagreement between news interviewees. In P. Drew and J. Heritage (eds.) *Talk at Work*. Cambridge University Press, pp. 268–301.

Greatbatch, David and Robert Dingwall. 1997. Argumentative talk in divorce mediation settings. *American Sociological Review*, 62: 151–70.

Gurevitch, Michael, T. Bennett, J. Curran, and J. Woollacott (eds.). 1982. *Culture, Society, and the Media*. London: Methuen.

Hall, Stuart. 1973. A world at one with itself. In Stanley Cohen and Jock Young (eds.) *The Manufacture of News*. London: Constable, pp. 85–94.

Hall, Stuart, Chas Critcher, Tony Jefferson, John Clarke, and Brian Roberts. 1978. *Policing the Crisis: Mugging, the State, and Law and Order*. New York: Holmes and Meier.

Hallin, Daniel C. 1994. The media, the war in Vietnam, and political support: a critique of the thesis of an oppositional media. In D. Hallin *We Keep American On Top of the World*. New York: Routledge.

1997. Commercialism and professionalism in the American news media. In James Curran and Michael Gurevitch (eds.) *Mass Media and Society*, pp. 243–64.

Hallin, Daniel C. and Paolo Mancini. 1984. Speaking of the President: political structure and representational form in US and Italian Television News. *Theory and Society*, 13: 829–50.

Halloran, James D., Philip Elliott, and Graham Murdock. 1969. *Demonstrations and Communication: A Case Study*. Harmondsworth: Penguin.

Harris, Sandra. 1986. Interviewers' questions in broadcast interviews. In *Belfast Working Papers in Language and Linguistics* Vol. 8, ed. J. Wilson and B. Crow, Jordanstown: University of Ulster, pp. 50–85.
    1991. Evasive action: how politicians respond to questions in political interviews. In P. Scannell (ed.) *Broadcast Talk*, pp. 76–99. London: Sage.
Heritage, John. 1984a. *Garfinkel and Ethnomethodology*. Cambridge: Polity Press.
    1984b. A change-of-state token and aspects of its sequential placement. In J. M. Atkinson and J. Heritage (eds.) *Structures of Social Action*. Cambridge University Press, pp. 299–345.
    1985. Analyzing news interviews: aspects of the production of talk for an overhearing audience. In T. A. Dijk (ed.) *Handbook of Discourse Analysis*, Volume 3. New York: Academic Press, pp. 95–119.
    1988. Explanations as accounts: a conversation analytic perspective. In C. Antaki (ed.) *Understanding Everyday Explanation: A Casebook of Methods*. Thousand Oaks, CA: Sage, pp. 127–44.
    1995. Conversation analysis: methodological aspects. In U. M. Quasthoff (ed.) *Aspects of Oral Communication*. Berlin: De Gruyter, pp. 391–418.
    1997. Conversation analysis and institutional talk: analyzing data. In D. Silverman (ed.) *Qualitative Research: Theory, Method and Practice*. London: Sage, pp. 160–82.
    Forthcoming a. Designing questions and setting agendas in the news interview. In J. Mandelbaum, P. Glenn, and C. LeBaron (eds.) *Unearthing the Taken-for-Granted: Studies in Language and Social Interaction*. Mahwah, NJ: Erlbaum.
    Forthcoming b. The limits of questioning: negative interrogatives and hostile question content. *Journal of Pragmatics*.
Heritage, John and David Greatbatch. 1986. Generating applause: a study of rhetoric and response at party political conferences. *American Journal of Sociology*, 92 (1): 110–57.
Heritage, John and David Greatbatch. 1991. On the institutional character of institutional talk: the case of news interviews. In D. Boden and D. H. Zimmerman (eds.) *Talk and Social Structure*. Berkeley: University of California Press, pp. 93–137.
Heritage, John and Andrew Roth. 1995. Grammar and institution: questions and questioning in the broadcast news interview. *Research on Language and Social Interaction*, 28 (1): 1–60.
Heritage, John and Marja-Leena Sorjonen. 1994. Constituting and maintaining activities across sequences: and-prefacing as a feature of question design. *Language in Society*, 23: 1–29.
Heritage, John and D. R. Watson. 1980. Aspects of the properties of formulations: some instances analyzed. *Semiotica*, 30: 245–62.

Hess, Stephen. 1981. *The Washington Reporters*. Washington: Brookings Institution.

Holt, Elizabeth. 1994. Reporting on talk: the use of direct reported speech in conversation. *Research on Language and Social Interaction*, 29 (3): 219–45.

Horn, Laurence. 1989. *A Natural History of Negation*. University of Chicago Press.

Hoynes, William. 1994. *Public Television for Sale: Media, the Market and the Public Sphere*. Boulder, CO: Westview Press.

Jefferson, Gail. 1974. Error correction as an interactional resource. *Language in Society*, 2: 181–99.

1981. The abominable "ne?": a working paper exploring the phenomenon of post-response pursuit of response. Occasional Paper No. 6, Dept. of Sociology, University of Manchester, England.

1984. On stepwise transition from talk about a trouble to inappropriately next-positioned matters. In J. M. Atkinson and J. Heritage (eds.) *Structures of Social Action*. Cambridge University Press, pp. 191–221.

1986. Colligation as a device for minimizing repair or disagreement. Paper presented at the Conference on Talk and Social Structure, University of California, Santa Barbara.

Jones, Bill. 1992. Broadcasters, politicians, and the political interview. In Bill Jones and Lynton Robins (eds.) *Two Decades in British Politics*. Manchester University Press, pp. 53–77.

Jucker, Andreas. 1986. *News Interviews: A Pragmalinguistic Analysis*. Amsterdam: John Benjamins.

Kernell, Samuel. 1986. *Going Public: New Strategies of Presidential Leadership*. Washington DC: Congressional Quarterly, Inc.

Koppel, Ted and Kyle Gibson. 1996. *Nightline: History in the Making and the Making of Television*. New York: Times Books.

Kotthoff, Helga. 1993. Disagreement and concession in disputes: on the context sensitivity of preference structures. *Language in Society*, 22: 193–216.

Kumar, Krishnan. 1975. Holding the middle ground: the BBC, the public and the professional broadcaster. *Sociology*, 9: 67–88.

Labov, William and David Fanshel. 1977. *Therapeutic Discourse: Psychotherapy as Conversation*. New York: Academic Press.

Levinson, Stephen C. 1983. *Pragmatics*. Cambridge University Press.

1988. Putting linguistics on a proper footing: explorations in Goffman's concepts of participation. In Paul Drew and Anthony J. Wootton (eds.) *Goffman: An Interdisciplinary Appreciation*. Oxford: Polity Press, pp. 161–227.

Macaulay, Marcia. 1996. Asking to ask: the strategic function of indirect requests for information in news interviews. *Pragmatics*, 6 (4): 491–509.

McCombs, M. E. and D. L. Shaw. 1972. The agenda-setting function of the Press. *Public Opinion Quarterly*, 36: 176–87.

MacNeil, Robert. 1982. *The Right Place at the Right Time*. New York: Penguin books.

Matheson, Hilda. 1933. *Broadcasting*. London: Thornton Butterworth.

Maynard, Douglas W. 1985. How children start arguments. *Language in Society*, 14: 1–29.

Molotch, Harvey and Lester, Marilyn. 1974. News as purposive behavior: the strategic use of routine events, accidents, and scandals. *American Sociological Review*, 39: 101–12.

1975. Accidental news: the great oil spill as local occurrence and national event. *American Journal of Sociology*, 81 (2): 235–60.

Nevin, Bruce. 1994. Quandary/abusive questions. *The LINGUIST Discussion List*, 5: 754.

Noelle-Neumann, Elizabeth. 1974. The spiral of silence: a theory of public opinion. *Journal of Communication*, 24: 24–51.

Olsher, David. Forthcoming. Inviting interplay in panel format news interviews.

Patterson, Thomas. 1993. *Out of Order*. New York: Vintage.

Pomerantz, Anita M. 1980. Telling my side: "limited access" as a "fishing" device. *Sociological Inquiry*, 50: 104–52.

1984. Agreeing and disagreeing with assessments: some features of preferred/dispreferred turn shapes. In J. M. Atkinson and J. Heritage (eds.) *Structures of Social Action: Studies in Conversation Analysis*. Cambridge University Press, pp. 57–101.

1988/9. Constructing skepticism: four devices used to engender the audience's skepticism. *Research on Language and Social Interaction*, 22: 293–313.

Quirk, R., S. Greenbaum, G. Leech, and J. Svartvik. 1972. *A Grammar of Contemporary English*. London: Longman.

Rather, Dan. 1994. *The Camera Never Blinks Twice: The Further Adventures of a Television Journalist*. New York: William Morrow and Co.

Raymond, Geoffrey. 2000. The structure of responding: conforming and nonconforming responses to yes/no type interrogatives. Unpublished PhD dissertation: University of California, Los Angeles.

Robinson, Jeffrey. Forthcoming. Soliciting patients' presenting concerns. In J. Heritage and D. Maynard (eds.) *Practicing Medicine: Structure and Process in Primary Care Encounters*. Cambridge University Press.

Robinson, Michael J. and Margaret A. Sheehan. 1983. *Over the Wire and on TV: CBS and UPI in Campaign '80*. New York: Russell Sage.

Roth, Andrew. 1996. Turn-final word repeats as a device for "doing answering" in an institutional setting. Paper presented at the Pacific Sociological Association annual meeting, Seattle, WA, April 1996.

1998a. Who makes news: descriptions of television news interviewers' public personae. *Media, Culture, and Society*, 20 (1): 79–107.

1998b. Who makes the news: social identity and the explanation of action in the broadcast news interview. Unpublished PhD dissertation: University of California, Los Angeles.

Roth, Andrew and David Olsher. 1997. Some standard uses of "what about"-prefaced questions in the broadcast news interview. *Issues in Applied Linguistics*, 8 (1): 3–25.

Sabato, Larry. 1991. *Feeding Frenzy: How Attack Journalism Has Transformed American Politics*. New York: Free Press.

Sacks, Harvey. 1972. On the analyzability of stories by children. In J. J. Gumperz and D. Hymes (eds.) *Directions in Sociolinguistics: The Ethnography of Communication*. New York: Holt, Rinehart and Winston, pp. 325–45.

1987. On the preferences for agreement and contiguity in sequences in conversation. In G. Button and J. R. E. Lee (eds.) *Talk and Social Organisation*. Clevedon, England: Multilingual Matters, pp. 54–69.

1992 [1964–72]. *Lectures on Conversation*, ed. G. Jefferson, 2 vols. Oxford: Blackwell.

Sacks, Harvey, Emanuel A. Schegloff, and Gail Jefferson. 1974. A simplest systematics for the organization of turn-taking for conversation. *Language*, 50: 696–735.

Sacks, Harvey and Emanuel A. Schegloff. 1979. Two preferences in the organization of reference to persons and their interaction. In G. Psathas (ed.) *Everyday Language: Studies in Ethnomethodology*. New York: Irvington Publishers, pp. 15–21.

Scannell, Paddy. 1991. Introduction: the relevance of talk. In Paddy Scannell (ed.) *Broadcast Talk*. London: Sage, pp. 1–13.

Schegloff, Emanuel A. 1968. Sequencing in conversational openings. *American Anthropologist*, 70: 1075–95.

1972. Notes on a conversational practice: formulating place. In D. Sudnow (ed.) *Studies in Social Interaction*. New York: Free Press, pp. 75–119.

1980. Preliminaries to preliminaries: "can I ask you a question." *Sociological Inquiry*, 50: 104–52.

1982. Discourse as an interactional achievement: some uses of "uh huh" and other things that come between sentences. In D. Tannen (ed.) *Analyzing Discourse (Georgetown University Roundtable on Languages and Linguistics 1981)*. Washington DC: Georgetown University Press, pp. 71–93.

1984. On some questions and ambiguities in conversation. In J. M. Atkinson and J. Heritage (eds.) *Structures of Social Action*. Cambridge University Press, pp. 28–52.

1986. The routine as achievement. *Human Studies*, 9: 111–51.

1987. Between macro and micro: contexts and other connections. In J. Alexander, R. M. B. Giesen, and N. Smelser (eds.) *The Micro-Macro Link*. Berkeley: University of California Press, pp. 207–34.

1988. On an actual virtual servo-mechanism for guessing bad news: a single case conjecture. *Social Problems*, 35 (4): 442–57.

1988/89. From interview to confrontation: observations on the Bush/ Rather encounter. *Research on Language and Social Interaction*, 22: 215–40.

1991. Reflections on talk and social structure. In D. Boden and D. H. Zimmerman (eds.) *Talk and Social Structure*. Berkeley: University of California Press, pp. 44–70.

1992a. Introduction. In Harvey Sacks, *Lectures on Conversation*, ed. G. Jefferson, vol. I (Fall 1964–Spring 1968). Oxford: Blackwell, pp. ix–1xii.

1992b. On talk and its institutional occasions. In P. Drew and J. Heritage, (eds.) *Talk at Work: Social Interaction in Institutional Settings*. Cambridge University Press, pp. 101–34.

1993. Reflections on quantification in the study of conversation. *Research on Language and Social Interaction*, 26: 99–128.

1996. Confirming allusions. *American Journal of Sociology*, 102 (1): 161–216.

1998. Word repeats as a practice for ending. Paper presented at the National Communication Association annual meetings, New York, November 1988.

1999. Discourse pragmatics, conversation analysis. *Discourse Studies*, 1 (4): 405–35.

2000. On granularity. *Annual Review of Sociology*, 26: 715–20.

Schegloff, Emanuel A. and Harvey Sacks. 1973. Opening up closings. *Semiotica*, 8: 289–327.

Schegloff, Emanuel A., Gail Jefferson, and Harvey Sacks. 1977. The preference for self-correction in the organization of repair in conversation. *Language*, 53: 361–82.

Schiffrin, Debra. 1987. *Discourse Markers*. Cambridge University Press.

Schlesinger, Philip. 1978. *Putting "Reality" Together: BBC News*. London: Constable.

Schlesinger, Philip, Graham Murdock, and Philip Elliott. 1983. *Televising "Terrorism": Political Violence in Popular Culture*. London: Comedia.

Schudson, Michael. 1978. *Discovering the News: A Social History of American Newspapers*. New York: Basic Books.

1982. The politics of narrative form: the emergence of news conventions in print and television. *Daedalus*. 111: 97–113.

1994. Question authority: a history of the news interview in American journalism, 1830s–1930s. *Media, Culture and Society*, 16: 565–87.

1995. Watergate and the press. In Schudson, *The Power of News*. Cambridge, MA: Harvard University Press.

1996. The sociology of news production revisited. In J. Curran and M. Gurevitch (eds.) *Mass Media and Society*. London: Arnold.

Schudson, Michael and Elliott King. 1995. The illusion of Ronald Reagan's popularity. In Theodore Glasser and Charles Salmon (eds.) *Public*

Opinion and the Communication of Consent. New York: Guilford Press.

Shoemaker, Pamela J. and Stephen D. Reese. 1996. *Mediating the Message: Theories of Influences on Mass Media Content.* Second edition. White Plains: Longman.

Sigal, Leon V. 1973. *Reporters and Officials.* Lexington, MA: Lexington Books.

Smith, Carolyn. 1990. *Presidential Press Conferences: A Critical Approach.* New York: Praeger.

Smith, Dorothy. 1978. K is mentally ill: the anatomy of a factual account. *Sociology,* 12 (1): 23–53.

Stengel, Richard. 1988. "Bushwhacked!" *Time,* 131 (6): 16–20.

Summerskill, Ben. 1998. Paxman wins award for Howard showdown. *The Evening Standard* (London), 15 May: sec. 1, p. 4.

Tannen, Deborah. 1998. *The Argument Culture: Stopping America's War of Words.* New York: Ballantine Books.

ten Have, Paul. 1999. *Doing Conversation Analysis.* Thousand Oaks: Sage.

Toner, Robin. 1988. Poll finds Rather clash is failing to ease Bush's Iran-Contra woes, *New York Times,* 2 Feb: sec. A, p. 1.

Tracey, Michael. 1977. *The Production of Political Television.* London: Routledge.

Tuchman, Gaye. 1972. Objectivity as strategic ritual: an examination of newsmen's notions of objectivity. *American Journal of Sociology,* 77: 660–79.

1978. *Making News: A Study in the Construction of Reality.* New York: Free Press.

1988. Mass media institutions. In Neil J. Smelser (ed.) *Handbook of Sociology.* Thousand Oaks, CA: Sage, pp. 601–26.

Tunstall, Jeremy. 1971. *Journalists at Work: Specialist Correspondents, Their News Organizations, News Sources, and Competitor-Colleagues.* London: Constable.

van Dijk, Teun. 1988. *News as Discourse.* Hillsdale, NJ: Lawrence Erlbaum.

Waisbord, Silvio. 2000. *Watchdog Journalism in South America.* New York: Columbia University Press.

Weaver, David H. and G. Cleveland Wilhoit. 1986; second edition 1991. *The American Journalist: A Portrait of US News People and Their Work.* Bloomington IN: Indiana University Press.

Weaver, Paul. 1975. Newspaper news and television news. In Douglas Cater and Richard Adler (eds.) *Television as a Social Force.* New York: Praeger.

Weber, Max. [1910] 1976. Towards a sociology of the press. *Journal of Communication,* 26 (3): 96–101.

Wedell, E. G. 1968. *Broadcasting and Public Policy.* London: Michael Joseph.

Weintraub, Bernard. 1988. Rather's role a matter of debate. *New York Times,* 11 Oct.: sec. A, p. 29.

Whale, John. 1977. *The Politics of the Media*. London: Fontana.

Whalen, Marilyn and Don H. Zimmerman. 1987. Sequential and institutional contexts in calls for help. *Social Psychology Quarterly*, 50: 172–85.

Wilson, John. 1990. *Politically Speaking: The Pragmatic Analysis of Political Language*. Cambridge, MA: Blackwell.

Wilson, Thomas P. 1991. Social structure and the sequential organization of interaction. In D. Boden and D. Zimmerman (eds.) *Talk and Social Structure*. Cambridge: Polity Press, pp. 22–43.

Wyndham Goldie, Grace. 1977. *Facing the Nation: Television and Politics 1936–1976*. London: Bodley Head.

Zaller, John. Forthcoming. *A Theory of Media Politics: How the Interests of Politicians, Journalists and Citizens Shape the News*. University of Chicago Press.

Zelizer, Barbie. 1990. Where is the author in American TV news? On the construction and presentation of proximity, authorship, and journalistic authority. *Semiotica*, 80: 37–48.

Zimmerman, Don H. 1988. On conversation: the conversation analytic perspective. In James A. Anderson (ed.) vol. II, *Communication Yearbook*, Newbury Park, CA: Sage, pp. 406–32.

Zimmerman, Don H. and Deidre Boden. 1991. Structure-in-action: an introduction. In D. Boden and D. Zimmerman (eds.) *Talk and Social Structure*. Berkeley: University of California Press.

Subject index

Index of names